Cambridge studies in medieval life and thought

CONQUEST, ANARCHY AND LORDSHIP

Focussing on Yorkshire, by far the largest English county, this book examines three of the most important themes in the period described by Sir Frank Stenton as 'the first century of English feudalism': the Norman conquest, the anarchy of Stephen's reign and the nature of lordship and land tenure. In each case the book offers a strong challenge to dominant interpretations, and seeks to alter in significant ways our conception of Anglo-Norman politics and government.

The first section of the book reveals that the Norman conquest of Yorkshire was a much more rapid and carefully controlled process than has hitherto been supposed; that, initially at least, it owed a great deal to the construction of castles and organisation of castleries; that during the reign of the Conqueror's youngest son, Henry I, its character changed as the king sought to bring Yorkshire under tighter central administrative control and promote monasticism there; and that its impact upon tenurial structure and terms of land tenure, although considerable, has been overestimated.

The second section of the book examines the anarchy of King Stephen's reign and its consequences in Yorkshire. It challenges the view that Stephen's creation of earls was a deliberate attempt to impose an alternative conception of government, and illustrates how the greater magnates profited from, and in some cases sought to promote, a failure of royal control.

The final section of the book deals with lordship, one of the most significant aspects of medieval society. It challenges Stenton's conception of twelfth-century society as a 'seignorial world' organised principally around the honour and dominated by baronial lordship. It reveals that on some (perhaps many) honours the bonds of association between the tenantry, and the powers of lords over their men, were weaker than Stenton supposed, and that royal intervention in the honour was far more regular. In doing so it undermines one of the basic premises of those legal historians who argue that the origins of the English Common Law are to be found in the legal reforms of He̶̶̶ ̶̶̶̶̶̶̶ ̶. The book will therefore be essential reading on both 'the first cent̶ ̶̶̶̶̶ ̶̶̶̶̶̶̶ of English feudalism.

Cambridge studies in medieval life and thought
Fourth series

General Editor:
D. E. LUSCOMBE
Professor of Medieval History, University of Sheffield

Advisory Editors:
R. B. DOBSON
Professor of Medieval History, University of Cambridge, and Fellow of Christ's College

ROSAMOND MCKITTERICK
Reader in Early Medieval European History, University of Cambridge, and Fellow of Newnham College

The series Cambridge Studies in Medieval Life and Thought was inaugurated by G. G. Coulton in 1921. Professor D. E. Luscombe now acts as General Editor of the Fourth Series, with Professor R. B. Dobson and Dr Rosamond McKitterick as Advisory Editors. The series brings together outstanding work by medieval scholars over a wide range of human endeavour extending from political economy to the history of ideas.

For a list of titles in the series, see end of book.

CONQUEST, ANARCHY AND LORDSHIP

Yorkshire, 1066–1154

PAUL DALTON

Lecturer in Medieval History,
Liverpool Institute of Higher Education

CAMBRIDGE
UNIVERSITY PRESS

PUBLISHED BY THE PRESS SYNDICATE OF THE UNIVERSITY OF CAMBRIDGE
The Pitt Building, Trumpington Street, Cambridge, United Kingdom

CAMBRIDGE UNIVERSITY PRESS
The Edinburgh Building, Cambridge CB2 2RU, UK
40 West 20th Street, New York NY 10011–4211, USA
477 Williamstown Road, Port Melbourne, VIC 3207, Australia
Ruiz de Alarcón 13, 28014 Madrid, Spain
Dock House, The Waterfront, Cape Town 8001, South Africa

http://www.cambridge.org

First published 1994
First paperback edition 2002

A catalogue record for this book is available from the British Library

Library of Congress Cataloguing in Publication data
Dalton, Paul.
Conquest, anarchy and lordship: Yorkshire, 1066–1154 / Paul Dalton.
p.   cm. – (Cambridge studies in medieval life and thought; 4th ser., 27)
Includes bibliographical references and index.
ISBN 0 521 45098 5 (hc)
1. Yorkshire (England) – Politics and government.   2. Great Britain – History
Norman period, 1066–1154.   3. Land tenure – England – Yorkshire – History.
4. Feudalism – England – Yorkshire – History.   5. Normans – England – Yorkshire
– History.   I. Title.   II. Series.
DA670.Y4D35   1994
942.8′102–dc20   93-13985   CIP

ISBN 0 521 45098 5 hardback
ISBN 0 521 52464 4 paperback

In memory of my parents
Joyce and Geoffrey Dalton

CONTENTS

MAPS

TABLES

ACKNOWLEDGMENTS

This book began as a doctoral thesis submitted to the University of Sheffield in April 1990. During the course of writing it I have incurred many debts, both professional and personal. My thanks must go first of all to the British Academy for the award of a major state studentship, which supported me during the first three years of my doctoral research, and for the three-year Post Doctoral Fellowship which I took to the University of Sheffield. The Department of History at Sheffield provided me with financial support on a number of occasions during my research, the most notable being a grant which enabled me to present a paper on the earl of York to the Haskins Society conference in Houston, Texas, in 1989. My thanks are due also to the Institute of Historical Research, London, for the award of a Scouloudi Fellowship for the academic year 1989–90, which supported me during the course of writing up my thesis.

Many scholarly friends have offered constructive criticisms and valuable suggestions which have greatly improved the book. They include Sir James Holt and David Luscombe, who examined the original thesis, David Carpenter, Michael Clanchy, Robin Fleming, Judith Green, John Hudson, Chris Lewis, David Palliser, Susan Reynolds, David Roffe and Kathleen Thompson. In addition, Robin Fleming, David Palliser, David Roffe, Frank Thorn and Ann Williams were kind enough to allow me to see drafts of their articles in advance of publication. My thanks go out to them all. During the course of preparing the book for publication, the advice and editorial skills of Professor R.B. Dobson and Mr William Davies have been greatly appreciated. My greatest academic debt is to Edmund King, whose supervision of the original thesis was exemplary, whose advice has always been invaluable and whose work is an inspiration. The responsibility for any errors and shortcomings which remain in the book is, of course, my own.

Acknowledgments

I would also like to pay tribute to my family and friends outside the field of medieval history, who have helped and supported me in various ways over the last few years. They include my sisters, Kate and Mandy, and their respective husbands, Derrick and Stewart. Among them also are my friends in Bradford: Tony Atack, Sean Briggs, Brendan and Stella Kilgallon and Chris Ridgway. The help and friendship of Joan Howe in London will always be remembered, as will that of Don and Lisa MacRaild and Cathy Clark in Sheffield.

It remains only to mention my greatest debt of all: the one I owe to my parents. Although both died before the completion of this book, without their help and encouragement it would never have been started, let alone brought to a conclusion. It is in memory of them that I dedicate it.

ABBREVIATIONS

Acta Sanctorum	*Acta Sanctorum*, ed. J. Bollandus *et al.* (Antwerp, 1643–1867)
Anderson, *Hundred-Names*	O.S. Anderson, *The English Hundred-Names* (Lund, 1934)
ANS	*Anglo-Norman Studies*
ASC	*The Anglo-Saxon Chronicle*, ed. and trans. D. Whitelock *et al.* (London, 1961)
Barlow, *Jurisdictional Peculiars*	F. Barlow, *Durham Jurisdictional Peculiars* (London, 1950)
Barlow, *Rufus*	F. Barlow, *William Rufus* (London, 1983)
Barrow, *Anglo-Norman Era*	G.W.S. Barrow, *The Anglo-Norman Era in Scottish History* (Oxford, 1980)
Barrow, *David I*	G.W.S. Barrow, *David I of Scotland (1124–1153): The Balance of New and Old* (The Stenton Lecture 1984: Univ. of Reading, 1985)
Barrow, *Kingdom of the Scots*	G.W.S. Barrow, *The Kingdom of the Scots* (London, 1973)
BIHR	*Bulletin of the Institute of Historical Research*
BL	British Library
BNJ	*British Numismatic Journal*
Book of Fees	*Liber Feodorum: The Book of Fees Commonly Called Testa de Nevill*, 3 vols. (London, 1920–31)
Brooke, *English Coins*	G.C. Brooke, *A Catalogue of English Coins in the British*

	Museum: The Norman Kings, 2 vols. (London, 1916)
Cal. Chart. Rolls	*Calendar of the Charter Rolls*, 6 vols. (London, 1903–27)
Cal. Inq. P. M.	*Calendar of Inquisitions Post Mortem...*, 16 vols. (London, 1904–74)
Cartularium de Gyseburne	*Cartularium Prioratus de Gyseburne*, ed. W. Brown, 2 vols. (Surtees Soc., 1889–94)
Cartularium de Rievalle	*Cartularium Abbathiae de Rievalle*, ed. J.C. Atkinson (Surtees Soc., 1889)
Cartularium de Whiteby	*Cartularium Abbathiae de Whiteby*, ed. J.C. Atkinson, 2 vols. (Surtees Soc., 1879–81)
Chartularies of Monkbretton	*Abstracts of the Chartularies of the Priory of Monkbretton*, ed. J.W. Walker (Yorks. Arch. Soc. rec. ser., 1924)
Chartulary of Fountains	*Abstracts of the Charters and Other Documents Contained in the Chartulary of the Cistercian Abbey of Fountains*, ed. W.T. Lancaster, 2 vols. (Leeds, 1915)
Cheney, Hubert Walter	C.R. Cheney, *Hubert Walter* (London, 1967)
Chester Charters	*The Charters of the Anglo-Norman Earls of Chester, c. 1071–1237*, ed. G. Barraclough (Rec. Soc. of Lancs. and Cheshire, 1988)
CHJ	*Cambridge Historical Journal*
Chronica de Melsa	*Chronica Monasterii de Melsa*, ed. E.A. Bond, 3 vols. (RS, 1866–8)
Chronicle of Langtoft	*The Chronicle of Pierre de Langtoft*, ed. T. Wright, 2 vols. (RS, 1866–8)
Chronicles of the Reigns	*Chronicles of the Reigns of Stephen, Henry II, and Richard I,*

	ed. R. Howlett, 4 vols. (RS, 1884–9)
Clanchy, *England and its Rulers*	M.T. Clanchy, *England and its Rulers 1066–1272* (London, 1983)
CLJ	*Cambridge Law Journal*
Colvin, *White Canons*	H.M. Colvin, *The White Canons in England* (Oxford, 1951)
Complete Peerage	*Complete Peerage*, by G.E.C., revised edn, V. Gibbs *et al.*, 13 vols. (London, 1910–59)
David, *Curthose*	C.W. David, *Robert Curthose, Duke of Normandy* (Cambridge, Mass., 1920)
Davis, *King Stephen*	R.H.C. Davis, *King Stephen 1135–1154* (3rd edn, London, 1990)
DB	*Domesday Book seu liber censualis…*, ed. A. Farley *et al.*, 4 vols. (London, 1783–1816)
Dickinson, *Austin Canons*	J.C. Dickinson, *The Origins of the Austin Canons and their Introduction into England* (London, 1950)
Domesday Geography	*The Domesday Geography of Northern England*, ed. H.C. Darby and I.S. Maxwell (Cambridge, 1962)
Domesday Studies	*Domesday Studies. Papers Read at the Novocentenary Conference of the Royal Historical Society and the Institute of British Geographers Winchester, 1986*, ed. J.C. Holt (Woodbridge, 1987)
EcHR	*Economic History Review*
EHR	*English Historical Review*
English, *Holderness*	B. English, *The Lords of Holderness 1086–1260* (Oxford, 1979)
English Lawsuits	*English Lawsuits from William I to Richard I*, ed. R.C. Van

	Caenegem, 2 vols. (Selden Soc., 1990–1)
Episcopal Acta	*English Episcopal Acta, V: York 1070–1154*, ed. J.E. Burton (Oxford, 1988)
ESC	*Early Scottish Charters Prior to A.D. 1153*, ed. A.C. Lawrie (Glasgow, 1905)
EYC	*Early Yorkshire Charters*, vols. I–III, ed. W. Farrer (Edinburgh, 1914–16); vols. IV–XII, ed. C.T. Clay (Yorks. Arch. Soc. rec. ser. extra ser., 1935–65)
EYF	C.T. Clay and D.E. Greenway, *Early Yorkshire Families* (Yorks. Arch. Soc. rec. ser., 1973)
Farrer, *Kendale*	W. Farrer, *Records Relating to the Barony of Kendale*, ed. J.F. Curwen, 2 vols. (Cumb. and Westmld. Ant. and Arch. Soc. rec. ser., 1923–4)
Fleming, *Kings and Lords*	R. Fleming, *Kings and Lords in Conquest England* (Cambridge, 1991)
Florence, *Chronicon*	Florence of Worcester, *Chronicon ex Chronicis*, ed. B. Thorpe, 2 vols. (Eng. Hist. Soc., 1848–9)
Foundation of Kirkstall	*The Foundation of Kirkstall Abbey*, ed. and trans. E.K. Clark, in *Miscellanea* (Thoresby Soc., 1895), 169–208
Freeman, *Norman Conquest*	E.A. Freeman, *The History of the Norman Conquest*, 5 vols. and index (London, 1867–79)
Furness Coucher	*The Coucher Book of Furness Abbey*, vol. I (in three parts), ed. J.C. Atkinson (Chetham Soc., n.s., 1886–7); vol. II (in three parts), ed. J. Brownbill (Chetham Soc., n.s., 1915–19)

Gesta Stephani	*Gesta Stephani*, ed. K.R. Potter and R.H.C. Davis (Oxford, 1976)
Gestis Regum	*Willelmi Malmesbiriensis Monachi De Gestis Regum Anglorum*, ed. W. Stubbs, 2 vols. (RS, 1887–9)
Glanvill	*Tractatus de Legibus et Consuetudinibus Regni Anglie qui Glanvilla vocatur*, ed. G.D.G. Hall (London, 1965)
Green, *Government*	J.A. Green, *The Government of England under Henry I* (Cambridge, 1986)
Green, *Sheriffs*	J.A. Green, *English Sheriffs to 1154* (London, 1990)
Hartshorne, *History of Northumberland*	C.H. Hartshorne, *Memoirs Illustrative of the History and Antiquities of Northumberland*, Proceedings of the Archaeological Institute, Newcastle on Tyne, 1852 (London, 1858)
Hedley, *Northumberland Families*	W. Percy Hedley, *Northumberland Families*, 2 vols. (Newcastle upon Tyne, 1968–70)
Henry of Huntingdon	Henry of Huntingdon, *Historia Anglorum*, ed. T. Arnold (RS, 1879)
Hey, *South Yorkshire*	D. Hey, *The Making of South Yorkshire* (Ashbourne, 1979)
Hey, *Yorkshire*	D. Hey, *Yorkshire from AD 1000* (London, 1986)
Historia Novella	William of Malmesbury, *Historia Novella*, ed. K.R. Potter (London, 1955)
Historians of York	*The Historians of the Church of York and its Archbishops*, ed. J. Raine, 3 vols. (RS, 1879–94)
Hodgson, *Northumberland*	J.C. Hodgson, *A History of*

	Northumberland, vol. VII: *The Parish of Edlingham. The Parish of Felton. The Chapelry or Parish of Brinkburn* (Newcastle upon Tyne, 1904)
Hollister, *Military Organization*	C.W. Hollister, *The Military Organization of Norman England* (Oxford, 1965)
Hollister, *Monarchy*	C.W. Hollister, *Monarchy, Magnates and Institutions in the Anglo-Norman World* (London, 1986)
Holt, *Magna Carta*	J.C. Holt, *Magna Carta* (2nd edn, Cambridge, 1992)
Holt, *Northerners*	J.C. Holt, *The Northerners. A Study in the Reign of King John* (Oxford, 1961)
HRH	D. Knowles *et al.*, *The Heads of Religious Houses: England and Wales 940–1216* (Cambridge, 1972)
Hugh the Chantor	Hugh the Chantor, *The History of the Church of York 1066–1127*, ed. and trans. C. Johnson (London, 1961)
JBAA	*Journal of the British Archaeological Association*
JEH	*Journal of Ecclesiastical History*
JLH	*Journal of Legal History*
JMH	*Journal of Medieval History*
Kapelle, *Norman Conquest*	W.E. Kapelle, *The Norman Conquest of the North: The Region and its Transformation, 1000–1135* (London, 1979)
Keefe, *Feudal Assessments*	T.K. Keefe, *Feudal Assessments and the Political Community under Henry II and his Sons* (Berkeley, 1983)
King, *Castellarium Anglicanum*	D.J.C. King, *Castellarium Anglicanum. An Index and Bibliography of the Castles in*

	England, Wales and the Islands, 2 vols. (Millwood, 1983)
Kirkby's Inquest	*Kirkby's Inquest*, ed. R.H. Skaife (Surtees Soc., 1867)
Kirkstall Coucher	*The Coucher Book of the Cistercian Abbey of Kirkstall*, ed. W.T. Lancaster and W. Paley Baildon (Thoresby Soc., 1904)
Knowles, *Monastic Order*	D. Knowles, *The Monastic Order in England* (2nd edn, Cambridge, 1963)
Lennard, *Rural England*	R. Lennard, *Rural England 1086–1135* (Oxford, 1959)
LHP	*Leges Henrici Primi*, ed. L.J. Downer (Oxford, 1972)
LHR	*Law and History Review*
Maitland, *Domesday Book*	F.W. Maitland, *Domesday Book and Beyond* (Cambridge, 1897)
McDonald and Snooks, *Domesday*	J. McDonald and G.D. Snooks, *Domesday Economy* (Oxford, 1986)
Memorials of Fountains	*Memorials of the Abbey of St. Mary of Fountains*, ed. J.R. Walbran and J.T. Fowler, 3 vols. (Surtees Soc., 1863–1918)
Miller, *Ely*	E. Miller, *The Abbey and Bishopric of Ely* (2nd edn, Cambridge, 1969)
Milsom, *Historical Foundations*	S.F.C. Milsom, *Historical Foundations of the Common Law* (2nd edn, London, 1981)
Milsom, *Legal Framework*	S.F.C. Milsom, *The Legal Framework of English Feudalism* (Cambridge, 1976)
Monasticon	W. Dugdale, *Monasticon Anglicanum*, ed. J. Caley et al., 6 vols. in 8 (London, 1817–30)
Mowbray Charters	*Charters of the Honour of Mowbray 1107–1191*, ed. D.E. Greenway (British Academy, 1972)

Newburgh, *English Affairs*   William of Newburgh, *The History of English Affairs Book I*, ed. P.G. Walsh and M.J. Kennedy (Warminster, 1988)

Nicholl, *Thurstan*   D. Nicholl, *Thurstan Archbishop of York (1114–1140)* (York, 1964)

North, *Hammered Coinage*   J.J. North, *English Hammered Coinage*, 2 vols. (2nd edn, London, 1980)

Orderic   *The Ecclesiastical History of Orderic Vitalis*, ed. M. Chibnall, 6 vols. (Oxford, 1969–80)

Painter, *English Feudal Barony*   S. Painter, *Studies in the History of the English Feudal Barony* (Baltimore, 1943)

Palliser, *York*   D.M. Palliser, *Domesday York* (Univ. of York, Borthwick Paper, no. 78, 1990)

Pollock and Maitland, *English Law*   Sir F. Pollock and F.W. Maitland, *The History of English Law before the Time of Edward I*, 2 vols. (2nd edn, Cambridge, 1968)

Pounds, *Medieval Castle*   N.J.G. Pounds, *The Medieval Castle in England and Wales: A Social and Political History* (Cambridge, 1990)

PR   *Pipe Roll*

PR 2–4 Henry II   *The Great Rolls of the Pipe for the Second, Third, and Fourth Years of the Reign of King Henry II*, ed. J. Hunter (London, 1844)

PR 31 Henry I   *Magnum Rotulum Scaccarii vel Magnum Rotulum Pipae de anno tricesimo-primo regni Henrici Primi*, ed. J. Hunter (London, 1833)

Priory of Hexham   *The Priory of Hexham*, ed. J. Raine, 2 vols. (Surtees Soc., 1864–5)

Raistrick, *West Riding*	A. Raistrick, *West Riding of Yorkshire* (London, 1970)
Recueil des Actes	*Recueil des Actes de Henri II...*, ed. L.V. Delisle and E. Berger, 4 vols. (Paris, 1906–27)
Red Book	*Red Book of the Exchequer*, ed. H. Hall, 3 vols. (RS, 1896)
Regesta	*Regesta Regum Anglo-Normannorum 1066–1154*, ed. H.W.C. Davis, C. Johnson, H.A. Cronne and R.H.C. Davis, 4 vols. (Oxford, 1913–69)
Regesta Scottorum	*Regesta Regum Scottorum 1153–1371*, ed. G.W.S. Barrow *et al.*, 6 vols. (Edinburgh, 1960–87)
Register of Holm Cultram	*The Register and Records of Holm Cultram*, ed. F. Grainger and W.G. Collingwood (Cumb. and Westmld. Ant. and Arch. Soc. rec. ser., 1929)
Register of St. Bees	*The Register of the Priory of St. Bees*, ed. J. Wilson (Surtees Soc., 1915)
Register of Wetherhal	*The Register of the Priory of Wetherhal*, ed. J.E. Prescott (Cumb. and Westmld. Ant. and Arch. Soc. rec. ser., 1897)
Registrum Antiquissimum	*The Registrum Antiquissimum of the Cathedral Church of Lincoln*, ed. C.W. Foster and K. Major, 10 vols. (Linc. Rec. Soc., 1931–73)
Ritchie, *Normans in Scotland*	R.L.G. Ritchie, *The Normans in Scotland* (Edinburgh, 1954)
Rolls of the Justices	*Rolls of the Justices in Eyre for Yorkshire 1218–19*, ed. D.M. Stenton (Selden Soc., 1937)
RS	Rolls Series
Sallay Chartulary	*The Chartulary of the Cistercian*

	Abbey of St. Mary of Sallay in Craven, ed. J. McNulty, 2 vols. (Yorks. Arch. Soc. rec. ser., 1933–4)
Sanders, *Baronies*	I.J. Sanders, *English Baronies: A Study of their Origin and Descent 1086–1327* (Oxford, 1960)
Searle, *Women*	E. Searle, *Women and the Legitimisation of Succession at the Norman Conquest* (California Institute of Technology Social Science Working Paper 328, July 1980)
Selby Coucher	*The Coucher Book of Selby*, ed. J.T. Fowler, 2 vols. (Yorks. Arch. and Top. Ass. rec. ser., 1891–3)
Select Charters	*Select Charters and Other Illustrations of English Constitutional History from the Earliest Times to the Reign of Edward the First*, ed. W. Stubbs (9th edn, Oxford, 1913)
SHR	*Scottish Historical Review*
Stenton, *First Century*	F.M. Stenton, *The First Century of English Feudalism 1066–1166* (2nd edn, Oxford, 1961)
Symeon, *Opera*	*Symeonis Monachi Opera Omnia*, ed. T. Arnold, 2 vols. (RS, 1882–5)
Tabuteau, *Transfers of Property*	E. Zack Tabuteau, *Transfers of Property in Eleventh-Century Norman Law* (Chapel Hill, 1988)
TCWAAS	*Transactions of the Cumberland and Westmorland Antiquarian and Archaeological Society*
TRHS	*Transactions of the Royal Historical Society*
VCH	*The Victoria History of the Counties of England* (London, 1900– , *in progress*)

Visitations of Southwell	*Visitations and Memorials of Southwell Minster*, ed. A.F. Leach (Camden Soc., n.s., 1891)
Vita Ailredi	*The Life of Ailred of Rievaulx by Walter Daniel*, ed. F.M. Powicke (Oxford, 1978)
Wardrop, *Fountains Abbey*	J. Wardrop, *Fountains Abbey and its Benefactors 1132–1300* (Kalamazoo, 1987)
Warren, *Governance*	W.L. Warren, *The Governance of Norman and Angevin England 1086–1272* (London, 1987)
Warren, *Henry II*	W.L. Warren, *Henry II* (London, 1973)
West Yorkshire	*West Yorkshire: An Archaeological Survey to A.D. 1500*, ed. M.L. Faull and S.A. Moorhouse, 3 vols. (Wakefield, 1981)
White, *Custom, Kinship and Gifts*	S.D. White, *Custom, Kinship and Gifts to Saints* (Univ. of North Carolina, 1988)
Wightman, *Lacy Family*	W.E. Wightman, *The Lacy Family in England and Normandy 1066–1194* (Oxford, 1966)
Williams, *Anglo-Saxons*	A. Williams, *The Fate of the Anglo-Saxons: The English and the Norman Conquest* (forthcoming)
YAJ	*Yorkshire Archaeological Journal*
YMF	*York Minster Fasti*, ed. C.T. Clay, 2 vols. (Yorks. Arch. Soc. rec. ser., 1957–8)
Yorkshire Domesday	*The Yorkshire Domesday*, ed. G.H. Martin and A. Williams (London, 1992)
Young, *William Cumin*	A. Young, *William Cumin: Border Politics and the Bishopric of Durham 1141–1144* (Univ. of York, Borthwick Paper, no. 54, 1979)

INTRODUCTION

The hundred years after 1066, which Stenton termed the 'first century of English feudalism', was full of remarkable developments which dramatically changed the nature of society. This book is a study of three of the most important of these developments: the Norman conquest, the anarchy of King Stephen's reign and the transformation in the nature of lordship and land tenure. Its aim is to contribute to our understanding of these developments by examining them within a county context. The county to be studied is Yorkshire, by far the largest in England.

The first three chapters reassess the nature and impact of the Norman conquest of Yorkshire. Employing a novel approach to the interpretation of the evidence of Domesday Book, Chapter 1 argues that the conquest was a more rapid and controlled process than has hitherto been supposed, and one in which the construction of castles formed a key element. In doing so, it suggests that the level of destruction in Yorkshire attributed to the famous harrying of the north has been overestimated, and makes a contribution to the recent debate concerning the effect of the conquest on patterns of land tenure. Chapter 2 reveals that under the Conqueror's successor, William Rufus, the size and number of the Norman lordships was deliberately increased, so that they covered the entire county and consolidated Norman tenurial domination there. It also reveals that under the next monarch, Henry I, this domination was reinforced by royal administration, as the king strengthened the links between central and local government. This was achieved through the grant of key local offices and institutions to a group of 'new men', who were dependent upon royal favour and in regular attendance at the royal court. Chapter 3 examines the scale and pattern of enfeoffment on the Norman lordships in 1135, and the terms on which the tenants of the Norman magnates held their lands. It reveals that the Norman settlement of lowland

Yorkshire was well advanced by 1135, whereas in the uplands it was still in its very early stages. It adds to the evidence suggesting that Norman military tenancies were held on terms which would have been very familiar to pre-conquest landholders, and that in large parts of the north military 'feudalism' was just a thin veneer laid over pre-existing forms of tenure. But it also argues that this veneer was deeper on the tenancies organised by the Normans for the garrisoning of castles, that Norman castle-guard obligations marked a significant innovation in the terms of landholding. Finally, the chapter turns from military to monastic enfeoffment, and argues that the establishment of monasteries in Yorkshire, like the establishment of honours, was coordinated by the crown and formed a crucial element in the programme of conquest.

The next section of the book deals with the anarchy of King Stephen's reign and its consequences. Chapter 4 reveals how the political troubles of the years 1135–54 led to a failure of royal control in Yorkshire, and a reversal of the centralising trend in Anglo-Norman administration. It examines the demise of royal administration which followed Stephen's appointment of William, count of Aumale, as earl of York in 1138. It reassesses the notion that Stephen's creation of earls was an attempt to impose an alternative conception of government, and offers a revision of accepted views concerning Earl William. He is revealed as a self-interested magnate, who was intent on building up a vast network of power in Yorkshire through the exploitation of royal rights entrusted to his charge, the acquisition of jurisdiction over a series of hundreds and the domination of the lesser aristocracy. But the chapter goes deeper than this. It illustrates that the lesser aristocracy had their own agenda in Stephen's reign, and throws light on their simmering ambition. They took advantage of the troubles to build their own castles, found their own monasteries and treat these foundations as private property; and in doing so, they undermined lordship and exacerbated social and political instability. But this instability was never total, and the chapter goes on to explore some of the forces within society which served to pacify Yorkshire and bring the anarchy to an end. Chapter 5 examines the most serious consequence of this anarchy: the significant and dangerous increase of Scottish power in Yorkshire and the north; and how this threatened to detach the region from the rest of England.

The third and final section of the book deals with lordship, one of the most significant aspects of medieval society. Chapter 6 examines lordship within the context of the honour, the 'community' of tenants and collection of tenancies over which the lord exercised certain rights. It does so by studying the *cartae baronum* of 1166. It argues that the magnates objected to providing the information required of them, and explores their motives. These motives help to explain the questions Henry II asked his magnates in 1166, and suggest that the politics of Stephen's reign served to undermine the coherence of the honorial community. By analysing some of the pre-1135 information contained within the *cartae baronum* in conjunction with other evidence, the chapter also illustrates other forces already undermining this coherence before Stephen's accession to the crown. It reveals that the strength of honorial ties, and the lordship essential to them, has been overestimated; a revelation with very serious implications for the history of the 'first century of English feudalism' and the origins of the English Common Law. These implications are explored in the final chapter of the book, which seeks to contribute to the debate concerning the nature of seignorial lordship before 1154, and the impact on this lordship of the legal reforms of Henry II. It does so by arguing that seignorial courts were not always autonomous jurisdictional entities free from outside interference, which had the power to settle the disciplinary and proprietary disputes of tenants; and that lords did not always have the right and power to control the alienation of land by tenants, and the succession of these tenants to their tenements. The chapter reveals that on some honours lordship was already crucially limited before the inception of the Angevin legal reforms, and that inheritance and property rights were already a reality.

The term 'Yorkshire' requires definition. Before 1066 Yorkshire was the only one of the six modern counties of northern England to have been shired. It is first explicitly described as a shire in 1065.[1] Its western boundaries at, before and shortly after that date are uncertain. The area described under the heading *Eurvicscire* in Domesday Book, included a number of districts outside the three ridings: Amounderness, Cartmel, Furness, Kendale, parts of Copeland, Lonsdale and Cravenshire (that is, modern Lancashire north of the Ribble and parts of Cumberland and Westmorland). Whether these districts were included in 'Yorkshire' in 1086 is unclear. It is possible that they were only attached to the county

---

[1] F. R. Thorn, 'Hundreds and wapentakes', in *Yorkshire Domesday*, 40.

for administrative convenience.[2] What is reasonably certain is that the 'shiring' of Lancashire, Cumberland and Westmorland only took place after 1086, and that when this 'shiring' occurred these regions were no longer regarded as part of Yorkshire, the boundaries of which remained relatively stable thereafter until 1974.[3] It is this 'historic' county to which the term Yorkshire refers in this book. It is a county bounded in the north by the River Tees, in the south by the Rivers Sheaf and Humber and by Meersbrook and in the west by the Pennines. It includes the three ridings of Domesday Book, with the addition of Cravenshire and parts of eastern Lonsdale.[4]

The region here defined has a varied topography.[5] It contains three extensive areas of upland: the Pennines, which rise to 2,415 feet above sea level; the North Yorkshire Moors, which are mainly over 1,000 feet; and the Wolds of the East Riding, which rarely exceed 800 feet. Nearly all of the many rivers which traverse the county rise in these uplands, most of them extending from the Pennines eastwards across the lowland Vale of York to join the Rivers Ouse or Humber. The rivers flowing out of the North Yorkshire Moors include the Esk, which runs west-east along Eskdale to enter the sea at Whitby, and the Derwent, which flows south to join the Humber near Howden. The land through which these rivers cut their paths is covered by a variety of soils. The Pennines and North Yorkshire Moors are characterised by poor quality acid moorland soils, whereas the limestone and chalk Wolds have high quality freely drained calcareous loams. Good agricultural land is also to be found in several of the lowland districts of Yorkshire, the most notable being the Vale of York, with its light to medium loams, and Holderness and Cleveland, with their medium to heavy loams. The exceptions include the Vale of Pickering and the region immediately to the south-west of

[2] For a discussion of this problem, see D. M. Palliser, 'An introduction to the Yorkshire Domesday', in *Yorkshire Domesday*, 4–5; Thorn, 'Hundreds and wapentakes', 41, 55–60; Hey, *Yorkshire*, 4; D. R. Roffe, 'The Yorkshire Summary: a Domesday satellite', *Northern History*, 27 (1991), 257.

[3] Cumberland may have been shired in 1092. There was a sheriff of Westmorland by 1129, and a sheriff of Lancashire by 1164.

[4] In this definition I follow that given in Palliser, 'Yorkshire Domesday', 5.

[5] For the details in this paragraph I rely mainly on the following: Hey, *Yorkshire*, Introduction; J. A. Sheppard, 'Pre-conquest Yorkshire: fiscal carucates as an index of land exploitation', *Inst. of Brit. Geographers Trans.*, 65 (1975), 67–78; *Domesday Geography*, 7–18, 78–82, 92–101, 159–62, 170–9, 228–32; Palliser, 'Yorkshire Domesday', 18–21; *VCH, Yorkshire*, II, 455–75.

the Humber, which are covered by ill-drained alluvial silt soils, clays and thin peat; and the broad area immediately to the east of the Pennines, with its mixture of light soils on Coal Measure sandstones and poorly drained clay loams on shales. This pattern of relief and soils had an obvious impact on the pattern of settlement. As we might expect, in Domesday Book the greatest concentration of vills occurred in the lowlands and those upland areas covered by better soils, while the Pennines, North Yorkshire Moors and marshy Humberhead levels appear to have been relatively sparsely populated. It is a pattern of settlement which has endured until modern times.

By far the largest and most important settlement in Yorkshire was York, from which the county took its name, and which was independent of the three ridings.[6] Until its capture by the Danes in 867, York was the capital of the ancient kingdom of Deira which covered the region between the Humber and the Tees. From 735 it was also the seat of an archbishopric which encompassed what is now Cumberland, Westmorland, Lancashire, Yorkshire and Nottinghamshire, and which had subcathedrals at Ripon, Beverley and Southwell. On the eve of the Norman conquest York was clearly a major city. Domesday Book records that it then contained 1,607 inhabited houses, and was divided into seven 'shires'. Other details reveal the existence of a market, archbishop's hall, mint and pool, and the presence of a council of judges (*iudices*). A good proportion of the large number of churches recorded in York in 1086 had probably been founded before the arrival of the Normans. The importance of the city is also reflected by the fact that eighty-four carucates distributed in thirteen neighbouring villages were said to be in the tax of York, suggesting that they were in some way subject to its authority.[7]

Just as York was the focus of the administration of Yorkshire, it was also the focus of its communications system.[8] It was situated on the River Ouse, which formed one of the main branches of an

---

[6] For a more comprehensive discussion of the pre-conquest history of Yorkshire, see Palliser, 'Yorkshire Domesday', 1–2; Kapelle, *Norman Conquest*, 3–105; Thorn, 'Hundreds and wapentakes', 41–3.

[7] *DB*, I, 298a-b; *Domesday Geography*, 157. For the best analysis of the Domesday Book account of the city, see Palliser, *York*.

[8] The following details are derived from F. M. Stenton, 'The road system of medieval England', *EcHR*, 7 (1936), 1–21, reprinted in *Preparatory to Anglo-Saxon England*, ed. D. M. Stenton (Oxford, 1970), 234–52. As Stenton noted, the reconstruction of the medieval road system is an extremely difficult task, and the highways discussed here may represent only a fraction of those in use in the Anglo-Norman period.

extensive network of water courses in Yorkshire stemming from the Humber estuary. This network provided access to the sea and, via the Trent, to the rivers of Lincolnshire and the midlands (Maps 12, 21).[9] York was also at the centre of the road system of Yorkshire. On the mid-fourteenth-century Gough map, depicting an English road system which was probably already ancient, a number of highways can be seen to radiate outwards from York. These highways connect the city with Leeming via Helperby; with Malton; with Market Weighton via Pocklington; with Market Weighton direct; and with Howden. The road from York to Leeming intersected the Great North Road at Leeming; and the road from York to Market Weighton continued on to Beverley, where it joined another highway connecting Beverley with Bridlington, Scarborough, Whitby and Guisborough (Maps 3–22).[10] There are indications in the Gough map that a road may also have extended northwards from York to Thirsk, North-allerton, Croft, Darlington, Durham, Chester le Street and Newcastle. Another important focus of communications in Yorkshire was Doncaster. This settlement was situated at the point where the Great North Road crossed the River Don at its highest navigable point for coastal traffic. From Doncaster the Great North Road extended northwards to Pontefract, Wetherby, Boroughbridge, Leeming, Catterick and Gilling, before branching north-westwards across the Pennines via Bowes and Stainmore to Brough, Appleby, Penrith and Carlisle. Doncaster was also the starting-point of an important road running through Wakefield, Bradford, Skipton, Settle and Kirkby Lonsdale, where it was joined by a road which extended over the Pennines from Richmond. In addition to these main highways, it is almost certain that Yorkshire was criss-crossed by a series of ancient drovers' roads, along which livestock were driven between estates and markets.[11]

[9] Palliser, *York*, 17.
[10] Some of the roads referred to here do not appear in the maps cited. This is because the precise course of these roads has not been determined with any degree of certainty. The roads which are depicted in the maps connect settlements which the Gough map informs us were connected by major highways in the middle ages, and they follow the line of modern A roads and/or ancient Roman roads. Although the correlation between the course of these A/Roman roads and medieval roads may not be exact, it is more than likely to be very close.
[11] Stenton noted that one of these roads connected Long Sutton (Lincs.) with Tadcaster (Yorks.) via Doncaster and Ferrybridge: 'Road system', 249–50. I am grateful to Professor Holt for drawing my attention to a drovers' road connecting the important

The name York is derived from the Anglo-Scandinavian name *Jorvic*, and reflects the powerful influence exercised by the Danes and Norsemen over Yorkshire in the centuries before the arrival of the Normans. After its capture by the Danes in 867, York was ruled until 954 by a series of Danish and Norse kings. They and their followers were responsible for changing the language spoken in Yorkshire and many of its place-names, and (probably) for establishing the three ridings and twenty-five wapentakes into which the county was divided for administrative purposes (Map 24).[12] Scandinavian domination ended when the West Saxon king, Eadred, killed the Viking leader, Eric Bloodaxe, on Stainmore in 954, and annexed Yorkshire. Thereafter, the county and the entire region to the north of the Humber was governed by a succession of earls, appointed by the West Saxon kings from the local nobility. Sometimes one earl governed the whole of Northumbria, sometimes the region was divided between two earls; one controlling Yorkshire from York, and another, usually drawn from the descendants of the old Northumbrian kings, governing the region between Tees and Tweed. To some extent, however, the Tees remained a cultural and political frontier between the Anglo-Scandinavians and Northumbrian English. As Professor Palliser points out, when Cnut reestablished Scandinavian power in England in 1016 after removing Uhtred, earl of Northumbria, and defeating King Edmund in battle, he was careful to choose his earls from the local Scandinavian population of Yorkshire.[13] His first earl, Eric, was succeeded by Siward, who was earl of Yorkshire by 1033 and of the whole of Northumbria from 1041 until his death in 1055. Edward the Confessor's choice of Tosti Godwinson as earl, in place of Siward's son, Waltheof, marked a new departure in the government of the north. Tosti was the first West Saxon earl of Northumbria, and his attempt to impose his authority ended with his deposition at the hands of the northern nobility, who chose Morcar, the younger brother of Edwin, earl of Mercia, to replace him in 1065. Edward the Confessor was forced to accept the *fait accompli*, and although his

---

Lacy demesne manors of Pontefract (Yorks.) and Clitheroe (Lancs.), which passed through Kirkstall, Eccleshill, Manningham, Haworth and Colne.

[12] The number of wapentakes includes five in the East Riding and two in the lands of Count Alan of Richmond, which, although not specifically mentioned until the twelfth century, were probably already in existence at the time of the Domesday survey. See Roffe, 'Yorkshire Summary', 246, 248.   [13] Palliser, 'Yorkshire Domesday', 2.

successor, Harold, replaced Morcar with Maerlesveinn, an important thane in the northern Danelaw, he did so only after Morcar's defeat in 1066 by a Norwegian invasion force at Fulford, and his own victory over the Norwegians at Stamford Bridge.

The reluctance of Edward and Harold to challenge the independent actions of the northern nobility is hardly surprising when we consider the limitations of their territorial power base north of the Rivers Sheaf and Humber. Although they held the governmental seat of York, outside it their control of the local centres of administration and power was limited. The most important of these centres were the complex soke manors, which were the most extensive and wealthy estates in Yorkshire, and which often served as the administrative focus of the county's wapentakes and hundreds. Domesday Book reveals that of the fifty or so complex manors in Yorkshire, Edward the Confessor held just five, with a combined value of £137; whereas the earls of Northumbria, Mercia, the north midlands and Wessex held thirty, which were worth a total of approximately £1,237.[14] Eight of the remaining fifteen complex manors were held by Archbishop Aldred of York, whose total landed estate in Yorkshire was valued at £270.[15]

In total, over 300 thanes are named as landholders in Yorkshire in 1066, and (because of the possibility that some of them shared the same name) the number may have been considerably greater. Farrer calculated that they held a total of some 1,583 manors, and Palliser notes that no landholder had an overwhelming dominance.[16] Besides the king and the earl, the most privileged thanes were those listed in Domesday Book as holding rights of 'sake and soke and toll and team'. The list includes the names of Earl Harold, Maerlesveinn, Ulf Fenisc, Lagr, Thorgautr, Toki, Edwin, Morcar, Gamall Fitz Osbert, Copsi and Cnut.[17] If Dr Roffe is correct in equating sake and soke with rights of full ownership, it could be that these nobles enjoyed overlordship of all the other thanes in Yorkshire. The existence of such overlordship in certain parts of the county is implied by a number of features in the Domesday text, including multiple manor entries, the interlocking of manors with larger estates and the existence of extensive territorial liberties

---

[14] See *ibid.*, 30. For the importance of the complex manors, see G. R. J. Jones, 'Multiple estates and early settlement', in *English Medieval Settlement*, ed. P. H. Sawyer (London, 1979), 9–34. [15] *DB*, I, 302a–4a.
[16] *VCH, Yorkshire*, II, 145; Palliser, 'Yorkshire Domesday', 30. [17] *DB*, I, 298b.

or franchises incorporating large numbers of holdings.[18] It is possible, therefore, that the vast majority of Anglo-Scandinavian thanes in Yorkshire in 1066 were subtenants. But even if this was the case, the power of some of these thanes was immense. Ormr son of Gamall was the predecessor of the Norman lord Hugh Fitz Baldric in twelve of his forty-four Yorkshire manors, and Gamalbarn held twenty-seven manors and shares in two more.[19] Another Yorkshire noble, Arnketill, is described by Orderic Vitalis as 'the most powerful of the Northumbrian nobles': a power reflected in his tenure with Gospatric (his son) of some 285 carucates of land in the county, in his family relationship with the House of Bamburgh, and in his joint-leadership of the northern rebellions of 1068 and 1069.[20] Gospatric was the only native lord to be named in the Yorkshire Domesday as a tenant-in-chief in 1086, and is recorded as holding 148 carucates of land valued at over £9.[21] The leaders of the northern rebellions also included the four sons of the powerful Yorkshire thane Karle, whose family was engaged in a blood-feud with the House of Bamburgh, which continued from 1016 down to the early 1070s. One of these sons, Thorbrand, held approximately seventy carucates in Yorkshire, which may have been administered from his hall at Settrington in the North Riding. Thorbrand's father and his brothers, Cnut and Sumarlithr, are recorded as holding another sixty-three carucates in Yorkshire.[22] Those of Cnut lay in Holderness, a region which Dr Williams suggests may once have been administered in its entirety by Cnut's grandfather, Thorbrand the Hold.[23]

The story of the resistance offered by these and other northern nobles to Norman power has been told many times, and need only be related in outline here.[24] Although the Conqueror secured the allegiance of some of these nobles at Barking shortly after the battle of Hastings, and was crowned in London by Archbishop Aldred of York, the majority of the powerful Northumbrian thanes remained aloof. William's determination to impose his authority in the north is reflected in his choice of a new earl of Northumbria before his departure to Normandy in March 1067.

[18] D. R. Roffe, 'From thegnage to barony: sake and soke, title, and tenants-in-chief', *ANS*, 12 (1990), 157–76.   [19] Palliser, 'Yorkshire Domesday', 30.
[20] Orderic, II, 218; Williams, *Anglo-Saxons*.   [21] *DB*, I, 330a.
[22] For Karle's family, see Williams, *Anglo-Saxons*.   [23] *Ibid*.
[24] J. Le Patourel, 'The Norman conquest of Yorkshire', *Northern History*, 6 (1971), 1–21; Kapelle, *Norman Conquest*, 105–57. For the most recent account, see Williams, *Anglo-Saxons*.

But this choice was a disastrous one. The new earl was Copsi, an old associate of the deposed Earl Tosti who had assisted the Norwegian invasion of England in 1066. Within a short time of arriving in the north Copsi was confronted by a major rebellion, which ended with his murder at Newburn in March 1067. The man chosen by William to succeed him, Gospatric son of Maldred, a cousin of King Malcolm III of Scotland, and a leading member of the House of Bamburgh, was hardly an improvement. When the earls Edwin and Morcar revolted shortly after May 1068, Gospatric was among the group of northern nobles who joined them, which also included Maerlesveinn, Arnketill and the four sons of Karle, all of whom held important estates in Yorkshire. The Conqueror's response was dramatic. He immediately marched north, building castles as he went at Warwick and Nottingham; actions which frightened some of the leading rebels into submission, and others into seeking refuge in Scotland. After taking hostages, establishing a castle at York under the command of Robert Fitz Richard and appointing William Malet as sheriff of Yorkshire, the king returned south via Lincoln, Huntingdon and Cambridge, where additional fortresses were constructed. Before departing for Normandy towards the end of the year William replaced Gospatric as earl of Northumbria beyond the Tees with Robert de Commines, a Frenchman, who established his base at Durham. This was a new departure in northern government, and it ended in disaster. The Conqueror's attempt to undermine the traditional political independence (or semi-independence) of the region beyond the Humber, and to impose direct rule from the south, provoked bitter opposition. Within a month of the arrival of Commines in the north, the Northumbrians launched an armed attack on Durham, in which the new Norman earl and his men were butchered.

The murder of Commines signalled the start of a major northern rebellion, which brought the Northumbrian and Anglo-Scandinavian exiles back from Scotland, and which soon spilled over from the land of St Cuthbert's, Durham, into Yorkshire. During the spring of 1069 a major force led by Edgar the Aetheling, Earl Gospatric, Maerlesveinn, Arnketill and the four sons of Karle marched into Yorkshire, slaughtered Robert Fitz Richard and his men after catching them out in the open and laid siege to the Norman castle of York. The Conqueror was once again quick to respond. In another lightning campaign he returned from Normandy, marched north, dispersed the rebels and built a second castle at York. After leaving the city and castles in the charge of William Fitz Osbern, William Malet and Gilbert of Gant, the Conqueror returned to the south and held his Easter court at Winchester. Most of the rebel leaders remained at large, and on 8 September were reinforced by the arrival of a Danish fleet in the Humber sent by King Swein Estrithson, who probably had his own ambitions towards the English crown. On 21 September 1069 the Danes joined the English in an assault on the castles at York, which ended with the slaughter of the Norman garrison and the capture of its commanders, William Malet and Gilbert of Gant. The Conqueror responded by going to Yorkshire, and the Danes fled to the banks of the Humber.

To deal with the situation the Conqueror despatched Robert, count of Mortain, and William, count of Eu, to contain the Danes in Lincolnshire, while he marched to put down a subsidiary rebellion which had broken out in the region of Stafford. After successfully quelling the rising at Stafford, William marched north, but was held up for three weeks at Pontefract, where the Anglo-Scandinavians had destroyed the bridge over the River Aire. When William eventually reached York the rebels had withdrawn, and the king commanded the castles to be repaired. He dealt with the Danes by offering them tribute and rights of plunder, in return for an agreement to depart from England in the following spring. The Anglo-Scandinavian rebels received sterner treatment. William was determined to hunt them down, and embarked upon a campaign, known as 'the harrying of the north', designed to wipe out resistance to his rule beyond the Humber. William's determination to impose his authority in the north was reflected not only in his use of force, but also in his decision to wear his crown at York during the Christmas festival of 1069. When the festivities were over the harrying continued; and William is said to have laid waste to the entire region between the Humber and the Tyne. Whatever the cruelties involved, it was a campaign which achieved results. Before the start of February 1070 the earls Waltheof and Gospatric had submitted to William in Teesdale, Edgar the Aetheling had withdrawn to Wearmouth and Bishop Aethelwine of Durham and his community had fled to Lindisfarne. The native-led Northumbrian rebellion was at an end. In 1071 William replaced Bishop Aethelwine with a Lotharingian, Walcher, and in the following year installed Waltheof son of Siward in place of Earl Gospatric. Waltheof remained in favour for a time, but after his involvement in the rebellion of the earls of East Anglia and Hereford in 1075, and his subsequent execution, power in Northumbria passed to Bishop Walcher; and with this, native governance of Yorkshire had passed away forever.

By 1075 the Normans had overcome Anglo-Scandinavian opposition to their authority in Yorkshire, and they had also taken steps to protect this authority from external threats. The most immediate of these threats was posed by the king of Scotland, Malcolm III. When the Conqueror succeeded to the crown, Scottish power to the west of the Pennines extended as far south as the Rere Cross on Stainmore at the north-western tip of Yorkshire, and King Malcolm was determined to extend it further.[25] In 1070 he ravaged Teesdale and Cleveland. The Conqueror responded by launching a major invasion of Scotland, which ended with Malcolm's acknowledgment of William's overlordship at the treaty of Abernethy in 1072. Thereafter, the Scots were unable or unwilling to penetrate as far south as Yorkshire until after William's death. The Danes, who posed the other major external threat to Norman power in Yorkshire, were only marginally more successful than the Scots. Between 1070 and 1087 they launched only one invasion of Yorkshire, which achieved little more than the sack of York, and which was over within a few weeks. Yorkshire was effectively at peace in the decade before the Domesday survey, and in that period the development of Norman authority within the county went largely unchallenged.

The original sources available for the study of Anglo-Norman Yorkshire are abundant. The main source for the history of land tenure in the eleventh century is Domesday Book. The Domesday text employed in this book is that published by Farley in 1783.[26] Domesday Book provides a mass of detailed information on the lands held by the Norman magnates in 1086, including the names of their Anglo-Scandinavian predecessors, geld assessments, annual seignorial income and the agricultural resources generating that income. In the case of Yorkshire, it also includes a section dealing with tenurial disputes (*clamores*), and a Domesday 'satellite' text

---

[25] G. W. S. Barrow, 'The Anglo-Scottish Border', *Northern History*, 1 (1966), 24–30; Thorn, 'Hundreds and wapentakes', 43–4.

[26] *DB*. Shortly before this book went to press Farley's text was superseded by a new facsimile edition. See *Yorkshire Domesday*.

commonly known as the Summary.[27] Although the Yorkshire Domesday is deficient in many respects, because Yorkshire was probably the first county in Circuit VI to be enrolled, it is still an important source for determining the pattern and extent of Norman power in 1086, and the process by which this power had been established.[28] When used in conjunction with later sources, the Yorkshire Domesday can also help to reveal the descent of estates, and to study the transformation of the structure of lordship, in Yorkshire between 1066 and 1154. The later sources include the returns of knights' fees in 1166, commonly known as the *cartae baronum*, and thirteenth-century feodaries and surveys, which mainly deal with land held by military service. Additional details on the descent of land held by military and other forms of service are provided by the *Inquisitions Post Mortem*.[29]

Charters provide another major category of source material, and here the historian of Yorkshire is particularly fortunate. Between the twelfth and the fifteenth centuries thousands of charters issued in the Anglo-Norman period were copied into the cartularies of Yorkshire's thirty or so major monasteries; the survival rate of which compares favourably with those produced in the religious houses of southern England. A good number of these cartularies have been published, with varying degrees of accuracy, by the Yorkshire Archaeological, Surtees and Thoresby Societies.[30] English translations of abstracts of the cartulary of Bridlington Priory, and one of the Fountains Abbey cartularies dating from the fifteenth century, were published privately by Lancaster.[31] Many monastic charters, both originals and cartulary copies, have also been printed in the *Monasticon Anglicanum*.[32] Other documents relating to the history of the northern bishoprics were published by Raine.[33] For the charters of most of the major secular lords of Yorkshire, reference must be made to the monumental work entitled *Early Yorkshire Charters*. The first three volumes of this work were published between 1914 and 1916 by

---

[27] For a detailed discussion of the Yorkshire Domesday, see Palliser, 'Yorkshire Domesday', 12–14; Roffe, 'Yorkshire Summary', 242–60.

[28] For the deficiencies of the text, see D. R. Roffe, 'Domesday Book and northern society: a reassessment', *EHR*, 105 (1990), 310–36.

[29] *Red Book*; *Book of Fees*; *Yorkshire Inquisitions of the Reigns of Henry III and Edward I*, ed. W. Brown, 3 vols. (Yorks. Arch. Soc. rec. ser., 1892–1902); *Cal. Inq. P. M.*

[30] See Bibliography.

[31] *Abstracts of the Charters and Other Documents Contained in the Chartulary of the Priory of Bridlington in the East Riding of the County of York*, ed. W. T. Lancaster (Leeds, 1912); *Chartulary of Fountains*.   [32] *Monasticon*.   [33] *Historians of York*, III.

the antiquarian, William Farrer, who tended to date charters on intuitive grounds. Between 1935 and 1965 the historian Sir Charles Clay added another nine volumes, in which he printed transcripts of the charters connected with the Yorkshire lordships of Richmond, Paynel, Skipton, Warenne, Stuteville, Trussebut, Percy and Tison. Further charters relating to Anglo-Norman Yorkshire were printed by Clay in the *Yorkshire Deeds* series of volumes, published by the Yorkshire Archaeological Society, and in two volumes devoted to the lands and rights of St Peter's, York, entitled *York Minster Fasti*. Clay's work on Yorkshire charters also enabled him to publish a volume providing details on over thirty of the county's baronial and knightly families.[34] To these sources Dr Greenway and Dr Burton have added excellent editions of the charters of the Mowbray family and of the archbishops of York respectively.[35] The royal charters relating to Yorkshire in the period 1066–1154 can be found in the volumes published under the title *Regesta Regum Anglo-Normannorum*.[36]

A great deal of information on political and ecclesiastical affairs in Yorkshire can also be derived from the accounts of chroniclers. The 'major' works containing information relevant to Yorkshire include those of the Anglo-Saxon chronicle, Orderic Vitalis, 'Florence of Worcester', Henry of Huntingdon, William of Malmesbury and the author of the *Gesta Stephani*, all of whom were writing in the Anglo-Norman period.[37] To these can be added the works of a number of monks based in the north of England, who often provide many details about Yorkshire not found elsewhere. These include the *Historia Regum*, attributed to Symeon of Durham, which relies heavily on the chronicle of 'Florence of Worcester' for its description of events between 1066 and 1118, but which is an original source for the period 1119–29.[38] Where the *Historia Regum* left off, the story was taken up by two priors of Hexham, Richard and John. Richard attained office in 1141, and wrote a history of the deeds of King Stephen and the battle of the Standard.[39] John served as prior between 1160 and c. 1209, and his historical work covers the period 1130–54.[40] Another Durham tract, the *De Injusta Vexatione Willelmi*, provides

[34] EYF.   [35] *Mowbray Charters*; *Episcopal Acta*.   [36] *Regesta*, I; II; III.
[37] ASC; Orderic; Florence, *Chronicon*; Henry of Huntingdon; *Gestis Regum*; *Historia Novella*; *Gesta Stephani*. I rely for most of the information in this paragraph on A. Gransden, *Historical Writing in England c. 550 to c. 1307* (London, 1974), which provides an excellent discussion of all these sources.   [38] Symeon, *Opera*, II, 3–283.
[39] *Chronicles of the Reigns*, III, 139–78.   [40] Symeon, *Opera*, II, 284–332.

useful information on the administration of Yorkshire, and the fate of the estates there belonging to the bishopric of Durham, during the quarrel between William Rufus and Bishop William of St Calais in 1088.[41] Other works by northern chroniclers or hagiographers of particular interest include Hugh the Chantor's *History of the Church of York* for the years 1066 to 1127, which contains interesting material on the archbishops of York from Thomas I to Thurstan, and on the primacy dispute between York and Canterbury; two anonymous lives of Archbishops Thurstan and William Fitz Herbert; the description of the battle of the Standard by Ailred, abbot of Rievaulx, probably written between 1155 and 1157; Walter Daniel's *Life* of Ailred, written shortly after 1167, which provides vital information on the spread of the Cistercian order in the north, and the influence of the Scots there; the *Historia Selebiensis*, written in 1174, recording the foundation and early history of Selby Abbey; William of Newburgh's *Historia Rerum Anglicarum*, written between 1196 and 1198, which was intended as a general chronicle of English events covering the period 1066–1197; and the chronicle of Pierre de Langtoft, a late thirteenth- or early fourteenth-century work by a canon of Bridlington Priory, which provides valuable details on the local wars conducted in Yorkshire and Lincolnshire in the reign of Stephen.[42] More information on the spread of Cistercian monasticism in Yorkshire can be gleaned from the foundation histories of the houses of Byland, Jervaulx, Fountains and Kirkstall written in the late twelfth and early thirteenth centuries.[43]

Pipe rolls provide the final category of original documentary source material. These survive for the year 1129–30 and in a continuous series from the early years of the reign of Henry II. They contain a considerable amount of information which casts valuable light on a number of themes and topics, including royal administration and finance, the exercise of patronage, tenurial descent, legal disputes, opposition to royal government and baronial wealth, to name just a few.[44] In studying these themes and topics the pipe rolls can be supplemented by information contained within the Red Book of the exchequer.[45]

[41] Symeon, *Opera*, I, 170–95.
[42] Hugh the Chantor; *Historians of York*, II, 259–91; *Chronicles of the Reigns*, III, 181–99 (*Relatio de Standardo*); *Vita Ailredi*; *Selby Coucher*, I, [1]–[54]; *Chronicles of the Reigns*, I, 3–408; Newburgh, *English Affairs*; *Chronicle of Langtoft*.
[43] *Monasticon*, v, 349–54, 568–74; *Memorials of Fountains*, 1–129; *Foundation of Kirkstall*.
[44] *PR 31 Henry I*; *PR 2–4 Henry II*; *PR 5 Henry II to 4 Henry III*.   [45] *Red Book*.

In addition to the original sources, there is a considerable body of secondary material on the history of Anglo-Norman Yorkshire. Before 1800 very few works of importance were published on this subject. The only ones worthy of mention are the studies of York by Widdrington and Drake, Gale's account of the estates of Earl Edwin in Richmondshire and Burton's survey of Yorkshire's monasteries.[46] The nineteenth century witnessed the publication of Allen's general history of Yorkshire, and a series of notable regional works by antiquarian scholars, including Whitaker's studies of Cravenshire and Richmondshire, Poulson's history of Holderness, and Hunter's account of south Yorkshire, which has been referred to as 'The foundation of the county's historical studies'.[47]

In the last hundred years a great deal of work has been done to collect details on the aristocratic families and lordships of Yorkshire. The fruits of some of the best of it can be found in the *Victoria County History*, which provides detailed studies of York, the North Riding and the bulk of the East Riding, but which does not encompass the West Riding. Another outstanding work is the series of volumes entitled *Early Yorkshire Charters* noted above. In addition to charters, the three volumes published by Farrer incorporate information on a large number of Yorkshire honours derived from a variety of other sources. Farrer's work in this respect was surpassed by Clay, whose detailed studies of the lords, lands, tenants and tenancies of nine Yorkshire lordships are remarkable for their erudition. Valuable work on the descent of the aristocratic families of Yorkshire has also been published in the *Complete Peerage*, and in Walker's study of Yorkshire pedigrees.[48] Mention should also be made of the detailed work undertaken by Michelmore on townships and tenure in the West Riding.[49]

[46] T. Widdrington, *Analecta Eboracensia*, ed. Caesar Caine (London, 1897) (Widdrington wrote around 1660); F. Drake, *Eboracum* (London, 1736); R. Gale, *Registrum Honoris de Richmond* (London, 1722); J. Burton, *Monasticon Eboracense* (York, 1758).

[47] T. Allen, *A New and Complete History of the County of York*, 3 vols. (London, 1828–31); T. D. Whitaker, *The History and Antiquities of the Deanery of Craven in the County of York*, ed. A. W. Morant (3rd edn, Leeds, 1878); idem, *History of Richmondshire*, 2 vols. (London, 1823); G. Poulson, *The History and Antiquities of the Seigniory of Holderness*, 2 vols. (Hull, 1840–1); J. Hunter, *South Yorkshire: The History and Topography of the Deanery of Doncaster*, 2 vols. (London, 1828–31). The quotation is from Hey, *South Yorkshire*, 5.

[48] *Complete Peerage*; *Yorkshire Pedigrees*, ed. J. Walker, 3 vols. (Harleian Soc., 1942–4).

[49] D. J. H. Michelmore, 'Township and tenure' and 'Township gazetteer', in *West Yorkshire*, II, 231–64, 294–579.

Although many historians have made use of this information on family and tenure to highlight other aspects of Yorkshire's history, the bulk of their work has been published in the form of articles on specialised topics, many of which can be found in the bibliography at the end of this book. A review of all these articles is beyond the scope of this introduction, which will confine itself to a discussion of works of greater length. The nearest thing to a general history of Yorkshire in this period is Kapelle's book on the Norman conquest of the north. This is a lively work, full of interesting and original ideas, which contains much valuable information on Yorkshire. However, the work is not specifically concerned with Yorkshire, only takes the story down to 1135 and advances some general arguments which are open to serious doubts.[50] Dr Hey's recent study of Yorkshire from the year 1000 to 1974 is more sober and less controversial, but is intended only as an outline survey, and devotes only forty-three pages to the Anglo-Norman period.[51] Raistrick's book in the series of volumes on the making of the English landscape, incorporates some incisive views about the Norman conquest, but confines itself to the West Riding.[52] A large amount of valuable information on the Norman conquest of Yorkshire, including some important and original ideas about Norman tenurial redistribution, can be found in Professor Fleming's recent study of eleventh-century England; but her work should be read in conjunction with the important series of articles by Roffe on Domesday Book, and with Palliser's wide-ranging and highly informative introduction to the *Alecto* facsimile edition of the Yorkshire Domesday.[53] Much of the information in the Yorkshire Domesday has been mapped and tabulated in Darby and Maxwell's edition of *The Domesday Geography of Northern England*.[54] General histories of individual Yorkshire lordships are few, the only full length monographs being those of Dr Wightman on the Lacys, and Dr English on the lords of Holderness.[55] Both these works contain stimulating accounts of the formation and development of the Norman lordships, the political careers of the magnates who governed them, the terms of land tenure and the nature of honorial economy and society. The same is true of Dr

[50] Kapelle, *Norman Conquest*. [51] Hey, *Yorkshire*, 24–67.
[52] Raistrick, *West Riding*.
[53] Fleming, *Kings and Lords*; Roffe, 'Domesday Book', 310–36; *idem*, 'Yorkshire Summary', 242–60; Palliser, 'Yorkshire Domesday', 1–38. See also D. Bates, *A Bibliography of Domesday Book* (Woodbridge, 1986). [54] *Domesday Geography*.
[55] Wightman, *Lacy Family*; English, *Holderness*.

Greenway's long introduction to her edition of the charters of the honour of Mowbray.[56] With regard to the spread of monasticism in Yorkshire, the magisterial study of Knowles remains the standard general work of reference and can be supplemented for additional details on specific orders by Dickinson's account of the Augustinians, Colvin's study of the Premonstratensians and Wardrop's work on the Cistercian house of Fountains.[57]

---

[56] *Mowbray Charters.*
[57] Knowles, *Monastic Order*; Dickinson, *Austin Canons*; Colvin, *White Canons*; Wardrop, *Fountains Abbey.*

Chapter 1

THE NORMAN CONQUEST OF YORKSHIRE

By 1071 the last native-led rebellion against Norman authority in Yorkshire had been suppressed, and most of the leading Anglo-Scandinavian thanes in the region who had resisted William the Conqueror and his followers were either dead, in prison or in exile. Any intentions the Conqueror may have entertained of working with the Anglo-Scandinavian aristocracy on anything like a position of equality had been cast away. Over the next fifteen years nearly all of the families belonging to this aristocracy were either deprived of their lands or reduced to the level of subtenants.[1] Domesday Book in 1086 records that twenty-five continental magnates introduced into Yorkshire by the Conqueror were in possession of over 90 per cent of the county's manors.[2] A very large number of these manors appear to have been underdeveloped. If the Domesday figures are totalled and tabulated they suggest that, taken as a whole, agricultural land in Yorkshire had suffered a dramatic decline in value in the twenty years following the arrival of the Normans (Table 1). Much of the county was apparently characterised by low population and plough-team densities. Many estates were described as waste, and recorded without resources or value.[3] In several areas the survey provides almost no information beyond tax assessment figures. In only a few had estates apparently weathered the twenty years of Norman rule well.[4] All this begs a number of questions concerning

[1] DB, I, 298a-332b.
[2] The term 'manor' is used to describe those estates described as such by the compiler of the Yorkshire Domesday. It should be noted, however, that Roffe has shown that the compiler may have included as manors in Yorkshire holdings which he did not count manorial in other counties: Roffe, 'Domesday Book', 328-31.
[3] *Domesday Geography*, 31-40, 59-71, 114-22, 139-50, 192-7, 212-21, and Figs. 9-11, 15-18, 28-30, 33-6, 47-9, 53-5.
[4] To some extent the decline in Yorkshire's agricultural prosperity is an illusion resulting from the deficiencies and omissions in the Domesday text. See R. W. Finn, *The Making and Limitations of the Yorkshire Domesday* (Univ. of York, Borthwick Paper, no. 41, 1972); Roffe, 'Domesday Book', 310-36.

what happened in Yorkshire between 1071 and 1086. The concern of this chapter is with two of the most important of them. How far had the Normans established their authority in Yorkshire by 1086? And what were the stages and methods by which this establishment was achieved?

As Professor Davies has argued, the Normans conquered and imposed their domination of other peoples through a complex, rich-textured and many faceted process. It was a process which involved the establishment of military, tenurial and political mastery; the formation of perceptions of dependence, norms of superiority, alliances, marriages and ties of friendship; the winning over of men through gifts, flattery, invitations to social occasions, cooperation and intimidation; the establishment of economic superiority and strangleholds; the settlement of colonists; and the imposition of cultural forces, such as ecclesiastical conformity, monasticism, learning and habits.[5] In Yorkshire and elsewhere many of these facets of the Norman conquest have already been admirably examined and elucidated by a number of historians.[6] But two of these facets will repay further attention, and it is here that this chapter seeks to make a particular contribution to our understanding of the conquest. In examining the extent of Norman authority in Yorkshire in 1086, and the chronology and methodology by which this authority had been established, the chapter will concentrate on the tenurial and military facets of the Norman take-over. It will reassess the evidence for the establishment of Norman authority within the lordships described in Domesday Book, for the methods by which the Normans redistributed land and for the construction and functions of Norman castles and castleries.

In tenurial terms, the Norman conquest of Yorkshire has traditionally been portrayed as a slow, ill-organised and piecemeal affair. Dr Wightman argued that the creation and organisation of the great compact lordships of Pontefract, Richmond, Tickhill and

---

[5] R. R. Davies, *Domination and Conquest* (Cambridge, 1990), Chapter 1.
[6] Le Patourel, 'Norman conquest', 1–21; *idem*, 'The Norman colonization of Britain', *I Normanni e la loro espansione in Europa nell'alto medioevo* (Centro Italiano di Studi sull'Alto Medioevo, Settimana xvi, 1968, Spoleto, 1969), 418–19; *idem*, *The Norman Empire* (Oxford, 1976), 41–2; Kapelle, *Norman Conquest*, 105–57; Wightman, *Lacy Family*, 20–54; Williams, *Anglo-Saxons*; Fleming, *Kings and Lords*, 153–79. Searle, *Women*, 10–11, 13, 22–3, 32–5, 38–40; D. Bates, *William the Conqueror* (London, 1989), 75–85, 122–34, 140–8, 163–5; English, *Holderness*, Chapter 1.

possibly Conisbrough was delayed until the 1080s.[7] The argument
was based on the apparent absence of castles on these lordships in
1086, the Domesday evidence that Ilbert I of Lacy only acquired
Pontefract and several other Yorkshire estates very shortly before
the completion of the Domesday survey, the continuation of the
construction of some of the compact lordships after 1086 and the
survival of large numbers of Anglo-Scandinavian tenants. Accepting this interpretation, Professor Le Patourel suggested that the
development of Norman tenurial control was a very gradual and
dislocated process lacking firm direction from above:

> The redistribution of land, as the Normans came to dominate Yorkshire,
> must have been a fairly rough-and-ready affair. In so far as it was
> controlled, it could only be operated by assigning to each of William's
> followers who were seeking property in Yorkshire the lands, or part of
> the lands, of some English landholder ... This would often bring it about
> that the total holding of any one Norman baron was a scattered, untidy
> and perhaps almost unworkable affair.[8]

The ideas of Wightman and Le Patourel were readily adopted in
turn by Professor Kapelle, who found that they complemented his
interpretation of the pre-conquest political separatism of the
north; and by Professor Searle, who argues that the Normans
could not hope to control or govern the north in 1070, and that
while Earl Waltheof lived the area was closed to Norman
ambition, only becoming ripe for real conquest after 1075.[9] Most
recently, Dr Golding's study of the honour of one Yorkshire
tenant-in-chief, Robert count of Mortain, concludes that 'it is
doubtful if [Robert's] hold over the Yorkshire estates was ever
more than nominal ... control of the north was more theoretical
than real till the reign of Henry I. It is likely, by analogy with the
holdings of Ilbert of Lacy (Pontefract) or Alan of Brittany
(Richmond) that Robert only assembled his Yorkshire lands in the
1080s'.[10]

The major source on which these historians have based their
conclusions is Domesday Book. This chapter will adopt a new and
more systematic approach to the information contained within
Domesday Book. It will employ this information to establish a
model for measuring the extent of seignorial authority achieved

[7] Wightman, *Lacy Family*, 21–8, 40–2, 54.
[8] Le Patourel, 'Norman conquest', 12–13.
[9] Kapelle, *Norman Conquest*, 3–49, 86–157, esp. 144–5; Searle, *Women*, 11, 19–20.
[10] B. Golding, 'Robert of Mortain', *ANS*, 13 (1991), 125.

on the various Norman honours in 1086. It is possible to use Domesday Book for this purpose because of the way in which it was compiled. The Domesday commissioners relied on the men of the vill, wapentake, division, riding and shire, who made presentations concerning tenure and title on the basis of pre-existing geld lists in an open session of the county court; while the tenants-in-chief provided (privately) the bulk of the information on estate organisation, including details concerning plough-teams, population and values.[11] In the settlements for which information of this nature appears in Domesday Book the Normans were exercising at least enough administrative control to compel the attendance of the villagers at the county court sessions, and to secure local knowledge of the land and its resources. In the settlements for which this information was either partly or wholly absent, Norman authority is likely to have been weaker or more limited.

The Domesday model for assessing the level of Norman authority is described in the first section of this chapter. The model is then applied to the various Norman lordships, and used to divide them into broad categories of development. Finally, the results of this study are analysed in conjunction with other evidence for the conquest of Yorkshire, derived from the chroniclers and from strategic and military considerations. It is an analysis which, despite certain limitations resulting from the inadequacies and ambiguities of the Domesday information, suggests that on several lordships (or parts of lordships) Norman authority was far from negligible in 1086, that some of these lordships incorporated compact castleries and that the construction of these castleries had begun much earlier and proceeded more rapidly than has hitherto been supposed.

It is important to stress at the outset that this approach to the study of the conquest is only one of many possible approaches, and that it is intended as a contribution to an on-going debate, rather than the last word on the subject. The limitations and problems associated with the information contained within the Yorkshire Domesday, and the many unknown or partially known variables which influence the interpretation of that information, preclude a definitive history of the Norman conquest of Yorkshire. The historian of Yorkshire will often be forced by the limitations of the

---

[11] Roffe, 'Domesday Book', 311.

evidence to make assumptions. If some of the assumptions incorporated within the following analysis turn out on closer inquiry to be misplaced, it is to be hoped that by provoking or stimulating further investigation they will help to advance our knowledge of the Norman conquest.

SEIGNORIAL AUTHORITY IN 1086: FIVE MEASURES

I. *Waste*

Hundreds of vills distributed throughout Yorkshire were described in Domesday Book as having no population, resources or values; and many of these were termed 'waste'. Although a number of historians have argued that many (or most) of these vills had been devastated by the Conqueror's armies or those of the Scots and Danes, particularly during the harrying of the north in the winter of 1069–70, there are grounds for doubting their conclusions, and for disposing of the myth that the Norman devastation of Yorkshire was almost total.[12]

Although the drastic decline in estate values in Yorkshire between 1066 and 1086, and in the geld assessment of the county between 1086 and the early twelfth century, together with the graphic and corroborative accounts of several chroniclers, leave little doubt that there was major destruction of some kind, it is likely that the geographical scope of this destruction was relatively limited. Recent research has indicated that the hundreds of highly abbreviated Domesday entries in which estates are recorded without population, resources and values are more likely to reflect compilation problems resulting from changes of plan and a lack of information, rather than physical destruction.[13] This suggests that the harrying of the north may well have been exaggerated; and

---

[12] For the argument for a connection (direct or indirect) between waste and military operations, see F. Baring, 'The Conqueror's footprints in Domesday', *EHR*, 13 (1898), 17–25; J. Beddoe and J. H. Rowe, 'The ethnology of West Yorkshire', *YAJ*, 19 (1907), 31–60, esp. 50–1, 58–9; T. A. M. Bishop, 'The Norman settlement of Yorkshire', in *Studies in Medieval History Presented to Frederick Maurice Powicke*, ed. R. W. Hunt *et al.* (Oxford, 1948), 1–14; R. W. Finn, *The Norman Conquest and its Effects on the Economy: 1066–86* (London, 1971), 27, 205; *Domesday Geography*, 63, 144; Kapelle, *Norman Conquest*, 163–7; S. Harvey, 'Domesday England', in *The Agrarian History of England and Wales*, vol. II, ed. H. E. Hallam (Cambridge, 1988), 135. For the supposed systematic devastation of Yorkshire, see D. C. Douglas, *William the Conqueror* (London, 1964), 220; McDonald and Snooks, *Domesday*, 26, 122–3.

[13] Roffe, 'Domesday Book', 323.

the suggestion is strengthened by a consideration of the military, chronological and climatic limitations within which the Conqueror was working in the winter of 1069–70. It is questionable whether William had the manpower, time and good weather necessary to reduce vast areas of the region between the Humber and the Tyne to a depopulated, uncultivated desert. In the late 1060s the bulk of his troops must have been stationed in the castles that were under construction everywhere in the south of England and Welsh marches, and his visit to Yorkshire in 1069–70 lasted no longer than three months, and may have been considerably shorter.[14]

The key to the extent of the harrying of the north is provided by Orderic Vitalis. Although his general description of the appalling scale and horror of the devastation is one of the most vivid, Orderic makes two precise and consistent statements which serve to qualify his account in one crucial respect. He begins by stating that the Conqueror 'continued to comb forests and remote mountainous places, stopping at nothing to hunt out the enemy hidden there', and concludes with a description of William spending fifteen days 'encamped on the bank of the Tees [where] Waltheof and Gospatric submitted to him'.[15] Upper Teesdale would certainly fit the description of a remote and mountainous place, and was exactly the sort of area where rebel Anglo-Scandinavians might have taken refuge from a hostile Norman king. Although Orderic's knowledge of northern geography is suspect in places, when considered in conjunction with the military and chronological realities of the conquest, his account of the Conqueror's movements in 1069–70 strongly suggests that, although severe, the harrying of the north was largely confined to the more remote upland regions of northern England, and that its purpose was to seek out and secure the submission of the native leaders who had assisted the Danish capture of York.

The corollary of this interpretation of the harrying of the north is that the *universal* equation of waste with physical devastation is inaccurate. This is supported by Professor Palliser's observations that not one of the Yorkshire entries for waste attributes the cause

---

[14] The Danes captured York on 21 September 1069. On his way to York William was prevented by opposing forces from crossing the River Aire for three weeks, which makes it unlikely that he began the harrying earlier than late October. In January William 'left the Tees and returned to Hexham' before marching to York and then departing to deal with a rebellion at Chester: Orderic, II, 230, 234 and note 1. See also Symeon, *Opera*, II, 188.   [15] Orderic, II, 232.

directly to military harrying, that only one entry in the whole of Domesday does so, and that one other entry (for Wiggington which 'was and is waste') would seem to rule out any link with the harrying because it suggests that land could already be waste in 1066.[16] Although this does not preclude the possibility that some waste was physical, it does suggest that the term might often have had other meanings unconnected with devastation.[17]

The most plausible interpretation of the meaning of waste was put forward by Wightman, who argued from his examination of Yorkshire Domesday that estates were written off as waste as an administrative or accounting device, and that there were several reasons why this was done. These included the destruction of the estate and killing or dispersal of its peasants; the attachment of it to some other estate for administrative purposes; the lack of suitable or willing tenants prepared to pay full rents (or the attempt to attract settlers by writing off renders); afforestation; poor agricultural development and the absence of arable; and the exemption of the estate from geld and resultant lack of concern about its value.[18] Wightman's general conclusion that ultimately waste seems to have meant that 'for administrative purposes the land to which it applied was worthless or nearly so' has much to recommend it.[19] Since most of the estates described as waste at the time of Domesday had not been waste twenty years earlier, it would appear reasonable to conclude that waste was often, although by no means universally, used to describe land where there had been some form of serious administrative and/or agricultural disruption in the period 1066–86; and that there were many possible causes for this disruption besides the physical devastation of the land.[20] Conversely an absence of waste suggests either a less severe form of disruption, or no disruption at all.

[16] D. M. Palliser, 'Domesday Book and the "harrying of the north"', *Northern History*, 29 (1993), 9–10; *idem*, 'Yorkshire Domesday', 35–6. Professor Palliser and I have been working independently towards the same broad conclusions with regard to the harrying.

[17] The equation of waste with physical devastation is implied by the description of the Poitevin fee in Amounderness: *DB*, I, 301b.

[18] W. E. Wightman, 'The significance of "waste" in the Yorkshire Domesday', *Northern History*, 10 (1975), 55–71 and note 47; *idem*, *Lacy Family*, 43–53.

[19] Wightman, 'Waste', 70.

[20] It is possible that the attachment of some of the estates described as waste to other estates for administrative purposes was done for reasons of efficiency and convenience, rather than because the Normans were experiencing difficulties in exercising direct control. It would be useful, but extremely difficult, to attempt to quantify the number of cases where waste relates to this form of administrative transference.

2. *Estate values and income*

The meaning of the 1066 and 1086 values ascribed to the settlements of Yorkshire in Domesday Book was called into question long ago by Maitland, who pointed out that these values often look artificial.[21] This is most apparent in Holderness, where several complex manors belonging to Drogo de la Beuvrière were each valued at £56 in 1066 and at either £10 or £6 in 1086. But if we consider that these figures represent annual values of dues and renders (farms) to the tenant-in-chief, rather than capital values of land and equipment, and that dues and renders of this sort are often expressed in round figures, then their 'artificiality' is neither surprising nor prohibitive of their use as a measure of seignorial authority.[22]

Declining estate values are a common feature in the Yorkshire Domesday. Although it is possible that some of them were due to natural causes, such as population migration or flooding, it is quite likely that most of them reflect the disruptive influence of the Norman conquest. They might be due to allowances made by lords on account of physical devastation, a shortage of suitable tenants prepared to render full rents (leading to competition for service), difficulties in collecting rents or Norman administrative reorganisation.[23] Conversely, it would seem reasonable to suppose that where the level of values had been maintained or increased over the period 1066–86 the Norman lords had gained knowledge about the land and the renders due from it, and had established themselves in a position strong enough to ensure that these renders were paid and collected in full. It is difficult to imagine why a Norman lord would wish to inform the Domesday commissioners that he was obtaining as much or more income from an estate in 1086 than his predecessor had done in 1066, if this was not in fact the case. Indeed, the comparative rarity of Yorkshire estates which

---

[21] Maitland, *Domesday Book*, 473.

[22] For Domesday values, see Roffe, 'Thegnage to barony', 170–1; McDonald and Snooks, *Domesday*, 77–8, 98; A. R. Bridbury, 'Domesday Book: a re-interpretation', *EHR*, 105 (1990), 290–1. Palliser tentatively suggests that it may be safer to measure changes in wealth in the period 1066–86 by using the ratio of carucates to ploughlands: that is, by comparing the tax assessment of estates in 1066 with their assumed revised assessment in 1085. As Palliser notes, however, the meaning of the term ploughland is a matter of debate: 'Yorkshire Domesday', 37. Another difficulty is that the size of carucates might vary from region to region.

[23] Fleming has noted a correlation between higher incidences of value decline and Norman tenurial reorganisation: Fleming, *Kings and Lords*, 123–6.

had either maintained or increased their values, suggests that information of this nature was likely to be genuine.[24]

3. *Plough-teams*

For Bridbury, the plough-teams recorded in Domesday represent only those which contributed towards the taxable income of the lord, and many teams operated by the peasants for their own purposes are left out of the picture.[25] Whether this view is correct or not, when considered against the background of the agricultural potential of the land, the number of plough-teams on an estate in 1086 would appear to offer another reasonable indication of Norman estate management and seignorial authority. Although it is likely that the presence of large numbers of plough-teams in areas of good agricultural potential reflects pre-conquest conditions, quite unaltered, the recording of these teams in Domesday would still have been dependent upon Norman knowledge of the estate and some form of control over its administration. It is difficult to imagine the continuation of peasant ploughing on the demesne in the absence of seignorial supervision. It is also worth remembering that the presence of low numbers of teams need not necessarily indicate a relative absence of, or decline in, seignorial estate management. A small plough force might be due instead to the poor quality of the land, a failure on the part of the tenant-in-chief to report the teams to the Domesday commissioners, or the physical devastation of the estate during the conquest period.

The assessment of plough-team levels in 1086 in these terms, and the conclusions drawn from this assessment about Norman seignorial authority, can only be impressionistic. A major difficulty is that no comparisons can be made between plough-team levels in 1066 and 1086, since Domesday contains little or no information on these levels at the former date. The only way of obtaining a general impression of 'high' and 'low' levels of plough-teams is to compare individual Norman estates and lordships in 1086. And

---

[24] It is important to stress that comparisons between the level of value preservation on the various Norman lordships in Yorkshire in 1086 will be comparisons of 'official' annual seignorial income only. It is more than likely that the Norman tenants-in-chief were in receipt of revenues in excess of this income, which they were not required to admit to the Domesday commissioners. I am grateful for this observation to Dr Roffe.

[25] Bridbury, 'Domesday Book', 284–309.

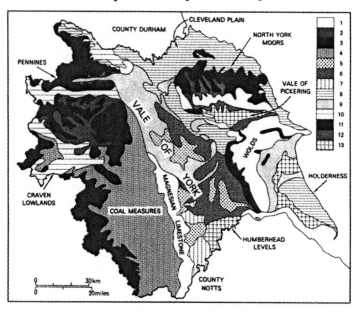

1. Freely drained calcareous loams on limestone and chalk.
2. Thin soils with many rock outcrops on Carboniferous limestone.
3. Acid moorland soils with areas of peat.
4. Alternating light soils on Coal Measure sandstones and poorly drained clay loams on shales.
5. Heavy loams with high water-table.
6. Sands with high water-table.
7. Well-drained sands.
8. Medium to heavy loams over glacial drift.
9. Light to medium loams over glacial drift.
10. Medium to heavy but freely drained calcareous loams.
11. Flinty loams over chalk gravel.
12. Calcareous loams over glacial drift containing limestone.
13. Alluvial silt loams and clays with some thin peat.

Map 1 The soils of Yorkshire, based on a map in W. Harwood Long, *A Survey of the Agriculture of Yorkshire* (1969), 15

Source: J.A. Sheppard, 'Pre-conquest Yorkshire: fiscal carucates as an index of land exploitation', *Institute of British Geographers Transactions*, 65 (1975), 75.

here there is always the danger of not comparing like with like. In part this is due to the absence of direct information in Domesday Book about the area of arable land, in part it is because the pre-conquest agricultural potential of land, which almost certainly had an uneven influence on its post-conquest development, is difficult to assess and, within the scope of this book, can only be discussed in broad regional terms.

Relief and soil quality are two of the major determinants of agricultural potential, and we are fortunate in possessing a map relating to these against which the Norman lordships can be compared (Map 1). It is significant that this map corresponds reasonably closely with a map of the intensity of fiscal carucation in early eleventh-century Yorkshire which Dr Sheppard argues reflects the intensity of land exploitation at that time (Map 2).[26]

4. *The progress of enfeoffment and condition of tenant estates*[27]

Enfeoffment represents a further stage in the extension of seignorial authority over the land. It is likely that in the very early stages of the Norman conquest most of the followers of the Norman tenants-in-chief would have been retained in the households of their lords. It is equally likely that the enfeoffment of these followers would only have proceeded when the lords had secured some knowledge of the geography and tenurial structure of their lordships. Once enfeoffed, the followers had the responsibility of taking stock of the resources on their estates, and of managing these resources so as to provide for themselves and render service to their lords. Since Domesday Book is partly a record of resources and renders (values) compiled from information supplied by tenants-in-chief and their men, it provides some measure of the success of the Norman subtenants in establishing their authority over the land.

[26] Sheppard, 'Pre-conquest Yorkshire', 67–78, map on p. 74. Sheppard's maps probably provide a more accurate representation of land exploitation than the maps of plough-teams or population in 1086 drawn by Darby and Maxwell, since they are not distorted by either the effects of the harrying of the north or the deficiencies of the Domesday text.

[27] The term 'enfeoffment' might be considered to refer to the grant of land held by hereditary fee in return for knight service. If so, as will become clear in Chapter 3, the use of the term to describe the alienation of land to tenants in the eleventh century is anachronistic in some cases. However, for the sake of convenience, I propose to use the term in this way, but without any implication of heritability, actual military service, tribute or anything similar.

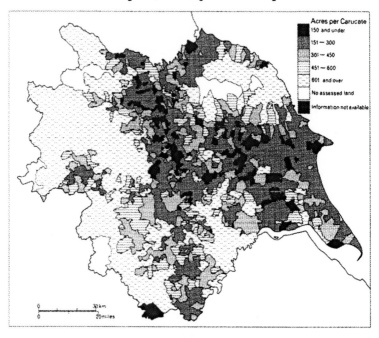

Map 2 The intensity of fiscal carucation in eleventh-century Yorkshire

Source: J.A. Sheppard, 'Pre-conquest Yorkshire: fiscal carucates as an index of land exploitation', *Institute of British Geographers Transactions*, 65 (1975), 74.

One of the problems with using Domesday Book in this way springs from its failure to record all subtenants.[28] Although it is a problem which will not weaken the general argument of this chapter, it may distort any comparisons which are made between levels of tenant enfeoffment on different lordships. Another problem with these comparisons is the danger of regarding the correlation between the number of tenants and the level or extent of seignorial estate management and authority as uniform. A low level of tenant enfeoffment need not necessarily be equated with a low level or extent of seignorial authority. It could have been due to other causes. Some lords may have had less capacity or desire to enfeoff tenants than others. Although it is difficult, if not impossible, to assess accurately the different objectives and skills of

---

[28] Palliser, 'Yorkshire Domesday', 33.

different lords, it is possible to take some account of honorial variations by examining enfeoffment in terms of the proportion of honorial resources alienated to tenants.

5.   Castles and castleries

Castles served a variety of purposes in this period, depending upon (among other things) who owned them, their location and their size. In most cases they served as residences, and as symbols of seignorial authority and status.[29] But they commonly had additional functions. One of these functions might be military, and this could vary from castle to castle depending on their size and location. Another function was administrative. In a recent study Mr Pounds has argued that most of the royal castles established in the Anglo-Norman period were intended to dominate and control urban centres and to serve as 'instruments of civil administration'; while in the case of most baronial castles,

local and tenurial factors predominated in the choice of site ... [the baron] was motivated primarily by his own convenience and security. Above all, he wanted access to the lands from which he derived his income and support ... Ease of defence was a significant factor, but possibly not one of overwhelming importance ... the vast majority of English and Welsh castles were established on lowland or valley sites.[30]

These arguments are in accord with a recent study of the distribution of castle sites in Yorkshire, which concludes that 'It is clear ... that their locations were determined by the nature and distribution of land-holdings ... and that they acted more as administrative centres for estates of both tenants-in-chief and mesne tenants, rather than as sites chosen for their strategic positions.'[31] It would appear, therefore, that the construction of Norman castles and the establishment of Norman estate management and administrative authority often went hand in hand.

The remains of motte and bailey or ringwork earthworks survive throughout England, and are numerous in Yorkshire. Although many of these castles cannot be dated with absolute certainty to within a hundred years of 1066, Stenton maintained that most of them were the product of the period 1066–1135.[32] His views have found support in one of the most recent studies of

---

[29] Pounds, *Medieval Castle*, 184–201.
[30] *Ibid.*, 57–8, 60–5, quotations from pp. 58, 61, 64–5, 69–70.
[31] *West Yorkshire*, III, 734.   [32] Stenton, *First Century*, 198–201.

castles in Anglo-Norman England, which argues that 'The total [number of castles] rose dramatically from almost nothing [in 1066] to a near peak figure of more, perhaps much more, than 500 in the decade after 1066.'[33] If many of the earthwork castles were founded in the conquest period, and if the agricultural resources and values recorded in Domesday Book do provide a measure of Norman seignorial estate management, we would expect a degree of correlation between the distribution of earthwork sites and the distribution of estates recorded in Domesday with reasonably large numbers of peasants and plough-teams, and reasonably well-preserved values. And in Yorkshire this is exactly what we find.[34]

These are the measures of seignorial estate management by which the Domesday lordships of Yorkshire are to be divided into broad categories of development, and by which the extent of Norman authority in the county in 1086 and the chronology of its growth are to be established. The categories which follow are distinguished and defined on the basis of the overall organisational profile produced by the application of all five measures, rather than the individual and limited picture produced by each of them. It is possible, therefore, that lordships with markedly different internal structures may appear within the same category of organisation. In five out of six cases the categories provide a basis for establishing the order in which the various lordships began to be constructed. It should be noted that on each lordship only the estates where Domesday Book provides both 1066 and 1086 values have been considered.

---

[33] R. Eales, 'Royal power and castles in Norman England', in *The Ideals and Practice of Medieval Knighthood III*, ed. C. Harper-Bill and R. Harvey (London, 1990), 60. See also Pounds, *Medieval Castle*, 10–11.

[34] It is possible that castle construction followed the pattern of administrative organisation rather than vice-versa, in which case some of the castles may belong to the period after 1086. However, given the military exigencies of the conquest period, the danger from brigandage, the likelihood that Norman lords would have required a secure base from which to take stock of their holdings, assess their resources and to ensure the maintenance of their exploitation, castle construction is more likely to have preceded, or to have been concurrent with, Norman administrative take-over.

NORMAN AUTHORITY ON THE HONOURS OF YORKSHIRE IN
1086: SIX CATEGORIES

Conisbrough

The complex estate of Conisbrough, with more than twenty sokelands, stretched across the gap between the Humberhead marshes and the Pennine hills (Map 21), and was the sole constituent of the Yorkshire lordship held in 1086 by William I of Warenne, a distant cousin of the Conqueror.[35]

The Domesday account of the estate is unusual in both form and content. It appears to have been inserted postscriptally into the main body of the text, and it includes a long list of entries for each of the sokelands recording details of population and resources, in addition to the normal composite sokeland entry following the description of the main settlement.[36] When viewed in conjunction with several other extraordinary features, this account suggests that Conisbrough may have been a liberty or franchise. These features include the exalted status of the pre-conquest tenants, and the very low level of military service which appears to have been owed to the crown from the estate in the twelfth century.[37]

An early date of alienation for Conisbrough would be consistent with the high level of estate management evident there in 1086. This suggests that William of Warenne had enjoyed sufficient time in which to take stock and establish control of the existing resources. No part of the estate was waste, and even the outlying sokelands were recorded with demesne and peasant plough-teams and a large peasant population (Table 2). The ratio of seignorial plough-teams to peasant teams (16:92) is another sign that Warenne had extended his knowledge, and almost certainly his management, of agriculture far beyond the estates he farmed directly. In total, he had secured command of around 300 peasants and 108 plough-teams, and appears to have been exploiting his lands relatively intensely by Yorkshire standards. The number of plough-teams per carucate was nearly three times the county average.[38] To some extent this is probably a reflection of the

---

[35] *DB*, I, 321a. [36] Roffe, 'Domesday Book', 313, 317.
[37] Michelmore, 'Township and tenure', 242; *idem*, 'Township gazetteer', 577; *DB*, I, 321a; *EYC*, VIII, 139–40.
[38] The county average referred to is the average for the lordships of the secular tenants-in-chief. On both the demesne and tenanted portions of these lordships the average was 0.42 plough-teams per carucate.

location of Conisbrough and some of its sokelands in the belt of land extending south from the River Aire to the county boundary with Nottinghamshire which, despite the prevalence of poor sandy soils, appears to have been reasonably well exploited agriculturally before 1066 (Maps 1–2). However, the fact that Domesday Book reflects the continuation of these conditions after 1066 indicates that Norman authority in Conisbrough and its outliers was more than nominal, that William of Warenne knew his land and had taken charge of its administration. There are indications that he had gone further, and had either expanded the agriculture of the Conisbrough complex or was exploiting it more efficiently. One of these indications is the dramatic increase in the value of the estate from £18 to £40, a remarkable feature in a county where the majority of estate values had declined sharply.[39] Another is the location of some of the sokelands with the largest numbers of plough-teams near the peripheries of the lordship, several miles from Conisbrough, in areas where the pre-conquest level of agricultural exploitation appears to have been very low and the soils were of poor quality.[40]

Conisbrough is known to have been the site of a powerful castle in the twelfth century, and had probably been fortified before the Normans arrived in England. The name Conisbrough derives from the Old English Cyningesburh, 'the stronghold of the king', and the Normans appear to have been quick to make use of the site and to construct a castle there. The structure of the earthworks at Conisbrough suggests that this castle may have been built in the reign of the Conqueror.[41] The lordship of Conisbrough, in short, was probably a highly organised and profitable castlery in 1086.

The honours of William I of Percy and Hugh Fitz Baldric

The Domesday accounts of the lordships of William I of Percy and Hugh Fitz Baldric bear sufficient comparison to warrant their incorporation within the same category. Both lordships were well placed to control the road and river approaches to York (Maps 3–4).

The level of estate organisation on the lordships of Percy and Fitz Baldric reflected in Domesday Book suggests that in 1086

---

[39] £10 of the £40 was attributed to tallage: *DB*, I, 321a.
[40] This was true, for example, of Fishlake, Thorne and Hatfield: *DB*, I, 321a.
[41] S. Johnson, *Conisbrough Castle* (London, 1984), 3.

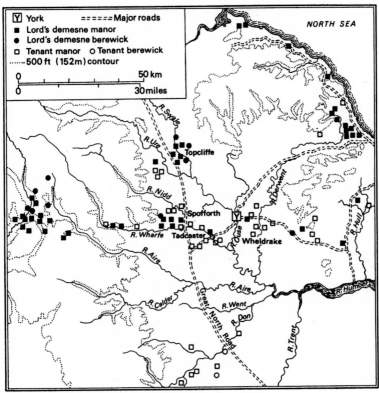

Map 3   The honour of William of Percy: 1086

these lords were well aware of their resources, were managing a large proportion of them and had been in charge of their estates for a considerable period of time. The maintenance of reasonably well-developed demesne agriculture on both lordships may have been due to the need to provide for a large body of Norman soldiers and administrators (Table 3).[42] Of the thirty-seven Percy manors farmed directly by the lord, twenty-three supported plough-teams, twelve had increased in value and fourteen were

[42] In the case of the Fitz Baldric fee the figures for carucates, ploughlands, peasant plough-teams, peasants and values on the demesne are maximums, and the corresponding figures for tenanted estates are minimums. This is because portions of certain manors were in the hands of tenants, some of whose resources are not clearly distinguished in the Domesday text from those of their lord. In these cases the resources and wealth of the manor have been counted with the demesne.

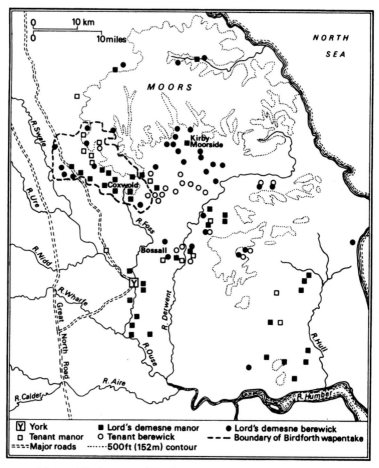

Map 4   The honour of Hugh Fitz Baldric: 1086

either wholly or partly waste.[43] In the case of Hugh Fitz Baldric's twenty-eight demesne manors, the development was even greater. Twenty-six supported plough-teams, four had preserved their value, nine had increased their value, and only three were described

---

[43]   Here and elsewhere, the practice adopted by the Domesday scribe, when dealing with composite entries for groups of manors, of listing the resources of all the settlements together rather than recording them separately manor by manor, may artificially increase the number of manors which supported teams and which had increased in value. It is possible, for example, that the three plough-teams listed in the entry for the four manors of Catton were situated in only one of these manors.

as either wholly or partly waste.[44] The demesne estates of both lordships had retained a comparatively high proportion of their 1066 values: in the case of Percy, 69 per cent, in that of Fitz Baldric, 71 per cent (Table 3). The number of peasant plough-teams on the demesne (Percy 44.5; Fitz Baldric 121.8) suggests that this was probably due in part to the extension of Norman administrative authority beyond the estates farmed directly by the lords. The level of this authority is also reflected to some extent in the intensity of agricultural exploitation evident from the Domesday figures. On both lordships the number of plough-teams per carucate was higher than the county average.[45]

The level of tenant enfeoffment and the condition of tenant estates provides another indication that Norman seignorial authority on the lordships of Percy and Fitz Baldric was far from negligible in 1086, and may have been in existence for a considerable period of time. William of Percy had enfeoffed seventeen tenants, a number which compares very favourably with the numbers enfeoffed on the considerably larger lordships of Richmond, Holderness and Pontefract. Although Hugh Fitz Baldric had alienated land to fewer tenants, their number (eight) is not insubstantial by Yorkshire standards (Table 4). A good proportion of the tenanted estates are recorded as supporting seignorial plough-teams: in the case of Percy, thirty-four of the forty-five manors, in the case of Fitz Baldric, six of the fourteen manors; suggesting that the tenants were aware of (and managing) many of their resources. Their active administration of their tenements is also reflected in the recording of a considerable number of peasant teams on these tenements in Domesday Book (Table 3). On both lordships the number of plough-teams per carucate was well above the county average, a good proportion of the tenant estates had either preserved or increased their value and very few of these estates were described as waste.[46] Taken as a whole, in 1086 the lands under the control of the Percy tenants

---

[44] *DB*, I, 327a–8a. It is possible that some of the value increases are an administrative illusion resulting from the Domesday compiler's practice of combining the values of certain manors.

[45] In the case of Percy 0.43, in that of Fitz Baldric 0.54. The latter result is subject to the distorting influence of the problems discussed in note 42.

[46] There were 0.55 teams per carucate on the Percy lordship, and 0.73 on that of Fitz Baldric. Eleven Percy manors had either preserved or increased their value, and only two were described as waste. On the lordship of Fitz Baldric the corresponding numbers were six and none respectively.

were worth just over 50 per cent of their value in 1066, and those in the charge of the men of Hugh Fitz Baldric were worth just under 85 per cent (Table 3).

The comparatively high level of organisation evident on the Percy and Fitz Baldric lordships almost certainly owed something to pre-conquest levels of agricultural potential. Almost all the Percy and Fitz Baldric estates which had either preserved or increased their value in the period 1066–86 were situated either in the Vale of York, the eastern part of the East Riding, or the Wolds, areas of good soils which appear to have been intensively exploited for agricultural purposes before 1066 (Maps 1–2). However, even where pre-conquest conditions were favourable, the maintenance and expansion of agriculture and estate values in the period 1066–86, and the recording of these features in Domesday Book, is unlikely to have occurred without the imposition of Norman authority and the maintenance of some form of administrative continuity.

It is possible that several castles had been constructed on the Fitz Baldric lordship by 1086, and that at least some of them date from the first decade of the conquest. Slight traces of the earthworks of a small fortification still survive at Bossall, which appears to have been a berewick of the manor of Scrayingham in the wapentake of *Bolesford*. The comparatively high level of estate organisation evident there and in several other nearby estates belonging to the lordship in 1086 is exactly what we might expect if this castle dates from the period of the conquest (Table 5).[47] In and around Scrayingham, Hugh Fitz Baldric's estates incorporated a large number of seignorial and peasant plough-teams, a sizeable peasant community and a number of functioning mills and churches; and in some cases had already been granted to Norman tenants. With the exception of only Buckton Holms, they had either increased or had preserved a reasonable proportion of their 1066 values. Although not as well developed as Bossall, it is possible that the Fitz Baldric estates at Felixkirk and Kirby Moorside also incorporated castles by 1086.[48]

On the lordship of Percy it is possible that each of the four separate clusters of estates in the West and East Ridings in-

---

[47] King, *Castellarium Anglicanum*, II, 514; *DB*, I, 327b–8a.
[48] King, *Castellarium Anglicanum*, II, 517, 520. Kirby Moorside had declined in value from £12 to 100s, but was still reasonably prosperous by Yorkshire standards in 1086 and incorporated two seignorial plough-teams and fifteen peasant teams: *DB*, I, 327b.

corporated a castle by 1086. In the most northerly cluster the castle may have been at the manor of Topcliffe, where motte and bailey earthworks can still be seen.[49] In 1086 Domesday Book records the manor as incorporating three seignorial plough-teams, fourteen peasant teams, a peasant population of nearly fifty, a functioning mill and a church and as having increased its value; a record which suggests administrative continuity and the establishment of Norman authority.[50] Similar conditions prevailed at the manors of Spofforth, Tadcaster and Wheldrake, all of which contain castle earthworks which may date from the reign of the Conqueror.[51]

The compact lordships: Richmond, Pontefract, Holderness and Tickhill

The lordships of Richmond, Pontefract, Holderness and Tickhill, held in 1086 by Alan I of Brittany, Ilbert I of Lacy, Drogo de la Beuvrière and Roger I of Bully respectively, display an obvious similarity of tenurial structure which sets them apart from other Yorkshire Domesday fees. All four lordships were extensive and compact. The regions which they covered encompassed few estates belonging to other fees, and the boundaries of these regions coincided for the most part with those of wapentakes. In the east, the lordship of Holderness dominated the peninsula of the same name which, although not specifically described as such in Domesday Book, was almost certainly already a wapentake by 1086.[52] In the west, the lordship of Pontefract extended over the wapentakes of Osgoldcross, Staincross, Barkston, Agbrigg, Skyrack and Morley. In the north, the lands of Count Alan incorporated almost all the settlements within the wapentakes of Gilling and Hang, administrative districts which are first mentioned in the twelfth century, but which were probably already in existence at the time of the Domesday survey.[53] And in the south, the estates of Roger of Bully extended throughout the wapentake of Strafforth (Maps 5–8).

[49] King, *Castellarium Anglicanum*, II, 527. Clay stated that William of Percy built a castle at Topcliffe, but provided no evidence: *EYC*, XI, 1.   [50] *DB*, I, 323a.
[51] Spofforth had four seignorial plough-teams, four peasant teams and a working mill, and had increased its value three-fold in the period 1066–86. Tadcaster had increased in value from 40s to 100s, and incorporated three seignorial plough-teams and four peasant teams. Wheldrake had preserved its 1066 value. See *DB*, I, 322a, 321b, 322b; Symeon, *Opera*, II, 323; King, *Castellarium Anglicanum*, II, 532, 527, 531.
[52] Roffe, 'Yorkshire Summary', 246–7.
[53] Thorn, 'Hundreds and wapentakes', 51–2, 61.

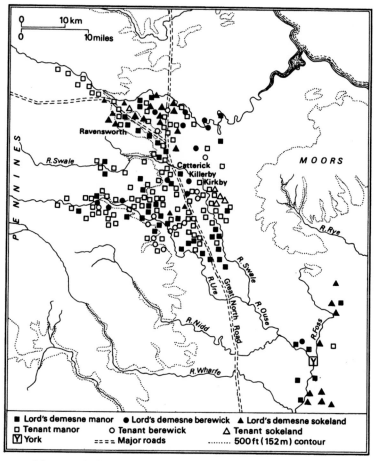

Map 5   The honour of Richmond: 1086

In comparison with the level of estate management on most
other Yorkshire fees in 1086, that on the compact lordships was
reasonably high; and by any standards was far from negligible. At
first sight this appears to be more apparent in the case of Tickhill
and Holderness. In the lordship of Tickhill only nine of the fifty-
five demesne manors were waste. In the lordship of Holderness the
corresponding number was eleven out of thirty-three, eight of
which were concentrated in just three vills. The Tickhill demesne
had preserved approximately 56 per cent of its 1066 value, one of
the highest overall levels of value preservation in the county.

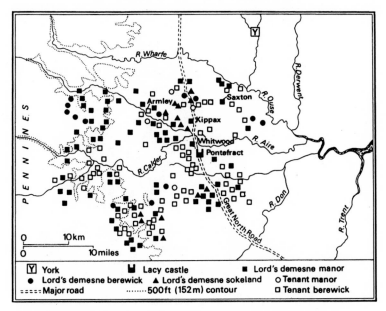

Map 6   The honour of Ilbert of Lacy: 1086

Although in the case of Holderness the corresponding figure was
only approximately 13 per cent, the wealth of its demesne, and
particularly the wealth of a number of large manors within the
demesne, remained high by Yorkshire standards (Table 6).[54] The
partial maintenance of wealth on both lordships suggests a degree
of administrative continuity after 1066, and the imposition of
Norman seignorial authority over some agricultural resources;
something also indicated by the recording of considerable numbers
of plough-teams in Domesday Book. Thirty-six of the fifty-five
Bully manors were recorded with seignorial plough-teams, forty-
two with peasant teams, and thirty-three with both seignorial and
peasant teams. In the case of the thirty-three Holderness demesne
manors the corresponding figures were seventeen, nineteen and
sixteen respectively. The extent of the Norman supervision of
agricultural resources is probably also reflected by the intensity of
the agriculture evident in the Domesday figures. On the Bully fee

---

[54] The figures for carucates, ploughlands, peasant teams, peasants and values on the
demesne of the compact lordships are maximums, and the corresponding figures for
the tenanted estates are minimums, for the same reason as outlined above in the case of the
Fitz Baldric fee: see note 42.

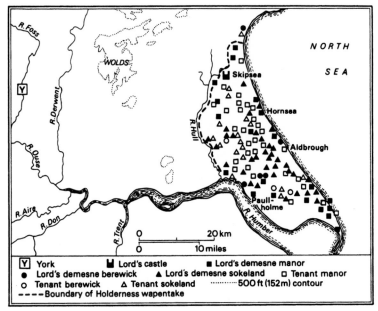

Map 7   The honour of Drogo de la Beuvrière: 1086

the number of plough-teams per carucate (0.93) was well in excess
of the county average. Although this does not appear to have been
the case on the lordship of Holderness, the results here (0.22) may
be an illusory function of the smaller than average size of the
carucates in the region.[55]

W aste was far more prevalent in the lordships of Richmond and
Pontefract than in those of Tickhill and Holderness. In the lordship
of Richmond, thirty-five of the fifty-one demesne manors were
either partly or wholly described as such; in the lordship of
Pontefract the proportion was forty-nine out of ninety-three.
However, these bald figures conceal a geographical bias in the
evidence. The bulk of the waste estates were concentrated in the
western portions of the lordships, in and around the fringes of the
Pennines. The more easterly regions display a lower (in the case of
Pontefract, a much lower) concentration of waste estates, and a
higher level of wealth and agricultural exploitation.[56] It was there

---

[55] See English, *Holderness*, 142; *EYC* indexes. The results for the numbers of plough-
teams per carucate are subject to the distorting influence of the problems discussed in
note 42 above.

[56] For waste distribution, see *Domesday Geography*, 60, 66, 140, 146.

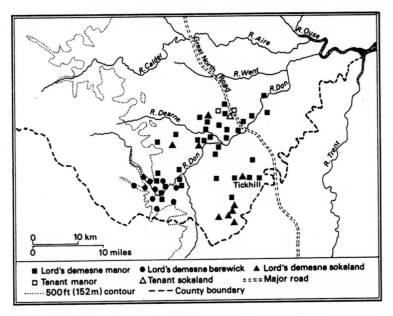

Map 8   The honour of Tickhill: 1086

that the eight manors of Count Alan, and the twenty of Ilbert of
Lacy, which had either maintained or increased their 1066 values,
were situated. Overall, the demesne of the lordship of Richmond
had maintained approximately 27 per cent of its 1066 value, and
that of the lordship of Pontefract approximately 55 per cent.
However, if the waste estates on both lordships are excluded from
our calculations, the figure for the lordship of Richmond rises to
approximately 80 per cent, and that for the lordship of Pontefract
to approximately 75 per cent.[57] These high levels of value
preservation suggest the maintenance of a considerable degree of
administrative continuity, and the effective imposition of Norman
seignorial authority, in certain parts of these lordships after 1066.
This is also indicated by the recording of agricultural resources in
Domesday Book. Nine of the lordship of Richmond's fifty-one
demesne manors were worked by seignorial plough-teams,
eighteen by peasant teams and eight by both seignorial and peasant
teams. Of the ninety-three demesne manors on the lordship of
Pontefract, nineteen were worked by seignorial plough-teams,

[57] Only Count Alan's castlery estates are included in these calculations.

forty-five by peasant teams and seventeen by both seignorial and peasant teams. These figures suggest that on the demesne estates of both lordships the Normans had extended their management of land and agricultural resources beyond the estates they farmed directly; a suggestion which is strengthened by the fact that large numbers of peasant plough-teams were recorded on both lordships (Richmond 77.4; Pontefract 135). The lower than average number of plough-teams per carucate on both lordships (0.27 and 0.41 respectively) was almost certainly due to the very low level of agricultural exploitation in their western regions.

According to Wightman, the survival of large numbers of Anglo-Scandinavian tenants on the lordships of Pontefract and Richmond in 1086 may indicate that Ilbert of Lacy and Alan of Brittany had not had time to dispossess them, and that these lordships were of recent creation.[58] However, there are problems with Wightman's implied premise that native tenants were absent from most Yorkshire lordships because the Normans had dispossessed them. It is far more likely that this absence is an illusion resulting from the demotion of these tenants to the ranks of the subtenantry and the failure of Domesday Book to record details about their tenure.[59] If this is correct, the problem becomes one of explaining why in many places on the lordships of Richmond and Pontefract this demotion had only progressed one stage; why, in other words, the native tenants we see there in Domesday Book had not been subjected to the lordship of the continental retainers of the Norman magnates. Although it might be that the Normans had not had time to establish their retainers on the land, it is also possible that they had no wish or capacity to establish them, or that for some reason these retainers were not recorded in the Domesday text.

In terms of the extent of tenant enfeoffment, and the development of tenant estates, three of the four compact lordships (Holderness, Richmond and Pontefract) appear among the more advanced fees in Yorkshire in 1086. In all three cases the proportion of seignorial land and resources granted out to tenants was considerable, and the number of tenants enfeoffed by 1086 was far in excess of the number enfeoffed on the other lordships of Yorkshire (Tables 6 and 4). This undoubtedly reflects the great size of the compact lordships and the abundance of the resources on

---

[58] Wightman, *Lacy Family*, 41.
[59] See Michelmore, 'Township and tenure', 252.

them which were available for alienation; but it could hardly have occurred without some degree of Norman knowledge and administrative management of the land.

The description of the alienated lands in Domesday Book suggests that the Norman tenants established by the lords of Richmond, Pontefract and Holderness were not slow to take advantage of the opportunities granted to them; that by 1086 they had made significant progress in establishing their authority over their estates. On the Holderness fee, this is reflected in the absence of waste, and in the far from inconsiderable level of value preservation (approximately 41 per cent: Table 6). This must have been due in part to the extension of Norman authority over many agricultural resources. Thirty-seven of the fifty-five Holderness tenant manors were recorded with seignorial plough-teams, forty-three with peasant teams and thirty with both seignorial and peasant teams. The ratio of seignorial to peasant teams (37:32.5) also indicates that, although primarily concerned with direct farming, the continental tenants of Holderness were also aware of, and possibly supervising, a considerable amount of peasant agriculture. The level of their knowledge and supervision may also be reflected in the intensity of agricultural exploitation which, expressed in terms of the number of plough-teams per carucate (0.48), was greater than the county average.

On the lordships of Richmond and Pontefract the tenant estates display a rather different organisational profile. Waste was far more abundant. Sixty of the 130 Richmond tenant manors, and twenty of the 101 on the lordship of Pontefract, were either wholly or partly waste. As with the demesne, however, these figures obscure a geographical bias in the evidence. Most of the waste estates were situated in the western upland peripheries of the lordships. Further east, value preservation was much greater. Thirty-two tenant manors in the more easterly areas of the lordship of Richmond, and fifteen in those of the lordship of Pontefract, had either increased or preserved their pre-conquest values. This explains why the tenant manors on both lordships had maintained a reasonable proportion of their 1066 values (despite the heavy level of wasting): approximately 48 per cent in the case of Richmond, and 47 per cent in that of Pontefract. Value preservation on this scale must reflect Norman knowledge and management of a considerable proportion of the productive capacity of the tenant estates. Fifty-seven of the 130 Richmond tenant estates are recorded in Domesday Book with seignorial plough-teams, sixty-five with peasant teams and fifty with both seignorial and peasant teams. On the Lacy lordship, with its 101 tenant manors, the corresponding figures were sixty-nine, seventy-six and sixty-two respectively. Once again, the ratio of demesne to peasant teams on both lordships (72.5:184.4 in the case of Richmond, and 77.5:123.5 in that of Pontefract) suggests that the tenants had progressed far beyond managing the estates they farmed directly. This is also indicated by the intensity of the agriculture on their estates reflected in Domesday Book. Despite the wasting of the western portions of both lordships, the number of plough-teams per carucate on the Richmond fee (0.33) was not greatly exceeded by the county average, and the number on the fee of Pontefract (0.67) was actually in excess of that average (Table 6).

The patterns of estate management and agricultural organisation displayed by the compact lordships in 1086 were undoubtedly influenced to some extent by geographical relief, soil conditions, pre-conquest levels of agricultural exploitation and military devastation. The more developed estates in the eastern portions of the lordships of Richmond and Pontefract were situated in lowland areas covered by good soils, which had been cultivated relatively intensely before 1066, and which had probably escaped the worst of the devastation inflicted by the Conqueror's troops. By contrast, the less developed and waste estates were situated in, or on the fringes of, the Pennine hills, which were covered with soils of poor quality, and which were the most likely areas to have suffered from the harrying of the north. Pre-conquest conditions probably also had an important influence on the organisational profile of the lordships of Tickhill and Holderness, although, given the comparatively low numbers of waste estates, the impact of the harrying (which was one of the many possible causes of wasting) is likely to have been much less marked. The absence of sharp regional variations in the level of organisational development was probably partly a result of the absence of similar variations in relief and soil conditions. Both lordships were situated for the most part in lowland areas covered by good quality soils, which had been intensively farmed before 1066 (Maps 1–2).

A number of settlements on each of the four compact lordships preserve the remains of earthwork castles, and there is evidence that several of them were constructed before 1086. The portion of the Yorkshire Domesday known as the Summary records that the lord of Richmond 'has in his castlery (*castellatu*) 200 manors less one'.[60] Although the term castlery was sometimes used to refer to the entire honour of a magnate rather than to a district supporting and dominated by a castle, this cannot be the case in this instance since Count Alan is also described as holding forty-three manors which were outside his castlery. The count's castlery appears to correspond with his lands in the north-western corner of Yorkshire, a region known later as Richmondshire, and probably incorporated one or more castles. Although at a later date Richmond castle was the *caput* of the descendants of Count Alan in Yorkshire, it was probably not in existence in 1086 when the demesne portion of the manor was described as waste.[61] It is more than possible that the castlery referred to by Domesday Book was focussed instead on castles at Catterick, Killerby, Kirkby Fleetham and Ravensworth, all of which appear to incorporate castle earthworks.[62] The reasonably well-developed estate organisation evident on all four estates in Domesday Book is exactly what we might expect if they were centres of Norman administration in 1086.[63]

References in the Domesday *clamores* provide evidence of another castle in the charge of the lord of Pontefract, Ilbert of Lacy.[64] The *clamores* state that the settlement of Thorner 'is situated within the bounds of Ilbert's castle (*castelli*), according to the first measurement, and, according to the most recent measurement it is situated outside it'; and that land in the settlement of *Saxehale* is 'within the castle (*castelli*) boundary'.[65] That the term *castelli* was used in this context to refer to an actual castle rather than a castlery corresponding to the entire honour, and that the castle was in existence by 1087 at the latest, is indicated by a charter of William Rufus issued between 1088 and *c.* 1095 which concedes to Ilbert of Lacy, 'consuetudinem de castellaria

---

[60] *DB*, I, 381a.   [61] *Ibid.*, 311a.

[62] King, *Castellarium Anglicanum*, II, 515, 519, 523.

[63] Catterick and its berewicks, which included Killerby, had preserved their 1066 value of £8 and are attributed with nine seignorial plough-teams: *DB*, I, 310b. Nearby Kirkby Fleetham was also well developed and known to the Normans in 1086. Further north, Ravensworth had been granted by Count Alan to Bodin. Although not as well developed in 1086 as the other castle settlements, it is significant that Ravensworth and a number of nearby estates were recorded in Domesday as having seignorial plough-teams and/or preserving a good proportion of their pre-conquest values, despite the fact that they were situated in an area which was otherwise largely waste. See *DB*, I, 309b–10a.   [64] *Ibid.*, 373b.   [65] *Ibid.*

castelli sui, sicut eam habuit tempore patris ipsius regis Willelmi et tempore Baiocensis episcopi'.[66] It is even possible that there was more than one castle on the lordship of Pontefract by 1086. The remains of castle earthworks on estates belonging to this lordship survive at Pontefract, Kippax, Whitwood, Saxton and Armley, and it is significant that in most of these settlements the Normans had gained knowledge of, and were managing, a considerable amount of agricultural resources and wealth in 1086.[67]

Domesday Book makes no mention of a castle or castlery in Holderness. However, it is recorded elsewhere that the builder of Skipsea castle was Drogo de la Beuvrière, who must have established it before 1087 when he lost his lands.[68] Other castles may have been constructed on the lordship by 1086 at Hornsea and Paullholme, which incorporate the earthworks of what may be early mottes or military towers, and at Aldbrough where a castle is possibly referred to in a charter issued in the early twelfth century.[69] Although greatly devalued in 1086, all three settlements remained wealthy by Yorkshire standards, and incorporated a plough force likely to have been sufficient for the support of a castle-based Norman community.[70]

Several castles may also have been constructed by 1086 on the lordship of Tickhill. The existence of one at Tickhill itself by 1100, and possibly earlier, is suggested by Orderic Vitalis.[71] In Domesday Book the settlement is probably represented by the well-developed borough of Dadsley, which incorporated seven seignorial plough-teams, two and a half teams belonging to a *miles*,

---

[66] *EYC*, III, no. 1415.

[67] Pontefract, which was represented by the settlement of Tanshelf in Domesday Book, is recorded with four seignorial plough-teams, eighteen peasant teams, sixty lesser burgesses, forty peasants, a church, a priest and three mills, and had retained 75 per cent of its 1066 value of £20. Kippax and its berewick of Ledston had preserved their pre-conquest value of £16, and were recorded with twelve seignorial plough-teams, sixteen peasant teams, sixty peasants, three mills, three churches and three priests. Although not nearly so well developed, estate organisation in the manors of Saxton and Whitwood may reflect the existence of more early castles. See King, *Castellarium Anglicanum*, II, 523, 519, 528, 524, 529; Michelmore, 'Township gazetteer', 420; *West Yorkshire*, II, 561; III, 736–7; *DB*, I, 315a–16b, 317b. [68] English, *Holderness*, 7.

[69] King, *Castellarium Anglicanum*, II, 531; English, *Holderness*, 9, 136 and note 5.

[70] Aldbrough incorporated three plough-teams belonging to the lord, three belonging to *milites* and nine belonging to the peasants: *DB*, I, 324a. Hornsea incorporated two seignorial plough-teams and 3.5 peasant teams: *DB*, I, 323b. Paullholme was a berewick of the manor of Burstwick. In total, Burstwick's five berewicks incorporated two seignorial plough-teams and seven peasant teams. The remainder of the manor supported another six seignorial teams: *DB*, I, 323b.

[71] See Orderic, VI, 22, and compare Florence, *Chronicon*, II, 50.

twenty-four peasant teams and a population of sixty-six peasants and thirty-one burgesses; and which had increased its value from £12 to £14.[72] The second possible castle site was Laughton en le Morthen, a settlement which contains the earthwork remains of a motte and bailey castle.[73] The existence of this castle in 1086 would be consistent with the Norman management of agricultural resources which is reflected in Domesday Book. Laughton en le Morthen and its appurtenances incorporated ten seignorial plough-teams, two teams belonging to two *milites*, twenty-eight peasant teams and a population of nearly 130 peasants, and were valued in 1086 at £15.[74]

The lordship of the count of Mortain

In its structure and organisation the fee of Robert, count of Mortain, was distinct from any other Yorkshire lordship. The count's extensive estates, both demesne and tenanted, were distributed widely throughout the three ridings of the county and display an amorphous quality (Map 9).

Compared with the estates Count Robert granted to tenants in Yorkshire, his demesne manors were fewer in number, more poorly equipped with resources and of lower value (Table 7). Of the twenty-four demesne manors, ten were wholly or partly waste, only five had preserved their 1066 value and only one had increased in value. Overall, the demesne displays one of the worst rates of value preservation in Yorkshire (29 per cent), and was worth less than £15 in 1086; a feature which must reflect a low level of estate management or agricultural exploitation (Table 7). The overall number of seignorial teams (nine) was small. Moreover, the average number of teams per carucate (0.28) was well below the county average. The Domesday account of the count of Mortain's demesne lands suggests that most of them were agriculturally or administratively underdeveloped, and that the count was an absentee lord who was primarily concerned with extracting peasant services and renders, rather than with farming his estates directly.

The underdevelopment of the count of Mortain's demesne cannot be attributed to pre-conquest conditions and poor agricultural potential, since the bulk of it was situated in the Cleveland plain, the Vale of York and the region surrounding the Vale of

---

[72] *DB*, I, 319a.   [73] Hey, *South Yorkshire*, 41.   [74] *DB*, I, 319a.

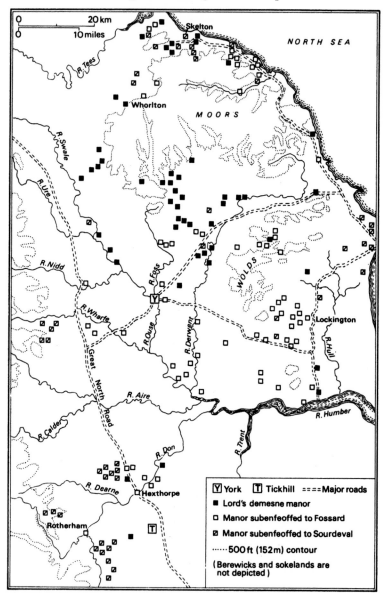

Map 9   The honour of Robert of Mortain: 1086

Pickering: areas of good soils and high levels of pre-conquest agricultural exploitation (Maps 1–2). It was mainly in these areas that the few demesne manors which had either preserved or increased their values were situated. The exception was the Cleveland plain, where all except two demesne manors were waste.[75] Although this wasting may have resulted from the harrying of the north or the Scottish invasion of 1070, there is another possible explanation. The underdeveloped nature of Mortain estates in less remote areas than Cleveland which probably escaped military devastation suggests that the wasting in Cleveland was at least as likely to have resulted from the exclusion of the area from the ambit of Norman administration throughout the period of the conquest.

The main burden of administering the count of Mortain's estates in Yorkshire appears to have fallen on his tenants, who controlled nearly three-quarters of his lands and an even greater proportion of most of his resources (Table 7). Two tenants, Nigel Fossard and Richard of Sourdeval, held nearly all of the 114 or so tenant manors between them. In total, these manors had preserved a greater proportion of their 1066 value than those of the count of Mortain (approximately 36 per cent). This was probably due to the fact that the tenant estates display a higher level of agricultural exploitation than those on the demesne, and a lower level of waste. However, when compared with the tenant estates on the other categories of lordship examined so far, those on the Mortain fee appear more underdeveloped. Thirty of the 114 tenant manors were wholly waste, three were partially waste, only nine had preserved their 1066 values and only one had increased in value. Although fifty-five manors were recorded with seignorial plough-teams, sixty-nine with peasant teams and forty-nine with both seignorial and peasant teams, and although the number of peasant teams (163.8) suggests that the Norman tenants had extended their knowledge and possibly their management of estates and resources far beyond the land they farmed directly, the average number of teams per carucate (0.34) was comparatively low.

As with the demesne, the general statistics for the tenant estates obscure regional variations in the level of estate organisation reflected in Domesday Book. The most developed region was south Yorkshire, where the thirty-two tenant manors had

[75] *Ibid.*, 305b.

51

preserved approximately 50 per cent of their pre-conquest value, sixteen of the thirty-two supported a total of sixteen seignorial plough-teams and only four manors were waste. In the East Riding the forty-four tenant manors had preserved only about 32 per cent of their value. Although only four of the manors were waste, and approximately twenty-four supported demesne agriculture, the total number of seignorial plough-teams did not exceed the number working in south Yorkshire. Elsewhere in the lordship, Domesday Book gives the impression that seignorial agriculture on the tenanted estates was even more scarce, particularly in Cleveland where nearly all the estates were waste.

The low overall level of estate development on the tenanted portion of the lordship of Mortain, and the regional differences in this level, cannot be adequately explained by soil distribution and pre-conquest agricultural patterns, or by military devastation. The quality of the soils and the level of agricultural intensity in Cleveland, the East Riding and south Yorkshire were among the highest in Yorkshire. As for military devastation, the comparative absence of waste in south Yorkshire and the East Riding suggests that these regions suffered little from the passage of armies. Although Cleveland was more wasted, and more vulnerable to the Scots, the low level of development there reflected in Domesday Book is at least as likely to be attributable to a lack of Norman estate management. It is possible that the Mortain land in Cleveland was well endowed with resources, which the Normans did not record in Domesday Book because they did not know about them or were not managing them.

The estates held by Nigel Fossard and Richard of Sourdeval of the count of Mortain were confined to Yorkshire, suggesting that Robert intended these men to live and work in the county; and it is possible that Fossard and Sourdeval had constructed a number of castles by 1086.[76] The most likely site for an early fortress was the composite manor of Hexthorpe in Strafforth wapentake. In 1086 the manor had attached to it sokeland in neighbouring Doncaster, a settlement which later came to absorb Hexthorpe, and which was certainly fortified in the twelfth century. Situated at the point where the Great North Road crosses the River Don at its highest navigable point for coastal traffic, Hexthorpe must have been of considerable strategic importance to a Norman king wishing to

[76] I. N. Soulsby, 'The fiefs in England of the counts of Mortain, 1066–1166' (Univ. of Wales, Cardiff, MA thesis, 1974), 179–80.

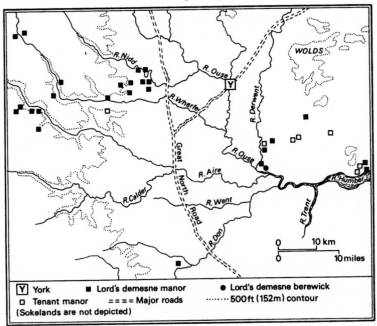

Map 10   The honour of Gilbert Tison: 1086

protect his access to the north and the city of York (Map 9). As a former possession of Earl Tosti, and the focus of a large number of appurtenant sokelands, Hexthorpe was also a significant administrative, jurisdictional and population centre. Although it had declined in value from £18 in 1066 to £12 by 1086, it was still a wealthy and well-organised estate by Yorkshire standards.[77]

Other castles on the lordship of Mortain which may have had conquest origins include those of Rotherham and Lockington, situated on the Fossard fee; Skelton, which formed part of the Sourdeval estate; and Whorlton, which belonged to the count's demesne.[78]

[77] DB, I, 307b–8b; King, *Castellarium Anglicanum*, II, 530, 534; Hey, *South Yorkshire*, 44.
[78] King, *Castellarium Anglicanum*, II, 525, 530, 521, 528. Rotherham supported one seignorial plough-team and 2.5 peasant teams, a mill, a priest and a church, but had declined in value from £4 to 30s. Lockington incorporated one seignorial plough-team and three peasant teams, but had declined in value from £6 to 30s. Skelton incorporated one seignorial plough-team and three peasant teams. Although it had declined in value from 40s to 16s it was still reasonably wealthy compared with most estates in Cleveland. Whorlton appears to have incorporated no seignorial plough-teams, but was the only unwasted sokeland of the complex manor of Hutton Rudby and supported eight peasant plough-teams and a population of twenty peasants. See DB, I, 307b, 306b, 305b.

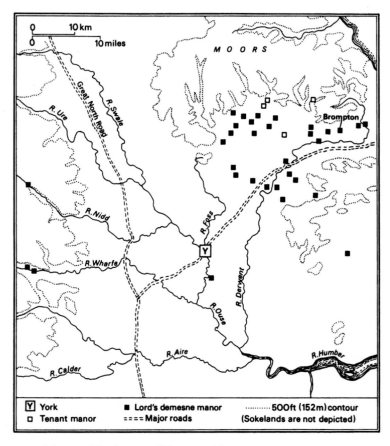

Map 11   The honour of Tosny: 1086

Embryonic lordships

Included in this category are the fees of Gilbert Tison, Robert and Berengar of Tosny, Ralph Paynel, Ralph of Mortemer, Hugh earl of Chester, Erneis of Burun and Osbern of Arches, most of which were widely distributed throughout Yorkshire (Maps 10–16).

Compared with the lordships examined so far, the level of estate organisation on the embryonic fees as it appears in Domesday Book was retarded. In some lordships we can discern a sharp contrast between a few highly organised estates, and many manors with little or no organisation at all. In others a moderate amount

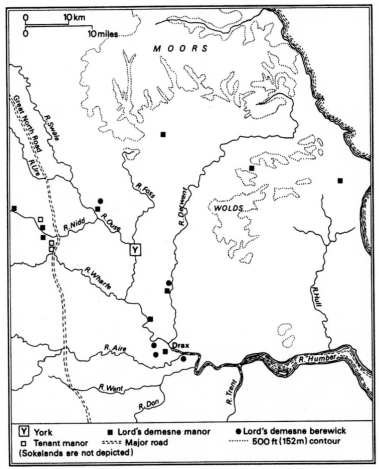

Map 12   The honour of Ralph Paynel: 1086

of development appears to characterise the majority of estates. There are also cases of lordships combining a reasonably well-developed demesne with poorly organised tenant estates.

Some of these contrasts can be seen in the case of the Tosny fee. The demesne resources of Robert of Tosny and his son Berengar were greater, and in some cases considerably greater, than those in any of the other lordships considered under this heading (Table 8). As a whole, the Tosny demesne manors for which we have both 1066 and 1086 valuations appear to have weathered the twenty years of Norman rule well. They had maintained very nearly 98

Map 13   The honour of Ralph of Mortemer: 1086

per cent of their wealth, and the intensity of agriculture practised upon them (0.43 teams per carucate) appears to have been slightly greater than the county average (Table 8). When we look more closely, however, the organisation of the demesne was not uniform across the entire lordship, but concentrated in a handful of highly developed estates. Only five of the fifteen demesne manors had either increased or preserved their 1066 value, and just as many manors were wholly or partly waste. Eight manors were worked by seignorial plough-teams, nine by peasant teams and only six by seignorial and peasant teams. With the exception of seven or eight

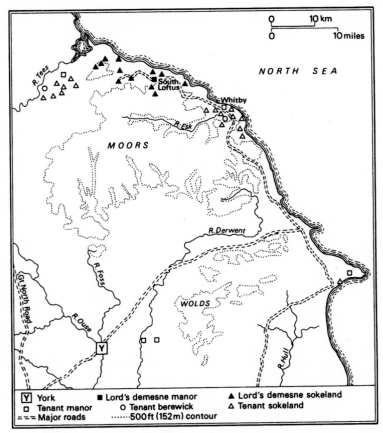

Map 14   The honour of Hugh earl of Chester: 1086

manors, the Tosny demesne appears in Domesday Book as largely underdeveloped. It is a feature which seems to owe little either to soil conditions or to pre-conquest agricultural exploitation. Some of the waste manors were situated on the better soils of the East Riding hundreds of *Sneculfcros*, Acklam and Warter, which were intensely exploited for agricultural purposes before 1066. More-over, some of the better developed manors like Brompton, which had doubled its value, and Sinnington, which was populated and worked by both demesne and peasant plough-teams, lay within the Vale of Pickering, one of the poorest agricultural areas in Yorkshire (compare Maps 11 and 1–2). It is far more likely that the apparent underdevelopment of the Tosny estates is a Domesday

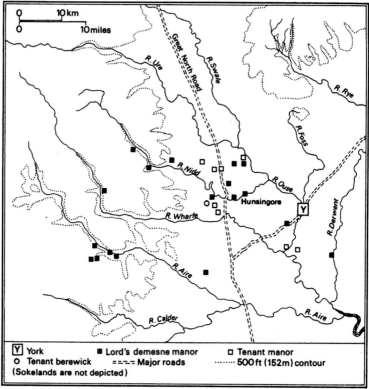

Map 15 The honour of Erneis of Burun: 1086

illusion, resulting from a lack of information about the lordship
and a weakness or limitation of Norman authority there.

Domesday Book gives the impression that the Tosnys had made
little progress towards the establishment of a locally based tenant
community by 1086. Only five manors had been granted out, and
all of them to St Mary's Abbey, York. Despite this, the tenant
estates were reasonably well developed. Of the four manors for
which details are provided, one had increased its value, two had
preserved their values and one was waste. Although it is possible
that the waste manor had been included for administrative
purposes in the manor which had increased its value, which was
located in the same vill (Kirby Misperton), the combined 1086
value of the two estates still exceeded their combined value in 1066
(Table 8).

Domesday Book indicates that the fee of Osbern of Arches was

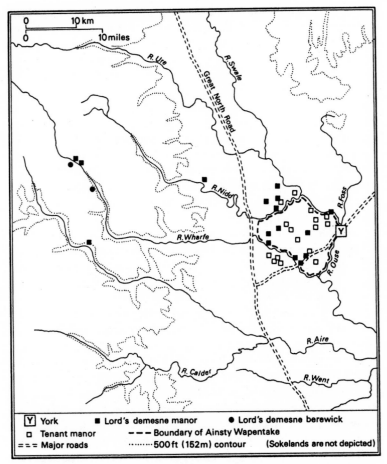

Map 16   The honour of Osbern of Arches: 1086

also among the more developed embryonic lordships, but that it had a very different internal organisation to the Tosny estate. Although the Arches demesne incorporated fewer waste manors (three) than that of the Tosny lordship, it had preserved a much lower proportion of its 1066 value, and the agriculture recorded upon it was less intensive and distributed over a greater number of estates. The Domesday figures suggest that in the period 1066–86 the Arches demesne had declined in value by approximately 65 per cent (Table 8).[79] Only four of its twenty-two manors had either increased or preserved their 1066 value, and these were all situated in the vill of Steeton. Although sixteen manors are listed with seignorial plough-teams, nineteen with peasant teams and sixteen with both seignorial and peasant teams, these figures are an illusion resulting from the Domesday compiler's penchant for multiple manor entries. In total, Domesday Book records only seven seignorial plough-teams and twelve peasant teams on the demesne in 1086, an average of just 0.35 teams per carucate (Table 8).

A contrast between the honours of Arches and Tosny is also evident in the structure of tenant enfeoffment. Domesday Book records that Osbern of Arches had established fifteen tenants in Yorkshire by 1086, a far higher number than on any other embryonic lordship, and one of the highest numbers in the county as a whole (Table 4). With the exception of only the lordship of Chester, a greater proportion of total honorial resources had been alienated to tenants on the Arches fee than on any other embryonic lordship (Table 8). The tenanted portion of the Arches fee is also notable for the absence of waste and the comparatively high level of value preservation (almost 50 per cent). As with the demesne, however, the productive resources of the tenanted lands appear to have been spread thinly over the lordship. Although sixteen of the thirty-seven manors are listed with seignorial plough-teams, thirty-five with peasant teams and sixteen with both seignorial and peasant teams, there were actually only 33.5 teams in total, an average of only 0.38 per carucate. This suggests that some tenants knew very little about the resources of some of their estates, and that their authority over these estates was little more than nominal.

The development of agriculture on the embryonic fees appears retrograde when compared with the other categories of lordship examined so far. It is a backwardness which in most cases cannot be explained in terms of soil quality or agricultural potential. Only on the lordships of Paynel and Tison were a significant proportion of estates situated in regions where the quality of the soils and intensity of pre-conquest agriculture were low. In a number of cases, most notably Arches and Chester, the bulk of the lordships were actually situated in regions where soils and agricultural

---

[79] In the case of the Arches lordship the figures for carucates, ploughlands, seignorial plough-teams, peasant teams, peasants and values on the demesne are maximums, whereas the corresponding figures on the tenanted estates are minimums, for the same reason as outlined in the case of the lordship of Hugh Fitz Baldric: see above note 42.

potential were extremely good (compare Maps 16, 14 and 1–2). Another possibility is that the lack of development evident on the embryonic lordships was due, at least in part, to military devastation. The fact that most of these lordships incorporated estates which were situated in upland and remote areas and/or which were waste might be taken as evidence to support this proposition.[80] However, the distribution of waste is not always in accord with the likely movement of armies. It is possible that the backwardness of the embryonic lordships is actually a Domesday illusion, resulting from a lack of Norman knowledge of, and authority over, the resources on the land.

The hypothesis concerning the underdevelopment of Norman authority on the embryonic lordships is in accord with the paucity and uncompelling nature of the evidence for early castle construction. The strongest case is that for the manor of Brompton on the honour of Tosny, the site of a motte.[81] The manor had increased in value from 10s to 20s, was served by one seignorial and five peasant plough-teams and incorporated a functioning mill, a priest and a church.[82]

The underdevelopment of Norman authority on the embryonic lordships suggests that they were either formed at a somewhat later date than the other categories of fee examined so far, or that Norman authority within them had developed more slowly, perhaps as a result of piecemeal construction.

The lordship of Roger the Poitevin

The lordship of Roger the Poitevin was situated in the region of Cravenshire and incorporated nearly all the estates there.[83] Two of its constituent estates are said to lie within Roger's castlery, a term which could refer either to Cravenshire or to a much larger area consisting of Amounderness and the region 'between Ribble and Mersey', which Roger had either forfeited or exchanged shortly before the completion of the Domesday survey.[84]

The Domesday description of the Poitevin fee in Cravenshire is highly abbreviated. It might be that this was a result of the

---

[80] Seven of the twelve Mortemer manors for which 1066 values are provided were either partly or wholly waste in 1086. On the lordship of Chester the proportion was three out of five; on that of Paynel seven out of ten; on that of Tison five out of twenty-one; and on that of Burun six out of sixteen.

[81] King, *Castellarium Anglicanum*, II, 514.   [82] *DB*, I, 314a.   [83] *Ibid.*, 332a.

[84] *Ibid.*; Thorn, 'Hundreds and wapentakes', 45 note 76, 57.

devastation of the region during the harrying of the north. This was the opinion of Professor Maxwell, who believed that the whole of Cravenshire was waste in 1086.[85] However, for a number of reasons, this opinion is difficult to accept. The first reason is that approximately two-thirds of the estates in Cravenshire, including those on the Poitevin fee, are not specifically described as waste. A second springs from Raistrick's observation that the 'uninhabited' areas mapped by Darby and Maxwell coincide very closely with the wapentakes of Ewcross and Staincliff (that is, Cravenshire), with plenty of inhabited vills just east of the boundary. It is difficult to believe, as Raistrick states, that 'William's army worked, in their wasting, to the map of the wapentakes, and worked so accurately'.[86] This does not necessarily mean that Cravenshire was entirely free from the effects of the harrying (the Domesday description of the Poitevin estates in neighbouring Amounderness suggests that many waste vills had been destroyed), but it does highlight the difficulties in using the harrying to explain the abbreviated form of the Domesday account of the Poitevin fee.

From the discussion above it will have become clear that the measures of Norman authority used to establish the six categories of Yorkshire lordships are not without their weaknesses and limitations, and that the categories themselves are to some extent artificially rigid. Conclusions drawn from a model based upon the Yorkshire Domesday must be qualified to some extent by the inconsistencies, omissions, compressions and other deficiencies which have been shown by recent research to characterise the text.[87] There are also difficulties in projecting conditions in 1086 backwards into the past in order to determine the chronology by which the Normans established their authority in Yorkshire. Although it is quite likely that in most of the lordships where the Normans appear to have been exercising a considerable amount of authority in 1086 the establishment of this authority had been under way for many years, it would be dangerous to assume that this is true of them all.[88] Some of the lordships exhibiting a similar

---

[85] *Domesday Geography*, 67, 80.   [86] Raistrick, *West Riding*, 40.

[87] Roffe, 'Domesday Book', 310.

[88] The impact of a number of the factors which are likely to have influenced the rate at which Norman authority evolved is difficult to measure precisely. These factors include the different objectives, abilities and resources (human and agricultural) of individual

level of Norman authority in 1086, and placed in the same category of development, may actually have been created at different dates and evolved at different speeds. Some, perhaps many, of these lordships may have been created in piecemeal fashion over a considerable period of time. If so, our artificial categories will obscure a degree of chronological overlap in the formation of the Domesday lordships, and in the development of Norman power within them.

For these and other reasons it should be stressed that the Domesday model outlined above cannot hope to produce a completely clear and accurate picture of Norman power in 1086, and of the stages and methods by which this power had been established. Given the limitations of the evidence, such a goal is unattainable. But what is possible, especially when the model is considered in conjunction with the evidence of the chroniclers, is the formation of an impressionistic picture, one which seeks to make a contribution to our understanding of the Norman conquest. For all its shortcomings and imprecision, it is a picture which strongly suggests that in Yorkshire this conquest was much more rapid, carefully controlled and (in 1086) advanced than we have been led to believe, and that one of the major instruments by which it was achieved was the castle.

THE NORMAN CONQUEST OF YORKSHIRE: CHRONOLOGY, CONTROL AND CASTLES

Even in very general terms the results of our analysis of Domesday Book suggest that the extent of Norman authority in Yorkshire was much more extensive, and had developed more quickly, than has hitherto been realised. At the most basic level, by 1086 the Normans had acquired knowledge of the names and tax assessments of some 1,830 settlements, a figure which has been said to represent 'some five out of six of all the hamlets and villages there ever were in medieval Yorkshire'.[89] Despite the probability that much of this knowledge had been derived from Anglo-Scandinavian administrative records, it was an important step in the

---

lords, the piecemeal fashion in which some of them must have acquired their lands and the tenurial reorganisation which sometimes accompanied these acquisitions.

[89] Palliser, 'Yorkshire Domesday', 18. Quotation from E. Miller and J. Hatcher, *Medieval England: Rural Society and Economic Change 1086–1348* (London, 1978), 3.

establishment of Norman power. In hundreds of vills many more steps had been taken. The Normans knew about the productive resources which generated seignorial income, such as demesne plough-teams; and in the many estates which were rendering dues (represented by values), they were almost certainly exercising supervision of these resources. The extent of this supervision is illustrated by the compact lordships, where over 275 seignorial plough-teams and 625 peasant teams were contributing to the income of Norman lords and their tenants in 1086. It is also illustrated by the high levels of value preservation on the lordships of Percy, Fitz Baldric and Bully, parts of which were clearly being exploited almost as efficiently as in the pre-conquest period. Although this level of management pales in comparison to that achieved by the Normans in most of England's counties, it is far from insignificant. It suggests that the formation of the lordships in the first four categories of our model, and the establishment of Norman administration there, began before, in some cases long before, the 1080s.

When we turn to the formation and organisation of individual lordships in detail it is instructive to examine the results of our Domesday model in conjunction with other evidence derived from Domesday Book, the chroniclers and strategic consider-ations. Although this evidence suggests that the model is too artificial and needs to be adjusted in places, generally speaking it tends to confirm that the lordships which display a high level of Norman authority in Domesday Book had been in existence for many years, and that at least some of those with a low level of authority were only formed or organised shortly before 1086.

The lordship on which the establishment of Norman authority appears to have been most advanced in 1086 was that of Conisbrough. This was the only great complex manor in Yorkshire to increase, let alone preserve, its value in the conquest period. It had been held before 1066 by Earl Harold, whose estates in other areas of England were some of the first to be granted out to Normans by the Conqueror.[90] Conisbrough's availability, due to Harold's death in 1066, its strategic location at a fording point on the River Don and its importance as a traditional centre of local administration and population are likely to have influenced the Conqueror to place the estate in safe hands at an early date. The

---

[90] Fleming, *Kings and Lords*, 170–1.

manor may well have been alienated to William of Warenne when the king went to Yorkshire in 1068 to deal with a major rebellion.[91] According to the Anglo-Saxon chronicler, William went 'to Nottingham and built a castle there, and so went to York and there built two castles, and in Lincoln and everywhere in that district'.[92]

The rebellion of 1068 may either have resulted in, or been partly caused by, the dispossession of a number of powerful Anglo-Scandinavian thanes, and their replacement by Normans. In 1086 Gilbert I of Gant, who was certainly active in Yorkshire by 1069 when he defended York against the Danes, held the manor of Hunmanby which had formerly been in the possession of Karle, a thane whose four sons were among the leaders of the 1068 rebellion. Several estates in Holderness belonging to Karle's son, Cnut, passed to William Malet before the destruction of York castle in 1069, possibly by illegal means.[93]

Little additional Norman honorial construction is likely to have taken place until after the defeat of the 1069 rebellion and the subsequent harrying of the north. Our Domesday model suggests that among the first lords to be established after this cataclysm were William of Percy and Hugh Fitz Baldric, and other evidence tends to strengthen the suggestion. The Percy lordship appears to have been created in piecemeal fashion. A portion of it was acquired from the fee of William Malet sometime after Malet's death, which occurred at some point in the period 1069–71.[94] However, in the Domesday *clamores* William of Percy claimed that he was in possession of Bolton Percy while William Malet was alive and held the sheriffdom of York.[95] His early presence in Yorkshire is also attested by an entry in Domesday Book which records a complaint made by the burgesses of York that Percy had taken a certain house into the castle after his return from the Scottish expedition of 1072. William responded by claiming that he had taken the house on the orders of the sheriff, Hugh Fitz Baldric, in the first year after the destruction of the castles at York, which would place the seizure in 1070.[96] Hugh Fitz Baldric's tenure of the sheriffdom at about this time and residence within Yorkshire is reported by the author of the late twelfth-century *Historia Selebiensis*, who records the assistance given by Hugh to Bernard of Auxerre in founding Selby Abbey, which possibly

[91] Orderic, II, 218.   [92] *ASC, s.a.* 1068.   [93] Williams, *Anglo-Saxons*.

[94] Fleming, *Kings and Lords*, 159–60; J. H. Round, 'The death of William Malet', *The Academy* (26 April 1884).   [95] *DB*, I, 374a.   [96] *Ibid.*, 298a.

occurred in 1069 or 1070.[97] Within a short time of this foundation Hugh may also have acquired land in Yorkshire. Professor Fleming has suggested that some of the Anglo-Scandinavian thanes to whose estates Hugh succeeded may have been implicated in the northern revolt of 1069, and that Hugh probably acquired their lands *c*. 1070.[98]

The evidence suggests that William of Percy and Hugh Fitz Baldric were the men chosen by the Conqueror to restore Norman authority in Yorkshire after the debacle of 1069. They had been given charge of York, and it was probably no accident that the lordships granted to them were distributed in a belt around the city. It is not completely beyond the bounds of reason that the formation of these lordships is what Orderic Vitalis had in mind when he declared that upon returning to York after harrying the Tees in 1070 the Conqueror 'restored the castles there and established order in the city and surrounding district'.[99]

The Domesday model indicates that the development of Norman authority on the compact lordships began later than on the Percy and Fitz Baldric fees. This is supported by what we know of the fate of some of the pre-conquest lords whose estates became important constituent elements of these lordships. Edwin, earl of Mercia, held the two largest complex manors in Richmondshire, may have enjoyed overlordship of nearly all the other estates within the region and also had possession of the complex manors of Kippax and Laughton en le Morthen which were later included in the lordships of Pontefract and Tickhill respectively. His brother Morcar, earl of Northumbria, held a number of important manors outside Richmondshire which formed part of Alan of Brittany's Yorkshire lordship, and several complex manors in Holderness later acquired by Drogo de la Beuvrière. As far as we know, both earls were in favour with the Conqueror at the end of 1069, and were not finally removed from political life until 1071.[100] Although it is possible that Alan of Brittany, Ilbert of Lacy and Drogo de la Beuvrière acquired some of the estates which formed their compact lordships before the fall of the earls, it is likely that most were acquired after this fall had taken place. This is best illustrated in the case of Drogo. Fleming has suggested that Drogo's antecessor, Ulf Fitz Tope, from whom Drogo acquired six Holderness manors, was probably deprived of his

[97] *Selby Coucher*, I, [14]–[15]; Symeon, *Opera*, II, 186, 201; Green, *Sheriffs*, 89.
[98] Fleming, *Kings and Lords*, 167–8   [99] Orderic, II, 234.   [100] *Ibid.*, 256–8.

lands either in 1070 or 1071.[101] In addition to Ulf's lands, Drogo's Holderness fee was made up of thirty manors formerly held by William Malet, and another six manors held by Earl Morcar, which were probably only acquired by Drogo after Malet's death and Morcar's rebellion, which occurred in the period 1069–71. For Orderic Vitalis there was no doubt that the removal of the earls Edwin and Morcar marked the point at which the Conqueror 'divided up the chief provinces of England amongst his followers'.[102]

In 1072 the Conqueror passed through Yorkshire on his way to and from Scotland. In the face of the Scottish threat, William is unlikely to have departed from Yorkshire without attempting to make the Norman position there more secure. It was probably at this point that the vacant estates of Earl Edwin, together with nearly all the other property in Richmondshire, passed under the control of Alan of Brittany, and that the count began the construction of fortresses there.[103] It was probably also at about the same time that Ilbert of Lacy and Roger of Bully secured and fortified Edwin's complex manors of Kippax and Laughton en le Morthen respectively. Although it was not until 1086 that Ilbert received the borough of Pontefract, which became the *caput* of his fee, it is more than likely that either he or another tenant-in-chief had been entrusted with custodianship of the estate, and had built a castle there, long before that date. In the light of the problems encountered by the Conqueror in 1069 when he was prevented from crossing a river and reaching York because of the destruction of the bridge at Pontefract, it is difficult to accept Wightman's argument that the Normans probably waited at least another seventeen years to build a castle at this vital settlement.[104]

The construction of the lordship of Robert, count of Mortain, is much more difficult to date. Our Domesday model indicates that in 1086 the establishment of Norman authority on the lordship was much more advanced on the tenanted estates than on the demesne, and that the degree of this authority varied widely from region to region. These variations appear to owe little to soil conditions or pre-conquest agricultural potential. The contrast between the demesne and tenanted land was almost certainly due

---

[101] Fleming, *Kings and Lords*, 168.   [102] Orderic, II, 260.
[103] One of the thanes to whose lands Alan succeeded was Arnketill who had fled from the harrying of the north: Fleming, *Kings and Lords*, 167.
[104] Symeon, *Opera*, II, 188; Orderic, II, 230; Wightman, *Lacy Family*, 24–5, 54.

instead to the fact that Robert spent little (if any) time in Yorkshire. Although in England in 1068–9 and possibly again in 1071–2 and 1080–2, Robert probably lived in Normandy for most of the Conqueror's reign.[105]

In contrast to their lord, the Mortain tenants, Nigel Fossard and Richard of Sourdeval, probably spent a considerable amount of time in Yorkshire, where they held almost all of their lands. Their administration of these lands is especially marked in the more southerly portions of the lordship in the wapentakes of Staincross, Strafforth and Osgoldcross, and in parts of the East Riding. The pattern suggests two possibilities. The first is that the count's tenants were concentrating their administrative efforts in particular areas. The second is that this concentration was due to the construction of the lordship in piecemeal fashion over a considerable period of time; something which is also indicated by the division of the count's Domesday *breve* into a number of separate sections.[106] In view of the importance of south Yorkshire for access to the north, and in the light of what we know of the activities of the count of Mortain in the late 1060s, the early establishment of Norman authority in the Mortain estates in this region would be logical. According to Orderic Vitalis, it was after Robert had fought the Danes in northern Lincolnshire in 1069 that he was granted major English estates and revenues.[107] It is surely more than coincidental that the most developed Mortain tenant estate in south Yorkshire in 1086, Hexthorpe, was situated on the Great North Road at the lowest bridging point on the River Don, immediately to the west of the region where this fighting had taken place. The evidence suggests that Robert and his tenants acquired their lands in south Yorkshire, and began to manage some of them, in or shortly after 1069. In the case of their lands in other areas of the county, however, the establishment of their authority may have been delayed for a number of years, particularly in Cleveland where this authority appears to have been very limited even in 1086.

With regard to the chronology of the establishment of Norman authority over the embryonic lordships, where evidence supplemental to the Domesday model can be found, it indicates that here the model is at its most distorted; that a low level of estate development need not necessarily be taken as evidence that

---

[105] Golding, 'Robert of Mortain', 124; Soulsby, 'Counts of Mortain', 19–20, 29–32.
[106] Roffe, 'Yorkshire Summary', 250–1. [107] Orderic, II, 230, 266.

Norman control was only established shortly before 1086. It is possible that some of the Normans in charge of the embryonic lordships had acquired their lands at an early date, but had not developed their authority within these lands because of a lack of desire or capacity to do so. Fleming suggests that Ralph Paynel, Robert of Tosny, Ralph of Mortemer and Gilbert Tison may have succeeded to the estates of their Anglo–Scandinavian antecessors shortly after the rebellion of 1069 and the subsequent harrying of the north.[108] In the case of Gilbert Tison this is supported by the fact that Edgar the Aetheling was accompanied in his escape to Wearmouth by Alwine Fitz Northmann, who may be the same man as the Alwine whom Tison succeeded in several Yorkshire manors.[109] Ralph Paynel's acquisition of estates in Yorkshire may have taken place even earlier when his antecessor, Maerlesveinn, appears to have been exiled around the time of Christmas 1067.[110] Professor Lennard noted a marked contrast on the Paynel honour in 1086 between the counties of Somerset, Gloucestershire and Northampton, where all the Paynel estates had been granted out to tenants, and those of Yorkshire, Lincolnshire and Devon where a considerable amount of land still belonged to the demesne.[111] It is a contrast which suggests that Ralph Paynel may have been organising his estates in stages, and may have left the more remote counties until last.

Two more embryonic lordships to be established relatively soon after 1066 were those of Berengar of Tosny and Hugh, earl of Chester. In the former case, as Fleming observes, this probably occurred shortly after Berengar's antecessor, Thorbrand, was killed while still in possession of his *setl* of Settrington in 1073.[112] In the latter case, it had certainly taken place by *c.* 1076 × *c.* 1078 when William of Percy granted land in Whitby held of Earl Hugh to the monastic pioneer, Reinfrid, for the foundation of an abbey.[113] The comparatively limited extent of Norman authority on the Chester fee in 1086 was almost certainly due to the fact that

[108] Fleming, *Kings and Lords*, 166–8.

[109] Symeon, *Opera*, II, 190, cited by Williams, *Anglo-Saxons*; *DB*, I, 326b. Williams notes that Alwine's son, Uctred, attested Gilbert Tison's charter to Selby Abbey. See *Selby Coucher*, II, 19.

[110] Fleming, *Kings and Lords*, 173. Not all the rebels were immediately dispossessed. Gospatric the son of Arnketill was a tenant-in-chief in 1086, and the sons of Karle were still in possession of some of their Yorkshire estates in 1074: Williams, *Anglo-Saxons*.

[111] Lennard, *Rural England*, 95–8. [112] Fleming, *Kings and Lords*, 169.

[113] *DB*, I, 305a; D. Bethell, 'The foundation of Fountains Abbey and the state of St Mary's York in 1132', *JEH*, 17 (1966), 17–18; *Cartularium de Whiteby*, I, xxxiv.

the fee constituted only a small and remote portion of an honour which extended across twenty shires.[114]

In one case, that of the lordship of Roger the Poitevin, corroborative evidence indicates that it would be correct to equate a limited level of Norman authority in 1086 with a late date for the start of the establishment of this authority. Roger is known to have been born *c.* 1060, and can only have received his estates on coming of age.[115] He appears to have been in possession of his lands in Lancashire in the early 1080s, and his acquisition of property in Yorkshire can hardly have taken place before this time.[116] It is likely that Roger received his Cravenshire estates in exchange for those in Lancashire and Amounderness, where his tenure is recorded in Domesday Book in the past tense.[117] The exchange probably occurred during the course of the Domesday survey. The Domesday Summary for Yorkshire, which pre-dates the main text, records only a handful of Cravenshire estates and assigns them no lord.[118] In the main text itself, with the exception of only the lordship of Brus (the information for which was entered in the second decade of the twelfth century), Roger's Cravenshire fee is the last fee to be recorded.[119] There is good evidence that this record may be a postscriptal addition.[120] As Professor Holt has pointed out, the description of Roger's lands in the Yorkshire Domesday was simply an extract from a geld roll.[121] It almost certainly represents the sum total of the information the Domesday compiler had to hand.[122] All of this evidence points to the conclusion that Roger the Poitevin knew very little about his Cravenshire estates in 1086, and had not been in possession of them for very long.

The chronology of the establishment and development of

---

[114] For the honour, see C. P. Lewis, 'The formation of the honor of Chester, 1066–1100', in *The Earldom of Chester and its Charters: A Tribute to Geoffrey Barraclough*, ed. A. T. Thacker (Journal of the Chester Arch. Soc., 1991), 37–68.

[115] *Complete Peerage*, XI, 688–9; J. F. A. Mason, 'Roger de Montgomery and his sons (1067–1102)', *TRHS*, 5th ser., 13 (1963), 14–15.

[116] For Lancashire, see K. Thompson, 'Cross channel estates of the Montgomery-Bellême family, *c.*1050–1112' (Univ. of Wales, Cardiff, MA thesis, 1983), 149–57.

[117] K. Thompson, 'Monasteries and settlement in Norman Lancashire: unpublished charters of Roger the Poitevin', *Trans. Hist. Soc. of Lancs. and Cheshire*, 140 (1990), 202 and note 4.

[118] *DB*, I, 380a. For the date of the Summary, see Roffe, 'Yorkshire Summary', 249–51.

[119] P. King, 'The return of the fee of Robert de Brus in Domesday', *YAJ*, 60 (1988), 25–9.

[120] Roffe, 'Domesday Book', 324; Palliser, 'Yorkshire Domesday', 11–12.

[121] J. C. Holt, '1086', in *Domesday Studies*, 61.

[122] Roffe, 'Yorkshire Summary', 257–8.

Norman authority proposed here accords reasonably well with that recently put forward in Fleming's important study of the conquest. Fleming argues that for the first seven years of the Conqueror's reign the lands of individual or small groups of Anglo-Scandinavian lords which became available through death or disgrace were bestowed in their entirety upon Norman lords designated as successors. By c. 1073, however, the supply of great Anglo-Scandinavian antecessors had been exhausted, and the Norman administration could not cope with the problems of assigning the small estates of minor English thanes to individual Norman successors. Faced with this problem, and with increasing commitments on the continent, the Conqueror had to decide how to dispose of the remaining Anglo-Scandinavian lands and, at the same time, to provide for the security of the north. It was at this point that he began to grant out lands by hundred to his most powerful and trusted magnates. All the estates within hundreds not already acquired by antecession, incorporated within the royal demesne or maintained by the church were bestowed in their entirety upon an individual Norman tenant-in-chief, thus creating a series of compact lordships made up of the estates, or portions of the estates, of several pre-conquest landholders. It was in this way, so the thesis runs, that Robert, count of Mortain, acquired lands in nineteen Yorkshire hundreds and wapentakes, Ilbert of Lacy in five and Roger of Bully, Hugh Fitz Baldric, Drogo de la Beuvrière and Osbern of Arches in one each. It was in this way also that Alan of Brittany acquired Richmondshire, and Roger the Poitevin secured most of Cravenshire.[123]

On some of the Yorkshire lordships established by antecession, including those of Warenne, Fitz Baldric and Percy, Norman authority appears to have been reasonably well established in 1086; an observation which tends to support the case that these lordships, or at least parts of them, were formed relatively soon after 1066. Although Norman authority on other lordships established by antecession, including all but one (Arches) of those categorised as embryonic, appears to have been far less developed, it has been suggested above that this need not be taken to indicate a substantial delay in the initial formation of these lordships. In the case of the 'hundredal lordships', Fleming's argument that these may have been created in the period c. 1073–86 is supported by

---

[123] Fleming, *Kings and Lords*, 153–62, 174–82.

evidence indicating that on some of them the establishment of Norman authority was highly advanced in 1086, and had probably been underway for several years, whereas on others (like that of Roger the Poitevin) it was still in the very early stages of evolution and had almost certainly begun only shortly before the completion of the Domesday survey. Moreover, Fleming's contention that some lords, like Robert count of Mortain and Ilbert of Lacy, received several 'hundredal grants' is in accord with the suggestion made above that their lordships appear to have been constructed in piecemeal fashion over a number of years. This is particularly true of the Mortain lordship, where Fleming has suggested that some of the 'hundredal grants' made to Count Robert may not have been made until eight years after 1066. The evidence for this suggestion is that the thane Thorbrand, who died while apparently still in possession of his Yorkshire lands in 1073, held extensively in a number of the wapentakes eventually used to construct the Mortain lordship.[124] It is significant, therefore, that most of Thorbrand's estates were situated in the North and East Ridings, that is in those regions of the Mortain lordship where (according to our Domesday model) the authority of the count appears to have been more limited in 1086. Although it would be valuable in the case of lordships like Mortain, where honorial construction had taken place partly by antecession and partly by 'hundredal grants', to compare estate organisation on the antecessorial and 'hundredal' portions of the fee, this is either extremely difficult or impossible because of the inadequacies of the Domesday text.[125]

Turning now from the chronology of the Norman tenurial take-over to its methodology, although accepting that a great deal of land was redistributed by the Normans on the basis of antecession, Fleming argues that the conquest brought about a tenurial revolution resulting from, among other things, grants of land on a territorial basis: in other words, grants by hundred.[126] This is a very valuable and, in the case of a large number of the lordships considered by Fleming, compelling argument. However, it might not be applicable to all these lordships. Roffe's

---

[124] *Ibid.*, 176–7.

[125] Neither the number of the count of Mortain's antecessors nor the degree to which pre-conquest patterns of overlordship lie behind the 'grants by hundred' made to the count, can be established with absolute certainty. In the case of the lordship of Hugh Fitz Baldric, although the methods of acquisition seem clearer, the impact of these methods on the development of estates in 1086 is difficult to interpret.

[126] Fleming, *Kings and Lords*, 111–61.

discussion of Domesday Book's failure fully to record pre-conquest patterns of overlordship must be taken into account. It could be that in some regions many or all of the Anglo-Scandinavian thanes whose estates appear to have formed the constituent elements of a 'hundredal grant', were subtenants of a single pre-conquest lord who was designated as the antecessor of the Norman Domesday tenant-in-chief to whom the grant was made. In that case the basis of acquisition would be antecessorial rather than hundredal. Roffe considers that pre-conquest overlordship of this nature is reflected in extensive liberties or franchises attached to the *capita* of post-conquest lordships (which suggest that these *capita* were royal or comital centres before 1066), in multiple manor entries and in the interlocking of some elements of post-conquest lordships with larger estates (indicating a common origin for whole groups of manors).[127]

It may be, therefore, that at least some of the compact lordships which have often been seen as Norman creations were already in existence before 1066.[128] If Roffe's methods for identifying patterns of pre-conquest overlordship are reliable this may be true of a good proportion, if not the whole, of the lordship of Richmond, where Alan of Brittany succeeded fifty-four thanes. The greatest estates in Alan's lordship were the complex manors of Gilling and Catterick. Both of these were held before 1066 by Earl Edwin, and both were almost certainly the respective administrative centres of the wapentakes of Gilling and Hang.[129] The impression that Earl Edwin's overlordship in Richmondshire may have been extensive is strengthened by the fact that the lordship of Count Alan interlocked in several vills with the estates of Edwin's former neighbouring complex manor of Northallerton, the administrative focus of Allerton wapentake.[130] It is an impression which gains further force from the fact that the lordship appears to have been coterminous with a region known as Richmondshire, from the probability that Richmondshire formed a franchise which was in some way administratively distinct from Yorkshire in 1086, and from the treatment of the lordship of Richmond as a

---

[127] Roffe, 'Thegnage to barony', 169. Dr Roffe has informed me that he has not discounted the possibility of 'hundredal grants', but that he has yet to see a convincing case of one.
[128] For the view that they were Norman creations, see Le Patourel, 'Norman conquest', 14–15; Wightman, *Lacy Family*, 19–21; Kapelle, *Norman Conquest*, 145; Fleming, *Kings and Lords*, 153–62, 180; Palliser, 'Yorkshire Domesday', 3, 33.
[129] See Thorn, 'Hundreds and wapentakes', 52.
[130] *EYC*, II, no. 931; *DB*, I, 299a, 309a–10a.

distinct earldom in Stephen's reign.[131] Such 'shires' occur in various places in the north, appear to be of pre-conquest origin and usually constitute wide districts administered from central estates.[132] It is unlikely, however, that Earl Edwin's overlordship extended over the whole of Richmondshire. A few estates there were held by pre-conquest thanes *cum saca et soca*, an expression which may be synonymous with rights of full ownership.[133] However, if *saca et soca* can be interpreted in this way, the limitation of these rights to only a small number of thanes and estates suggests that the bulk of the manors which formed the lordship of Count Alan were held prior to 1066 as subtenancies of a great lord, and that this lordship was already a tenurial entity before the Normans arrived in England.

The theory of 'grants by hundred' does not seem to apply to Roger of Bully's lordship of Tickhill. Fleming argues that Roger acquired his extensive estates in Strafforth wapentake by 'hundredal grant' and added them to his lands in Derbyshire.[134] On closer analysis it emerges that although Bully acquired considerable holdings in Strafforth wapentake from a large number of Anglo-Scandinavian lords, he did not acquire every estate there that had not been taken into the royal demesne, maintained by the church or alienated to Norman lords by antecession. A large number of estates in Strafforth also passed to Robert, count of Mortain. These had been held by nineteen pre-conquest lords, the majority of whom are not listed by Fleming among the count's antecessors.[135] There is some evidence that Roger of Bully may have acquired his estates by antecession. Roffe argues that 'part, probably even most, of Roger's honour was derived from the interests of the pre-Conquest earl'.[136] Another possibility is that the formation of the Bully and Mortain fees in south Yorkshire owed more to strategic considerations than either 'hundredal grants' or antecession. The castlery of Tickhill bestrode the Great North Road; and the Mortain estates probably constituted two more castleries, one close to the entrance into Yorkshire via the

[131] For the franchise, see Roffe, 'Domesday Book', 327; *idem*, 'Yorkshire Summary', esp. 247–8, 255–6. For Stephen's reign, see below pp. 166–7. But see also Thorn, 'Hundreds and wapentakes', 52.

[132] H. M. Cam, *Liberties and Communities in Medieval England* (London, 1963), 105, and see 86–7, 90.   [133] *DB*, I, 309a, 310b; Roffe, 'Thegnage to barony', 157–9, 164–8.

[134] Fleming, *Kings and Lords*, 148, 158.

[135] *DB*, I, 307b–8b; Fleming, *Kings and Lords*, 155.

[136] Roffe, 'Thegnage to barony', 169.

Snake pass, and the other at the point where the Great North Road crossed the River Don (Map 9).

As Fleming notes, strategic or territorial considerations may also have influenced the structure of the lordships of Hugh Fitz Baldric and William of Percy.[137] Although the former was made p partly of land acquired by 'hundredal grant' in the wapentake f Birdforth and partly of estates acquired by antecession, it did not incorporate all the property belonging to Hugh's antecessors, Gamall and Ormr. With the exception of a manor in Langbargh wapentake and about twenty more manors in the East Riding, only the lands of Gamall and Ormr in Birdforth and neighbouring wapentakes were acquired by Hugh, and many more of their estates passed to other Norman tenants-in-chief. The compactness of the honour, therefore, appears to have been the result of selective tenurial engineering. This also appears to have been true of the four clusters of estates which made up the fee of William of Percy, who acquired only a portion of the lands of his antecessors, Gamall, Northmann and Gamalbarn.[138]

Our Domesday model suggests that the early motte and bailey and ringwork castles which lay at the heart of these and other lordships in Yorkshire were situated at many of the centres of administrative, demographic and military importance in the county, and were one of the keystones of Norman power. In some areas within Yorkshire the Normans had not only constructed castles, they had organised regions to provide for their subsistence. We read in the Yorkshire Domesday of castleries, a term interpreted by Stenton as designating 'a well-defined district within which the whole arrangement of tenancies was primarily designed for the maintenance of the castle'.[139] It is an interpretation which seems unobjectionable when tested in Yorkshire. Thorner

[137] Fleming, *Kings and Lords*, 145–8.
[138] For the antecessors of Fitz Baldric and William of Percy, see Fleming, *Kings and Lords*, 138, 157–8, 167–8. Estates belonging to pre-conquest landholders with the same names as these antecessors also passed to Berengar of Tosny, Ilbert of Lacy, Robert Malet, Robert count of Mortain, Alan of Richmond, Osbern of Arches and Drogo de la Beuvrière. However, for a number of reasons the tenurial reorganisation may not be as great as it may seem. The first is the possibility that the names of the antecessors of Fitz Baldric and Percy were shared by more than one thane (on this, see *Domesday Book : Yorkshire*, ed. M. L. Faull and M. Stinson, 2 vols. (Chichester, 1986), II, Appendix). The second is the possibility that some of the estates of the antecessors of Percy and Fitz Baldric did not pass to them because they had been held as subtenancies of other lords before 1066. Similarly, some of the estates which passed to Percy and Fitz Baldric from thanes who were not their antecessors may have been held by those thanes as subtenancies of these antecessors.   [139] Stenton, *First Century*, 194.

we are told was 'situated within the bounds of Ilbert's castle', even though it was over ten miles from the nearest Lacy fortress; the castlery of Alan of Brittany incorporated '200 manors less one'; and the castlery of Roger the Poitevin encompassed manors in vills ten miles apart.[140] However, the interpretation needs to be broadened out. As Professor Hollister noted, 'The district of a castle, although normally composed of fees, might also be described as including particular manors, woods, hundreds, and, in one instance, an entire shire'.[141]

Evidence from Yorkshire suggests that castleries could have an administrative as well as a territorial basis. They were governmental as well as military entities. The castlery of Count Alan was almost certainly coterminous with Richmondshire. That of Ilbert of Lacy probably had the same boundaries as the wapentake of Skyrack. According to the Domesday *clamores*, 'the men of Barkston wapentake and Skyrack wapentake cite testimony to Osbern of Arches that Wulfbert, his predecessor, had all Thorner, they do not know by whose gift... But all Thorner is situated within the bounds of Ilbert's castle, according to the first measurement, and, according to the most recent measurement is situated outside [it]'.[142] This can only have been one of the many tenurial disputes resulting from conflicts between litigants basing their claims to title on antecessorial succession, and litigants basing their claims to title on 'hundredal grants'; conflicts which Fleming argues were at the heart of many of the legal cases recorded in the Domesday *clamores*.[143] The claim of Osbern of Arches was clearly antecessorial. What the men of the wapentake were trying to decide was whether the claim of Ilbert of Lacy was justifiably hundredal. Their difficulty may have lain in the fact that Thorner was situated only two miles from the boundary between Barkston and Skyrack wapentakes. This is probably why both wapentake courts were asked to give testimony, and why precise measurements were required. The Lacy wapentake was clearly that of Skyrack, the court of which was controlled by the family in the twelfth century.[144] However, it was not to the wapentake boundaries that the jurors referred in 1086, but to the boundaries of Ilbert's castlery; and there can be little doubt that the two were perceived by them as being the same.

---

[140] *DB*, I, 373b, 381a, 332a.   [141] Hollister, *Military Organization*, 150.
[142] *DB*, I, 373b.   [143] Fleming, *Kings and Lords*, 161.
[144] Wightman, *Lacy Family*, 107.

This is not to argue that every castle built by the Normans in Yorkshire lay at the heart of a hundredal or franchisal castlery. Besides those mentioned above the only other possible early fortresses of this type were Skipsea (Holderness), Conisbrough and Laughton en le Morthen (Strafforth) and Sheffield (Hallamshire). Whatever their individual roles, however, collectively the castles were the linchpins of the conquest; a point not lost on Orderic Vitalis. 'The fortifications called castles by the Normans', he declared, 'were scarcely known in the English provinces, and so the English – in spite of their courage and love of fighting – could put up only a weak resistance to their enemies'.[145]

CONCLUSION

There is no doubt, and the point should be stressed, that the Norman conquest of Yorkshire was very far from complete in 1086, and that its progress lagged a long way behind that achieved in many other counties. In considerable areas of Yorkshire the Normans knew very little about their lands beyond the names of vills and the numbers of carucates by which they were assessed for taxation; information derived from Anglo-Scandinavian records probably kept in York. This limitation of authority is reflected in the recording of hundreds of vills in Domesday Book without population and resources, and as waste. It is reflected also in the frequency with which those estates for which details are provided had declined sharply in value. The Yorkshire of Domesday Book was a region at the frontiers of Norman power. This was particularly true of the Pennine uplands and Cleveland. It was only slowly over the next half-century that these areas were brought within the ambit of Norman authority.

Having said all this, however, it is clear that the extent of Norman power within Yorkshire was greater, and the process by which this power had been established was more rapid, than historians have realised. When combined with evidence from other sources, a detailed analysis of the descriptions of the Norman lordships in the Yorkshire Domesday indicates that the conquest, colonisation and tenurial reorganisation of Yorkshire was achieved more expeditiously than has hitherto been supposed. Many of the Norman Domesday lordships, including several of the most underdeveloped in 1086, had probably been established within

[145] Orderic, II, 218.

five or six years of the arrival of the Conqueror, and very few remained to be organised after *c.* 1075. It is possible that the only fee originating in the 1080s was that of Roger the Poitevin.

And if the speed of the conquest has been underestimated, so has the level of control exercised over the process by the Conqueror. Although some Anglo-Scandinavian lands were undoubtedly seized arbitrarily, the vast majority were redistributed in an organised fashion either by antecession, 'hundredal grant' or on strategic grounds. The systematic way in which William and his followers went about the conquest of Yorkshire is illustrated most clearly, perhaps, by the likelihood that castles were constructed on most of their lordships. The landscape of the county was probably covered in castles in 1086, most of them carefully situated in old administrative and population centres or close to the major road and river routes which were the tentacles by which the Normans tightened their grip on Yorkshire; and some of them attached to castleries which corresponded to the hundreds, wapentakes and shires which were and remained the centres of wealth and local jurisdictional authority throughout the Anglo-Norman period. Administratively and militarily the castleries helped to give the Normans a stranglehold on the population, land and resources of Yorkshire. In summing up the progress of the Norman conquest and the extent of the Conqueror's achievement in the county in 1086, the words of another great statesman referring in 1942 to a similar struggle for control of England are probably the most appropriate. It was not the end. It was not even the beginning of the end. But it was, perhaps, the end of the beginning.

Chapter 2

THE TRANSFORMATION OF YORKSHIRE
1066–1135: TERRITORIAL CONSOLIDATION
AND ADMINISTRATIVE INTEGRATION

By 1086 William the Conqueror and the first generation of
Anglo-Norman magnates had laid the foundations of Norman
rule in Yorkshire. The county had undergone a social, military
and (in places) tenurial revolution. The vast majority of the
Anglo-Scandinavian aristocracy had been deprived of their lands
or demoted to the level of subtenants, their governmental offices
had been taken away, their honours had been partially reorganised
and many of their most important administrative and population
centres had been subjected to Norman military control. The
county probably bristled with Norman castles, around the
majority of which a resident continental tenantry was already
bringing Norman administration to bear. And coordinating this
administration was the Norman sheriff, based in one of the castles
at York, and directly responsible to the king.[1]

In the years that followed the Conqueror's death in 1087 it fell
to his sons, William Rufus and Henry I, to build upon these
tenurial, military and administrative foundations in order to
consolidate and extend the Norman grip on Yorkshire.[2] There
remained much to be done. The large areas of the county which
lay outside direct Norman control, such as Cleveland and the
eastern fringes of the Pennines, required organisation and colonisation. If the Normans were going to exercise effective royal
control of Yorkshire, it was also imperative that the local
administration be developed and brought under the closer
supervision of central government. In the half-century that
followed the Domesday survey the Conqueror's sons set about
achieving these objectives in a climate of repeated political
upheavals, which helped as well as hindered them. Although the
involvement of northern magnates in the rebellions of 1088 and

---

[1] For the early sheriffs, see Green, *Sheriffs*, 89.
[2] As stated in Chapter 1, the conquest of Yorkshire had many facets. The purpose of this
chapter is to develop those relating to tenure, military power and administration.

1095, and the political disturbances of the period 1101–6, probably impeded the emergence of royal power within the region in the short term, it was not without its benefits for the kings in the long run. When the uprisings eventually subsided, William Rufus and Henry I were able to replace several magnates who had acquired Yorkshire lordships from the Conqueror, and who had participated in the rebellions, and to reorganise the estates of these rebels to the royal advantage. The greatest strides were taken by Henry I who made use not only of the forfeited estates of the rebels, but also of the extensive royal demesne, to introduce an important breed of 'new men' into northern England who were closely attached to his court. By 1135 these 'new men' controlled the offices of local government, the royal castles and a large number of the county's wapentakes and hundreds. Their rise to power transformed the structure of magnate lordship and royal administration in Yorkshire, and consolidated the conquest and settlement which the Conqueror had begun.

William Rufus had been in power only a year when a political storm blew up which was to alter the structure of lordship in Yorkshire. Although the ringleader of the 1088 rebellion, organised to replace Rufus with Robert Curthose, was Odo bishop of Bayeux, and the main theatres of contention were the counties of Kent and Sussex and the Welsh marches, several magnates who were tenants-in-chief in Yorkshire were closely involved.[3] Robert, count of Mortain, was Bishop Odo's brother, and his castle of Pevensey was one of the three major rebel centres along the south coast; William bishop of Durham was Odo's protégé, and 'did whatever damage he could' in the north; and Ralph of Mortemer and the earl of Northumberland, Robert of Mowbray, were involved in a subsidiary rebellion in the Welsh marches.[4]

With the exception of Odo of Bayeux, the king appears to have dealt leniently with all these men when the rebellion ended in failure in the summer of 1088. Although it has been stated that the count of Mortain was exiled for his part in the affair, and suggested that his son, William, was never allowed to recover the Yorkshire portion of the Mortain fee, there is good evidence that Robert was

---

[3] For the rebellion, see Orderic, IV, 120–34; *Gestis Regum*, II, 360–4; *ASC, s.a.* 1088; Florence, *Chronicon*, II, 21–5; Barlow, *Rufus*, 70–82.

[4] Florence, *Chronicon*, II, 24; *ASC, s.a.* 1088; Orderic, IV, 98; Symeon, *Opera*, I, 170; Barlow, *Rufus*, 82.

reconciled with the king before the end of the rebellion, and that William inherited all of his father's estates.[5] Ralph of Mortemer was back in the king's favour shortly after the rebellion, and in 1090 was one of a group of magnates in north-eastern Normandy who fortified their castles in support of Rufus.[6] A year later the bishop of Durham, who had gone into exile after refusing to accept the jurisdiction of the king's court when brought to trial for deserting Rufus, was also restored to royal favour and recovered both his confiscated estates and the castle of Durham.[7] It was probably at about the same time that Robert, earl of Northumberland, who appears to have accompanied the bishop into exile, secured his pardon, and he was certainly back in control of his English fee by 1095 when he took part in another rebellion.

Most of the principal opponents of William Rufus in 1088 recovered the king's goodwill, but the rebellion was not without its political casualties. At least two Yorkshire tenants-in-chief may have been among them. Although it has been suggested that Hugh Fitz Baldric may already have been deprived of his Yorkshire estates by the death of the Conqueror, it is possible that the deprivation occurred as a result of participation in the 1088 rebellion.[8] It is certainly interesting that Hugh appears to have witnessed a charter of Robert Curthose in Normandy in 1089.[9] Neither of Hugh's daughters inherited any of his estates beyond what had been assigned to them as marriage portions. The bulk of his estates in Yorkshire and other counties passed instead to Robert I of Stuteville before 1100, almost certainly at the direction of the king who retained the remainder of the Fitz Baldric fee in his own hands and used it at a later date to endow other tenants-in-chief.[10] Another magnate holding lands in Yorkshire who may have participated in the 1088 rebellion was Robert Malet, whose lordship of Eye in Suffolk was granted by Rufus to Roger the Poitevin.[11]

More Yorkshire tenants-in-chief were to fall as a result of their participation in the rebellion of 1095. According to Florence of Worcester, this rebellion aimed to replace William Rufus with

---

[5] See Orderic, v, 208; Soulsby, 'Counts of Mortain', 42–6; Golding, 'Robert of Mortain', 121–2.   [6] Orderic, IV, 183; David, *Curthose*, 54.

[7] Symeon, *Opera*, I, 170–95; Barlow, *Rufus*, 82–90.

[8] For the possibility that he had been deprived by 1087, see *EYC*, IX, 72.

[9] *Ibid.*, xii.   [10] *Ibid.*, 73–5.

[11] C. P. Lewis, 'The king and Eye: a study in Anglo-Norman politics', *EHR*, 104 (1989), 569–87, esp. 578.

Stephen count of Aumale, the son of Odo count of Champagne, lord of Holderness.[12] As in 1088, the rebellion was a failure, but Rufus was far less inclined to be forgiving. The count of Eu was mutilated and blinded for his part in the affair, and his fellow conspirators, Odo of Champagne and Robert, earl of Northumberland, were deprived of their English estates and imprisoned or sent into exile for the remainder of the reign.[13]

William Rufus employed the lands confiscated from the rebels of 1088 and 1095, together with other estates derived from the on-going seizure of Anglo-Scandinavian tenancies and from natural escheats, to reorganise the tenurial structure of northern England and establish a number of 'new men' in lordships deliberately constructed to reinforce Norman power there. It was a re-organisation which involved the formation of a series of new lordships in Northumberland and Cumbria, and the establishment of Roger the Poitevin as lord of most of Lancashire; and much of it may well have taken place during or shortly after the king's visit to the north in 1092 when he fortified Carlisle and settled peasants from southern England within the vicinity.[14] It was a reorganisation which also embraced Yorkshire. As Dr Greenway has noted, the formation of strong lordships on the potential Scottish invasion routes into the county was 'in line with Rufus's vigorous northern policy'.[15]

One of the largest of these new lordships was that of Robert of Stuteville, whose Norman estates were centred on Valmont and Etoutteville sur Mer in the north-east of the duchy. This lordship was made up partly from the major portion of the honour formerly belonging to Hugh Fitz Baldric, and was situated mainly in the wapentakes of *Gerlestre* (Birdforth), *Maneshou* and *Dic*. The Fitz Baldric estates possibly already constituted two compact castleries in 1086, one of which may have been centred on the great soke manor of Kirby Moorside (Map 4). The two clusters of estates were situated on the eastern side of the Vale of York and at the entrance to several of the passes through the North Yorkshire Moors, and Rufus augmented them with a number of royal demesne estates, including a manor at Thirsk where a castle had

---

[12] Florence, *Chronicon*, II, 38.   [13] *ASC, s.a.* 1095–6.
[14] G. W. S. Barrow, 'The pattern of lordship and feudal settlement in Cumbria', *JMH*, I (1975), 117–38; Farrer, *Kendale*, I, viii–x, I; Thompson, 'Norman Lancashire', 201–25; Lewis, 'The king and Eye', 578.   [15] *Mowbray Charters*, xxiii.

been constructed by 1130.[16] On the western side of the Vale of
York, Stuteville acquired another compact body of lands formerly
in the possession of the Anglo-Scandinavian Domesday tenant-in-
chief, Gospatric, centred on Kirkby Malzeard which was also the
site of a castle in 1130.[17] And in addition to control of large
portions of the Vales of York and Pickering, Stuteville was
entrusted with the estates flanking another major lowland route
into Yorkshire further west when he acquired a lordship extending
from upper Ribblesdale to Lonsdale and Kendale after the death of
Ivo Taillebois (*c.*1094).[18] As at Thirsk and Malzeard, so at Burton
in Lonsdale, a castle had been constructed by 1130, and Robert of
Stuteville may well have been its founder (Map 17).[19]

Another new compact and strategically important lordship on
the northern frontier of Yorkshire probably constructed by Rufus
was that of Guy of Balliol, which was made up of estates formerly
belonging to Hugh Fitz Baldric, Robert earl of Northumberland
and the royal demesne.[20] The lordship dominated upper Teesdale
just north of the Roman road linking Yorkshire with Cumbria,
and within a short time of its formation the Balliols had
constructed a castle and borough at their *caput* of Barnard (Map
18).[21]

In conjunction with the great lordships of Richmond and
Cravenshire, the Yorkshire honours reorganised or created by
William Rufus formed a network of castleries extending from the
southern fringe of the North Yorkshire Moors in the east, to
Lonsdale and the Ribble valley in the west. It may have been with
the intention of strengthening this network that Rufus granted the
wapentake/soke manor of Northallerton to William bishop of
Durham, and the soke manor of Bolton in Craven to Robert of
Rumilly.[22] Northallerton and its outliers dominated the northern
end of the Vale of York between the North Yorkshire Moors and

---

[16] *Ibid.*, xxiii–xxiv; *PR 31 Henry I*, 138.
[17] *Mowbray Charters*, xxii and note 5; *PR 31 Henry I*, 137.
[18] *Mowbray Charters*, xxii. See also *EYC*, IX, nos. 41–3 and notes.
[19] *PR 31 Henry I*, 138.
[20] L. C. Loyd, *The Origins of Some Anglo-Norman Families*, ed. C. T. Clay and D. C. Douglas (Harleian Soc., 1951), 11, 17, 47, 108; *EYC*, I, 438–9; *VCH, Yorkshire*, II, 179, 183. See also Sanders, *Baronies*, 25 and notes; *Book of Fees*, I, 201; *Regesta*, I, no. 412.
[21] D. Austin, 'Barnard castle, co. Durham. First interim report: excavations in the town ward, 1974–6', *JBAA*, 132 (1979), 52.
[22] Robert of Rumilly had probably been granted Bolton by 1096: *EYC*, VII, 1–4. For the grant of Northallerton to the bishop of Durham, see *EYC*, II, no. 927; Symeon, *Opera*, I, 127.

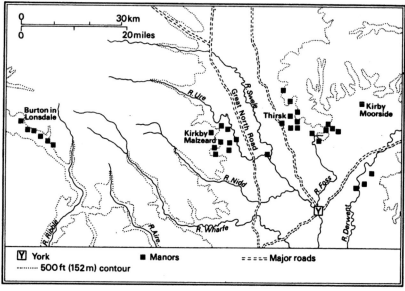

Map 17   The honour of Robert of Stuteville: *c.* 1100

the castlery of Richmond, through which ran one of the two
major roads between Durham and York; and the estates centred
on Bolton bestrode the river valley lowland route into Yorkshire via Lonsdale (Map 18). By the early twelfth century
castles had probably been constructed in a berewick of Bolton at
Skipton, and in the manor of Northallerton or one of its outliers.[23]
For William Rufus, as for his father, the 'hundredal' castlery was
a potent instrument for imposing Norman military and administrative power.

Rufus also consolidated the compact lordships along the eastern
frontier of Yorkshire. It may have been he, rather than his brother
Henry, who added a number of royal demesne estates in the East
Riding to the compact fee held there by the Gant family centred
on the manor (and possibly the castle) of Hunmanby, the probable
focus of *Turbar* hundred.[24] The most important of these estates was

---

[23] King, *Castellarium Anglicanum*, II, 526, 522, 520.
[24] Limitations of space prevent a comprehensive discussion of the evidence concerning the
location of the administrative centres of the wapentakes and hundreds of Yorkshire.
Some of this evidence may be found in Anderson, *Hundred-Names*, 3–27; Thorn,
'Hundreds and wapentakes', 50–5, 60–2, 67, 69–70; Roffe, 'Yorkshire Summary',
242–60. I hope to defend my assumption that the administrative centres of most of these

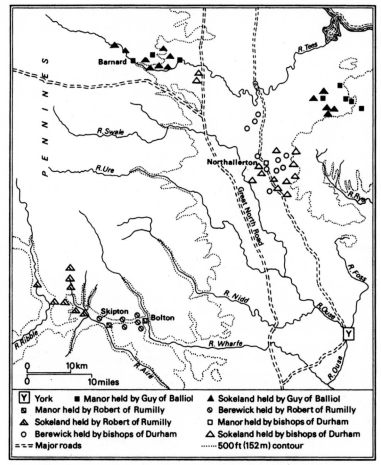

Map 18   The castleries of Barnard, Skipton and Northallerton: *c.* 1100

the great soke manor of Bridlington, which was almost certainly the administrative centre of neighbouring Hunthow hundred, and which was also a borough and a port.[25] The acquisition of

wapentakes and hundreds were located in wealthy and extensive soke manors in a forthcoming article.

[25] In one work Farrer stated that Bridlington was granted to the Gants by Henry I, in another that it appears to have been granted by William Rufus: *EYC*, II, 432; *VCH, Yorkshire*, II, 175. See also M. R. Abbot, 'The Gant family in England, 1066–1191' (Univ. of Cambridge, PhD thesis, 1973), 23, 77–9.

Bridlington and its appurtenances, together with other nearby royal estates, effectively doubled the size and resources of the Gant lordship, without sacrificing its compactness.[26]

The alienation of royal demesne estates within the vicinity of the great manor of Falsgrave in the North Riding may also have been undertaken by the king with a view to consolidating the coastal lordships. As well as the Gants, the main family to benefit from this were the Percys who already possessed important estates in the area centred on the great soke manors of Whitby and South Loftus, which had been held at the Domesday survey of the earl of Chester (Map 14).[27] Like his neighbour, Gilbert of Gant, William of Percy was a veteran of the warfare of the Conqueror's reign, a former custodian of York castle, and probably well suited to the role of providing for the security and administration of the coastal frontier. The shared experience and cooperation of the two old warriors may well explain the marriage of Percy's eldest son and heir, Alan, to Gant's daughter, Emma.[28]

Further south, Rufus was probably responsible for alienating another royal hundred, Burton Agnes, which bordered both Hunthow and *Turbar*, to the sheriff of Yorkshire, Geoffrey Bainard, a man new to the county and dependent upon the king.[29] Another newcomer to the north, Arnulf of Montgomery, a younger son of Roger II of Montgomery, was entrusted with the great wapentake castlery of Holderness after the fall of Odo, count of Champagne, in the rebellion of 1095.[30] On the southern shore of the Humber, Rufus granted Arnulf's brother, Roger the Poitevin, the confiscated Lincolnshire estates of Durand Malet.[31] Only a few miles to the west, Rufus granted custody of the important castle of Tickhill, which was situated close to the Great North Road, to another Montgomery brother, Robert of Bellême, whose expertise as a castle engineer was doubtless intended to be put to good effect in strengthening its fortifications.[32] Between

[26] For other royal estates acquired in this region by the Gants before 1135, see J. A. Green, 'William Rufus, Henry I and the royal demesne', *History*, 64 (1979), 344.

[27] *EYC*, II, nos. 855, 872; XI, 7–8, 11–14, 225–7, 233–4; and compare with *DB*, I, 299a, 300a; Green, 'Royal demesne', 344 note 49. [28] *EYC*, XI, 2.

[29] *EYC*, II, no. 676 and note.

[30] *Calendar of Documents Preserved in France I, A. D. 918–1206*, ed. J. H. Round (London, 1899), nos. 667, 1235; *EYC*, III, no. 1300 and note.

[31] Lewis, 'The king and Eye', 578.

[32] M. Chibnall, 'Robert of Bellême and the castle of Tickhill', in *Droit privé et institutions régionales: études historiques offertes à Jean Yver* (Paris, 1976), 151–6; K. Thompson, 'Robert of Bellême reconsidered', *ANS*, 13 (1991), 283.

Tickhill and the Humber, Rufus granted Robert of Stuteville the compact wapentake castlery of Axholme, originally created by the Conqueror to prevent a recurrence of the events of 1069 when the Danes had taken refuge in the area after sacking York.[33]

Wherever we look when examining the tenurial grants of William Rufus in Yorkshire we see the same thing: the alienation of extensive estates which had been confiscated from rebel magnates, or derived from the royal demesne, or taken from the Anglo-Scandinavian nobility, to experienced magnates already established in Yorkshire in 1086, and to a body of men who were new to the county and closely attached to the king. These estates stretched along the vulnerable frontiers of Yorkshire or across its major highways, and included several of the important wapentake, hundredal and soke manors which were a vital foundation of power in the localities. William Rufus had provided for the security of Yorkshire. It was to be Henry I and his 'new men' who would consolidate his efforts.

Within a year of Henry I's succession to the crown the supporters of Robert Curthose, and men with a variety of grievances against the new king, rebelled. England was thrown into a period of political upheaval that was to continue intermittently until 1106.[34] Several magnates in control of substantial Yorkshire lordships became involved in the opposition to the king, and suffered the confiscation of their estates for their trouble. They included Robert of Bellême and his brothers, Roger the Poitevin and Arnulf of Montgomery, William count of Mortain, Robert of Stuteville, Robert of Lacy, Ranulf Flambard bishop of Durham, and possibly Erneis of Burun, Gilbert Tison and William of Arches. The forfeited Yorkshire estates were vast, and they gave Henry I an opportunity to conduct a tenurial reorganisation of the county even more radical than that of William Rufus. Although the old conquest magnate families who had prospered under Rufus were to continue to receive a share of the political spoils, Henry I was also concerned with the establishment of a group of 'new men' closely connected with the court and skilled in matters of government as well as warfare.

Among the first rebels to be dispossessed by Henry I were the Montgomery brothers. Robert of Bellême's garrison of Tickhill

---

[33] *Mowbray Charters*, xxi. [34] Hollister, *Monarchy*, 77–115, 171–89.

surrendered to royal forces in 1102, and the castle remained in the king's hands for the rest of the reign.[35] It is likely that the estates of Robert's brothers were confiscated shortly afterwards. Although the lands of Roger the Poitevin's castlery of Cravenshire were divided at an uncertain date between the Rumilly lords of Skipton and Alan I of Percy, Henry I was clearly intent that Cravenshire should retain something of its compact tenurial structure. In addition to the Poitevin lands, both the Rumillys and the Percys received extensive estates in the region derived from other lordships which appear to have been confiscated, including those of Tison, Burun, Arches and Mortain, and from the royal demesne.[36] The result was the formation of two compact and partially interwoven castleries incorporating nearly all the land in Cravenshire. The Percy estates were mainly concentrated in the Ribble valley and probably focussed upon a castle at Gisburn, while the Rumillys dominated the upper Wharfe and Aire valleys and built their fortress at Skipton.[37] The Rumillys also acquired a cluster of former royal estates around Wath upon Dearne in south Yorkshire.[38]

Roger the Poitevin's opposition to Henry I may have been undertaken in response to, or in expectation of, the king's restoration to Robert Malet of the estates secured by Roger from the confiscated Malet fee in the reign of Rufus.[39] Robert Malet had been one of the first magnates to come to Henry's side in 1100, became one of his closest counsellors and was back in possession of his estates before his death in *c.* 1106. Although the Anglo-Saxon chronicle states that William Malet, whose exact relationship with Robert is uncertain, was deprived of his estates in 1110, he may never have succeeded Robert, and it is probable that the Malet lands were resumed by the crown in *c.* 1106. The Yorkshire estates were divided in the years that followed between Stephen of Blois, Robert I of Brus, Forne Fitz Sigulf, William Meschin, Anschetill of Bulmer, Robert I of Meinil and the powerful Nigel d'Aubigny.[40]

Nigel d'Aubigny was a younger son of Roger I d'Aubigny, lord of the small Norman honour of St Martin d'Aubigny, a younger brother of William d'Aubigny the royal *pincerna* and the most

[35] Chibnall, 'Robert of Bellême', 155–6.   [36] *EYC*, VII, 45–7, 194–5; XI, 14–16.
[37] King, *Castellarium Anglicanum*, II, 517, 529, 526.   [38] *EYC*, VII, 194–5.
[39] For this, and the following details, see Lewis, 'The king and Eye', 576–84.
[40] *EYC*, II, 358; III, 454–7; *Regesta*, II, no. 1357.

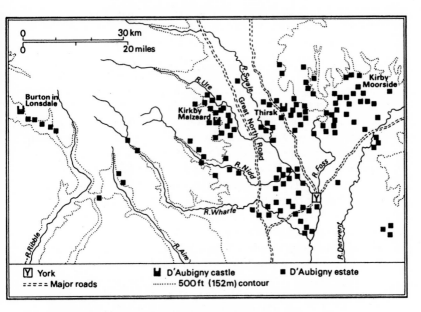

Map 19   The honour of Nigel d'Aubigny: *c.* 1115

prominent and richly rewarded member of the group of 'new
men' introduced by Henry I into the aristocratic community of
Yorkshire.[41] Although beginning his career as a landless knight at
Henry's court in 1101, during the following two decades Nigel
was elevated by royal patronage to a position rivalling that of the
most powerful magnates in Yorkshire. He appears to have secured
his extensive estates in the county, eight other English shires and
Normandy in the period 1107–*c.* 1115. The Yorkshire lands were
formed largely from the confiscated honour of Robert of
Stuteville, one of the rebels captured by the king at Tinchebrai in
1106, and included a lordship extending from upper Ribblesdale to
Lonsdale and Kendale, and two Stuteville castleries centred on
Thirsk and Kirkby Malzeard (Map 19). Although some of the
components of the castlery of Thirsk were withheld, Henry I
made up for them by granting Nigel several former Malet
holdings nearby. On the other side of the Vale of York, the
castlery of Malzeard was augmented by the addition of the portion
of the fee belonging in 1086 to Gospatric which had subsequently

---

[41] I am indebted for the details in this paragraph to *Mowbray Charters*, xvii–xxiv.

passed to Erneis of Burun (consisting of the tenancy-in-chief of Nidderdale, and an extensive subtenancy of the lordship of Richmond centred on Masham), and by Nigel's acquisition of a subtenancy in three estates belonging to the archbishop of York's manor of Ripon; an acquisition which, according to Greenway, provides 'further evidence that this large and compact lordship was the result of deliberate royal policy'.[42] A royal desire for tenurial uniformity and integration is also reflected by the fact that most of the more amorphous Stuteville estates in the East Riding of Yorkshire were withheld from Nigel, and passed instead to Geoffrey Murdac.[43] Henry I appears to have been just as determined as William Rufus to rationalise the often complicated and incoherent tenurial pattern resulting from the first generation of Norman settlement, and to replace it with a network of largely self-contained and regular castleries.

In addition to the Stuteville and Malet estates, Nigel d'Aubigny was granted the overlordship of two former tenants-in-chief and their fees. Before 1118 he had been given the service of Gilbert Tison, and by 1124 that of William of Arches.[44] Tison and Arches had suffered a tenurial demotion, which suggests that they may have become involved in the rebellions against the king. It is a suggestion strengthened by the partial disintegration of the Tison fee. Gilbert Tison carried only a portion of the fee he held in Yorkshire in 1086 to Nigel d'Aubigny.[45] Most of his lands in the West Riding passed either to the king or to the honours of Percy, Rumilly and Eustace Fitz John, and appear to have contributed either towards the creation of new castleries or the rounding-off of existing ones.[46] A similar pattern of redistribution is discernible in the descent of the Arches fee. The bulk of the Arches estates in Ainsty wapentake passed largely intact to Nigel d'Aubigny, the probable custodian of nearby York castle; the eight carucates belonging to the fee in Silsden were absorbed within the Rumilly castlery in Cravenshire; and the four Arches carucates in Oxton

---

[42] *Ibid.*, xxiii. [43] *EYC*, ix, 65–7, 74, 140. [44] *Mowbray Charters*, xxv.

[45] Out of a total of more than 160 carucates about 114 passed to Nigel d'Aubigny, and in 1166 constituted fifteen knights' fees held of Nigel's son, Roger of Mowbray, by William Tison the grandson of Gilbert Tison. They were almost certainly located in the East Riding. See *EYC*, xii, 1, 22–3.

[46] The lands passing to the king were situated in vills near the royal manor of Knaresborough. Those passing to the Percys and the lordship of Skipton were situated in Cravenshire. See *EYC*, xii, 19–21, no. 53 and note; xi, 14–15; vii, 46–7, 48 and note 2, 275 and note 3, 93, 178–80, 256.

were added to a compact group of Percy estates centred on Tadcaster (Map 16).[47] Whether by redistribution or tenurial subjection the old amorphous Domesday lordships were being woven by the king and his magnates into the compact castleries.

The same policy is discernible in the descent of the confiscated honour of William count of Mortain, the estates of which were widely scattered throughout Yorkshire in 1086 (Map 9). William initially accepted Henry I, but in 1104 went into opposition against him. He was among the barons captured by Henry at the battle of Tinchebrai in 1106, which was fought outside the gates of his castle, and was imprisoned and deprived of his English lands.[48] In the years that followed, his Yorkshire estates were dismembered and employed as components in the construction of new compact lordships.

After the fall of the count of Mortain the subtenancies held from his father in 1086 by Nigel Fossard and Richard of Sourdeval were transformed into tenancies-in-chief.[49] Although a portion of the Fossard estates in south Yorkshire centred upon Doncaster were leased to the crown at some time before 1130, and the remainder were in the king's hands at that date and may have been confiscated, Nigel Fossard's son, Robert, had been in possession of his father's lands at some point before 1129 and was given the opportunity to pay for their recovery.[50] Robert's son, William, returned a *carta* as a tenant-in-chief from Yorkshire in 1166.[51] The major portion of the Sourdeval estates passed at some point in Henry I's reign to the lord of Drax, Ralph Paynel, whose second wife, Maud, was probably a daughter of Richard of Sourdeval. From Ralph the estates passed to his younger son by Maud, Jordan Paynel, the ancestor of the Paynels of Hooton.[52] Almost all the Sourdeval estates in the North and East Ridings, consisting of a compact group of lands in the hundred of Hunthow, what possibly amounted to a hundredal castlery based upon the extensive manors of Hutton Rudby and Seamer in Langbargh wapentake, and two isolated manors in *Bolesford* wapentake,

---

[47] *EYC*, VII, 47, 194–5; XI, 15.
[48] William witnessed three charters issued by the king in 1100, and another issued in September 1101: *Regesta*, II, nos. 492, 497, 510, 544. For his later opposition to Henry, see *Gestis Regum*, II, 473–5; *Liber Monasterii de Hyda*, ed. E. Edwards (RS, 1866), 32–4; Florence, *Chronicon*, II, 53; *ASC*, s.a. 1104, s.a. 1106; *Regesta*, II, no. 677; David, *Curthose*, 159–60.   [49] See above, pp. 51–3, 68.
[50] *PR 31 Henry I*, 25, 30, 24; *Regesta*, II, nos. 1627, 1630; King, 'Robert de Brus', 25–8.
[51] *Red Book*, I, 407–8.   [52] *EYC*, VI, 4–5, 38–9, 58, no. 1.

appear to have been granted by Ralph Paynel to Robert of Meinil to hold of him for military service.[53] There is a clearly discernible pattern here. Ralph Paynel alienated the Sourdeval estates on a sharply delineated regional basis. The delineations were the county ridings, and part of the explanation for this probably lies in a desire to subject the more peripheral Sourdeval estates in the North and East Ridings, many of which had been 'waste', to resident lords with localised and manageable tenurial interests who could bring Norman authority to bear. There was a directing hand at work here, and it may well have received the support of the king. This is suggested by the rounding-off of the Meinil lands with nearby estates formerly belonging to the royal demesne and to Robert Malet.[54]

Royal influence in the tenurial restructuring of Yorkshire after 1100 is more evident in the descent of the thirteen former Sourdeval manors which did not pass to Ralph Paynel. These were confined exclusively to the wapentake of Langbargh, and were used in the construction of a compact lordship for Robert of Brus, a newcomer to England and one of Henry I's closest companions. The manors included Skelton, where the castle and borough which became the Brus *caput* may already have been in existence by the early twelfth century, and Guisborough, where Robert founded an Augustinian priory in 1119.[55] Brus probably made his first appearance in England in the reign of Henry I, is not known to have been related to the Sourdevals and may have acquired his Sourdeval estates from the king.[56] This is suggested by the composition of the remainder of his Yorkshire lordship. The major part of it was made up of over eighty manors which had been in the king's hands in 1086, and of estates recovered by the

---

[53] *Ibid.*, 185–7; II, 135–7; *DB*, I, 305b. The important manor of Hutton Rudby with its sokelands was held by the count of Mortain in demesne in 1086. It had been in the possession of Gospatric in 1066, and it is possible that after the Domesday survey it passed to Richard of Sourdeval who succeeded Gospatric in several other estates. For the possibility that a castle existed in Hutton Rudby's sokeland of Whorlton by 1086, see above, p. 53.

[54] For the royal estates, see *EYC*, II, 136. With the exception of only one carucate in Fridaythorpe, all of the estates were situated close to the clusters of former Mortain estates acquired by Robert of Meinil in the wapentakes of Langbargh and Hunthow: *DB*, I, 300a, 301a. The same was true of the Malet estates acquired by the Meinils in Great and Little Ayton in Langbargh wapentake: *EYC*, II, 358. It must be said, however, that the dates at which all these estates were acquired by the Meinils are uncertain.   [55] King, 'Robert de Brus', 29.

[56] Although Clay suggested that Robert may have married a daughter of Richard of Sourdeval there is no direct evidence for such a union: *EYC*, VI, 4 note 8.

crown from Robert Malet or confiscated from the former demesne lands of Gospatric, William of Mortain and Hugh Fitz Baldric.[57] The Fitz Baldric estates, which dominated Eskdale, were granted with other lands by Henry I to Brus in 1103 in exchange for property in Reighton and Collingham, situated some distance outside Langbargh wapentake.[58] It is an exchange which suggests a concern for tenurial uniformity and compactness. The same concern probably explains Brus's acquisition of a subtenancy in two knights' fees of the earl of Chester incorporating estates in several Cleveland vills.[59] The Brus fee was a deliberate creation, and one in which the king played a major part. Together with the neighbouring Fossard estates centred on Lythe castle, and those belonging to the Meinils in and around Hutton Rudby, it was a fee which formed an important link in a chain of compact lordships along the north-eastern frontier of Yorkshire which were under the control of resident lords who had been established or reinstated by the king (Map 20).[60] Through tenurial reorganisation and the establishment of 'new men', Henry I brought a region which had remained largely outside the control of his father firmly within the Norman structure of lordship. The canons of Guisborough remembered Robert of Brus as 'conquistor terrarum Clivelande'.[61]

Henry I's determination to maintain, consolidate and create compact lordships centred upon castles, hundreds or hundredal castleries is discernible in the tenurial history of several other areas within Yorkshire. This was certainly the case with the lordships along the east coast. When Arnulf of Montgomery was deprived of the lordship of Holderness in 1102 it was restored intact to Stephen of Aumale, whose father, Odo count of Champagne, had been deprived by Rufus in 1095. Further north, Henry I almost certainly had a part to play in the acquisition of the hundredal manor of Burton Agnes by Robert of Brus. Whether Robert secured the manor by direct royal grant or through marriage to a

---

[57] *EYC*, II, 16–19.

[58] *Regesta*, II, no. 648; *DB*, I, 327a–8a, 333a, 380b. The estates secured by Brus included twelve carucates in Danby, Crunkly Gill, Hangton, Hangton Hill and Lealholm. Reighton was in Hunthow hundred, and Collingham does not appear to have been situated in Yorkshire.   [59] *PR 14 Henry II*, 90.

[60] Although the vill of Lythe was greatly devalued in 1086 it is possible that the Fossards built a fortress there within a short time of the Domesday survey. A motte, or ringwork, and traces of a bailey still survive in the vill: *DB*, I, 305a; King, *Castellarium Anglicanum*, II, 521–2.   [61] *Cartularium de Gyseburne*, II, no. 1156.

93

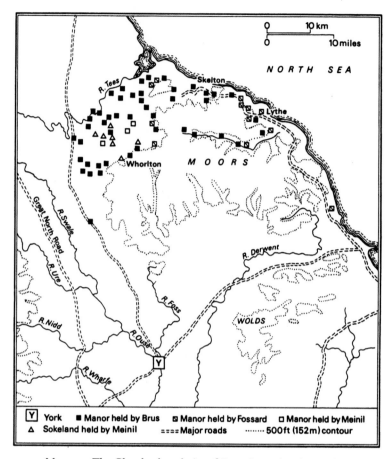

Map 20 The Cleveland castleries of Brus, Fossard and Meinil

daughter of the previous tenant, Geoffrey Bainard, is impossible to determine, but even in the latter case the consent of the king would have been required. Henry I's involvement is also suggested by his grant to Robert in 1103 of ten carucates of royal demesne land in Harpham and Gransmoor, which probably constituted berewicks belonging to the manor of Burton Agnes, in part-exchange for estates in Reighton and Collingham.[62]

As well as constructing new castleries, Henry I also preserved the integrity of old ones. This can be seen from the history of the

[62] *Regesta*, II, no. 648; *DB*, I, 299b, 331a, 382a.

Lacy fee which incorporated several wapentakes and probably a number of castleries in the West Riding of the county, and which remained intact despite the fact that it was taken back into the king's hands on two separate occasions during the reign (Map 6). Robert of Lacy was among the group of magnates supporting Robert Curthose in 1101, may have gone over to Henry I by 1102, but was finally deprived of his English lands in the period 1109 × 1116.[63] His Yorkshire estates passed in their entirety to a 'new man', Hugh of la Val, who held them until his death sometime before 1129, and then to another 'new man', William Maltravers, who proffered 1,000 marks and £100 to the king to marry la Val's widow and control his lands for a period of fifteen years, and who retained the estates until his murder at the hands of a knight of the honour in 1135.[64] The great Lacy castlery might be confiscated from a rebel or leased to an unscrupulous financier, but under no circumstances, it seems, was it ever to be dismantled.

The same was true of the Warenne lordship of Conisbrough, situated in the lowland gap between the Pennines and the Humberhead marshes. Although William II of Warenne opposed Henry I in 1101, and is described as departing for Normandy late in the year after being disinherited, by 1103 he had been restored to his English estates and subsequently 'throve as one of [Henry I's] closest friends and counsellors'.[65] Henry I not only restored Warenne to his Yorkshire estates, but was probably responsible for granting him the extensive and valuable royal wapentake manor of Wakefield.[66] In 1086 the manor and its berewicks had declined in value from £60 to only £15, and nearly all of its sokelands were waste; a lack of organisation which the grant to Warenne may have been designed to remedy.[67] But there was probably also a strategic purpose behind the grant. Situated on the River Calder between the Humberhead marshes and the mountains, Wakefield was a convenient base from which to control movement along

---

[63] Orderic's description of Robert's trial, dispossession and exile in 1102 has been called into question. See Orderic, IV, 309; Hollister, *Monarchy*, 132.

[64] Hugh was in control by the time of the Lindsey survey, which has been redated 1115 × 1116: Wightman, *Lacy Family*, 66; T. Foulds, 'The Lindsey survey and an unknown precept of King Henry I', *BIHR*, 59 (1986), 212–15. For Maltravers, see *PR 31 Henry I*, 34; *EYC*, III, 143–4, 148; Wightman, *Lacy Family*, 66, 68–72.

[65] Hollister, *Monarchy*, 141–4. The quotation is from Orderic, VI, 14.

[66] The exact date of the grant is uncertain and could have occurred at any point between 1086 and 1121. Clay suggested that it is not unlikely that the gift was made to reward William for his services at the battle of Tinchebrai in 1106: *EYC*, VIII, 178. See also Holt, *Northerners*, 215.   [67] *DB*, I, 299b.

Calderdale and to provide support for the neighbouring castleries of Conisbrough, Hallam and Pontefract (Map 21). If not already a castlery in the early twelfth century it probably soon became one, and, like the frontier lordships of the Welsh and Scottish marches, was held on very favourable terms of knight service.[68]

The tenurial engineering described above was probably completed within the first fifteen years of Henry I's reign. By dismantling the amorphous fees of the rebel barons in order to create or consolidate castleries and other compact lordships, Henry I rationalised the tenurial pattern of Yorkshire and strengthened Norman territorial and administrative domination there. He also began the process of introducing a group of 'new men' already attached to his court into the local tenurial community, of which Nigel d'Aubigny and Robert of Brus were pioneer members. In the second decade of the twelfth century the process continued, and Brus and d'Aubigny were joined by several other courtiers and talented local men seeking to make their political and administrative fortunes in the north. By this time the reservoir of estates confiscated from rebels was almost empty, and Henry I had to rely increasingly on the use of other means of patronage in order to establish or promote the 'new men' in Yorkshire.

The most prominent of these 'new men' established in the county in the period *c.* 1110–*c.* 1120 was David of Scotland. David had been brought up and educated at the royal court since at least 1103, and his marriage to a daughter and heiress of Countess Judith, widow of Waltheof, earl of Huntingdon, was arranged by the king in 1113 or 1114. Through his wife, David secured extensive estates in Huntingdon and Northamptonshire, and control of the 'shire' of Hallam in south Yorkshire which may have been a castlery (Map 21).[69]

Another 'new man' granted entry to the ranks of the northern political elite by a favourable marriage was Eustace Fitz John. As a younger son, Eustace appears to have inherited little of his father's modest fee in Essex, Suffolk and Norfolk, and owed his

---

[68] Wakefield and Conisbrough, incorporating some 212 carucates, appear to have owed the military service of only two knights. Clay suggested that the bulk of the Yorkshire lands of Warenne were held in socage or fee-farm: *EYC*, VIII, 139–40, 181. See also Michelmore, 'Township and tenure', 248–9.

[69] *ASC, s.a.* 1114; *Complete Peerage*, VI, 640–2; IX, 662–3; G. W. S. Barrow, 'Scottish rulers and the religious orders, 1070–1153', *TRHS*, 5th ser., 3 (1953), 85. For Hallam, see *DB*, I, 320a; *EYC*, III, 3. A castle was in existence at one of the outliers of the manor of Hallam (Sheffield) by 1184: King, *Castellarium Anglicanum*, II, 530.

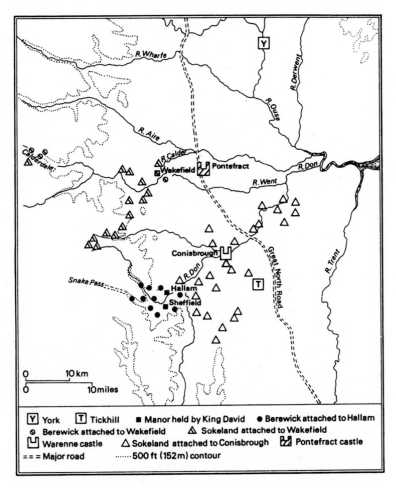

Map 21 The castleries of Hallam, Wakefield and Conisbrough in
Henry I's reign

marriage and promotion in the northern shires to the king.[70] He
may have been at the royal court by 1116, and almost certainly
before 1130 had married Beatrice, daughter and heiress of Ivo of
Vescy.[71] Through his wife, Eustace acquired the extensive and
compact lordship centred on the castle of Alnwick in Northum-

[70] *Complete Peerage*, XII, part ii, Appendix B; *DB*, II, 217a–b; *PR 31 Henry I*, 95.
[71] *Regesta*, II, no. 1130; *Complete Peerage*, XII, part ii, 272–4.

97

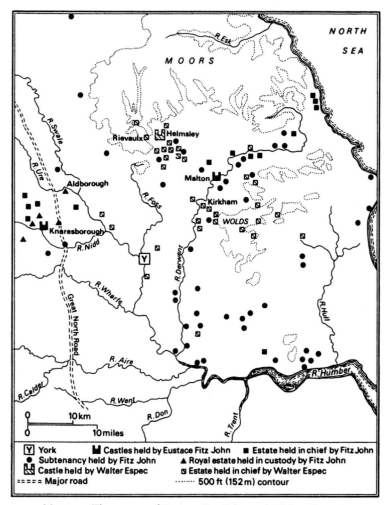

Map 22 The estates of Eustace Fitz John and Walter Espec in
Henry I's reign

berland, the former royal manor of Old Malton on the River
Derwent in the North Riding of Yorkshire where a castle existed
by 1138, and probably five and a half knights' fees in Yorkshire
formerly belonging to the baron Ralph of Mortemer (Map 22).[72]

---

[72] Sanders, *Baronies*, 103; Symeon, *Opera*, II, 292; *Red Book*, I, 68; *Cal. Chart. Rolls*, III,
114. A portion of the Mortemer estates appears to have been situated in Gilling in
Ryedale: *EYC*, III, no. 1877; *DB*, I, 325b. The remainder was probably located in a

A second marriage to Agnes, daughter of William Fitz Nigel, constable of Chester, which probably also occurred before 1130, brought Eustace additional estates in Loddington (Northants.) and Hilderthorpe near Bridlington (Yorks.), held of the earl of Chester.[73] His acquisition of several more subtenancies in Yorkshire, held of the archbishop of York, bishop of Durham, lord of Richmond, William Fossard, William I Paynel, Nigel d'Aubigny and count of Aumale, probably owed something to his connection with the royal court.[74] During the minority of Roger of Mowbray, son and heir of Nigel d'Aubigny, Henry I was certainly responsible for granting Eustace land belonging to the Mowbray fee in Brompton.[75] It was also to the king that Eustace owed his tenure of the important royal manors of Knaresborough, Aldborough and Tickhill, and his custody of the castles there.[76] Entries in the pipe roll of 1129–30 reveal Eustace receiving allowances against debts owed to the king for expenses incurred in work on the fortifications of Knaresborough and Tickhill, and for repairs to the gate of Bamburgh castle in Northumberland, which was also in his custody. They are entries which suggest that these fortresses had been placed in the charge of an experienced and skilled engineer.[77] Even in 1130 the military reinforcement of lowland Yorkshire was not quite at an end. What had changed was that it was now being undertaken more often by men who came from the middling ranks of the aristocracy.

Closely involved with Eustace Fitz John in the administration of the north, and established in the area at about the same time, was Walter Espec. Like Eustace, Walter was the son of a landholder of middling rank from the south of England, a newcomer to the north, and held the bulk of his estates in Northumberland and Yorkshire, where he was lord of Wark and Helmsley respectively.[78] He first appears in a great assembly of northern magnates held at Durham in 1121, by which time he was clearly already well

number of vills in the East Riding: *EYC*, III, v, 486–7, 494, 498, 501; XII, 32–3, 36; *PR 33 Henry II*, 93.   [73] *Complete Peerage*, XII, part ii, 274; *EYC*, II, nos. 1109–11.

[74] Multiple subtenancies of this kind were common among Henry I's administrators: Green, *Government*, 182 and note 194.   [75] *Regesta*, II, nos. 1722, 1730.

[76] *PR 31 Henry I*, 24, 31, 36.

[77] *Ibid.*, 31, 35–6. For his custodianship of Bamburgh, see Symeon, *Opera*, II, 291–2. See also *Regesta*, II, nos. 572, 1279.

[78] W. Farrer, 'The honour of Old Wardon', *Bedfordshire Hist. Rec. Soc.*, 11 (1927), 1–46, cited in Green, *Government*, 245–6 and note 164; Sanders, *Baronies*, 149; *Book of Fees*, II, 1120.

established.[79] A year or so later he founded the Augustinian priory of Kirkham in the East Riding of Yorkshire.[80] Kirkham was a component of a small and relatively amorphous Yorkshire lordship, composed mainly of estates in the East and North Ridings formerly belonging to the demesne of the count of Mortain and the king (Map 22).[81] By 1134 Walter had built a castle at Helmsley and founded a Cistercian abbey at nearby Rievaulx in Ryedale. Together with the neighbouring d'Aubigny castleries of Thirsk and Kirby Moorside, his lordship covered the southern entrances of the passes through the North Yorkshire Moors and bestrode the Roman road linking the east coast with the Great North Road.

The remaining members of the group of 'new men' established or promoted in Yorkshire by Henry I after 1110 were Anschetill of Bulmer, who was probably a native of Yorkshire, and who obtained the sheriffdom, the important and extensive royal wapentake manor of Easingwold in *Bolesford* wapentake, and several other manors formerly belonging to the king held in chief or as subtenancies of the Rumilly and Mowbray families; Forne Fitz Sigulf, who was probably also a native from the north, and who received a small group of former royal estates in Warter hundred in the East Riding, and land formerly belonging to Robert Malet in Thornton le Moor; Geoffrey Fitz Pain, who was granted the remnants of the former honour of Erneis of Burun, and lordship of the royal hundredal manors of Warter and Market Weighton; and Turgis Brundos, who secured control of Rosedale and a small cluster of nearby estates derived from the royal demesne and the dismembered fee of Gospatric.[82] Like Eustace Fitz John and Walter Espec, some of these 'new men' acquired extensive lordships bordering the land of the Scots, and were

---

[79] Symeon, *Opera*, II, 261.

[80] *Cartularium de Rievalle*, 159, 243; *Vita Ailredi*, lxxiii.

[81] Sanders, *Baronies*, 53 note 2; *Red Book*, I, 432–3; *EYC*, x, 146. For the component estates of the lordship, see *EYC*, x, 144, 148–9, 151–3, 157, 162–3, 166, 168–9, 173, no. 95 and note; II, 55, 382; *Cartularium de Rievalle*, 16–21, 131, 159, 243; *Vita Ailredi*, lxxiii; *Kirkby's Inquest*, 62, 71, 113–15, 119, 262, 274–5; *Cal. Inq. P. M.*, VIII, no. 474.

[82] For Anschetill of Bulmer, see Green, *Sheriffs*, 90; *idem*, *Government*, 248; *Red Book*, I, 407, 417, 420, 425, 428–9; *EYC*, II, 113–32, 341, 363–5; VII, 153–65; XI, 180–1; *Mowbray Charters*, 265. For the estates acquired by Forne Fitz Sigulf, see *EYC*, II, 509. For the grant of Thornton, see *Regesta*, II, no. 1357. For Geoffrey Fitz Pain, see Sanders, *Baronies*, 56; *Mowbray Charters*, xxii; *EYC*, VI, 57; x, 1–4, 8, 14, 24, 108–9, no. 71. For the fee of Turgis Brundos, see *VCH, Yorkshire*, II, 185; *VCH, North Riding*, II, 454–5, 457; T. H. B. Graham, 'Turgis Brundos', *TCWAAS*, 29 (1929), 49–56.

responsible for the security of the frontier region.[83] But their smaller and more scattered holdings in Yorkshire, few if any of which incorporated a castle by 1135, suggest that the provision of security was not their primary duty in this county. When these 'new men' arrived or were promoted in Yorkshire the process of constructing compact lordships was already virtually complete. It was a process which paved the way for another, and equally important, element in the Norman conquest of the county: the integration of Yorkshire within the system of royal administration and justice. It was through Henry I's 'new men' that this integration was to be considerably advanced.

THE ESTABLISHMENT OF ROYAL GOVERNMENT

Norman kings, like their Anglo-Scandinavian predecessors, rarely visited the English counties north of the Humber estuary which was viewed by some chroniclers as a dividing line between northern and southern England.[84] William the Conqueror and William Rufus paid only four visits to York, and Henry I only one or two.[85] Royal government in Yorkshire was exercised at second hand by local agents. One of the most important of these agents was the archbishop of York, who presided over the shire court with the sheriff. The Norman kings were always careful to ensure that the post was filled with men who were drawn from a group of clerics closely attached to the royal court and household, and who had no previous interests within Yorkshire.[86] In the case of the secular agents of Norman government, the first generation were clearly the men established as tenants-in-chief within the county. They included several relatives of the king, or the retainers of these relatives, and their duties were military as well as

---

[83] Forne Fitz Sigulf and Turgis Brundos held the Cumbrian lordships of Greystoke and Liddell respectively: Sanders, *Baronies*, 50, 129; *VCH, Cumberland*, I, 421; Graham, 'Turgis Brundos'. Forne also held Coquetdale in Northumberland, Coniscliffe in the region between Tyne and Tees, and probably several estates in upper Teesdale: *EYC*, II, 505–7.   [84] See, for example, Symeon, *Opera*, II, 267.

[85] *Regesta*, I, xxi–xxii; II, xxix–xxxi; Barlow, *Rufus*, 449–52.

[86] See Hugh the Chantor, 12, 34; Freeman, *Norman Conquest*, IV, 339–41; V. H. Galbraith, 'Girard the chancellor', *EHR*, 46 (1931), 77–9; *idem*, 'Notes on the career of Samson, bishop of Worcester (1096–1112)', *EHR*, 82 (1967), 87–92; *Episcopal Acta*, xxv; Nicholl, *Thurstan*, 5, 8; C. N. L. Brooke, 'The composition of the chapter of St Paul's, 1086–1163', *CHJ*, 10 (1950–2), 124 and note 71; F. Barlow, *The English Church 1066–1154* (London, 1979), 83; D. R. Bates, 'The character and career of Odo, bishop of Bayeux (1049/50–1097)', *Speculum*, 50 (1975), 1–20.

administrative.[87] It was the sheriff of York, William Malet, who defended York castle against the Danes in 1069 with the assistance of the king's cousin, Gilbert of Gant.[88] When we catch a glimpse of the activities of the next sheriff, Hugh Fitz Baldric, who held office between 1069 and c.1080, we find him patrolling the Humber and moving through the county with an army at his back.[89] His deputy, William of Percy, a man of equal stature, when not away with the king campaigning in Scotland, was entrusted with the custody of York castle.[90] The first generation of secular Norman officials in Yorkshire were clearly warriors drawn from the upper ranks of the aristocracy.[91] Their identity, and the nature of their duties, reflects the insecurity of the region entrusted to their charge.

The reign of Rufus began in the same way as the reign of the Conqueror had ended. Erneis of Burun, who succeeded Hugh Fitz Baldric as sheriff of Yorkshire before 1086, may have remained in office until 1088 when the shrievalty was held by another local tenant-in-chief, Ralph Paynel.[92] The continued reliance placed by the king on powerful magnates in the government of Yorkshire is also illustrated during the course of the quarrel between William Rufus and William bishop of Durham, which began in 1088. Ralph Paynel confiscated the bishop's estates in Yorkshire, while the counts Odo of Champagne, Roger the Poitevin and Alan of Brittany were sent with an army to negotiate with the bishop at Durham and encourage him to come to terms by ravaging his see.[93] The castle of Durham and the episcopal estates were eventually taken into the king's hands in November 1088 by Erneis of Burun and Ivo Taillebois, the lord of Kendale and Lonsdale, and a former sheriff of Lincolnshire.[94]

Within a few years of 1086, however, a change had taken place. Ralph Paynel was replaced as sheriff, possibly as early as 1089, not by another local magnate but by Geoffrey Bainard who may have

---

[87] The king's relatives included Robert, count of Mortain, a half-brother; Drogo de la Beuvrière, the husband of a kinswoman; William I of Warenne, a cousin; Countess Judith, a niece; Odo, count of Champagne, a brother-in-law; and Gilbert I of Gant, a first cousin once removed. The tenants of the king's relatives included Ilbert I of Lacy, who held considerable estates of Odo bishop of Bayeux.

[88] Freeman, *Norman Conquest*, IV, 204, 258, 268; Round, 'William Malet'.

[89] Green, *Sheriffs*, 89; *Selby Coucher*, I, [14]-[15].   [90] *DB*, I, 298a.

[91] Some of the early sheriffs of Yorkshire were among the wealthiest magnates in England: J. A. Green, 'The sheriffs of William the Conqueror', *ANS*, 5 (1983), 129-45, esp. 140-2.   [92] Green, *Sheriffs*, 89.   [93] Symeon, *Opera*, I, 171-3, 176-9.

[94] *Ibid*, 192.

been a landless younger brother of the Essex tenant-in-chief, Ralph
Bainard, and who was certainly a newcomer to Yorkshire. It was
after 1086 that Geoffrey acquired possession of the royal hundredal
manor of Burton Agnes, and it is possible that his tenure only
began when he secured control of the shrievalty. Geoffrey's
successor, who was sheriff at some point between 1096 and 1100,
is even more obscure and is known only by his initial ('H'). The
history of the shrievalty of Yorkshire in the later years of the reign
of Rufus suggests that the governmental emphasis in the county
was beginning to shift from territorial consolidation and military
security to civil administration and justice.[95] It is a suggestion
strengthened by the possible appearance of the office of local
justice at about the same time; though it has to be said that the first
two local justices (if such in fact they were), Ralph Paynel and
Robert of Lacy, were drawn from the ranks of the community of
local magnates.[96]

It was in the reign of Henry I that the greatest advances towards
integrating Yorkshire within the system of royal administration
and justice were made. The key role in this belonged to the 'new
men' entrusted with charge of the local arm of the king's
government. These men were either talented lesser nobles from
the north who were probably brought to the king's attention by
powerful northern magnates, and introduced into the court circle;
or they were younger sons and men of middling status who started
political life at the court, were enriched by the king, obtained
establishment in the north through his patronage and acquired
additional lands there from the local magnates because of their
position as his favourites. These 'new men' formed the vital link
between court and countryside.

Among the 'new men' employed by Henry I in the administration of Yorkshire were those appointed to the shrievalty. The
first of their number may have been Bertram of Verdon, who held
some form of administrative office (not necessarily the shrievalty)
in Yorkshire during the course of 1100. The second was Osbert the
priest, who was sheriff of Yorkshire from December 1100 until

---

[95] This change may also have been in progress in other counties. Green notes that whereas
the sheriffs of the Conqueror were a 'mixed bag' in terms of their landed endowment,
'in the reigns of Rufus and Henry I the office was increasingly filled by men of…
modest status': Green, 'Sheriffs', 144–5. See also the comments in Barlow, *Rufus*,
189–90.

[96] Barlow, *Rufus*, 190; H. A. Cronne, 'The office of local justiciar in England under the
Norman kings', *Univ. of Birmingham Hist. Journal*, 6 (1957–8), 28–9; Green, *Sheriffs*, 89.

approximately 1115, and of Lincolnshire in the period 1093 x 1116.[97] In 1086 Osbert held land from the Percys, and subsequently acquired tenancies in at least another ten honours in Yorkshire and Lincolnshire, and a small tenancy-in-chief in Yorkshire. Whether Osbert began his career as a royal courtier or was brought to the king's attention by William of Percy is uncertain; but what is more than probable is that he owed his administrative and tenurial elevation after 1086 to his connection with the king. This is suggested by evidence which records that Stephen, count of Aumale, granted Osbert (styled 'de Humbria') three knights' fees and four carucates in Yorkshire because Osbert was of the king's household.[98] Osbert's career was mirrored to some extent by those of Anschetill of Bulmer and his son Bertram, who held the shrievalty of Yorkshire in succession to each other after Osbert, and who acquired tenancies in several Yorkshire lordships.[99] Anschetill of Bulmer was almost certainly a native Anglo-Scandinavian landholder from Yorkshire who probably owed his elevation to his administrative skills and to the patronage of a lord willing to bring him to the attention of the king.[100]

Henry I not only continued Rufus's policy of governing Yorkshire through 'new men' closely attached to the royal court and dependent upon the king, he extended it. After 1100 the employment of 'new men' was not confined to the shrievalty. The number of these royal agents acting in an administrative or judicial capacity within the county increased considerably. They included Nigel d'Aubigny, Eustace Fitz John, Walter Espec and Robert of Brus, some (possibly all) of whom were younger sons or middling magnates from the west of Normandy, who had probably been in the service of Henry I before he became king, and who had attached themselves to his royal court after 1100.[101] It was to him that all of them owed their Yorkshire tenancies-in-chief. They were expected to govern the county as his men, as an extension of the royal court.

---

[97] Green, *Sheriffs*, 54–5, 89; *EYC*, XI, 213–18.   [98] *Chronica de Melsa*, I, 85–6.

[99] Green, *Sheriffs*, 90; *idem, Government*, 238–9.

[100] Anschetill was endowed with linguistic skills, and could translate English and French: *Visitations of Southwell*, 191.

[101] Nigel d'Aubigny and Eustace Fitz John were both younger sons: *Mowbray Charters*, xvii–xix; *Complete Peerage*, XII, part ii, Appendix B; Green, *Government*, 251. Robert of Brus was probably lord of Brix in the Contentin. The family of Walter Espec may well have come from the same Norman neighbourhood as the d'Aubignys. For this, and Henry I's promotion of men from western Normandy or Brittany generally, see Green, *Government*, 146–8, 246.

Although Henry I may have continued to employ the local justiciar (possibly sheriff), Robert of Lacy, for a time, the administration of royal justice within Yorkshire (and northern England as a whole) was expanded and entrusted primarily to the 'new men'.[102] Among the more prominent northern justices was Nigel d'Aubigny, lord of Thirsk, who may also have received the custodianship of York castle.[103] For Nigel, service in northern government during the first and early part of the second decades of the twelfth century appears to have been part of an administrative apprenticeship. Thereafter, as Greenway observes, from around 1118 until his death in 1129 Nigel 'was constantly at the king's side, acting as adviser and military commander, and travelling with the court throughout England and Normandy'.[104] His involvement with the government of northern England, however, was far from over. He retained his important estates there, and the frequency with which he attested royal charters dealing with northern affairs after 1118, sometimes in the company of the local officials who worked there, suggests that his specialised knowledge of the region continued to be put to good effect by the king when formulating northern policy.[105] The liaison between Nigel, Walter Espec and Eustace Fitz John appears to have been particularly close, and it is almost certain that Eustace and Walter were Nigel's judicial successors in Yorkshire and other counties in the north.

From the latter part of the second decade of the twelfth century Walter Espec and Eustace Fitz John were the leading figures in the government of the north, and operated what amounted to an administrative and judicial partnership. The pipe roll of 1129–30 records allowances granted to both men for restocking royal manors and from the farm of the bishopric of Durham. Together with charter evidence, these allowances suggest that Eustace and Walter had been entrusted with joint management of the royal demesne, and joint custody of the temporalities of the see of Durham during the five-year vacancy that followed the death of Bishop Ranulf Flambard in September 1128. Payments for pleas in the 1129–30 pipe roll also reveal that at some point before 1129 Eustace and Walter had heard pleas together in Yorkshire,

---

[102] For Lacy, see Green, *Sheriffs*, 89.   [103] *Mowbray Charters*, xvii–xviii, xxv.
[104] *Ibid.*, xviii.
[105] *Regesta*, II, nos. 1241, 1272, 1285–7, 1319–20, 1322–3, 1460, 1491, 1494, 1541, 1617, 1627–8.

Northumberland, Carlisle and Westmorland; that Eustace had
also heard them in Durham; and that Walter had heard pleas of the
stag and was probably in control of the jurisdiction of the royal
forests.[106] As Dr Green has remarked, 'Nothing is a clearer witness
to the reality of royal authority in the north than [these] laconic
entries in the pipe roll for payments from pleas of itinerant
justices.'[107]

The joint role of Eustace Fitz John and Walter Espec in the
administration of royal justice in Yorkshire and other northern
counties is also clear from the royal charters addressed to, or
witnessed by, them (Table 9). Half of the twelve charters addressed
to Walter Espec concern Yorkshire, and the other half deal with
matters relating to Northumberland, Durham and Cumberland.
Of the six Yorkshire charters, five are also addressed to Eustace
Fitz John, and in three of these the king conveys specific
instructions concerning the tenure of lands and rights, implying
that the addressees were to act in a judicial capacity. In one charter,
for example, Walter and Eustace were commanded to cause the
prior and canons of Nostell to have the land in Bramham given to
them by Anschetill of Bulmer, and to restore any estates that had
been unjustly seized by Robert Fossard and Bertram of Bulmer
since Anschetill's death.[108] Of the twenty-six royal charters
witnessed by or addressed to Walter Espec, sixteen concern
Yorkshire, nine deal with Northumberland, Cumberland and
Durham and one is addressed to the men of Bedfordshire where
Espec was a landholder.[109] Eustace Fitz John attests five of the same
charters and, like Walter, was clearly in regular attendance at the
royal court.[110]

The royal charters addressed to or witnessed by Walter Espec
reveal his close cooperation not only with Eustace Fitz John, but
also with several other 'new men' working for part of their time
as northern officials. Among those addressed with Walter in a
judicial capacity in some of the charters were Ranulf bishop of
Durham, Nigel d'Aubigny, Odard sheriff of Northumberland,

---

[106] *PR 31 Henry I*, 24, 27, 32–3, 35–6, 131–2, 142–3. See also *Regesta*, II, nos. 1561, 1604, 1825. [107] Green, *Government*, 133. [108] *Regesta*, II, no. 1662.
[109] *Ibid.*, nos. 1264, 1279, 1312, 1326, 1332–3, 1335–6, 1451, 1463–4, 1491, 1494, 1532, 1557, 1560, 1603–4, 1662, 1679, 1685, 1756, 1759–60, 1825, 1891.
[110] Eustace attested twenty-eight charters of Henry I in the period 1114–35, and was addressed by the king in a further eight: *Regesta*, II, nos. 1130, 1217, 1284, 1312, 1327–8, 1459, 1464, 1575, 1654, 1710, 1723, 1740, 1752–3, 1758–60, 1766, 1770, 1773, 1809, 1811, 1832, 1856, 1868, 1870–1.

Forne Fitz Sigulf, Anschetill and Bertram of Bulmer sheriffs of Yorkshire, and Geoffrey Escolland steward of the bishopric of Durham (Table 9). And witnessing some of the same charters, either alone or in various combinations of groups, were Archbishop Thurstan, Nigel d'Aubigny, Robert of Brus, Forne Fitz Sigulf, Geoffrey Fitz Pain and William Maltravers. Walter himself was frequently among groups of northern officials attesting royal charters addressed to their colleagues in Yorkshire, Cumberland, Northumberland and Durham, despite the fact that the charters were issued in places as far from the north as Rockingham, Woodstock, Winchester, Westminster and Portsmouth. Walter Espec's membership of a group of men who were frequently, though far from exclusively, involved in the implementation of justice in the north is perhaps best illustrated by a royal charter addressed to Serlo of Burg, the custodian of the royal manors of Knaresborough and Aldborough.[111] The charter is witnessed by Nigel d'Aubigny, and warns Serlo that if the canons of St Peter's, York, were not placed in possession of the lands and rights pertaining to the church of Aldborough as they had held them in the past, Walter Espec, Forne Fitz Sigulf and Anschetill of Bulmer would cause it to be done, so that the king would hear no further claims for want of justice.[112] This royal charter, and others like it, clearly reveal the cooperation of Henry I's officials in the north, the close ties and coordination they maintained between the royal court and the localities, and the resultant expansion of royal justice and administration in Yorkshire and northern England generally.

The strength of Henry I's administrative grip on Yorkshire is reflected not only in the 1129–30 pipe roll and the royal charters, but also in the number of key centres of local government placed in the hands of his 'new men'. These included York castle, the focus of city and county administration, which was probably in the custody of Nigel d'Aubigny; and the other major royal fortresses of Knaresborough and Tickhill, entrusted to Eustace Fitz John.[113] As well as being important military and demesne centres, Knaresborough and Tickhill were probably also the administrative centres of wapentakes or hundreds, the important institutions of

---

[111] The operations of some of the officials active in the north often extended outside this region. For example, of the seventy charters attested by Geoffrey Fitz Pain, only about ten concerned Yorkshire and the regions to the north of it: *Regesta*, II, index.

[112] *Ibid.*, no. 1541, and see also nos. 1357, 1532, 1604, 1662.

[113] *VCH, City of York*, 29–31, 522–3; *Mowbray Charters*, xxv; *PR 31 Henry I*, 31, 36.

justice and law enforcement which Professor Sawyer and Dr Harvey argue were the key to local power in this period.[114] It is a striking fact that of the thirty-one or so wapentakes and hundreds of Yorkshire in secular hands in 1135, at least twelve were under the control of the king's 'new men', and several others were in the possession of old-established magnates who had benefited greatly from Henry I's patronage.[115]

It must be said, however, that although the integration of Yorkshire within the royal system of justice was greatly advanced under Henry I, the process was far from complete in 1135. Large areas of the county, including a good number of wapentake and hundredal centres, remained outside the influence of the 'new men' and under the control of old conquest magnates who were less dependent upon the king and not nearly so frequently in attendance at his court. The count of Aumale's lands in Holderness, and the lord of Richmond's estates in Richmondshire, were probably outside the jurisdiction of the royal sheriff; and this was certainly true of the ecclesiastical liberties of Beverley, Ripon and St Peter's, York.[116] The availability and effectiveness of royal justice in Yorkshire generally must remain open to question, especially in view of the local customs and language barriers which were still causing the Normans difficulties in the twelfth century.[117] There is evidence that the judicial eyres of Henry I were neither regular nor countrywide, that his itinerant justices were appointed on an *ad hoc* basis to hear particular cases in particular counties, that these justices merely presided over special sessions of the county courts rather than making judgments there and that the law applied at these sessions was the customary law of the county rather than the more general custom of the king's court which was

[114] S. P. J. Harvey, 'The extent and profitability of demesne agriculture in England in the later eleventh century', in *Social Relations and Ideas. Essays in Honour of R. H. Hilton*, ed. T. H. Aston *et al.* (Cambridge, 1983), 45–72; P. Sawyer, 'The royal *Tun* in pre-conquest England', in *Ideal and Reality in Frankish and Anglo-Saxon Society*, ed. P. Wormald *et al.* (Oxford, 1983), 280–3.

[115] The twelve were Morley, Skyrack, Agbrigg, Staincross and possibly Osgoldcross, held by William Maltravers; Burghshire, held by Eustace Fitz John; *Bolesford*, held by Anschetill and Bertram of Bulmer; *Maneshou* and *Gerlestre*, held by Nigel d'Aubigny; Warter and Weighton, held by Geoffrey Fitz Pain; and probably a hundred within Langbargh wapentake, held by Robert of Brus. Stephen of Aumale had been restored by Henry I to his father's lordship of Holderness which incorporated three hundreds and was almost certainly already a wapentake in 1086.

[116] English, *Holderness*, Chapter 3, esp. 98–107; *DB*, I, 298b, 303b, 304a; G. R. J. Jones, 'The portrayal of land settlement in Domesday Book', in *Domesday Studies*, 189.

[117] See *Visitations of Southwell*, 191.

of nationwide applicability. These limitations in the integration of Yorkshire within the royal system of justice were only to be remedied after 1154.[118]

Judicial and administrative integration was also limited by the fact that the king had to compromise with his officials. Despite their lowly origins and debts to royal patronage, the 'new men' were often capable of rapacious and independent actions undertaken to further their own interests rather than those of the king. In 1106 Henry I was forced to send Robert bishop of Lincoln, Ralph Basset, Geoffrey Ridel, Ranulf Meschin and Peter of Valognes to Yorkshire to preside over an inquest after Archbishop Gerard of York complained that the sheriff of Yorkshire, Osbert, was attempting to deprive the canons of St Peter's of their liberties and do them harm.[119] Some years later Henry commanded his castellan of Knaresborough, Serlo of Burg, who had been entrusted with custodianship of the archiepiscopal estates during the exile of Archbishop Thurstan from 1118 to 1121, to cause the canons of St Peter's to have their lands, tithes and rights pertaining to the church of Aldborough; a command which suggests that Serlo may not have returned all of the church's property after Thurstan's restoration.[120] Another northern official, Nigel d'Aubigny, confessed to a series of illegal land seizures from the church and other tenants when he thought he was dying.[121]

Just as Henry I was forced to compromise with his new officials in matters of justice, this was also true in matters of finance. Although he had increased the financial efficiency of royal government in order to compensate for the considerable erosion of demesne resources since 1086, and in 1129–30 collected a total revenue that was surpassed only three times in the reign of Henry II, it is clear that Henry I was having to share this wealth with his local officials.[122] Green has calculated that the crown collected only £23,000 of the £68,000 it demanded from the shires of England in 1129–30, and that over £38,000 still remained outstanding after the Michaelmas audit. Most of the unpaid debts go back well before 1129 and had been allowed to run on for several years, and a considerable number of them, amounting to

---

[118] P. Brand, '"Multis vigiliis excogitatam et inventam": Henry II and the creation of the English Common Law', *Haskins Society Journal*, 2 (1990), 197–222, esp. 199–206.
[119] *Visitations of Southwell*, 191.   [120] *Regesta*, II, no. 1541.
[121] *Mowbray Charters*, nos. 2–9.
[122] See Green, 'Royal demesne', 337–52; *idem*, *Government*, 55.

some £5,000, were written off in pardons.[123] Debts and pardons created obligations, and the creation of such obligations was a method of political control throughout the Anglo-Norman period and beyond. But it was a method which had a high price.

Yorkshire was no exception to the general pattern in this respect. The proportion of the demanded revenue that was left outstanding as debt or pardoned in 1129–30 was slightly higher than that for the country as a whole. Of the £3,963 demanded, £2,322 is described as owing, £333 as pardoned, and only £1,205 as paid into the treasury.[124] Although some of the more fortunate beneficiaries of Henry I's relaxed attitude to payment were the heads of old conquest families, the 'new men' appear to have been particularly privileged. The fourteen Yorkshire tenants pardoned danegeld in full or in part included Eustace Fitz John, Walter Espec, Geoffrey Fitz Pain, William Maltravers and Bertram of Bulmer, who probably all received a complete exemption.[125] The pardon granted to Maltravers of £14 10s was by far the highest in the county, and his privileges in other areas of finance were even more remarkable. His immense proffer of 1,000 silver marks and £100 to have the wife and land of Hugh of la Val for a period of fifteen years, was the largest individual debt left outstanding in Yorkshire, and he was pardoned forty silver marks in pleas.[126] The privileges were even extended to his tenants. Peter of Arches, for example, was pardoned ten marks 'for the love of William Maltravers'.[127] Walter Espec and the sheriff, Bertram of Bulmer, were also highly privileged and allowed large outstanding debts. Walter owed £100 for pleas of the stag; while Bertram's debts comprised 145 silver marks for his father's debts, land and office, £55 6s for land which his father had taken from Robert Fossard and £27 10s for the county aid of the previous year.[128] Roger of Mowbray, the son of Nigel d'Aubigny, received a large pardon of forty marks for pleas.[129] It is even possible that some of the sums actually paid in full by the 'new men' for custodianships and other

---

[123] Green, *Government*, 87–8.

[124] The figures are my own. I have included the accounts for the area between the Ribble and the Mersey which appear to be mainly concerned with Yorkshire. The difference between the amount demanded (£3,963) and the sum of the amounts paid, owing and pardoned (£3,860) is accounted for by sums written off as expenditure. See *PR 31 Henry I*, 24–36.

[125] *Ibid.*, 34; *EYC*, x, 3 and note 3; *VCH, Yorkshire*, II, 180, 140.

[126] *PR 31 Henry I*, 34, 29.   [127] *Ibid.*, 28.   [128] *Ibid.*, 24, 26.

[129] *Ibid.*, 29.

offices represented only a small fraction of the revenues they were actually collecting. The king demanded only £22 from Eustace Fitz John for the farm of the royal manors of Aldborough and Knaresborough, despite the fact that it was probably worth far more by 1129. Sixty years later William of Stuteville proffered £2,000, and immediately paid £1,000, for the custody of Knaresborough and its appurtenances, a sum which, even allowing for inflation and the possibility that Stuteville never expected to pay all of his proffer, suggests that Eustace Fitz John had struck a very favourable bargain with Henry I.[130]

The integration of Yorkshire within the system of royal administration and justice was still in its early stages in 1135, but it would be wrong to underestimate the extent of Henry I's achievement. Although Henry was forced to compromise with the 'new men' entrusted with control of the local machinery of government, that machinery was operated in the king's name and served to enforce his justice and collect his taxes. The vehemence of the criticisms launched against the group of 'new men' by some contemporary chroniclers was perhaps as much a response to their administrative efficiency as their allegedly dubious social origins.[131] This is implied by one description of the activities of two of the most powerful members of the group in the West Country, Payn Fitz John and Miles of Gloucester. According to the author of the *Gesta Stephani* these men had 'raised their power to such a pitch that from the River Severn to the sea, all along the border between England and Wales, they involved everyone in litigation and oppressed them with forced services'.[132] Had he been more familiar with the men and the area, the author might have said the same about Payn's brother, Eustace Fitz John, and his partner, Walter Espec, in northern England. It is significant that the one thing he did know about Eustace, or at least considered worthy of record, was that he was 'a great and influential friend of King Henry'.[133] The government of the 'new men', for all its shortcomings, was royal government.

---

[130] *PR 2 Richard I*, 68. [131] For an example of the criticism, see Orderic, VI, 16.

[132] *Gesta Stephani*, 24.

[133] *Ibid.*, 54. The author's words were echoed by Ailred abbot of Rievaulx, who wrote that 'of all the great nobles of England Eustace Fitz John was the most intimate with the late King Henry': *Chronicles of the Reigns*, III, 191.

The half-century that followed the completion of the Domesday survey witnessed a transformation in the structure of magnate lordship and local administration within Yorkshire. By 1135 the tenurial map of the county had been substantially and, in large part, deliberately redrawn. Most of the more amorphous and unwieldy Domesday honours had been replaced with more compact and manageable military lordships, constructed with estates confiscated from rebels and alienated from the royal demesne. The new castleries reflect the establishment of Norman occupation and administrative authority in regions along the frontiers of Yorkshire, which had remained largely outside the influence of the Conqueror and the first generation of continental magnates. The lords who controlled them were probably resident, and belonged to a new breed of royal official promoted in the county by William Rufus and Henry I. They were largely men of moderate social status, either talented local lesser nobles probably brought to the king's attention by powerful patrons, or young courtiers, some of them younger sons, from the middling ranks of aristocratic society, who owed everything to the king. These 'new men' were entrusted with control of the local administration of Yorkshire, and came to rival the local power of the old conquest magnates. They served as archbishops, sheriffs, justices and demesne custodians, and held the major royal castles and nearly half of Yorkshire's wapentake and hundredal centres. They brought the business of the countryside to the royal court, and the authority of the court to the countryside. Through them Henry I had made considerable progress by 1135 in increasing royal control over its own administration in Yorkshire. In the 'nineteen long winters' that followed, as we shall see in a later chapter, this control was to disintegrate.

Chapter 3

THE TRANSFORMATION OF YORKSHIRE
1086–1135: MILITARY ENFEOFFMENT AND MONASTERIES

In 1086 nearly all of the land in Yorkshire was in Norman hands, but Norman settlement was mainly confined to the shadow of the castles. The tenants-in-chief, most of whom had interests in other counties, in Normandy and at court, probably spent little time in the region between the Humber and the Tees. Most of their men appear to have been enfeoffed outside Yorkshire or were retained in the seignorial households.[1] Less than 175 of these men are recorded in possession of Yorkshire estates in the Domesday survey. By 1135, however, the number of subtenants in Yorkshire had risen substantially, and included many ecclesiastics as well as laymen. Many of these subtenants had tenants of their own. The Norman conquest of the county had become firmly rooted in the land.

The Domesday survey, the military returns of 1166 (known as the *cartae baronum*) and early charters make it possible to study the evolution of Norman settlement between 1086 and 1135 in some detail. In spite of its limitations, notably a failure to record all subtenancies, Domesday Book provides a record of the distribution, size, resources and value of both demesne and tenant estates in 1086. Although the *cartae* of 1166 are much less detailed (recording only the number of knights' fees established on the lands of tenants-in-chief in 1135 and 1166, the number which remained to be created on the demesne in order to make up the *servitium debitum*, and the names of the military subtenants), Sir Charles Clay and other historians have used them, in conjunction with later evidence, to reconstruct the constituent estates of the military tenancies comprising several Yorkshire lordships. Since a comprehensive examination of all these tenancies is beyond the scope of this book, the most feasible method of establishing

---

[1] The term enfeoffment is used in this chapter in the same sense as in Chapter 1 (note 27). I use the terms 'military enfeoffment', 'military tenancies', 'military tenants' and 'military settlement' when referring to those tenements later recorded in the 1166 *cartae baronum*.

general conclusions about the settlement in 1135 is to study the tenancies on three honours of differing size, distribution and tenurial history. The honours to be examined are those of Mowbray, Percy and Skipton.

As well as helping to throw light upon the pattern and scale of Norman enfeoffment, the Domesday survey and the *cartae baronum* help to illuminate the terms of tenure, especially when the information they provide is examined in conjunction with the evidence of early charters. What is revealed is that before 1135 many of the Normans whose tenancies were later recorded in the *cartae* of 1166 held their lands on terms which differed very little from those on which pre-conquest thanes held, and that these terms were hardly military. But what is also revealed is that other Normans held on terms which bore little resemblance to those in existence before 1066, which had a military *raison d'être*, and which resulted from the necessity of providing garrison forces for the castles which were under construction everywhere.

In addition to introducing a new form of military tenure into Yorkshire, the Normans were also responsible for ushering in a new wave of monastic settlement. In 1066 there were apparently no fully fledged religious houses in Yorkshire, but by 1135 there were nearly twenty. An examination of this phenomenon suggests that it may have resulted partly from a conscious policy on the part of the Anglo-Norman kings to harness the ecclesiastical reform movement to the on-going programme of conquest and colonisation; that the establishment of monks and monasteries, as much as knights and castles, may have been geared towards the consolidation and extension of Norman power.

THE SCALE AND PATTERN OF TENANT SETTLEMENT IN 1086

There had already been an extensive degree of tenant enfeoffment in Yorkshire by 1086. Domesday Book reveals that on some honours Norman tenants were in control of considerable portions of the lands and resources of their lords (Tables 3, 6–8). And because the Domesday survey is inconsistent in the recording of the names of tenants, the degree of demesne alienation may have been far greater than appears in the record.[2] Moreover, the survey provides almost no information on the level of subenfeoffment,

---

[2] Roffe, 'Thegnage to barony', 171.

which may have been substantial. The extent of tenant enfeoffment within individual honours appears to have depended to some
extent on whether or not the lord was resident within the county.
In the case of the honours of Mortain and Chester, where the lords
held the bulk of their most valuable possessions outside Yorkshire
and were probably rarely, if ever, resident within the county,
alienation had taken place on a grand scale by 1086.[3] This
doubtless reflects a need to delegate authority in order both to
establish effective lordship over the land, and to secure the most
effective economic means of exploiting estates far removed from
the centres of seignorial power, where direct demesne cultivation
was impractical. Within Yorkshire the count of Mortain and the
earl of Chester had endowed their tenants with far more lands and
resources than they had retained in demesne (Tables 7–8). The
estates alienated by the count were mainly situated in the more
accessible parts of his lordship near Doncaster, within easy reach of
the Great North Road. In contrast, the majority of his manors near
the remote Vale of Pickering and within Cleveland were retained
in his demesne, despite the fact that they were probably of better
agricultural quality.[4] Although the tenurial pattern on the Chester
and Mortain lordships may be distorted to some extent by the
shortcomings of the text of the Yorkshire Domesday, it suggests
that settlement and estate organisation was in a relatively early
stage and was being directed by lords who were absent from
Yorkshire. This is also indicated by the fact that the count of
Mortain had enfeoffed only four tenants in Yorkshire, and the earl
of Chester just two.[5]

The lower concentration of lands and resources in the hands of
tenants on the remaining Yorkshire lordships suggests that the
lords are more likely to have been resident within the county for
at least part of their time (Tables 2–3, 6, 8). On the majority of
these lordships the larger and more populated estates of higher

[3] Mortain and Chester each held lands in twenty counties. Mortain's Yorkshire manors
comprised 18 per cent of the total number on his honour (184 out of 1,002) and only
14 per cent of the total value of the honour (4.25 per cent of the 1086 value). Mortain
appears to have been absent from England in Normandy for long periods during the
1070s and 1080s. See Soulsby, 'Counts of Mortain', 12–36; Golding, 'Robert of
Mortain', 119, 124, 128–9. Although Yorkshire was the most important county in the
English honour of the earl of Chester after Cheshire in 1066, accounting for about 22
per cent of its total value, by 1086 this figure had fallen to only 1.2 per cent: Lewis,
'Honor of Chester', 41–3.
[4] For the Vale of Pickering and Cleveland, see Sheppard, 'Pre-conquest Yorkshire',
67–78.   [5] *DB*, I, 305a–8b.

value were usually retained in demesne, especially the manors which had been held in 1066 by Anglo-Scandinavian earls, which were usually attached to great sokes, and which were often the administrative centres of wapentakes and hundreds.[6] This suggests that the lords were intent on retaining direct control of the administrative centres of their Yorkshire holdings. It was common, however, for much of the remainder of the seignorial demesne to be situated on the geographical peripheries of the honour, rather than close to the administrative centres. This was doubtless a reflection of the administratively underdeveloped nature of lordship in Yorkshire in 1086, and of the military considerations that governed the way the Normans secured what was essentially a frontier region.

An illustration of this feature is provided by the lordships of Pontefract and Richmond. In the former, although approximately twenty-seven and a half of the eighty-four and a half knights' fees recorded in the *carta* of 1166 had probably already been established by 1086, with only one exception the estates forming these tenancies appear to have been confined to the eastern portion of the honour.[7] Most of them were situated within a ten mile radius of the major demesne centres of either Kippax or Pontefract (Map 6). Very few Norman tenants appear to have been enfeoffed west of a north–south line drawn through East Ardsley, a region where the great majority of manors were waste.[8] In the case of the lordship of Richmond the estates outside Richmondshire situated close to York had all been retained in demesne (Map 5). The establishment of tenants was confined to the castlery of Richmondshire, and principally to areas within a ten mile radius of the probable castle sites of Catterick, Killerby, Kirkby Fleetham and Ravensworth (Map 5). Although some enfeoffment had taken place in the remote Pennine valleys in the western portion of the castlery, the estates here were waste and as yet outside the sphere of direct Norman administration. As in other areas of England, so in Yorkshire, it is more than likely that the Normans were establishing their military tenants in the protective shadow of their castles and major administrative and demesne centres.[9]

---

[6] For examples, see *DB*, 1, 309a, 310b, 315a, 316b, 323b–4a.
[7] Wightman, *Lacy Family*, 38–40. [8] *Ibid.*, 52–3.
[9] J. H. Round, 'The origin of Belvoir castle', *EHR*, 22 (1907), 508–10; Le Patourel, 'Norman colonization of Britain', 424–5; S. P. J. Harvey, 'The knight and the knight's fee in England', *Past & Present*, 49 (1970), 21–6.

The structure of the settlement pattern in 1086 suggests that lords were exercising a strong measure of control over the process of tenant enfeoffment. This control may be reflected to some extent by the absence of large or compact tenancies. Dr English has noted that only four *homines* of Drogo de la Beuvrière, lord of Holderness, held land in more than one vill. The average estate held by these tenants incorporated only about five carucates and was valued at less than £1. Out of the nine large manors with extensive sokes and berewicks on the honour worth over £5 at the depressed 1086 values, Drogo retained eight in his own hands.[10] The same carefully controlled division of land and resources is discernible on several other Yorkshire lordships.[11] An exception appears to be the honour of Richmond, where a number of continental tenants acquired extensive holdings. Despite their size, however, the Richmond tenancies were not the result of a disorderly scramble for lands. They reflect the supervisory care with which the settlement was effected. The individual continental tenants were succeeding to almost the entire estates held by one or more Anglo-Scandinavian thanes in 1066.[12] On the honour of Richmond, therefore, there was a degree of continuity between Anglo-Norman military tenancies and pre-conquest patterns of landholding; continuity which reveals the application of the principal of antecessorial succession in the settlement of the land, and the seignorial control which underpinned it.

Tenant enfeoffment continued apace after the completion of the Domesday survey, even on those honours where a considerable proportion of land and resources had already been granted to tenants. Dr Wightman has shown that in the honour of Lacy, Anglo-Scandinavians continued to be either dispossessed or demoted to the level of subtenants, and their lands resumed into the lord's demesne or regranted to Norman retainers. Gradually the Normans established their tenants in the more remote westerly wapentakes on the fringes of the Pennines, such as Agbrigg and Morley, where the vills had mostly been described as waste in 1086.[13]

---

[10] English, *Holderness*, 139–40.
[11] On the lordship of Ilbert I of Lacy the average size of estates belonging to continental tenants was just eighteen carucates, and no tenant held more than nine manors. On the lordship of Hugh Fitz Baldric only one tenant, Gerard, held more than two manors. The largest tenancy on the Percy lordship was that of Eburhard which incorporated eight manors valued at £4 8s in 1086. For these and other examples, see *DB*, I, 321b–3a, 327a–8a, 329a–b, 315a–18a, 328b, 326b–7a.　　[12] *VCH, Yorkshire*, II, 157.
[13] Wightman, *Lacy Family*, 42; *VCH, Yorkshire*, II, 157–8.

The *cartae baronum* of 1166 record the number of knights' fees in existence when Henry I died, that is fees of the old enfeoffment. When used in conjunction with evidence from charters, feodaries and other tenurial surveys they can be employed to illustrate the evolution of the military settlement pattern, and the scale, structure and terms of tenure on the lordships of Yorkshire by 1135. The large number of these old enfeoffment fees, and the difficulties of reconstructing the constituent estates of many of them, calls for a measure of selection. In order to draw general conclusions from the evidence, therefore, I have chosen to examine three honours of differing tenurial history, size and geographical distribution, where the composition of the military tenancies has been established with some degree of clarity. These honours are those of Mowbray, Percy and Skipton.

THE SCALE, PATTERN AND TERMS OF TENANT SETTLEMENT IN 1135: THREE CASE STUDIES

The honour of Mowbray

The Yorkshire portion of the honour of Mowbray was a vast tenurial complex, extending over the three ridings of the county. It incorporated several compact castleries centred on Burton in Lonsdale, Kirkby Malzeard, Thirsk and (possibly) Kirby Moorside. In addition, there were a number of more amorphous holdings immediately to the west and south of York, and in the East Riding.

The tenurial structure of the honour has been examined in detail by Dr Greenway.[14] The *carta* returned by Roger of Mowbray in 1166 records that sixty knights' fees had been in existence when his father, Nigel d'Aubigny, received his lands, that Nigel had created another twenty-eight fees and that Roger himself had added a further eleven and three-quarters fees out of the demesne. The individual old-enfeoffment returns give a total of eighty-eight and one twelfth knights' fees, a figure which requires adjustment in view of the inclusion here of the eight knights' fees of Robert III of Stuteville created after 1154.

The tenancies of the individual Mowbray vassals ranged in extent between one thirteenth of a knight's fee and fifteen knights' fees. The first to be established were chiefly situated in the

---

[14] For what follows, see *Mowbray Charters*, xxxiii–xliii.

midlands, and were also usually the largest. In Leicestershire, Warwickshire and Northamptonshire the pattern of military enfeoffment was largely complete by *c.* 1114. In the north enfeoffment progressed much more slowly:

the Pennine lordships of Burton in Lonsdale and Kirkby Malzeard had scarcely any knights' fees established until *c.* 1150. Hired knights... and household knights... doubtless provided the honour's main force in the north in the first half of the twelfth century. Enfeoffment in Yorkshire ...largely took the form of settling household knights on the land. Consequently, few military tenants in the northern estates owed more than one knight's service, and most of the fractional fees in the entire honour belonged to Yorkshire.[15]

With the aid of Greenway's material establishing the location of military tenancies, it is possible to calculate that between twelve and twenty-one knights' fees (approximately) had been established in Yorkshire by 1135. Even if we include the fifteen knights' fees of the Tison family and the seven and a quarter fees of the Arches family, which came to be incorporated in the honour in exceptional circumstances, the level of military enfeoffment on the Yorkshire portion of the Mowbray lordship, an estate comprising well in excess of 600 carucates, is hardly impressive.

The retarded development of military settlement in the Yorkshire portion of the Mowbray honour is reflected not only in the pattern of tenure, but also in the terms on which land was held, which differed very little from those on which thanes held socage tenements before 1066. In the twelfth century, as Greenway notes,

Much of the tenanted land of the honour was held by free tenants for rent in money or in kind. This had probably been true also at the time of Domesday Book ... Sometimes we have glimpses of tenures going back into Nigel d'Aubigny's time, and many of those in the hands of men of native ancestry must have originated in the pre-conquest period. In Yorkshire and Lincolnshire there was a substantial class of free tenants, many of whom bore Scandinavian names. They were particularly numerous in the area round Kirkby Malzeard and Masham, where even some of the estates held as fractional fees were in the hands of men of native descent ... A feudal veneer had been laid in patches on the existing pattern of tenancies, so that in social and economic terms there was little to distinguish the tenants on fractions of fees from rent-paying socage tenants.[16]

[15] *Ibid.*, xxxiv–xxxv.   [16] *Ibid.*, xxxix.

That the terms governing the tenure of these small post-conquest military tenancies differed little from those of pre-conquest socage estates is also suggested by the assessment of knight's fees on the honour of Mowbray in numbers of carucates, ranging from ten and a half to twenty-four.[17] Dr Roffe argues that ministerial tenure was apparently the essence of these holdings, which are likely to have had their ultimate origin in pre-conquest thanages and drengages, that many of them may not have been held on hereditary terms in 1086 and that in the thirteenth century many emerged as sergeanties.[18] The notion that at this social level the Normans always distributed and held land in return for actual military service has also been challenged from another direction by Dr Mortimer. He argues that lands were initially granted out by the Normans for reward and loyalty rather than actual military service, and that such service remained a matter of personal agreement between lord and tenant.[19]

The honour of Percy

At the Domesday survey the honour of William I of Percy was mainly confined to Yorkshire and Lincolnshire, with the majority of the estates, including the *caput* of Topcliffe, in the former county.[20] The bulk of the estates in Yorkshire appear to have formed component parts of three compact castleries centred on Topcliffe, Spofforth and Tadcaster. The small number of estates outside the castleries were situated in the upland area of Cravenshire, the East Riding, the Don valley and on the east coast near Scarborough. In addition, William of Percy held a Domesday tenancy of the earl of Chester centred on the manors of Whitby and Catton, which either he or his immediate descendant, Alan I of Percy, probably converted into a tenancy-in-chief (Map 14).

There had already been a considerable degree of tenant enfeoffment on the Yorkshire portion of the honour of Percy by 1086 (Tables 3–4). The tenant estates were well distributed throughout the lordship, although in greatest concentration in the Don valley, East Riding and around the demesne centres of

[17] *Ibid.*, xxxvii note 6.
[18] Roffe, 'Thegnage to barony', 171–2; *idem*, 'Domesday Book', 335–6 and notes.
[19] R. Mortimer, 'Land and service: the tenants of the honour of Clare', *ANS*, 8 (1986), 177–97.   [20] *EYC*, XI, 11–19.

Spofforth and Tadcaster (Map 3). They are notably absent from the Cravenshire estates in the foothills of the Pennines. Fifty years later the entire honour is recorded as incorporating twenty-nine military tenants holding a total of twenty-eight knights' fees. Of these fees, between twenty and five sixths and twenty-two and five sixths were situated in Yorkshire. The vills incorporating them were widely distributed throughout the county, located as far afield as Marske in Cleveland, Wigglesworth in Cravenshire, Carnaby in the East Riding and Brinsworth in the Don valley (Map 23). Some regions were more heavily encumbered with military tenancies than others. This can be illustrated by comparing the level of military enfeoffment with the number of carucates in the four major distinct regions of the honour in Yorkshire: the Don valley; the 'central region' (incorporating the wapentakes of Ainsty, *Bolesford*, Halikeld, Burghshire, Skyrack, *Gereburg* and *Gerlestre*); the 'coast region' (encompassing the estates of the east coast plain in the North Riding); and Cravenshire.[21]

The choice of regions may appear arbitrary and artificial, but has been made on the basis of several criteria. The first criterion is geographical definition. The 'coast', Don valley and Cravenshire regions incorporated estates detached from the main body of Percy holdings and the major centres of Percy authority, and display a degree of internal geographical coherence. The second criterion is the distribution of knights' fees. The component estates of some Percy military tenancies were dispersed over a wide geographical area, and it is often impossible to discern what proportion of the service owed by the fee was attached to each part. In choosing the regions to be studied it was essential, therefore, to limit this problem as much as possible by ensuring that most, if not all, of the component estates comprising the knights' fees were confined to only one region, in order that the level of enfeoffment within the region as a whole could be determined with some degree of accuracy. The third criterion used in determining the choice of regions is the tenurial history of the Percy honour. After 1086 the Percys acquired an extensive body of estates to augment their Domesday fee.[22] The majority of

---

[21] A thoroughly detailed analysis of the apportionment of service owed by individual tenancies between the vills constituting these tenancies is impossible in many cases because of the limitations of the evidence. To some extent, therefore, this study must remain impressionistic.   [22] *EYC*, XI, 14–16.

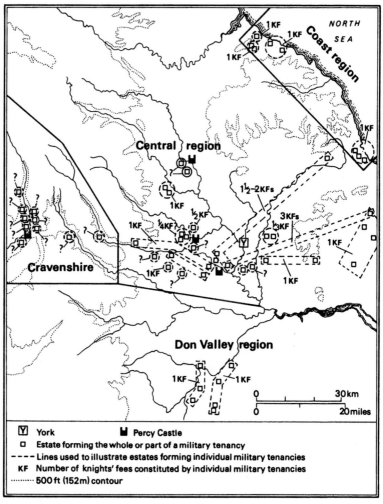

Map 23 The pattern of military enfeoffment on the honour of
Percy in 1135

these estates comprised the confiscated lands of Roger the Poitevin
in Cravenshire, which had almost certainly been acquired by 1135.
Although William of Percy held some estates in this area in 1086
these were small in comparison to those subsequently acquired.
The Cravenshire portion of the honour, therefore, had a peculiar
history, and is studied as a distinct region.

All the estates in the Don valley region had been alienated by

1135 to form component parts of two military tenancies, each held for the service of one knight. In 1166 one of these tenancies was in the hands of William the Vavasour, and formed part of a family estate of two knights' fees of the old enfeoffment. It comprised the manors of Barnby upon Don and Edlington (including the berewicks of Braithwell and Doncaster) which had been held in 1086 by William's grandfather, Malger.[23] The lord of the second tenancy in 1166 was William of Neville. His knight's fee was composed of the manors of Thrybergh, Brinsworth, Dalton and Bolton upon Dearne, of which all except Bolton had been held in 1086 by the Percy tenant Rozelin, whose relationship to William is uncertain.[24] The estates comprising the Vavasour knight's fee incorporated almost six carucates in 1086, while those within the Neville fee were assessed at almost thirteen carucates. When compared with the Percy honour as a whole, the Don valley region accounted for approximately 10 per cent of the fees, and just 2 to 3 per cent of the carucates, on the lordship in 1135.

The total number of knights' fees established in the 'central region' in 1135 was between eleven and one third and thirteen and five sixths. The figure is imprecise because the location of the old-enfeoffment tenancies of the families of Steward, Arches and Foliot has not been fully ascertained.[25] Of the twelve tenants holding military tenancies in the region recorded in the *carta* of 1166, the familial ancestors of five (possibly six) held land of the Percys in 1086.[26] The tenure of the families of another four can be traced back to the early twelfth century.[27] The total number of carucates on the Percy estates within this region was approximately 326, accounting for around 47 per cent of the total number of carucates on the lordship in 1135.[28] The number of knights' fees

---

[23] *Ibid.*, 118–21. [24] *Ibid.*, 286–9. [25] *Ibid.*, 89–90, 146–7, 202.

[26] *Ibid.*, 89–90, 104–8, 118–22, 137–9, 213–18, 252–5.

[27] *Ibid.*, 146–54, 186–91, 196–201, 180–1, 213–18, 222, 248.

[28] The total carucage figures for regions which follow may not be absolutely accurate because they are based on Domesday Book assessments and take no account of possible changes in the period up to 1135 resulting from the expansion of estates through land clearance and assarting. However, it has been argued that such developments were unlikely to affect assessments: D. Hall, 'Fieldwork and fieldbooks: studies in early layout', in *Villages, Fields and Frontiers: Studies in European Rural Settlement in the Medieval and Early Modern Periods*, ed. B. K. Roberts and R. E. Glasscock (British Archaeological Reports Int. Ser., 185, 1983), 115–29. In the case of this region, the figure of 326 carucates includes the Domesday assessments of all the estates acquired by the Percy lords after 1086, some of which may have been acquired after 1135. See *EYC*, XI, 14–16.

within the region in 1135 made up between 54 per cent and 61 per cent of the entire number established on the honour at that date.

Four knights' fees had been established in the 'coast region' by 1135: one incorporating the manors of Osgodby, Killerby, Deepdale and Cayton, held in part in 1166 by Durand of Cayton, whose father was possibly the tenant here in the early twelfth century; one at Lazenby, Wilton and West Coatham, held jointly in 1166 by William Fitz Richard and Walter Fitz Ralph, whose predecessors are unknown; one based on the manor of Kirkleatham, held in 1166 by Ilger Fitz *Roeri*, the first known tenant; and one centred on the manors of Upleatham, Marske, South Loftus and possibly Ugthorpe, under the control in 1166 of William of Argentom, whose father, Robert, preceded him in the tenement.[29] The Percy estates in this region incorporated approximately sixty-nine carucates in 1086. To these must be added the large estate constituted by the manor of Whitby and its outliers, held in 1086 by William of Percy of the earl of Chester. By the early twelfth century the tenancy-in-chief in Whitby appears to have passed to William's son, Alan, who probably acquired another Chester estate of ten carucates in Upleatham which had been in the earl's demesne in 1086.[30] In addition, approximately another twenty-eight carucates in the region were acquired by Alan through marriage and other means.[31] This gives a total carucage of around 179, accounting for approximately 26 per cent of the total carucage of the entire honour in 1135. The military tenancies in the 'coast region' accounted for four of the honour's twenty and five sixths to twenty two and five sixths knights' fees; that is, between 17 and 19 per cent.

By 1135 the number of knights' fees established within the Cravenshire region was at least three, and possibly four and a half. The four tenancies incorporating these fees which certainly existed at this date included a knight's fee in the manors of Long Preston, Painley and Wigglesworth, held in 1166 by Ralph of Amundeville, whose elder brother, Walter, held the tenancy before 1135; a knight's fee in Halton West, Hellifield, Long Preston, Paythorne and Swinden, held in 1166 by William of Humez, who held the tenancy in the early twelfth century; a half knight's fee in the manor of Rimington and its outliers, held in 1166 by Adam Fitz Norman, whose grandfather may have been the tenant in the

---

[29] *EYC*, XI, 233–4, 232–3, 225–7.   [30] *Ibid.*, 334–5.   [31] *Ibid.*, 353–6.

reign of Henry I; and a half knight's fee in Carleton, held in 1166 by William Fitz Robert, whose grandfather may have been a Domesday tenant of Percy at Wetherby.[32] The 177 carucates within this region comprised approximately 25 per cent of the total number of carucates on the lordship in 1135. The number of knights' fees within the region accounted for between 13 per cent and 21 per cent of the honorial total.

What emerges from this study of the Percy estates is that the level of military enfeoffment varied between the different geographical areas within the honour. In proportion to the number of carucates, the region most heavily encumbered with knights' fees was the Don valley, and the region least heavily encumbered was probably Cravenshire. To some extent this pattern must reflect the wealth of the land granted. The Don valley region was an area characterised for the most part by good agricultural soils, which appear to have been relatively intensively exploited for agricultural purposes before 1066; and the same was true to some extent of the 'central' district of the Percy lordship. Cravenshire, on the other hand, was an upland area, with poor soils and a harsh climate hardly conducive to the more profitable forms of agriculture capable of sustaining high levels of service.[33] Here the pattern of settlement on the Percy lordship closely resembles that in the Pennine regions of the Mowbray fee. It is a pattern which suggests that the Normans were still in the process of establishing themselves in the area in 1135, and viewed it as a military as well as an economic frontier region.[34] Within this region the Mowbrays had castleries centred on Kirkby Malzeard and Burton in Lonsdale by 1130, and the Percys may either have constructed, or acquired from Roger the Poitevin, a castle at Gisburn close to one of the major routes running from the West Riding through the Pennines into Lancashire.[35] It is significant that in 1135, all except one of the military tenancies of the Percys in Cravenshire were situated within ten miles of Gisburn (Map 23). Here again the Norman tenurial take-over appears to have been proceeding within the protective shadow of castles.

Just as the level of Norman military enfeoffment varies between

---

[32] *Ibid.*, 172–6, 227–30, 243–9, 252–5.

[33] See *Ibid.*, no. 50; *Foundation of Kirkstall*, 177–8; *Domesday Geography*, 79–80.

[34] This is supported by the fact that the majority of the Cravenshire tenancies recorded in the Percy *carta* of 1166 had been formed or taken over by the Normans in the period after 1135. See *EYC*, xi, 89, 146, 255, 261.   [35] See above, pp. 88–9.

the different regions of the Percy lordship, so does its form. In the three outlying areas of the lordship (Cravenshire, the Don valley and the north-east coast) the military tenancies were either single or fractional knight's fees made up of lands situated in one vill or adjacent vills. By contrast, in the 'central region' of the lordship some military tenancies were composed of multiple knights' fees, and were distributed over wide geographical areas. They seem to have been honours in miniature, divided between estates held in demesne and let out for service. And the men who held them can be equated with Professor Stenton's 'honorial barons'.

One of these men was Robert Fitz Picot, whose 1166 tenancy of three knights' fees was composed of estates in vills as far afield as Nesfield in the Wharfe valley and Carnaby near Bridlington in the East Riding. Robert was the son of a man who is known to have employed the surname of Percy, which if not necessarily implying a family connection with the lord, at least indicates a close relationship of some kind. Picot's influential status is also reflected in the fact that he attested three of Alan I of Percy's seven extant charters; his name appearing in a prominent place in the list of witnesses immediately after those of the lord's brothers, and before that of the Percy steward, Fulk Fitz Reinfrid. A comparison of the Domesday survey and the 1166 returns reveals that Picot's family gradually built up their estate. In 1086 Picot held two and a half carucates of William of Percy in Bolton upon Dearne, and six carucates in nearby Sutton upon Derwent. By 1135 he, or his son Robert, had considerably augmented the family estate with the addition of lands in the vills of Bolton Percy, Carnaby and Nesfield.[36]

Another holder of a multiple fee who fits the description of a 'honorial baron' is Robert Fitz Robert the steward, who held three knights' fees of the old enfeoffment and a half knight's fee of the new enfeoffment of Percy in 1166. The ancestor of his family was Reinfrid, prior of the Percy foundation of Whitby Abbey, whose son, Fulk, grandson, Robert, and great-grandson, Robert Fitz Robert, served as stewards of the Percy lords and witnessed many of their charters. Here again, the family appears to have gradually built up its estate. By 1135 the Domesday holdings, consisting of two carucates in Pallathorpe and one and a half carucates in Snainton, had been considerably augmented by the addition of

[36] *EYC*, XI, 104–18.

between one and a half and two knights' fees in the vills of Bolton Percy, Ouston, Healaugh, Pallathorpe and Snainton.[37]

Roffe has recently suggested that these 'honorial barons' held their lands on very different terms from the tenants of smaller fees. These terms are seen as no mere vestige of those on which pre-conquest ministerial or drengage tenures were held:

In addition to the grant of the rights of justice, the estate was conferred *in feudo et hereditate*, that is, it was to be held hereditarily as opposed to a life or term of lives; and the new lord, for such we can now call him, was to hold *in nemoribus et in planis, in villa et vico, et campis et pratis, in aquis et omnibus locis*, or words to that effect, that is he was endowed with all the rights which Domesday Book calls *terra* [full economic rights].

The 'honorial baron' 'was a king's thane in all but name', he held a *feudum* and he held it in return for actual military service.[38]

The existence of such a sharp distinction between 'honorial barons' and lesser tenants, who Roffe appears to believe held by non-hereditary socage tenure (ministerial/drengage tenure), may apply in some places, but possibly not in all. It is interesting that some of the holders of fractional knight's fees, men who cannot be construed as 'honorial barons', appear to have held lands on similar terms to those of their greater neighbours. At some point between *c.* 1155 and 1165 Apolitus de Braham, whose son Henry held only a half knight's fee of William II of Percy in 1166, gave land in Middleton owing forinsec service on the basis of sixteen carucates per knight's fee to Arthur Fitz Serlo, 'in villa et extra villam. in bosco et in plano. in aquis. in viis et in semitis. in pratis et pascuis. et in omnibus locis eidem ville pertinentibus'.[39] Here the rights assumed to have been the exclusive preserve of the 'honorial baron' appear to have been held by a tenant of lesser status; although it is possible that by the time this charter was issued the words formerly conveying full economic rights had become common form, and had ceased to be indicative of tenure.

What is reasonably certain is that if the expression of knight's fees in terms of numbers of carucates is an indication of the continuity of pre-conquest socage tenure, then such tenure was just as widespread on the lordship of Percy as it was on that of Mowbray. A number of military tenancies created both before and after 1135 incorporated estates which were held on the basis of

---

[37] *Ibid.*, 93–6, 89–91; *DB*, I, 321b, 323a. [38] Roffe, 'Thegnage to barony', 175–6.
[39] *EYC*, XI, 243, 248, no. 202.

either five, ten, twelve, twelve and a half or fourteen carucates per knight's fee, and which were distributed throughout the three ridings of the county.[40] Tenure of this nature survived into the late twelfth century and beyond. Between *c.*1160 and 1175, for example, Robert Fitz Robert the steward, who as an 'honorial baron' may himself have rendered actual military service to his lord, gave twelve bovates of land in Coniston Cold to Gilbert Fitz Richard 'making the service that pertains to the aforesaid bovates where twelve carucates make a fee of one knight'.[41] One late twelfth-century charter indicates that some military sergeanty tenures were the direct descendants of ministerial thanage holdings. Between 1175 and (?)1184, one of the daughters and co-heiresses of William II of Percy, Maud, issued a charter in favour of Fountains Abbey granting two bovates of land in Malham, which had belonged to Adam the sergeant (*servientis*) and his brother, and two more bovates which had been in the possession of Reginald the horseman (*equestrarius*), to be held by the render of 2s yearly, and doing the forinsec service on the basis of fourteen carucates per knight's fee.[42] It is a charter which reveals that on some Percy estates the 'feudal' veneer laid by the Normans over pre-conquest socage tenures was spread very thinly indeed.

Although the terms of tenure may have altered little from pre-conquest times, the structure of the socage tenements may have been transformed by the Percys and their retainers. The best example of this is provided by the tenancy of two knights' fees of the old enfeoffment held by William the Vavasour in 1166, which were held by William's predecessor, Malger, in 1086. In 1066 these manors had been held by Arnketill, Wulfstan, Gamall, Ulf, Asulfr and Northmann.[43] Even where, as in the case of the knight's fee held by William of Humez, and in that of the knight's fee held by Thomas Darel, Percy military tenements were composed of the estates of just one pre-conquest Anglo-Scandinavian landholder, it appears as though they did not constitute all the estates belonging to that landholder.[44] It is possible, however, that owing to the

---

[40] *Ibid.*, 248, 268, and nos. 109, 168 and note, 208, 220.
[41] *Ibid.*, 89 and no. 90. For the equation of the formula 'in pratis ... ', and similar phrases, with socage tenure, see Roffe, 'Thegnage to barony', 165–6, 175–6.
[42] *EYC*, XI, no. 40, and see nos. 35, 44, 72, 134, 137–9, 242, 245, 252, 259, 262.
[43] *Ibid.*, 118–19; *DB*, I, 321b.
[44] The Humez lands in Hellifield, Paythorne and Swinden had all been held in 1066 by Bjornulfr, who was also in possession of numerous other estates in Cravenshire: *DB*, I, 322a. The Darel lands in Wheldrake and possibly Warter were held in 1066 by

failure of Domesday Book to record patterns of overlordship adequately, this tenurial discontinuity may be more apparent than real.

The honour of Skipton

The honour of Skipton held by the Rumillys, which came into being after 1086 and was centred on the castle of Skipton, was constructed for the most part from a large portion of the former Domesday estates of Roger the Poitevin, and from a body of royal demesne lands centred chiefly on the manor of Bolton.[45] The estates within the Yorkshire portion of the honour were situated mainly in a compact block of territory in Cravenshire, with a small outlying cluster of lands in the parish of Wath upon Dearne in south Yorkshire.

The *carta* returned by Alexander Fitz Gerold, lord of Skipton, in 1166 records twelve knights' fees on the honour in 1135. Clay has shown that the correct number was probably thirteen.[46] Of these, however, only two and a half were situated in the Yorkshire portion of the honour, even though the honorial estates there incorporated approximately 210 carucates.[47] The two and a half fees were held by the Mauleverer (one), Bulmer (one) and Vavasour (half) families, all of whom could trace their ancestors back to the reign of Henry I, and in the case of the Vavasour family back to the Domesday survey.[48] The very limited extent of enfeoffment tends to confirm the impression gained from a study of the Percy lordship that the organisation of military tenure in Cravenshire was still underdeveloped in 1135, and that it was probably restricted to the settlement of knights partially maintained in the seignorial household in estates close to castle sites.[49] Outside this area progress was even slower. The military settlement of the Skipton estates in south Yorkshire between Pontefract and Conisbrough was delayed until after 1135.[50]

It is probable that all of the knights' fees belonging to the honour of Skipton in Yorkshire were held on similar terms to pre-

Northmann. But Northmann also held lands which passed by 1086 to Rozelin, Picot and Malger (the ancestor of the Vavasour family), who all held of William of Percy. See *DB*, I, 321b–3a; *EYC*, XI, 104, 186–7. [45] *EYC*, VII, 42–9.
[46] *Red Book*, I, 430–2; *EYC*, VII, 90. [47] *EYC*, VII, 47–9, 90.
[48] *Ibid.*, 114–16, 153–4, 166–7.
[49] For the settlement of household knights generally, see M. Chibnall, *Anglo-Norman England 1066–1166* (Oxford, 1986), 16; D. F. Fleming, 'Landholding by *milites* in Domesday Book: a revision', *ANS*, 13 (1991), 92. [50] *EYC*, VII, 193–4.

conquest socage estates. In the 1166 *carta*, the tenancies of seventeen of the twenty new-enfeoffment tenants were assessed in terms of numbers of carucates and bovates.[51] Later evidence indicates that the two and a half knights' fees of the old enfeoffment in Yorkshire shared between the Vavasour, Mauleverer and Bulmer families were assessed in the same way.[52] It is significant that one of the subtenants in both the Bulmer and Vavasour fees was Uctred Fitz Dolfin, the grandson of the great Yorkshire pre-conquest landholder, Gospatric, and a tenant of the Mowbrays in military tenancies within the region of Masham which appear to have been based on pre-conquest socage holdings.[53]

The three tenancies which made up the two and a half knights' fees of the old enfeoffment in the Yorkshire portion of the honour in 1166 appear to have been composite holdings formed from the estates, or portions of the estates, of several pre-conquest land-holders. To some extent this probably reflects the fact that the honour of Skipton itself was a composite lordship, made up mainly of lands held by the king and by Roger the Poitevin in 1086; to some extent it was almost certainly produced by the tenurial engineering undertaken by the lords and their military tenants in the fifty years after the Domesday survey, as they gradually built up and rounded off their estates. This engineering can be seen if we examine the composite holdings in detail. The knight's fee held by the Mauleverer family in 1166 was made up of several pre-conquest tenements, including some (but not all) of the lands which were dependent on Earl Edwin's manor of Bolton; a carucate in Hellifield held by either Ulf or Karle, which was a dependency of other estates which did not pass to the Mauleverers; and a manor of three carucates in Hawkswick held by Gamall.[54] The knight's fee held by the Bulmer family incorporated land in Burnsall held in 1066 and 1086 by Heardwulf the king's thane, land in Coniston Cold which was attached to the royal manor of Bolton, three manors in Cracoe (*Holedene*) held by the king's thanes Ketill, Gospatric and Ulfketill and land in Airton held by Arnbrandr.[55] The half knight's fee of the Vavasour family also appears to have been a composite estate, but may provide us

[51] *Red Book*, I, 431–2. See also *EYC*, VII, 216, 222, 226, 230, 252–3, and nos. 26, 120, 143, 156, 161, 173–4.   [52] *EYC*, VII, xiii, 153, 166, nos. 6, 92, 96–7, 104, 106.
[53] *Ibid.*, nos. 92, 106; *Mowbray Charters*, xxxix and note 6, xl.
[54] *EYC*, VII, 45–7, 114; XI, 14–15; *DB*, I, 301b, 332a.
[55] *EYC*, VII, 45–7, 153; *DB*, I, 301b, 331b, 332a.

with an example of a post-conquest tenant family attempting to reconstitute at least part of a dismembered pre-conquest thanage tenure. The fee incorporated three carucates in Addingham which had been held by Gamalbarn in 1066. One of these carucates was held by the king in 1086, and the other two by Gilbert Tison, possibly as a dependency of Gilbert's manor of Swinton, which had formerly been held by the thane Adestan.[56] What may have happened is that after 1066 Adestan's lands and their dependencies had passed to Tison, and that sometime after 1086 either the lords of Skipton or the Vavasours had secured control of the entire estate formerly belonging to Gamalbarn in order to consolidate their existing holdings in Addingham. Thus, even on the composite honours created after 1086, threads of continuity in the structure of subtenancies can still be found.

The case studies of Norman settlement in the honours of Mowbray, Percy and Skipton reveal that military enfeoffment developed more slowly in Yorkshire than in other more southerly areas of England, particularly in the more remote frontier areas of the county. In 1135 the military tenancies in these frontier areas were few in number, often composed of only fractions of knight's fees and largely confined to the immediate vicinity of the castles. In the more accessible lowland/central areas of the county, by contrast, the military tenancies were larger and more complex, often composed of lands dispersed in widely separated vills, and held by more important honorial retainers who were the ancestors of Stenton's 'honorial barons'. The pattern suggests that military enfeoffment began in these more accessible areas with the granting of small parcels of land to men from the upper echelons of honorial society, who proceeded over the next fifty years to augment their estates and grant them out to their own tenants. It also suggests that the military settlement of the less accessible/upland areas was much slower, but that it too was underway by 1135 and was spreading outwards from beneath the shadow of small fortresses. The progress of tenant settlement, both military and non-military, is reflected in the fact that whereas approximately 47 per cent of the carucates and 48 per cent of the value of the Yorkshire portion of the Percy honour had been alienated to tenants in 1086 (Table 3), by 1135 the figure for carucates was at least 60 per cent, and

---

[56] *EYC*, vii, 45–7, 166; *DB*, i, 301b, 326b.

probably far more.[57] However, the tenurial settlement of York-shire was still incomplete in 1135, the county remained a military frontier region and the terms of military tenure were often retrograde.[58] These terms differed little from the socage obli-gations owed by pre-conquest thanes for their estates. What had changed on some lordships was the structure of tenure itself. Although the estates of some thanes passed undivided into the hands of Norman subtenants, others appear to have been dismembered. The tenurial changes wrought by the Norman conquest may have been exaggerated by some historians, but were important nonetheless.

ENFEOFFMENT, CASTLES AND QUOTAS

It has been illustrated that the knights' fees established by the Normans in Yorkshire were often held on terms which differed little from those of pre-conquest thanages. This is not to suggest, however, that everything stayed more or less the same. The construction of dozens of new castles in the period 1066–1135, which required specialised arrangements for their maintenance and defence, and which amounted, however optimistically the evidence for pre-conquest fortifications is interpreted, to a military revolution, must have transformed the nature of tenure to some extent.[59] Many tenants-in-chief are known to have owed ward service at royal castles, and to have demanded the same service from their tenants in order to garrison their private fortresses. This was so on the lordship of Richmond by the early years of the twelfth century (and probably earlier) when 187 $\frac{1}{4}$ knights were expected to provide ward at the private castle during the course of the year. These knights served for two months at a time, in groups ranging between twenty-six and forty-three; the larger groups during the summer months when the risk of Scottish attack was presumably greatest.[60] Similar arrangements had developed on the

---

[57] P. Dalton, 'Feudal politics in Yorkshire 1066–1154' (Univ. of Sheffield, PhD thesis, 1990), Appendix 2.

[58] For the widespread assessment of knight's fees on the basis of carucates, see *EYC*, III, nos. 1311, 1361, 1364; VII, 90; X, 94–6, 98, 104, 152–3, 166, 168, 172; XII, 16, 80–1, 83. On the lordship of Richmond drengage tenure was widespread: *EYC*, IV, no. 33, 108–9, 114, 116 note 7, 121, 143; V, 26.

[59] See Eales, 'Royal power and castles', 52–4.

[60] *EYC*, V, 2–9, 11–12; Keefe, *Feudal Assessments*, 259 note 125; S. Painter, 'Castle-Guard', *AHR*, 40 (1935), 451; Sanders, *Baronies*, 140 notes 5 and 6.

lordship of Tickhill, where sixty knights owed ward service at the castle; on the lordship of Mowbray, where a knight and ten sergeants were garrisoning the castle of Burton in Lonsdale in 1129–30; and on the lordship of Skipton, where a number of tenants referred to ward service in their charters.[61] In time this service was often commuted to an annual payment, but initially at least must have been performed by some tenants in person.[62] On some lordships personal service in royal and private castles appears to have remained a tenurial obligation well into the twelfth century. Between 1165 and 1179, William count of Aumale issued a notification that he had granted land to Ingelbert de Mainers in the vill of Skeffling, to hold by the service of a sixth part of one knight, 'ad custodiam castelli de Skipse ad servitium regis'.[63]

Whether there was any relationship between the dues involved in pre-conquest socage/ministerial tenure and post-conquest ward service is open to question. An early thirteenth-century charter from Yorkshire suggests that the two forms of obligation may have been distinct. Sometime either in or shortly after 1217, Benedict of Stapleton, a subtenant on the military tenancy held by the Scalers family of the lords of Richmond, gave three carucates of land in Stapleton to the abbey of Easby, 'making as much forinsec service as pertains to three carucates of land where ten carucates make the service of one knight, and doing as much ward service at the castle of Richmond on the day of the Purification of Saint Mary as pertains to the service of one knight, namely half a mark for all demands which pertain to me or my heirs'.[64] The basic distinction here between forinsec service and ward service was probably made because the former was owed ultimately to the king, and the latter to the lord.[65] But there is also a distinction in detail. Whereas the forinsec service is related to carucage in a manner which varied from tenancy to tenancy, the ward service is

---

[61] *PR 13 Henry II*, 101; *PR 31 Henry I*, 138; *EYC*, VII, 42, 107–9, 112; Painter, *English Feudal Barony*, 132.

[62] For the commutation, see Painter, *English Feudal Barony*, 45–7, 131, 133; Hollister, *Military Organization*, 154–9.   [63] *EYC*, III, no. 1400.

[64] *EYC*, v, no. 338A.

[65] The confinement of the fees owing ward service at Richmond castle to the lordship of Richmond suggests that the castle was regarded as the property of the lord rather than of the king. However, when the lordship was in the king's hands the castle was probably regarded as a royal fortress. This appears to have been the case in 1172 when scutage was levied on 176.6 knights, a figure close to the number of knights who owed ward at Richmond castle in the early twelfth century. See *EYC*, v, 2–9, 11–12; IV, 108–13; Keefe, *Feudal Assessments*, 259 note 125; Sanders, *Baronies*, 140 note 5.

described as a simple monetary render which appears to have been standard throughout the lordship.[66] This suggests that whereas forinsec service was related to pre-conquest terms of tenure, ward service may have been a new burden imposed arbitrarily throughout the lordship which bore little or no relation to socage obligations. Although it is possible that post-conquest castle-guard services at some of the larger royal borough castles were related to pre-conquest obligations, within the private lordships of Yorkshire this relationship may not have existed.

THE REVIVAL OF MONASTICISM IN YORKSHIRE

When the Normans arrived in England in 1066 Yorkshire was a county devoid of monastic foundations. The golden age of Northumbrian monasticism had long since passed away. The buildings of the famous monastic community of *Strenaeshalc* at Whitby lay in ruins.[67] The habit-clad soldiers of God, it seems, were almost nowhere to be found. During the next seventy years all this was to change. Religious orders came to flourish in Yorkshire, slowly at first, but with a marked acceleration after the promotion of Thurstan of Bayeux to the archbishopric of York in 1114. In 1114 there were six or seven religious houses in Yorkshire, by 1135 there were at least twenty.

The rapid emergence of religious orders in the north under Henry I was part of a broad reform movement within the church, which was older than his reign, continued far beyond it and was fuelled by a complex mixture of religious, social and economic factors. The motives which inspired and encouraged the foundation and development of the new houses were many faceted. The initial impetus sometimes came from churchmen (like Thurstan) anxious to reform and develop the church through the promotion of monastic and canonical ideals, and ready to encourage influential and wealthy secular lords to assist them in the task. The spiritual, practical and personal benefits to be derived explain why many of these lords were more than ready to help. Their religious foundations allowed them to fulfil the demands of piety, provided for the care of their souls, helped them to exploit

---

[66] On the lordship of Richmond the number of carucates making a knight's fee could be seven, eight and a half, nine, ten, twelve, fourteen, fifteen, sixteen or twenty: *EYC*, v, subject index (under 'carucates'). For the commutation of ward service on the basis of half a mark per knight, which had occurred by the early thirteenth century, see *ibid.*, 6, 16. [67] For Whitby, see *VCH, Yorkshire*, III, 101–2.

their lands more efficiently, served as symbols of their status and prestige, educated their children, provided careers for their younger sons and daughters and offered respectable places in which to retire, be buried and be remembered. That the development of religious orders in Yorkshire owed a great deal to a complex interaction of all these influences is not in question. What is open to investigation, however, is whether this development was related in any way to the reinforcement of Norman authority within Yorkshire; particularly in view of the fact that the foundation of monasteries was a tried and tested method of consolidating power in areas of territorial dispute or doubtful political allegiance.[68] In order to address this question it is instructive to examine the degree to which the Norman kings and their officials were involved in the expansion of religious orders in Yorkshire before 1135.

One of the earliest monasteries founded in Yorkshire after 1066 was the Benedictine abbey of Selby, possibly by 1070 and certainly by 1086. Although the vill of Selby belonged to the king, the origins of the new foundation owed far more to the initiative of Benedict, a maverick monk from Auxerre, than to the Conqueror.[69] Benedict apparently came to England at the command of St Germanus who had instructed him in a dream to found a house at Selby. After a brief stay at Salisbury, which he mistook for the site intended, Benedict finally settled and founded a hermitage on the banks of the River Ouse. Once established, the new hermitage soon received help from the king and his officials. Sometime within a year of its foundation Benedict was introduced to the Conqueror (probably at York) by the sheriff of Yorkshire, Hugh Fitz Baldric, who was instrumental in obtaining for the nascent monastery a gift of royal lands in Selby and some of its neighbouring vills. The Conqueror also gave the house the important rights of soke, sake, toll, team and infangenetheof, and all the liberties enjoyed by St Peter's, York. Help was also forthcoming from the archbishop of York, Thomas I, who recognised Benedict as abbot, granted him land in Lesser Selby and

---

[68] M. Chibnall, 'The Empress Matilda and church reform', *TRHS*, 5th ser., 38 (1988), 108–9.

[69] *Selby Coucher*, I, [6]–[19]. For a discussion of the foundation, see R. B. Dobson, 'The first Norman abbey in northern England. The origins of Selby: a ninth centenary article', *Ampleforth Journal*, 74 (1969), 161–76; *VCH, Yorkshire*, III, 95–6; J. E. Burton, 'The origins and development of the religious orders in Yorkshire c. 1069 to c. 1200' (Univ. of York, DPhil thesis, 1977), 3–10.

Monk Fryston and confirmed him in possession of land in Hillam; and from Fitz Baldric's successor as sheriff, Erneis of Burun, who offered the monks a loan of 100 marks.[70] In the reign of Rufus, however, relations between Benedict and the king turned sour. After hearing that Benedict had created uproar in his house by his cruel treatment of two miscreant monks, the king ordered his arrest. Although the orders were not carried out, Benedict was forced by his monks to resign. Rufus then granted Selby Abbey to the archbishop of York in settlement of the archbishop's claims to jurisdiction over the see of Lincoln.[71]

The establishment and development of Whitby Abbey, founded in or about 1078, followed a similar pattern to that of Selby. Whitby was also a Benedictine house and, like Selby, owed its origins to the initiative of a pioneering monk; in this case Reinfrid of Evesham. Reinfrid had travelled north with Aldwin prior of Winchcombe and a fellow monk of Evesham, Aelfwig, with the intention of visiting the old sites of Northumbrian monasticism and settling there as hermits. After founding a number of houses north of the Tees, Reinfrid decided to refound the monastery of St Peter of *Strenaeshalc* at Whitby, and approached the local lord, William I of Percy, who granted him the ruined buildings of St Peter's and two carucates of land within the neighbourhood.[72] A narrative account of the foundation which has been ascribed to Abbot Stephen of St Mary's, York, and which may not be entirely trustworthy, states that owing to the subsequent hostility of Percy and the raids of pirates the monks sought aid from the king, who granted them a new site at Lastingham, where some of them moved before departing to York to found St Mary's Abbey.[73] The only other assistance offered to the house by the Norman kings before 1100 was a grant of lands in Hackness, Northfield and Burniston, certain liberties and customs and the church of All Saints Fishergate, York.[74]

The foundation of the Benedictine abbey of St Mary's, York, had taken place by 1086 and was originally based upon the church of St Olave, which had been granted by Alan I, lord of

---

[70] *Selby Coucher*, I, nos. 1, 2, pp. [17]–[18]; *EYC*, I, nos. 41–2.

[71] Hugh the Chantor, 8–9; *Registrum Antiquissimum*, I, no. 4.

[72] *VCH, Yorkshire*, III, 101–2; Burton, 'Religious orders', 20–32; Knowles, *Monastic Order*, 168; A. Hamilton Thompson, 'The monastic settlement at Hackness', *YAJ*, 27 (1924), 388–405; *Cartularium de Whiteby*, I, xiii–xc.

[73] *Monasticon*, III, 544–6; *Cartularium de Whiteby*, I, li *et seq.*; Burton, 'Religious orders', 21–6. [74] *Cartularium de Whiteby*, I, xlviii–l, 147, 166, 331–2; *EYC*, II, no. 863.

Richmond.[75] Thereafter, as Dr Burton notes, the Conqueror and William Rufus played a prominent role in the development of the abbey.[76] The former gave permission for the removal of the monks from Lastingham to York, and endowed St Mary's with land in Appleton le Moor and several other vills, and with the churches of St Michael and St Saviour in York. The latter confirmed his father's grants, provided an expanded site, gave land in Grimston and Emswell, protected the monks in a dispute with Archbishop Thomas I and may even have laid the foundation stone of the new house in a formal ceremony conducted in 1089.[77] According to Abbot Stephen, while Alan I of Richmond was on his death-bed he surrendered the advowson of the abbey to Rufus.[78] Rufus himself spoke of Alan as 'after me and my father the beginner and founder of this abbey', and his views of the origins of the abbey were echoed later by Henry II.[79] There can be no doubt, as Burton states, that the Norman kings regarded St Mary's as a royal foundation, and that this is partly why the house secured major acquisitions of lands from the Yorkshire baronage in the period before 1135.[80]

Shortly after the foundation of St Mary's a second Benedictine abbey, Holy Trinity, was refounded in York by Ralph Paynel as a dependency of the abbey of Marmoutier.[81] Ralph, who may have been sheriff of Yorkshire at the time, endowed the house with some twelve parish churches and a moiety in a thirteenth; but his royal master, William Rufus, appears to have offered no help to the new foundation.[82]

The last monastic house to be founded in Yorkshire before the reign of Henry I was Pontefract Priory, and once again royal involvement was limited. The house appears to have owed its origins, and apparently its entire initial endowment, to the local magnate, Robert I of Lacy, lord of Pontefract, who may have founded it with the advice of Archbishop Thomas I.[83] In one sense, however, the foundation of the priory marks a new departure in the history of monasticism in Yorkshire. Established as a cell of the French Cluniac monastery of La Charité sur Loire in or about

[75] *VCH, Yorkshire*, III, 107–8.
[76] The details in this paragraph are derived from Burton, 'Religious orders', 34–8.
[77] *EYC*, I, no. 350; BL Add. MS 38816, fol. 33r–v.
[78] BL Add. MS 38816, fol. 33r.   [79] *EYC*, I, nos. 350, 354.
[80] Burton, 'Religious orders', 36.   [81] *EYC*, VI, viii–ix, 3–5, nos. 1–2.
[82] Green, *Sheriffs*, 89; *EYC*, VI, no. 1; Burton, 'Religious orders', 47–9.
[83] Burton, 'Religious orders', 60–8.

1090, Pontefract was the first reformed monastic house to be constructed in Yorkshire. But the Cluniacs were not to flourish in England in the same way as the Augustinians and Cistercians.[84] Pontefract remained the only Cluniac monastery in Yorkshire until the foundation of nearby Monk Bretton by the Lacy tenant, Adam Fitz Swain, in the early 1150s.

By 1100 the Normans had established only five monasteries in Yorkshire. The foundation of two of these, Selby and Whitby, owed more to the initiative of pioneering monks than to the influence of the king, the king's ministers or local lords; and the foundation of a third, St Mary's, resulted from the hostility of one of these local lords to the house he established at Whitby. Although the Conqueror, William Rufus and some of their ministers had provided important support to Selby and St Mary's, York, Rufus had been prepared to use Selby as a bribe to buy off the claims of the archbishop of York to the see of Lincoln. Moreover, the involvement of the Conqueror and Rufus in the foundation of Whitby, Holy Trinity and Pontefract appears to have been either limited or non-existent. It was undoubtedly in their capacity as local lords rather than royal officials that Ralph Paynel and Robert of Lacy founded their religious houses. When Henry I came to power, Yorkshire monasticism was developing with limited assistance from the crown, and it was developing slowly.

Under Henry I religious life in Yorkshire was transformed. Not only were the endowments of the existing Benedictine and Cluniac houses expanded, but fourteen new foundations, including eight reformed Augustinian houses, were established.[85] Numerous charters reveal the close and persistent involvement of the king and his principal officials.[86]

Of the old-established houses, Selby Abbey benefited most from the new initiative. Henry I gave the abbey the churches of the great royal demesne manor of Snaith; his justice, Nigel d'Aubigny, gave estates in Amcotts and elsewhere; his sheriff of

---

[84] Knowles, *Monastic Order*, 153.

[85] The Augustinian houses were Bridlington (*c*. 1113), Nostell (*c*. 1114), Guisborough (1119), Embsay (1120 × 1121), Kirkham (*c*. 1122), Warter (*c*. 1132?), Woodkirk (before 1135) and Drax (1130 × 1139). The remaining monasteries were the Benedictine houses of St Martin's Richmond (1100 × 1137), and St Clement's York (1125 × 1133); and the Cistercian houses of Rievaulx (1132), Fountains (1132), Handale (1133) and Byland (1135).

[86] For this phenomenon generally, see Dickinson, *Austin Canons*, 108–31.

Yorkshire, Osbert, gave further land in Duffield and Acaster Selby; and his archbishops of York, Thomas II and Gerard, made further donations.[87] By 1135 the abbey had also attracted the patronage of a number of local magnates, and was one of the wealthiest foundations in .Yorkshire.[88] Whitby Abbey secured a grant from Archbishop Thurstan of the important liberties enjoyed by the minster churches of Beverley and Ripon.[89] St Mary's Abbey, York, received a grant from Henry I of land in and near Airmyn and Ousefleet, and of whatever he had in Haldenby.[90] Holy Trinity Priory, York, obtained several confirmation charters from Henry I and Archbishop Thomas II, the archbishop's protection and permission to appropriate a number of churches and a grant from Nigel d'Aubigny of three houses and the tithe of his mills in York.[91] And Pontefract Priory procured charters from both Henry I and Archbishop Thomas II confirming agreements made with Nostell Priory concerning possession of various churches, rents and customs.[92]

The involvement of the king and his officials in the religious expansion is most apparent in the foundation of the new Augustinian houses. Very few of these houses had been founded in England until the establishment of Holy Trinity Priory, Aldgate, by Henry I's queen in 1107. Thereafter, with the help of the king, queen and greater magnates the Augustinian order flourished in England, and especially in Yorkshire. Walter of Gant, the founder of Bridlington Priory, endowed his new house 'by the order and with the agreement of King Henry'.[93] As well as directing the foundation of the priory, which took place in or about 1113, the king was also prepared to offer material support.[94] He granted land from the royal demesne in Bridlington, Hilderthorpe and Easton, and commanded that the canons were to enjoy specific judicial rights and acquittance from toll and customs.[95] Two of the

---

[87] *Regesta*, II, no. 495; *Selby Coucher*, I, no. 5; *EYC*, I, nos. 43, 45–6, 462.
[88] Burton, 'Religious orders', 6–7, 11, 19.   [89] *EYC*, II, no. 876.
[90] *Ibid.*, I, no. 470.   [91] *Ibid.*, VI, nos. 2–4, 8–11; *Mowbray Charters*, no. 3.
[92] *EYC*, III, nos. 1431, 1465.
[93] *Ibid.*, II, no. 1135. Henry I issued a charter confirming Walter's gifts and making grants of his own: J. S. Purvis, 'A foundation charter of Bridlington Priory', *YAJ*, 29 (1927–9), 395. A sixteenth-century source states that Walter founded the house, 'assensu et precepto ejusdem Henrici Regis Anglie', and also mentions the involvement of Archbishop Thomas II: Burton, 'Religious orders', 81.
[94] J. S. Purvis, 'The foundation of Bridlington Priory', *YAJ*, 29 (1927–9), 241–2.
[95] *Regesta*, II, nos. 1333, 1429; *EYC*, II, no. 1143; Purvis, 'Foundation charter of Bridlington', 395; BL Add. MS 40008, fol. 19.

king's principal northern administrators, Archbishop Thurstan of York and Eustace Fitz John, not only witnessed Walter of Gant's 'foundation' charter, but also made gifts of their own.[96] Several other men of important local standing followed suit, and by 1135 the new house had attracted the support of a large body of Yorkshire magnates.[97]

The king and his ministers were also closely involved in the foundation of Nostell Priory *c.* 1114. The history of the foundation is not without its difficulties, but what appears to have happened is that a group of hermits established by Robert of Lacy at Nostell, and living under the rule of St Augustine, were discovered by chance by a royal chaplain and confessor to Henry I, either Ralph Adlave or Adelulf, the future prior of the house. With the backing of the king, Archbishop Thurstan and several other royal officials, who made a number of grants of land and churches to the hermits, the royal chaplain was able to transform the hermitage into a fully fledged and prosperous Augustinian priory.[98]

Although Henry I does not appear to have been directly involved in the foundation and initial endowment of the other religious houses established in Yorkshire in his reign, his influence may have been exercised through his officials, who were closely associated with all the new Augustinian and Cistercian houses. The most prominent among them was Archbishop Thurstan, who had served as a royal chaplain under both William Rufus and Henry I, and whose involvement went beyond the normal duties and concerns of a diocesan.[99] As we have seen, Thurstan was closely associated with the establishment of Nostell Priory, and his influence can be detected again in the foundation of Guisborough Priory in 1119. Guisborough was established by Robert I of Brus, a frequent attestor of royal charters, who had been granted the lordship of Skelton by Henry I; and it was established, according to the document purporting to be the foundation charter, 'with

---

[96] See *EYC*, II, nos. 1144, 1148, 1151–2; *Episcopal Acta*, no. 37 and note; *Regesta*, III, no. 120.　　[97] See *EYC*, II, nos. 1144, 1148.
[98] This account of the foundation is derived from Burton, 'Religious orders', 87–95; W. E. Wightman, 'Henry I and the foundation of Nostell Priory', *YAJ*, 41 (1963–6), 57–60; *idem*, *Lacy Family*, 61–3. See also Michelmore, 'Township gazetteer', 376. For the gifts of Henry I and Thurstan to the house, see *EYC*, III, no. 1428; *Episcopal Acta*, nos. 17, 53–5; Nicholl, *Thurstan*, 127–37; J. Wilson, 'Foundation of the Austin priories of Nostell and Scone', *SHR*, 7 (1910), 141–59; *VCH, Yorkshire*, III, 231; *Regesta*, II, nos. 1207, 1241, 1285–7, 1312, 1319–20, 1432, 1450, 1494, 1532, 1662.
[99] Nicholl, *Thurstan*, 127–37, 142–5, 192–212.

the counsel...of Pope Calixtus II and Archbishop Thurstan of York'[100] Thurstan later issued his own charter confirming the new foundation.[101] He also gave advice and support to the founders of, or issued confirmation charters for, the Augustinian houses of Embsay, Worksop, Kirkham and Drax, and the Cistercian house of Rievaulx, all of which were founded in the 1120s and 1130s.[102] In or around 1130 Thurstan was also responsible for founding the nunnery of St Clement's in York.[103] And when in 1132 a body of monks from the Benedictine abbey of St Mary's, York, were exiled from their community because of their desire to reform their house along Cistercian lines, the archbishop provided them with lands in Skeldale near Ripon to establish a community, which developed into the Cistercian abbey of Fountains.[104]

The secular officials of Henry I worked hand-in-hand with their ecclesiastical counterparts in fostering the emergence of the new religious houses in Yorkshire. Two key figures in the administration of the north provided sites for the foundation of daughter houses of Nostell. Nigel d'Aubigny gave land on the Isle of Axholme in Lincolnshire, and in or about 1122 Walter Espec founded Kirkham Priory in the East Riding of Yorkshire with the assistance of his uncle, William, a canon of Nostell, who became the first prior.[105] Subsequently, Kirkham also received support from the king, who issued charters granting confirmations, privileges and protection.[106] At about the same time as the foundation of Kirkham another Augustinian house was established at Embsay by William Meschin, lord of Skipton, and his wife Cecily of Rumilly.[107] Although holding no formal administrative office in the north, William Meschin was one of the chief beneficiaries of royal patronage in the region and a frequent courtier of Henry I.[108] The same was true of Geoffrey Fitz Pain, who may have founded the Augustinian priory of Warter in the

---

[100] *Cartularium de Gyseburne*, I, nos. 1–2. For the foundation and endowment of the house, see Burton, 'Religious orders', 97–100; *VCH, Yorkshire*, III, 208–9; King, 'Robert de Brus', 28–9.　　　[101] *Episcopal Acta*, no. 48, and see nos. 49–51.

[102] Nicholl, *Thurstan*, 128, 192; *EYC*, VI, no. 13; VII, no. 3; *Chronicles of the Reigns*, I, 50; *Cartularium de Rievalle*, no. 218.　　　[103] Burton, 'Religious orders', 243–4.

[104] *VCH, Yorkshire*, III, 134–5; Bethell, 'Fountains Abbey', 11–27; L. G. D. Baker, 'The foundation of Fountains Abbey', *Northern History*, 4 (1969), 29–43; *EYC*, I, nos. 61–2.

[105] *VCH, Yorkshire*, III, 219, 232; Nicholl, *Thurstan*, 135–7; *HRH*, 168; *Cartularium de Rievalle*, 159–61, 243–5, xx–xxii; Dickinson, *Austin Canons*, 123 and note 3.

[106] *Regesta*, II, nos. 1334, 1459.

[107] *VCH, Yorkshire*, III, 195; *HRH*, 152; Burton, 'Religious orders', 110–12.

[108] *Complete Peerage*, VII, 667, 774; *EYC*, VII, 4–6; *Regesta*, II, nos. 1196, 1389, 1449.

East Riding of Yorkshire *c.* 1132.[109] At about the same time Walter Espec founded the first Cistercian monastery in Yorkshire at Rievaulx.[110] Shortly afterwards his administrative partner, Eustace Fitz John, saved the abbey of Fountains from early extinction by the timely provision of food.[111]

The close involvement of, and cooperation between, Henry I and his officials in the expansion of religious houses in Yorkshire after 1113 does not in itself prove that this expansion was influenced partly by a political motive to consolidate Norman power in Yorkshire; but it does suggest that the existence of such a motive cannot be ruled out. There can be no doubt that the expansion owed a great deal to the personal influence of Archbishop Thurstan whose motives may have been primarily religious, and whose reliance on men like Nigel d'Aubigny, Eustace Fitz John and Walter Espec is hardly surprising given the fact that they had served with him at the royal court. However, Thurstan was not only a capable archbishop he was also a capable politician. This is illustrated most clearly during the reign of King Stephen when he negotiated truces with the king of Scotland and organised the defence of northern England against Scottish invasions. Thurstan should be viewed as one of the 'new men' established by Henry I in Yorkshire, whose duties included the consolidation of Norman authority in the region. We have seen in a previous chapter how this consolidation was achieved partly through the cooperation of these 'new men' in the conduct of administration and the implementation of justice. The fact that they were also cooperating in the promotion of monasticism suggests that this promotion was also directed, at least in part, towards the same objective.

---

[109] *VCH, Yorkshire*, III, 235; *HRH*, 188; N. Denholm-Young, 'The foundation of Warter Priory', *YAJ*, 31 (1934), 208–13; *EYC*, x, 3–4, 110–12. For an alternative view, see E. King, 'The parish of Warter and the castle of Galchlin', *YAJ*, 52 (1980), 50. For Geoffrey's receipt of lands from the king, see *Regesta*, II, no. 424; *EYC*, XI, 307; x, 107–12.

[110] *Cartularium de Rievalle*, 16–21; D. Baker, 'Patronage in the early twelfth-century church: Walter Espec, Kirkham and Rievaulx', in *Traditio – Krisis – Renovatio aus theologisher Sicht. Fetschrift Winfried Zeller*, ed. B. Jaspert and R. Mohr (Marburg, 1976), 92–100; *VCH, Yorkshire*, III, 149–50; *Episcopal Acta*, no. 59 and note.

[111] *Memorials of Fountains*, I, 55, 57.

CONCLUSION

This study of the pattern, scale and terms of settlement in Yorkshire in the half-century following the Domesday survey has illustrated that Norman domination lagged behind that achieved in counties further to the south. This is most apparent, perhaps, in the survival of larger numbers of Anglo-Scandinavian landholding families, the comparatively limited amount of military settlement and the retrograde nature of the terms on which knights' fees were held. On many estates the native peasants and lesser landholders must have found it very difficult to distinguish between the authority exercised by their new Norman lords, and that which had been imposed by their pre-conquest masters. On some lordships 'knight service' and socage were almost the same, and the pattern of pre-1066 subtenure survived the conquest and can be traced into the twelfth century. Moreover, it has been pointed out that early Yorkshire charters are 'shot through with Middle English, and to a less extent Scandinavian, words and usages, and ... demonstrate the stubborn persistence of numerous native personal names far into the thirteenth century'; and that,

Knight-service and feudal incidents, castleries and castle-guard had no impact, or only the most gradual of impacts, upon distinctive social customs such as the division of the rent-paying year at Whitsun and Martinmas, the reckoning of productive land by ploughgates and oxgangs ... and the functioning of pre-feudal shires with their ministerial class of thegns and drengs.[112]

But along with continuity we can also discern change, both in the terms and the pattern of tenure. The change in terms involved the introduction of the burden of ward service in the new castles which were under construction everywhere in Yorkshire. The change in pattern resulted from the dismemberment or agglomeration of many pre-conquest thanages to form composite post-conquest military tenancies bearing little, if any, resemblance to what had gone before; tenancies which continued to be transformed after 1086 as the Norman families sought to build up and round off their estates.

The degree of continuity and change, and the degree of Norman control, varied from region to region. The most striking contrast is that between the poorly settled Pennine areas and the

---

[112] Barrow, *Anglo-Norman Era*, 106.

lowlands. In the former, tenant estates were few and confined to the immediate vicinity of the castles. Enfeoffment here was largely a post-1135 phenomenon. It has been suggested that this may have been due in part to 'the looseness of agrarian organization in the Northern Danelaw where a lord could exploit his holdings far less thoroughly than in the manorialised districts to the south', but it was also due to the vulnerability of the frontiers of Yorkshire to attack.[113] Even on the eve of King Stephen's reign the Normans huddled inside the small motte and bailey fortress of Burton in Lonsdale were still living in fear of an invasion from the north. The Norman conception of the Pennines as a frontier region at this date is also clear from the arrangements for the provision of permanent ward at the castles of Skipton and Richmond.[114] In the lowland areas, by contrast, the considerable scale of enfeoffment, complex tenant estates distributed over wide areas, firmly established pattern of lineal land succession and progress towards rationalisation and subinfeudation indicate that the Normans were more secure. The basic structure of tenant enfeoffment was virtually complete in the lowlands by 1135 and, at least in respect of the military tenancies, there was to be very little new enfeoffment here after this date. As for the non-military tenancies the greatest impact can be seen in the foundation of nearly twenty new religious houses in Yorkshire. By 1135 many of these were firmly established, very wealthy and already engaged in the settlement of their own tenants. In many areas of the county they probably played a crucial role in bringing the local vills within the Norman system of administration. Surviving as they did in many cases until the Dissolution they, better than anything perhaps, represent the permanence of the Norman settlement. At the level of the lords' immediate tenants, the pattern of settlement that was to continue to dominate estate organisation and tenurial relations in lowland Yorkshire well into the thirteenth century had already been constructed by 1135. In the shaping of this pattern no force had a greater influence than the castles and monasteries.

---

[113] For the agrarian argument, see Hollister, *Military Organization*, 57.
[114] See above, pp. 132-3.

Chapter 4

THE REIGN OF STEPHEN[1]

For John Horace Round the civil war of Stephen's reign was characterised by an 'anarchic spirit'.[2] In recent years the focus of historical research on this anarchy has shifted away from local destruction and baronial attitudes to monarchical authority, to questions concerning the nature and degree of royal control over its own administration, and the objectives and ambitions of the magnates. The work has concentrated upon the retrospective evidence for waste and exchequer activity in the early pipe rolls of Henry II, the regulation of the coinage, the competition for service, the rationale behind the creation of the new earldoms and the nature of allegiance.[3] It is against this background that this chapter will examine the fate of royal administration and authority in Yorkshire during the nineteen long winters when Christ and his saints are supposed to have slept.

The debate concerning the considerable increase in the number of earldoms in Stephen's reign and the position of the men who held them provides a point of departure. Whereas Round saw the

---

[1] An abridged version of this chapter first appeared as an article entitled, 'William earl of York and royal authority in Yorkshire in the reign of Stephen', *Haskins Society Journal*, 2 (1990), 155–65.

[2] J. H. Round, *Geoffrey de Mandeville* (London, 1892), v.

[3] E. King, 'The anarchy of King Stephen's reign', *TRHS*, 5th ser., 34 (1984), 133–53; R. Eales, 'Local loyalties in Norman England: Kent in Stephen's reign', *ANS*, 8 (1986), 88–108; K. Yoshitake, 'The exchequer in the reign of Stephen', *EHR*, 103 (1988), 950–9; Warren, *Governance*, 89–103; P. Latimer, 'Grants of "totus comitatus" in twelfth-century England: their origins and meaning', *BIHR*, 59 (1986), 137–45; E. King, 'Waleran, count of Meulan, earl of Worcester (1104–1166)', in *Tradition and Change. Essays in Honour of Marjorie Chibnall*, ed. D. Greenway *et al.* (Cambridge, 1985), 165–81; P. Dalton, 'Aiming at the impossible: Ranulf II earl of Chester and Lincolnshire in the reign of King Stephen', in *The Earldom of Chester and its Charters: A Tribute to Geoffrey Barraclough*, ed. A. T. Thacker (Journal of the Chester Arch. Soc., 1991), 109–34; G. J. White, 'Were the midlands "wasted" during Stephen's reign?', *Midland History*, 10 (1985), 26–46; E. Amt, 'The meaning of waste in the early pipe rolls of Henry II', *EcHR*, 44 (1991), 240–8; J. A. Green, 'Financing Stephen's war', *ANS*, 14 (1992), 91–114; P. Dalton, '*In neutro latere*: the armed neutrality of Ranulf II earl of Chester in King Stephen's reign', *ANS*, 14 (1992), 39–59.

earldoms simply as honorific titles, for Professor Davis these titles incorporated a responsibility to govern and defend the counties to which they were attached.[4] Taking the Davis interpretation a stage further Professor Warren argues that the new earldoms reflect a deliberate policy of decentralisation, involving an upgrading in the power of earls and a transference of executive authority from the centre to the localities. This was not simply a practical response to the state of war but 'an alternative conception of government'.[5] Yorkshire provides an appropriate local background against which to test these general ideas. In 1138 Stephen made William le Gros, count of Aumale, earl of York as a reward for conspicuous service at the battle of the Standard.[6] The circumstances and timing of the promotion reveal the king's motives, and are examined in the opening section of the chapter. They illustrate that for the first two years of the reign, far from dismantling centralised royal government Stephen actually attempted to preserve the northern administrative system of Henry I. Only when faced with an imminent military and administrative crisis in 1138 did he place the secular government of the county in the hands of William of Aumale.

While it is beyond question that the administrative and military responsibilities of several of the men styled *comes* in Stephen's reign were of a greater scope and importance than those of the earls of the first three Norman kings, Dr White has argued that the link between comital title and administrative function was neither defined nor consistent, and Dr Latimer has drawn a sharp distinction between grants of earldoms and grants of *comitatus*, which he defines as the regalian rights within a county.[7] Although this definition is questionable, it is true that some of the earls of Stephen's reign appear to have been granted private control of regalian rights within particular counties, and that these rights were an important cornerstone of their local authority.[8] The next section of this chapter, therefore, sets out to consider the nature and extent of the administrative and territorial authority exercised

---

[4] Round, *Geoffrey de Mandeville*, 266–77; Davis, *King Stephen*, 125–8.
[5] Warren, *Governance*, 89–103, esp. 92–4.
[6] Symeon, *Opera*, II, 295; *Chronicles of the Reigns*, III, 165.
[7] G. J. White, 'The restoration of order in England, 1153–1165' (Univ. of Cambridge, PhD thesis, 1974), 160–3; Latimer, 'Totus comitatus', 137–45. The situation in Lincolnshire supports White's argument: Dalton, 'Ranulf of Chester', 111–13.
[8] For a criticism of Latimer's views, see Davis, *King Stephen*, 126 note 1. For an earl endowed with regalian rights, see King, 'Waleran of Meulan', 168–70.

by Earl William in Yorkshire. The evidence that he secured possession of the county town and castle, the royal mints and forests and a considerable number of the royal wapentakes and hundreds of Yorkshire indicates that William was not merely acting as the king's administrative agent in the county, but that he was exercising, and had probably been granted, private control of the regalian lands and rights within the county, almost certainly before his receipt of the comital title.

The alienation of regalian property and rights need not necessarily imply the disintegration of royal control. Theoretically at least, as long as the man holding the reins of power was capable and loyal there was no reason why the authority of the king should not be maintained. William earl of York has always been portrayed as just such a man, and it is this traditional picture which the next section of the chapter sets out to reexamine. In order to assess the manner in which William employed the power entrusted to him, and the impact of his actions upon royal control, the continuity and integrity of three institutions crucial to the local machinery of royal government are considered in turn: the royal demesne manors, the exchequer system and the coinage. In each case it is possible to detect a fundamental failure of central control.

William's lack of concern for the preservation of royal authority is also illustrated by his role in the internal political affairs of Yorkshire, and his relationship with his fellow nobles. The chapter moves on, therefore, to examine his involvement in several local conflicts, including the York election dispute. It reveals that, frequently in direct opposition to the interests of the king, he exploited his position in order to pursue an aggressive and acquisitive territorial policy directed chiefly towards the seizure of estates of key governmental, military and economic importance, and the domination of his aristocratic neighbours. Far from preserving law and order as an agent of royal government, William directly provoked many of the worst disorders in Yorkshire by his reckless pursuit of private ambitions.

Having dealt with the power of Earl William and several other greater Yorkshire nobles, the chapter will then move on to deal with the limitations of that power, with the ability of the lesser magnates to establish their independence from seignorial control and go their own way. This is illustrated through an examination of the careers of two tenants from the second rank of aristocratic society who took advantage of the opportunities provided by the competition for service in progress in Stephen's reign to advance their social and political standing, and to pursue private ambitions at the expense of their lords.

The disintegration of royal authority in Yorkshire, and the limitations of the seignorial authority which replaced it, supports the traditional interpretation of Stephen's reign as a period of anarchy. But it is an interpretation which must be qualified. The final section of the chapter illustrates some of the safety valves built into aristocratic society which prevented it from self-destruction. These were tenurial, familial and spiritual, and they are considered in turn. They were responsible for the peace treaty of 1153 and the restoration of royal authority under Henry II. In the final analysis, the aristocratic society of Yorkshire emerges as always anarchic, and yet ultimately always controlled.

THE ADMINISTRATION OF THE NORTH, 1136–38

King Stephen paid his first visit to York within two months of his coronation in London on 25 December 1135. The expedition was almost certainly a response to the Scottish invasion of Northumberland, which had been in progress since his accession. After a meeting with David of Scotland at Durham between the 5th and the 20th of February, and a further conference at Newcastle, Stephen came to York where he received the homage of Henry of Scotland in return for a grant of Doncaster, Carlisle, the honour of Huntingdon and a promise that if he decided to bestow the earldom of Northumbria upon anyone he would first consider the claims of Henry.[9]

There is evidence that while at York, Stephen attempted to secure the support of Archbishop Thurstan, Walter Espec and Eustace Fitz John, the principal surviving northern officials of Henry I, and that he did so with the aim of continuing Henry's northern administrative system. He confirmed the charters of the religious houses founded or endowed by these officials, each of whom came to his court either at York or shortly afterwards at the Easter festival held at Westminster.[10] The officials, who had cut their administrative teeth at the court of Henry I, were doubtless already familiar with Stephen, who had been one of Henry's

[9] Symeon, *Opera*, II, 287; *Chronicles of the Reigns*, III, 145–6.
[10] *Regesta*, III, nos. 46, 99, 335, 421–6 (possibly later than 1136), 716, 919, 944–8.

closest companions.[11] In the case of Thurstan the relationship was probably even closer owing to the friendship of the archbishop with Stephen's mother, Adela of Blois, who had offered him shelter during his exile from England in 1119.[12] The two men had also worked together in the foundation of Furness Abbey in 1127.[13] During Stephen's absence from England in 1137 the archbishop appears to have been entrusted with joint control of the government. Together with Roger bishop of Salisbury he presided over a council at Northampton attended by many bishops and nobles, was responsible for organising the military defence of the north against a threatened Scottish invasion and conducted truce negotiations with King David at Roxburgh.[14] In the following year Thurstan headed another council at Northampton which met in the wake of Stephen's unsuccessful campaign against the Scots in February, and was also to be instrumental in organising the northern army that defeated the Scots at the battle of the Standard in August.[15]

Initially Stephen was also able to count on the support of Walter Espec and Eustace Fitz John. Walter's castle at Wark stoutly resisted Scottish sieges, and in 1138 he served as one of the commanders of the English force at the battle of the Standard.[16] For his part, Eustace Fitz John probably held the royal castle of Bamburgh against the Scots in 1136, and appears to have been employed by Stephen in a judicial capacity.[17] The northern administrative continuity aimed at by the king is also reflected in the minting of royal coins. The traditional northern mints of Carlisle, Durham, Lincoln, Nottingham and York all produced coins of Stephen Type I, a regular issue of good workmanship and weight probably minted until c. 1142, and in many cases the coins were produced by the same moneyers at work under Henry I.[18]

[11] *Ibid.*, II, *passim.*   [12] Symeon, *Opera*, II, 303; Nicholl, *Thurstan*, 194–5.
[13] *Furness Coucher*, I, 122–4; Nicholl, *Thurstan*, 143–4.   [14] Nicholl, *Thurstan*, 218.
[15] *Ibid.*, 219; Symeon, *Opera*, II, 292–3; *Chronicles of the Reigns*, III, 160–1, 182.
[16] Florence, *Chronicon*, II, 105; Symeon, *Opera*, II, 289–94; *Chronicles of the Reigns*, III, 157, 185–9.
[17] Bamburgh resisted a Scottish attack in 1136: *Chronicles of the Reigns*, III, 145. Eustace was deprived of Bamburgh castle by Stephen in 1138: Symeon, *Opera*, II, 291. For a charter suggesting that Stephen employed Eustace as a justice early in his reign, see *Regesta*, III, no. 257.
[18] Brooke, *English Coins*, I, lxix, lxxv, civ–ccv, ccxviii–ccxxi, ccl–ccli; R. P. Mack, 'Stephen and the anarchy 1135–1154', *BNJ*, 35 (1966), 39–46; M. Blackburn, 'Coinage and currency under Stephen', in *The Anarchy of King Stephen's Reign*, ed. E. King (Oxford, forthcoming). See below, note 71.

Although the indications are that Stephen attempted to preserve the northern administration of Henry I, by the end of 1138 he was in danger of losing control of the north and could no longer rely upon the officials who made the administration work. His campaign against the Scots in Northumberland and the Scottish lowlands in February 1138 had failed to establish any permanent security for the north against future Scottish attacks, and left Yorkshire in the position of a military frontier region. It was during this campaign that Stephen deprived Eustace Fitz John of Bamburgh castle, an action which some historians have argued was responsible for the participation of Eustace on the Scots' side at the battle of the Standard later in the year.[19] There are indications, however, that Eustace was already in opposition, or at least suspected of being in opposition, to Stephen before the loss of Bamburgh. According to Ailred of Rievaulx, Eustace 'left the English king because he had been seized by him in court, contrary to ancestral custom, and had been forced to give back the castles which King Henry had entrusted to him'.[20] The reason for Stephen's arrest of Eustace prior to the seizure of the castles is probably provided by Richard of Hexham's statement that Eustace 'had long secretly favoured the king of Scotland'.[21]

Eustace was almost certainly concerned by Stephen's failure to provide security for his Northumberland barony centred upon the castle of Alnwick, which stretched across the Scottish invasion route between the Cheviot hills and the North Sea. King David had captured Alnwick in 1136 before surrendering it in the first treaty of Durham.[22] Eustace may have valued the barony more highly than his less extensive Yorkshire estates, and possibly offered his loyalty to the Scots, with whom he already had close relations, in order to provide for its safety.[23] His allegiance to Stephen may also have been undermined by the arrangements made by the king for the descent of the West Country possessions of his brother, Payn Fitz John, who died in 1137. In December 1137 Stephen gave Payn's estates, including all the *maritagium* and jurisdictional rights Payn had bestowed upon his daughter Cecily

[19] Symeon, *Opera*, II, 291; Young, *William Cumin*, 13.
[20] *Chronicles of the Reigns*, III, 191.   [21] *Ibid.*, 158.   [22] *Ibid.*, 145–6.
[23] Although Eustace held more estates in Yorkshire, a far greater proportion of them were held as subtenancies: Green, *Government*, 182, 252. In 1129–30 Eustace was pardoned 72s danegeld in Northumberland and only 60s in Yorkshire: *PR 31 Henry I*, 34–5. For his close relations with the Scots, see below, pp. 201, 207, 209–11.

from his wife's lordship of Weobley, to Cecily's husband, Roger
Fitz Miles, the future earl of Hereford.[24] There is evidence that
Payn's wife, Sibyl of Lacy, daughter and heiress of Hugh of Lacy,
resisted the transfer of the Lacy estates by trying to claim the
portion of her husband's fee acquired by means other than
inheritance.[25] Although Eustace Fitz John had no legal title to any
part of the Lacy lordship he, like many paternal uncles of heiresses,
may also have fostered some form of claim.[26]

Although Walter Espec remained loyal to Stephen until 1138
and fought for the king at the battle of the Standard, there are
indications that thereafter he too could no longer be relied upon.
Walter died in the mid-1150s, but was never to attest a charter of
Stephen after 1138. Like Eustace, Walter held lands in Yorkshire,
centred upon the castle of Helmsley, but his main possessions were
in Northumberland. The *caput* was Wark which had been taken
and restored by the Scots in 1136 and was captured again after a
long and bitter siege in November 1138. Walter's communication
in that year allowing the garrison to surrender probably signified
his abandonment of King Stephen.[27] He had good reason to resent
Stephen's failure to come to the aid of the valiant garrison of Wark
after the defeat of the Scots at the battle of the Standard, especially
as the commander of the garrison was his nephew, Jordan of
Bussey. The efforts of this garrison must have seemed wasted
when Stephen concluded the treaty of Durham in 1139, which
effectively abandoned Northumberland to the Scots.[28] There were
now sound tenurial motives for Walter to offer his allegiance to
the opponents of Stephen, especially since the authority of King
David and his son Henry in Northumberland was probably more
effective than that of Stephen in Yorkshire.[29] The transference of
Walter's loyalty must also have been encouraged by a friendship
with Robert of Gloucester and a long and close association with
the Scottish court.[30]

The most serious blow to the continuity of northern administration came with the demise of Archbishop Thurstan, who had

[24] *Regesta*, III, no. 312.   [25] *Ibid.*, no. 313.
[26] For the danger posed by paternal uncles to the succession of heiresses, see J. C. Holt,
'Feudal society and the family in early medieval England: III. Patronage and politics',
TRHS, 5th ser., 34 (1984), 19.
[27] *Chronicles of the Reigns*, III, 145–6, 157–8, 165–6, 170–2; Symeon, *Opera*, II, 291–2.
[28] Symeon, *Opera*, II, 300.   [29] See below, pp. 203–11.
[30] Walter borrowed a copy of Geoffrey of Monmouth's *Historia Regum* from Robert:
Vita Ailredi, lxxxviii. For Walter's connections with the Scots, see below, pp. 201–2.

occupied the archiepiscopal chair for over twenty years before Stephen's accession. Thurstan's importance as a focus of baronial loyalties and guardian of order and stability in the north can be witnessed in the events leading up to the battle of the Standard, in which he served temporarily to unify a northern magnate community rent by internal suspicions.[31] By 1138, however, he was already old and failing and had to be carried around on a litter.[32] He died in February 1140 only eighteen months after the battle of the Standard, and for John of Hexham his passing immediately presaged the disintegration of order in the north: 'After his death, forthwith sprang up the insolence and roving licence of unrestrained disputes, shameless contempt of the clergy, irreverence of the laity towards ecclesiastical laws and persons; the unity of the kingdom was destroyed, because each man's will was his law.'[33]

By 1138, therefore, the threat of Scottish invasion, together with the loss, or impending loss, of his principal northern officials, and his own personal preoccupation with events in the south, left Stephen with the problem of providing for the security of Yorkshire and filling an administrative vacuum. When viewed against this background, William of Aumale's rise to prominence in Yorkshire and receipt of the comital title in 1138 emerges as a response to an immediate military and administrative crisis, rather than a preconceived attempt to impose a new vision of decentralised government based upon the upgraded authority of earls.

THE AUTHORITY OF WILLIAM EARL OF YORK

In the years following 1138 Earl William was left much to his own devices. The king appears to have paid only two or three visits to Yorkshire in the period 1139–53.[34] Only seven extant royal charters relating to Yorkshire officials or property can definitely be ascribed to the same period.[35] Of these only two were addressed

---

[31] *Chronicles of the Reigns*, III, 160–5, 189; Symeon, *Opera*, II, 292–4.
[32] *Chronicles of the Reigns*, III, 161, 173; Symeon, *Opera*, II, 288, 292, 299.
[33] Symeon, *Opera*, II, 305.
[34] Stephen visited York in 1136, 1138(?), 1142(?), 1148, 1149 and 1154: *Regesta*, III, xxxix–xliv.
[35] *Ibid.*, nos. 109, 798, 982–4, 991–2. It is possible, however, that another forty royal charters connected with Yorkshire were issued in this period: *ibid.*, nos. 100–2, 107–8, 121–4, 307a, 336, 421–6, 428, 430, 604, 620–2, 624–5, 816, 943, 976–8, 980–1, 985–90, 994–5.

to a named official. In each case this was Earl William.[36] The absence of royal charters addressed to a named archbishop is to be expected in view of the York election dispute in progress from 1140 until 1151, during which the rival candidates were usually absent from York, but the lack of reference in these charters to named sheriffs and justices suggests that Earl William had either taken the place of these officials or had been established as their superior.[37] The latter possibility is supported by evidence that one of William's tenants, Robert of Octon, may have served as sheriff of Yorkshire for at least part of Stephen's reign.[38] Even if this is not the case, the details of the royal charters addressed directly to the earl of York in the anarchy tend to confirm the impression that after 1138 William was in charge of the royal government of the county.

Probably in 1146 Stephen addressed a charter to 'William count of Aumale and all his foresters of Yorkshire' granting estovers in the royal forest to St Peter's Hospital, York, and commanding that the brothers should not be disturbed.[39] The charter suggests that William had been given charge of the royal forests, and in the early years of Henry II's reign he was among a group of men, some of them described as foresters, who surrendered land within the royal forest and 'wastelands' around Pickering to Rievaulx Abbey at the instigation of the king.[40]

Of even greater significance is a charter indicating that William had been given control of the city and castle of York. In 1140 Stephen commanded 'William earl of York and all his barons and

---

[36] *Ibid.*, nos. 991–2. Of the forty additional charters which may have been issued in this period twenty-six were simply grants, confirmations and concessions. Only fourteen of the forty contained specific instructions. Of these fourteen, two were addressed to the earl of York, one to Count Alan (of Brittany), and two to Archbishop Thurstan and Ilbert II of Lacy: *ibid.*, nos. 101, 122, 124, 621–2.

[37] For the itinerary of the archbishops of York, see Symeon, *Opera*, II, 307, 311, 313, 317–20, 322, 325, 329; *Episcopal Acta*, xxxi.

[38] Robert is described as sheriff in the chronicle of Meaux Abbey, and can only have held the post at some point between 1130 and 1154. Robert's attachment to William is illustrated by a charter issued by the earl between 1130 and 1160 granting Robert all the land in the Holderness vill of Holmpton, and referring to him as William's man. It is possible, however, that Robert was the sheriff of Holderness rather than Yorkshire: Green, *Sheriffs*, 90, citing *Chronica de Melsa*, I, 102; Bodleian Library Dodsworth MS 20, fol. 133d, cited in B.A. English, 'The counts of Aumale and Holderness 1086–1260', (Univ. of St Andrews, PhD thesis, 1977), Appendix A, no. 11. Although it is possible that Bertram of Bulmer, who was sheriff of Yorkshire between 1128 and 1130, and appears as such again in 1155, remained in office throughout the anarchy, there is no direct evidence to confirm this. [39] *Regesta*, III, no. 992.

[40] *Cartularium de Rievalle*, 131–9; *EYC*, I, nos. 401–12 and notes.

burgesses of York' that the master of St Peter's Hospital York, his men and possessions should have the king's peace and not be impleaded concerning the lands he held in the time of King Henry I until the consecration of a new archbishop, when he was to answer according to the laws and customs of St Peter's church and the city of York.[41] The implication is that the earl was exercising within York the jurisdictional authority normally in the hands of the sheriff. If so he probably also enjoyed custody (perhaps even private possession) of York castle, the centre of city and county administration, which was usually in the sheriff's charge.[42] Further evidence is provided by the Anglo-Saxon chronicler's statement that Stephen 'entrusted York' to William, by the earl's powerful influence in the city during the York archiepiscopal election dispute when he sat 'as the representative of the king' in the chapter house and commanded the election of the royal candidate, and by his implication in the exclusion of Henry Murdac from York in 1148.[43]

William was probably also in control of the royal mints of York, which were almost certainly situated in the castle.[44] In or around 1150 he gave the vill of Bonwick in Holderness to Thomas Fitz Ulvieth, sometime alderman of the Merchants' Guild of York, whose father was one of the hereditary lawmen of the city and can probably be identified with the moneyer Ulf who minted coins of both Henry I and Stephen Type I at York.[45] Thomas was almost certainly the 'Thomas filius Ulf' whose name appears on the reverse of a coin of Eustace Fitz John dating from Stephen's reign which, along with a coin of Robert III of Stuteville of similar style, has been ascribed to a mint at York. Although Mr Seaby has argued that these coins may have been issued in Flanders by Eustace, count of Boulogne, and Robert le Roux, lord of Béthune, the connection of Thomas Fitz Ulvieth with York, the EBORACI inscription on one of the 'Eustace' coins and the IOANIS inscription

---

[41] *Regesta*, III, no. 991.

[42] *VCH, City of York*, 29–31, 522–3. In early Norman times the administrative centre of the county was the King's Tofts or Houses on Toft Green in York: *EYC*, I, 405–7, nos. 525–6; D. M. Palliser, 'York's west bank: medieval suburb or urban nucleus?', in *Archaeological Papers from York Presented to M. W. Barley*, ed. P. V. Addyman and V. E. Black (York, 1984), 103, 108 note 2.

[43] *ASC*, s.a. 1138; Symeon, *Opera*, II, 307, 313, 322.

[44] *VCH, City of York*, 30, 522.

[45] C. T. Clay, 'A Holderness charter of William count of Aumale', *YAJ*, 39 (1956–8), 339–42; *PR 31 Henry I*, 34. For Ulf the moneyer, see Brooke, *English Coins*, I, ccli; II, 356; Mack, 'Anarchy', 45.

on another must place them firmly in Yorkshire.[46] It can be no coincidence that both Eustace Fitz John and Robert III of Stuteville came to be closely associated with the earl of York in Stephen's reign, and it is to his Flemish connections, or perhaps to his employment of Flemish mercenaries, that we should attribute the unusual continental style of the coins.[47]

The evidence points to the conclusion that Earl William had been entrusted with supreme administrative authority in Yorkshire, but it also suggests that he had been granted private control of regalian rights such as the minting of coins. It is possible that at least a part of this authority may have been bestowed upon him prior to his receipt of the comital title. The Anglo-Saxon chronicler indicates that William had already been entrusted with York *before* the battle of the Standard and the grant of the earldom, though in exactly what capacity is unknown.[48] It is likely that this occurred when Stephen returned from his unsuccessful Scottish campaign in February 1138. The impression that William's administrative authority and regalian rights were somehow distinct from his comital title is strengthened by the reference to him as count of Aumale rather than earl of York in Stephen's charter concerning the management of the royal forests. In the royal writs addressed to or witnessed by William in the period 1138–53, and in William's private charters, the style 'count of Aumale' was more frequently employed than 'earl of York'.[49]

---

[46] P. J. Seaby, 'A new "standard" type for the reign of King Stephen', *BNJ*, 53 (1983), 14–18; *idem*, 'Some coins of Stephen and Eustace and related issues of Western Flanders', in *Coinage of the Low Countries (880–1500)*, ed. N. J. Mayhew (Brit. Arch. Soc. int. ser., 54, 1979), 49–53; *idem*, 'Of seals and sceptres: King Stephen and the advocate of St Vaast's', in *Numismatics-Witness to History: Articles by Members of the IAPN to Commemorate its 35th Anniversary*, ed. R. Margolis and H. Voegtli (Int. Assoc. of Professional Numismatists Publication, 8, 1986), 141–52. For the attribution of the coins to York see North, *Hammered Coinage*, I, 171–2; Mack, 'Anarchy', 80–4; Brooke, *English Coins*, I, 93–4, 158; Blackburn, 'Coinage'.

[47] For the links between Eustace Fitz John, Robert of Stuteville and Earl William, see below, pp. 179–81. For the Flemish connections of William, see English, *Holderness*, 6–7, 137; A. Giry, *Histoire de la Ville de Saint-Omer* (1877), chart. III, pp. 371–5. I owe the latter reference to Peter Seaby. With regard to the style of the York coins, another possibility is that it was influenced by the Flemish merchant community at York.

[48] We do not know whether the chronicler was referring to the city, the castle or both. Moreover, if it was the castle we do not know whether Stephen permitted William to defend it with his own troops, or merely conferred the constableship of a royal garrison.

[49] Of the fifteen royal charters seven use the continental title, and six use the English title. One describes William simply as 'earl', and one simply as 'of Aumale' although listing him with other earls: *Regesta*, III, nos. 16, 100–1, 124, 272, 276, 402, 437, 638, 803, 814,

When the inevitable confrontation between Henry II and William over the extent of the earl's power eventually came, it is clear that the point at issue was not the comital title but William's possession of regalian properties. Besides York and the royal forests the most important of these properties were the royal hundredal/wapentake or soke manors and castles which were the key to local military, jurisdictional and economic power in this period.[50] According to William of Newburgh, when Henry II went to Yorkshire in the early months of 1155 during a tour to recover the royal demesne alienated by Stephen, William of Aumale, 'Hesitating a long while, and boiling with indignation, at last, though sorely hurt, submitted to his power and very reluctantly resigned whatever of the royal domains he had possessed for many years, more especially that celebrated and noble castle of Scarborough.'[51] Although Earl William built the castle, Scarborough itself was almost certainly attached to the adjacent royal demesne manor of Falsgrave, one of the two major royal soke manors in the wapentake of *Dic*, and probably the focus of a hundred (Map 24).[52] The other was at Pickering, the site of a royal castle which may have fallen under William's control in Stephen's reign, and was probably the seat of the wapentake

921, 981, 991–2. For the private charters dating from Stephen's reign, see *EYC*, III, nos. 1305–6, 1313–14, 1379–81; Clay, 'A Holderness charter', 339–42; *Registrum Antiquissimum*, III, no. 1018. That William attached relatively little importance to his English title is also reflected by the fact that he was prepared to sanction the compromise of 1153, even though the treaty document appears to spell the end of the earldom of York: *Regesta*, III, no. 272. Several of the witnesses are individually styled as earl of a particular county or county town. Although other witnesses, including William, are not ascribed the individual style *comes* they are linked with the county or county town from which they are known to have derived their comital title, and are listed collectively as earls. William is styled 'of Aumale' rather than 'of York'. Although William is not known to have used the title 'count of Aumale' until after the grant of his English earldom, his father, Stephen, employed it in the reign of Henry I. See G. H. White, 'King Stephen's earldoms', *TRHS*, 4th ser., 13 (1930), 60 and note; *Complete Peerage*, I, 352–3; English, *Holderness*, 14–19, 55 note 7; *Regesta*, II, no. 1427; *EYC*, III, nos. 1304, 1318, 1326.

50 For the importance of hundredal manors, see Harvey, 'Demesne agriculture', 45–72; Sawyer, 'The royal *Tun*', 280–3; King, 'Anarchy', 133–53. For the importance of soke courts, see D. R. Roffe, 'The Descriptio Terrarum of Peterborough Abbey', *Historical Research*, 65 (1992), 1–16; *idem*, 'The origins of Derbyshire', *Derbyshire Arch. Journal*, 106 (1986), 106, 110–15.   51 *Chronicles of the Reigns*, I, 103–4.

52 For the earl's construction of Scarborough castle, see *Curia Regis Rolls*, 16 vols. (London, 1922–, in progress), XVI, 491. I am grateful to Dr David Crouch for supplying this reference. For the location of the administrative centres of the wapentakes and hundreds of Yorkshire, see Chapter 2 note 24.

court.[53] Pickering and Falsgrave were also the principal administrative centres of the great royal forest of Pickering that covered almost the entire wapentake.[54] When viewed against the background of the royal charters addressed to Earl William, one of them concerning the royal forests, his possession of Falsgrave and (?)Pickering can only confirm that he had been granted supreme administrative authority within the county.

With the exception of Pocklington and Kilham, the history of which is obscure, and Tickhill, which was in the hands of William de Clerfeith, William earl of York secured possession of all the major royal wapentake, hundredal and soke manors in Yorkshire in Stephen's reign (Map 24).[55] In the East Riding his possession of Warter has been illustrated by Professor King, and the pipe rolls indicate that the manor and castle of Driffield remained in his possession until his death in 1179.[56] He almost certainly also held the great soke manors of Aldborough and Knaresborough, which were probably the jurisdictional centres of Burghshire wapentake in the West Riding. In 1130 these manors, together with the castle of Knaresborough, were in the custody of Eustace Fitz John, but a charter of Henry II dating from after 1157 indicates that they were probably subsequently under the control of Earl William.[57]

---

[53] English, *Holderness*, 19, 23. Dr English is not completely convinced that William held Pickering castle (personal correspondence). William's control of Pickering might explain the fact that both he and his tenant, Robert of Ros, held interests in the royal forests and 'wasteland' below the manor: see above, p. 153; *Cartularium de Rievalle*, 131, 133–4.

[54] M. L. Bazeley, 'The extent of the English forest in the thirteenth century', *TRHS*, 4th ser., 4 (1921), 140–72; C. R. Young, *The Royal Forests of Medieval England* (Leicester, 1979), 15, 20, 62. For the royal forest of Scarborough, see *PR 18 Henry II*, 56; *PR 19 Henry II*, 4.

[55] It is interesting that in 1241 William II de Forz, count of Aumale, held the manor of Pocklington at farm for £30 a year: R. Stewart-Brown, 'The end of the Norman earldom of Chester', *EHR*, 35 (1920), 44, 54. For the descent of the castle and honour of Tickhill, see J. C. Holt, 'Politics and property in early medieval England', *Past & Present*, 57 (1972), 52; *Regesta*, III, nos. 178, 180; Symeon, *Opera*, II, 308; *VCH*, *Yorkshire*, II, 166–7; Chibnall, 'Robert of Bellême', 151–6. Many of the great soke manors in the royal demesne in 1086 were alienated to magnates in the following half century. See *DB*, I, 299a–300a; *EYC*, II, 16–19, 114, 271, 431, nos. 677, 927, 1135 and notes; VIII, 178–9; IX, 28; X, 14; XI, 307; *VCH*, *East Riding*, II, 106; Green, 'Royal demesne', 340–1, 344, 348; *YMF*, II, 80–2.

[56] King, 'Parish of Warter', 49–54. The manor of Driffield is included among the *terris datis* next to the name of the count of Aumale in the pipe rolls from 1155 until William's death in 1179. For Driffield castle, see *Historians of York*, I, 307.

[57] *PR 31 Henry I*, 24, 31. Henry II's charter confirms the estates of Eustace to his son, William of Vescy, and includes land in the vills of Nidd, Killinghall, Newton, Hewick and Westwick held of the count of Aumale: Public Record Office, Chancery Miscellanea C 47/9/5, printed as an appendix to Hartshorne, *History of Northumberland*.

THE FATE OF ROYAL AUTHORITY IN YORKSHIRE: I. THE
CONTROL OF THE ADMINISTRATION

The earl of York had been established as the head of royal
administration in Yorkshire, and he had secured possession of
almost all the royal hundredal, wapentake and soke manors which
were key centres of power in the localities. The crucial question is
how far this elevation of his authority undermined royal control
over the administration of Yorkshire, and royal authority within
the county generally. One measure of this is to examine the
continuity and integrity of three principal administrative institutions through which the king exercised authority within the
localities: the royal demesne manors, the exchequer system and
the coinage.

The interpretation of William's acquisition of nearly all the
major royal demesne estates depends on whether this acquisition
had taken place by royal grant or by illegal seizure. The list of *terris
datis* in Yorkshire in the very early pipe rolls of Henry II's reign
comprises only the manors of Kilham and Driffield, of which the
former estate had been granted by Henry II to the archbishop of
Rouen in 1155.[58] But this does not necessarily mean that all the
other royal manors held by Earl William had been acquired by
encroachment. The pipe rolls do not reveal the true extent of
demesne alienation. White has illustrated that many royal manors
granted out by Stephen were not entered as *terris datis* and remain
hidden in the exchequer accounts.[59] It is possible that others were
recovered before the production of pipe rolls during the royal tour
of 1155. This may have been the case with Scarborough and
Pickering in Yorkshire. Although later pipe rolls incorporating
lists of purprestures suggest that some royal land in Yorkshire had
been seized in Stephen's reign, the only estate known to have been
held by Earl William to be included in this list was the manor of
Warter; and even in this case there is evidence that an alienation
viewed by Henry II as illegal had been considered by Stephen to

All of the vills were situated within a few miles of Knaresborough or Aldborough and,
with the exception of Newton, all were included in the purpresture lists of Henry II's
pipe rolls. See, for example, *PR 11 Henry II*, 51. It is significant that the vills of
Ouseburn, Timble, Stainley and Cattal, which were jurisdictionally attached to either
Knaresborough or Aldborough in 1086, were also included in the lists. See *DB*, 1,
299b–300a, 301b, 329b. Eustace Fitz John was almost certainly deprived of the manors
for supporting the Scots. For the forest of Knaresborough, see *PR 14 Henry II*, 90.
[58] *PR 2–4 Henry II*, 26, 86.   [59] White, 'Restoration of order', 228–9.

be legitimate.[60] Stephen's acceptance of William's possession of
the manor of Warter before 1154 is clear from the terms of two
royal charters which recognise the title of William's sister, Agnes,
to whom the earl appears to have granted the estate as a
maritagium.[61] When viewed in conjunction with the evidence that
William had been entrusted with charge of the royal administration in Yorkshire, which must have involved the management
of the king's demesne, the royal charters concerning Warter
strongly suggest that all the demesne held by the earl of York in
Stephen's reign had passed to him by royal grant rather than
seizure.

The fate of the exchequer in Stephen's reign is a matter of
debate. Mr Yoshitake has argued that (although retrograde)
exchequer practice probably continued in Stephen's reign in a
group of counties in eastern England, including Yorkshire.[62] The
crux of his case is the payment of the county farms in blanch in the
early pipe rolls of Henry II's reign, which he regards as an
indication of payment during the anarchy. As Dr Green has
pointed out, however, 'It seems more likely ... that it took the
exchequer a few years to enforce blanch payment generally.'[63]
Yorkshire was one of those counties which accounted for only
three-quarters of the financial year 1154–5, which some historians
regard as a sign of financial disorder.[64] Furthermore, the figure for
the sheriff's farm in the first full year account of 1155–6
corresponds closely to that recorded in the 1129–30 pipe roll, and
suggests that whereas Henry II was able to raise the farms of several
counties early in his reign, in Yorkshire his exchequer may have
been forced by the disintegration of normal accounting procedure
to rely on the assessment figures of his grandfather.[65]

[60] *PR 11 Henry II*, 51–2.
[61] *Regesta*, III, nos. 101, 583. The estate at Beverley mentioned in the first charter was
attached to Warter. See also *EYC*, III, nos. 1384, 1388; King, 'Parish of Warter', 51.
[62] Yoshitake, 'Exchequer', 950–9, esp. 952 note 2.
[63] Green, 'Financing Stephen's war', 103.
[64] *Red Book*, II, 652. Yoshitake argues that a shorter term of account need not imply a
breakdown of exchequer practice because the sums owed to the king for the remainder
of the year could have been paid into the chamber, for which no accounts survive.
Alternatively, the sheriff may have been changed at some point during the exchequer
year, and the part of the farm due from him paid then: 'Exchequer', 951–2. However,
the first of these propositions is weakened by the fact that several such payments to the
chamber, including one example from Yorkshire itself, were duly noted in the pipe
rolls and included in the total sums. The second proposition cannot apply to Yorkshire.
See *PR 2–4 Henry II*, 146.
[65] *PR 2–4 Henry II*, 26; *PR 31 Henry I*, 24; White, 'Restoration of order', 236–46, 220–3.

The disintegration of exchequer practice which may have occurred in Yorkshire during Stephen's reign need not necessarily reflect a breakdown of royal financial government within the county. It is very likely, as Green has argued, that Stephen introduced an 'alternative arrangement' in the financial system, which involved 'using different channels between the localities and the itinerant household'; an arrangement in which the many new earls entrusted with county administration and defence may have played a prominent role, passing on some revenues to Stephen and siphoning off others 'in recompense for their expenditure on the king's behalf'.[66] In Yorkshire it is possible that a charter of Earl William provides a glimpse of this alternative arrangement in operation. The charter was issued between 1138 and 1142 and commands that, 'vicecomiti meo, quicumque vicecomitatum teneat, quod annuatim, omni occasione postposita, sicut me timet et diligit, ad festum Sancti Michaelis illam marcam reddat apud Eboracum'.[67]

We must be wary, therefore, of regarding the alienation of royal demesne in Stephen's reign and the breakdown of exchequer procedure as evidence in itself of a loss of royal control over local administration. What appears to have happened is that King Stephen introduced a different system of local administration organised around, and headed by, the powerful earl of York. If the comparatively low level of danegeld written off as waste in Yorkshire in the early pipe rolls of Henry II's reign is anything to go by, it was a system which may have operated with a certain amount of efficiency.[68] But it was also a system with an important weakness. So long as the earl was loyal to Stephen royal authority was secure, but if the earl decided to go his own way the consequences for this authority were potentially disastrous.

As the head of the senior line of the House of Blois, to the junior line of which Stephen belonged, Earl William was a relative of the king and has traditionally been portrayed as a consistent supporter

[66] Green, 'Financing Stephen's war', 91–114, quotations from pp. 113–14, 102.
[67] *EYC*, III, no. 1313. It should be noted, however, that the sheriff referred to could be the sheriff of Holderness.
[68] In 1155–6 the sheriff paid £124 10s 10d from the levy of danegeld; £10 19s 4d was pardoned; £18 17s 7d was owing; and £11 20d was waste: *PR 2–4 Henry II*, 27. See also *ibid.*, 86. The most recent interpretation of waste concludes that it indicates disputes over tax liability, the effects of war (either direct or indirect) and possibly pardons and out-of-date information about tax liability: Green, 'Financing Stephen's war', 104 and note 99. For the case for war damage, see Amt, 'Meaning of waste', 240–8.

of Stephen throughout the succession crisis.[69] It is a portrait which is difficult to reconcile with Stephen's need to tax the citizens of York and Beverley in 1149 (an action which suggests a breakdown of the alternative financial system operated by the earl), and with the numismatic evidence from Yorkshire.[70] Although coins of Stephen Type I were struck at York until *c.* 1142, thereafter the minting of regular royal coinage of good weight in the city appears to have ceased until the issue of coins of Stephen Type VII between 1153 and 1158.[71] No coins of the substantive Types II and VI, nor of the local variant Types III, IV and V, can be attributed with certainty to the city.[72] The only other coins minted at York were those irregular issues of low weight and unusual Flemish style bearing the names of King Stephen, Eustace Fitz John, Robert III of Stuteville, Bishop Henry and the moneyer Thomas Fitz Ulvieth. Although usually attributed, on the grounds of their similarity to coins of Stephen Type I, to the period 1135-*c.* 1141 or to that of Stephen's imprisonment, some of the coins were probably issued at the direction of Earl William, who had close associations with Fitz John, Stuteville and Fitz Ulvieth, and should be correctly dated *c.* 1142 × *c.* 1150.[73] The only coin probably issued by someone other than William was that bearing the inscription HENRICUS EPS (or EPC). This coin was almost certainly issued from the archiepiscopal mint, and may refer either to Henry bishop of Winchester, who had a close relationship with both Archbishop William and the treasurer of York, Hugh du Puiset, or to Henry Murdac.[74] Whatever the

---

[69] White, 'Stephen's earldoms', 52; English, *Holderness*, 17, 20–1; Davis, *King Stephen*, 132; Green, 'Financing Stephen's war', 94.

[70] For the taxation of York and Beverley, see Symeon, *Opera*, II, 323–4.

[71] North, *Hammered Coinage*, I, 164–6. Seaman's argument that Type I coins were issued until *c.* 1150 was rejected by Miss M. Archibald. See R. J. Seaman, 'A re-examination of some hoards containing coins of Stephen', *BNJ*, 48 (1978), 58–72; M. M. Archibald, 'Dating Stephen's first type', *BNJ*, 61 (1992), 9–21.

[72] Mack, 'Anarchy', 48–58. The one exception may be a single coin which has been described as a 'variety' of Type VI: North, *Hammered Coinage*, I, 164.

[73] For these coins, see Mack, 'Anarchy', 72–85; North *Hammered Coinage*, I, 171–2.

[74] North, *Hammered Coinage*, I, 172, no. 934. Bishop Henry was related to William, supported his candidacy for the archbishopric, consecrated him in 1143 and offered him shelter after his deposition in 1147: Symeon, *Opera*, II, 315, 320. Hugh du Puiset was a nephew of Bishop Henry and had been promoted by Archbishop William to the treasurership *c.* 1143. While Henry was away at the papal court, Hugh defended his castle of Winchester: Symeon, *Opera*, II, 321–2. For Puiset and his family, see C. T. Clay, 'The early treasurers of York', *YAJ*, 35 (1940–3), 10–11. For the attribution of the coin to Henry Murdac, see Blackburn, 'Coinage'.

origins of the coin, there is no doubt that along with the 'Eustace' and 'Robert' coins it represents a serious deterioration of royal control over the administration of Yorkshire after 1138.

THE FATE OF ROYAL AUTHORITY IN YORKSHIRE: II.
POLITICS AND WARFARE

If the numismatic evidence illustrates that Earl William exploited his power to exercise royal authority in order to serve his own interests rather than those of the king, this is also reflected by his role in the internal politics of the county. His ambitions extended far beyond the confines of Holderness and the royal manors under his charge. They were largely directed towards the construction of a vast network of territorial and jurisdictional influence, based largely upon the acquisition of yet more wapentakes and hundreds, and were often pursued against the interests of the king. They provoked a series of local wars throughout the 1140s that reduced large sections of the county to a state of disorder. And they reveal William not as an advocate of royal justice enforcing the king's peace, but as an acquisitive and aggressive magnate whose primary concern was the pursuit of his own ends. In the face of his policy and its results royal authority and local order could only degenerate.

The independent line adopted by the earl can be seen in his efforts to secure control of the East Riding hundreds of *Turbar* and Hunthow, which were in the possession of the Gant family (Map 24). The policy lies behind, and makes sense of, a series of hostilities in progress in the region in the early 1140s. John of Hexham informs us that in 1140 Alan of Richmond, 'in a stealthy night attack, scaling the wall, stormed with his men the fortress of Galclint and seized the castle, having driven out William de *Albanih* with his men'.[75] In the following year Alan himself was obliged to surrender the castle after being captured, imprisoned and forced to do homage by Ranulf earl of Chester.[76] In 1142 Alan's hostilities were directed against the earl of York, and Stephen was forced to come north to put an end to a war that had broken out between them.[77] Finally, in 1143 the earl of York, 'troubled by the hostility of Ranulf earl of Chester and Gilbert of

---

[75] Symeon, *Opera*, II, 306. [76] *Ibid.*, 308–9; *Gesta Stephani*, 116.
[77] Symeon, *Opera*, II, 312.

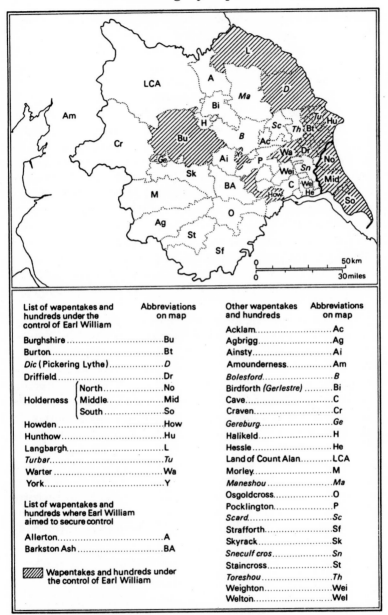

List of wapentakes and hundreds under the control of Earl William	Abbreviations on map
Burghshire	Bu
Burton	Bt
Dic (Pickering Lythe)	*D*
Driffield	Dr
Holderness { North	No
Holderness { Middle	Mid
Holderness { South	So
Howden	How
Hunthow	Hu
Langbargh	L
Turbar	*Tu*
Warter	Wa
York	Y

List of wapentakes and hundreds where Earl William aimed to secure control

Allerton	A
Barkston Ash	BA

▨ Wapentakes and hundreds under the control of Earl William

Other wapentakes and hundreds	Abbreviations on map
Acklam	Ac
Agbrigg	Ag
Ainsty	Ai
Amounderness	Am
Bolesford	*B*
Birdforth *(Gerlestre)*	Bi
Cave	C
Craven	Cr
Gereburg	*Ge*
Halikeld	H
Hessle	He
Land of Count Alan	LCA
Morley	M
Maneshou	*Ma*
Osgoldcross	O
Pocklington	P
Scard	*Sc*
Strafforth	Sf
Skyrack	Sk
Sneculf cros	*Sn*
Staincross	St
Toreshou	*Th*
Weighton	Wei
Welton	Wel

Map 24   William earl of York and the hundreds of Yorkshire

Source: based on *Domesday Book: Yorkshire*, ed. M.L. Faull and M. Stinson (Chichester, 1986), Map 1.

Gant converted the monastery of St Mary of Bridlington into a castle'.[78] The key to understanding this series of events, and Earl William's involvement in them, is provided by the identity of the mysterious castle of Galclint, which has long remained in doubt, and of the William 'de Albanih' who held it.

Galclint has been variously identified as Lincoln, Gilling in Ryedale in the North Riding of Yorkshire, Gaultney Wood in Rushton in Northamptonshire, Belvoir and Gildersdale in Warter in the East Riding of Yorkshire.[79] The arguments in each case are far from conclusive, and are outweighed by the evidence of a charter of 1172 linking Galclint with the parish of Willerby in the East Riding of Yorkshire.[80] William d'Aubigny *Brito*, who is always assumed to be the 'de Albanih' of John of Hexham, held no estates there. It seems certain that John wrote 'de Albanih' in error for 'de Albamarla', the continental toponymic surname of William earl of York, and that the struggle for control of Galclint in 1140 and 1141 was closely connected with William's war with Alan of Richmond in 1142 and his fortification of Bridlington a year later.[81]

In terms of both seignorial geography and genealogy Willerby ties in neatly with the series of hostilities described by John of Hexham. The vill belonged to the Gant family and was situated only five miles west of their castle and soke manor of Hunmanby, the probable administrative centre of *Turbar* hundred. Bordering *Turbar* to the east was Hunthow hundred centred upon the borough and soke centre of Bridlington, the major portion of which was held of the Gant family by the canons of the Augustinian priory founded there by Walter of Gant in *c.* 1113.[82] The earl of York also held important estates in the area. As well as his family lands in Holderness, to which the Gants may have fostered a claim, and an interest in Bridlington, he had secured control of the royal demesne manors and castles of Driffield, Scarborough and possibly Pickering.[83] The lord of Richmond's

[78] *Ibid.*, 315.
[79] *Priory of Hexham*, I, 132 note h; Symeon, *Opera*, II, 306 note a; *EYC*, IV, 90 note 1; Davis, *King Stephen*, 47 and note 10; King, 'Parish of Warter', 55–8.
[80] *EYC*, II, no. 1228.
[81] The same error regarding the count of Aumale's toponymic surname was made by a copyist of Stephen's Oxford charter of liberties for the church: *Regesta*, III, no. 271 and note. [82] *EYC*, II, no. 1135 and note.
[83] For a possible family relationship between the Gant family and Drogo de la Beuvrière, one of Earl William's predecessors in Holderness, see A. S. Ellis, 'Biographical notes on

interest derived from the fact that he was Gilbert of Gant's uncle and was doubtless concerned with the descent and security of the Gant honour after the death of Walter of Gant, Gilbert's father, in 1139. Through the marriage of Walter to Alan's sister the Gants had acquired important estates in Swaledale at the heart of the lordship of Richmondshire, and the lords of Richmond may have secured part of Hunmanby in return.[84] Gilbert of Gant was a minor when his father died, and is still referred to as a youth when fighting for King Stephen at the battle of Lincoln in 1141. When the young man was captured in battle by Ranulf earl of Chester and forced to marry the earl's niece, Rohese of Clare, William earl of York and Alan of Richmond had good cause for concern.[85]

When set against this background there is little doubt that the series of wars described by John of Hexham reflect the earls of York, Richmond and Chester competing for custody of the Gant honour during Gilbert's minority. All three must have been aware that the key to success was control of the hundredal and soke centres of Bridlington and Hunmanby. Topographical evidence indicates that Galclint castle was constructed for the purpose of controlling the communication routes to Hunmanby, and that it may have been a siege castle.[86] In the case of Bridlington the earl of York was more successful and built his castle in the Gant hundredal centre itself. What is most significant is that the earl's actions did not have the support of the king. A royal writ addressed to William commands him to let the canons of Bridlington have the port in peace.[87]

The hostilities in progress in the Willerby region may also have

---

the Yorkshire tenants named in Domesday Book', *YAJ*, 4 (1877), 216. For the Aumale tenurial interest in Bridlington, see *EYC*, II, 136, and no. 806; *Regesta*, II, no. 1333.

[84] *EYC*, II, 432; IV, 89; V, 340–7, no. 390; *Rotuli Litterarum Clausarum in Turri Londinensi asservati*, ed. T. D. Hardy, 2 vols. (Record Commission, 1833–44), I, 215b; *EYC*, V, 42.

[85] Symeon, *Opera*, II, 308.

[86] Earthworks illustrated on Ordnance Survey six-inch maps indicate two possible sites for the castle. The first is close to the junction of the modern B1249 with the A1039 from Malton to Filey, along a ridge of high ground extending west–east parallel to the A road. Philologically the word 'clint' can be equated with a rocky promontory, and therefore the location seems appropriate. The only problem is that it is some distance from the boundary of the parish of Wold Newton which incorporates the vill of Fordon, towards the 'outer bounds' of which vill Galclint is stated to have been situated. The second possible site is 'Castle Hill' at the junction of the A1039 and the road branching off into Hunmanby, on high ground known as 'White Gate Hill'. The difficulty here is that the site lies in the parish of Folkton and is at some distance from what might be construed as the 'outer bounds' of Fordon.

[87] *Regesta*, III, no. 124.

involved a struggle for control of the Brus hundred of Burton Agnes, which bordered those of *Turbar* and Hunthow (Map 24). The death of Adam I of Brus and succession of his infant son, Adam II, coincided with the earl of York's fortification of Bridlington in 1143.[88] William secured custody of the young heir and exploited his position by marrying Adam to his sister, Agnes, and detaching a number of Brus possessions from the young man's interest.[89] These included the hundredal and soke manor of Burton Agnes, which the earl appears to have granted to a minor branch of the Stuteville family as if it were of his own possession; the castle of Danby, one of the highly valuable forest and jurisdictional centres of Langbargh wapentake; a cluster of estates within the vicinity of Pickering; the manor of Loftus; and the churches (and possibly the manors) of Skelton, Kirklevington and Yarm.[90] His actions can only have alarmed Alan of Richmond, who was related to Adam II of Brus and held lands within or close to many of the areas dominated by Brus property, and affronted the earl of Chester, who held lordship over Adam II of Brus in certain Cleveland estates. Here again the earls of York, Richmond and Chester may have been competing for custodianship and control of a wealthy young ward.[91]

The competition between the earl of York and Alan of Richmond may also have resulted from a recognition by Stephen of the independent status of Richmondshire, a region which was probably already a liberty outside the jurisdiction of the sheriff of Yorkshire at the time of Domesday Book.[92] Such a recognition is

---

[88] *EYC*, II, 12.

[89] Adam II of Brus witnessed a charter of the earl issued *c.* 1150, another issued 1154 × *c.* 1168 and a third issued 1150 × 1167: *EYC*, III, nos. 1334, 1373, 1379. It is not completely certain that Adam's marriage to Agnes took place. If it did, then it must have occurred after the death of Agnes's first husband, William II of Roumare, which happened in or about 1151: King, 'Parish of Warter', 53 and notes.

[90] Although Burton Agnes was royal demesne in 1086, by the early twelfth century it had passed to the Brus family: *EYC*, II, 12, no. 676. For the estates acquired by Earl William near Pickering which were later held of the Bigod fee, see *EYC*, I, 491; *DB*, I, 299b, 300b, 332b–3a. The importance of Danby is reflected in the fine of £1,000 paid in 1200 by Peter of Brus for the restoration of the manor with the attached forest: *Rotuli de Oblatis et Finibus in Turri Londinensi asservati*, ed. T. D. Hardy (Record Commission, 1835), 109. For Earl William's control of Brus land and churches, see *Cartularium de Gyseburne*, II, 151; *EYC*, II, no. 660 and note; King, 'Parish of Warter', 53–4 and notes.

[91] Alan of Richmond's father, Stephen, was the half-brother of Ribald of Middleham, one of the most important tenants of the honour of Richmond, whose son, Ralph, married Agatha, a daughter of Robert I of Brus, between 1125 and 1135: *EYC*, IV, 84–6; V, 297–301; II, no. 650. For the earl of Chester's overlordship of certain estates held by Brus in Yorkshire, see *PR 14 Henry II*, 90.　　　[92] See above, p. 73.

perhaps implicit in Stephen's creation of Count Alan as earl of Richmond in 1136.[93] It gave Alan the same rank as William. It possibly also gave him the same administrative authority within a region which marched with the county governed by the earl of York, and which may have been regarded by the earl as forming part of that county.

The rivalry between Alan and William is most apparent in their attempts to secure control of the bishop of Durham's hundreds of Howden and Welton, his wapentake of Northallerton and the great soke manors of the same names from which these administrative divisions were almost certainly administered; and it was clearly pursued without regard for the interests of the king (Map 24).[94] As well as being important centres of jurisdiction, the episcopal wapentakes and hundreds were the focus of lucrative ecclesiastical liberties.[95] In the case of Howden and Welton, both Alan and William had a claim to the hundredal manors by virtue of the temporary tenure granted to their predecessors by William Rufus during his quarrel with Bishop William of St Calais in 1088, and (despite Rufus's restoration of the manors to the bishopric) both were intent on making the claim a reality in Stephen's reign. William's seizure of Howden is recorded by John of Hexham, and Alan's control of Welton is clear from a charter in which he disposed of land and churches belonging to the soke of the manor.[96] In addition, the two lords were also receptive to the overtures of William Cumin, who had secured control of Durham after the death of Bishop Geoffrey at Easter 1141, and who looked towards Stephen's enemies the Angevins and Scots for help in obtaining episcopal election and complete control of the temporalities of the see.[97] Earl William arranged a marriage between his niece and the nephew of William Cumin who held Northallerton and had built a castle there, and Alan of Richmond was bribed by Cumin to assist in the defence of Durham against the forces of Bishop William of Ste Barbe in 1143.[98] Alan had good cause to fear the earl of York's interest in Northallerton, which was close

[93] For the creation, see Davis, *King Stephen*, 141.
[94] For the tenure of the manors of Howden, Welton and Northallerton by the bishops of Durham, see *DB*, I, 304b; *EYC*, II, 266, 302–4; *Monasticon*, I, 238; Symeon, *Opera*, I, 127–8.
[95] Barlow, *Jurisdictional Peculiars*, xiii–xvi, 4, 53–61, 147, 151–2; Anderson, *Hundred-Names*, 8–9, 18. [96] Symeon, *Opera*, II, 320; *EYC*, IV, no. 17.
[97] Young, *William Cumin*, 10–29; Symeon, *Opera*, II, 309.
[98] Young, *William Cumin*, 20–2.

to Richmondshire and incorporated some estates which either fell within his castlery or were situated close to its boundaries, and responded by encroaching upon and fortifying episcopal property.[99] He appears to have seized the manor of East Cowton, and is known to have constructed a castle at Hutton Conyers.[100] The castle was probably intended as a base from which to dominate the adjacent archiepiscopal liberty of Ripon, where at some point in the 1140s Alan is known to have broken into the church with an armed force and ravaged the estate.[101] Aggressive competition of this nature provides another stark reflection of the fact that royal authority was breaking down.

Another powerful magnate with whom Earl William may have been competing for control of castles and hundreds was Roger of Mowbray, lord of Thirsk and Burton in Lonsdale, and a relative and important tenant of Alan of Richmond with whom he appears to have been on good terms in Stephen's reign.[102] Roger's father, Nigel d'Aubigny, seems to have been granted custody of York castle by Henry I, and Roger maintained a claim to the fortress in Stephen's reign and beyond.[103] At some point between *c.* 1143 and 1153 Roger granted his manor of Middlethorpe near York to Selby Abbey in satisfaction for the damage he had inflicted on the church, promising to give the monks an exchange 'when I shall recover the custody of York castle'. After the exchange had taken place Middlethorpe was to return to Roger's demesne.[104] These arrangements are highly unusual and beg obvious questions. Why did Roger alienate Middlethorpe to the monks, and why was the

---

[99] For Alan's tenure of appurtenances belonging to Northallerton, see *EYC*, II, no. 931. Several vills incorporated lands attached to the lordship of Richmond as well as the manor of Northallerton, see *DB*, I, 299a, 309a–10a.

[100] A charter of King Stephen, commanding Earl Alan to let the canons of Bridlington have the church of East Cowton in peace, suggests that Alan had begun to seize episcopal lands bordering his own estates. In addition to an estate belonging to Alan, East Cowton incorporated a berewick of the episcopal manor of Northallerton. The attachment of the church to the latter holding is suggested by the fact that it had been granted to Bridlington Priory before 1135 by Eustace Fitz John, who is known to have held lands of the bishop of Durham. See *Regesta*, III, nos. 119, 122; II, nos. 1722, 1730; *DB*, I, 299a, 310a; *EYC*, II, nos. 1144, 1152; V, no. 339 and note.

[101] Symeon, *Opera*, II, 306; *Memorials of Fountains*, I, 79 and note. For the castle, see King, *Castellarium Anglicanum*, II, 519.

[102] Roger was the brother-in-law of Alan's nephew, Gilbert II of Gant. For evidence that Roger and Alan were on good terms, see *EYC*, IV, nos. 18–19, 23 and note, 32; IX, no. 119 and note; *Mowbray Charters*, xxvii–xxviii, xli–xlii, nos. 172, 174, 255; *Monasticon*, V, 351–2, 568; Green, *Sheriffs*, 90.   [103] *Mowbray Charters*, xxv, xxx, no. 292.

[104] *Ibid.*, no. 255.

alienation to last only until he recovered control of York castle? Further light is cast on the problem by a notification issued in the same period by Roger to Leising and Chetell, his men of Acaster (Selby), of his gift to Selby Abbey of the land of Acaster, promising that if the monks were disseised by anyone he would reseise them by his charters.[105] Roger clearly expected that the tenure of the monks might be disturbed, and his expectations may have been realised. In a charter dated September 1143 × 1147, or October 1153 × June 1154, Roger notified Archbishop William Fitz Herbert of his restoration and concession ('reddidisse et concessisse') to Selby Abbey of the land of Acaster Selby.[106] Land within the same vill belonged to Alan of Richmond, and was held of him by St Mary's Abbey, York, and of the abbey in turn by Roger of Mowbray's man, Chetell.[107] Acaster Selby and Middlethorpe were situated within ten miles of one another within the wapentake of Ainsty. When viewed against this background, it is highly significant that Ainsty wapentake appears to have been administered from York, and that the bulk of the estates within it were probably the subject of a 'hundredal grant' made by William the Conqueror to Osbern of Arches, whose fee was later made subject to the lordship of Nigel d'Aubigny.[108] Although Roger of Mowbray's arrangements concerning the manor of Middlethorpe, and the tenurial insecurity of the monks of Selby at Acaster, can be interpreted in more than one way, it is possible that both were linked to a competition for control of the castle of York and its appurtenant wapentake of Ainsty; that Roger granted Middlethorpe and Acaster to the monks of Selby in order to safeguard his interests there (and possibly those of Alan of Richmond) until he regained power in the region; and that the man he was afraid of and competing with was the current custodian of York castle, William earl of York.[109]

The earl of York's pursuit of territorial ambitions at the expense of public order and royal authority can even be traced during the course of the York archiepiscopal election dispute. Although promoting the election of Stephen's candidate, William Fitz Herbert, in the king's name in 1141 and preventing, at the expense

[105] *Ibid.*, no. 254.   [106] *Ibid.*, no. 256.
[107] DB, I, 313a; *EYC*, IV, no. 87 and note.
[108] See Fleming, *Kings and Lords*, 153–8.
[109] For another possible, and not necessarily contradictory, interpretation of these documents, see below, pp. 288–9.

of his own excommunication, the entry of Fitz Herbert's rival, Henry Murdac, into York in 1148, Earl William's policy in the dispute was not as 'royalist' as it might at first appear.[110] He had initially offered his support to his kinsman Waldef, prior of Kirkham, who was opposed by Stephen on the grounds that he was a stepson of King David of Scotland and had been brought up at the Scottish court.[111] In spite of the royal veto, however, Waldef was offered the archbishopric by William on the condition that the earl would be allowed to obtain the important archiepiscopal wapentake manor and liberty of Sherburn in Elmet in the West Riding.[112] Only after Waldef refused the proposition did William switch his allegiance to William Fitz Herbert.

There were sound practical motives for securing the favour of an incumbent archbishop. As well as holding an extensive honour in Yorkshire encompassing private wapentakes, hundreds, soke centres, jurisdictional liberties and royal demesne churches, the archbishop of York was a powerful figure within the county town where he occupied a palace, controlled his own mint and administered one of the city's seven shires and the revenues of a third of another.[113] For a magnate like Earl William, seeking to extend his jurisdictional and territorial influence, the candidacy of William Fitz Herbert must have seemed particularly attractive, especially after the failure of Prior Waldef. In addition to being a kinsman of the earl, Fitz Herbert was archdeacon of the East Riding and held an important prebend there based upon the church of the hundredal manor of Weighton, and an interest in the church of the important soke manor of Weaverthorpe, which may have been the focus of *Toreshou* hundred.[114]

[110] Symeon, *Opera*, II, 307, 313, 322.

[111] *Acta Sanctorum*, I, August 3rd, 256–7; *Vita Ailredi*, xiii, xxxii, xliv; Nicholl, *Thurstan*, 240.

[112] For Sherburn in Elmet, see *DB*, I, 302b; A. J. Robertson, *Anglo-Saxon Charters* (2nd edn, Cambridge, 1956), 164–7; *VCH, Yorkshire*, II, 210; *Visitations of Southwell*, 190–6.

[113] *DB*, I, 302a–4a; *Regesta*, II, nos. 518, 837; *VCH, City of York*, 19–24, 29, 38–9; F. Liebermann, 'An English document of about 1080', *YAJ*, 18 (1904–5), 412–16; A. G. Dickens, 'The "shire" and privileges of the archbishop in eleventh century York', *YAJ*, 38 (1952–5), 131–47; Palliser, *York*, 11–12, 25. The wapentake whose administrative centre was under the control of the archbishop was that of Barkston, and the hundred was that of *Toreshou*.

[114] Fitz Herbert was the son of Herbert of Winchester and Emma of Blois. His mother was a daughter of Stephen, count of Blois, and a half-sister of King Stephen: *Episcopal Acta*, xxx. For Earl William's connection with the House of Blois, see above, p. 160. For Fitz Herbert's holdings, see *YMF*, I, 22, no. 50 and note; II, vii, 80–2; *EYC*, I, nos. 26–9; *Episcopal Acta*, nos. 54–5; *Regesta*, II, no. 1759.

The earl of York's desire to secure control of the archiepiscopal manor of Sherburn in Elmet may provide the explanation for the outbreak of a war at nearby Selby in the early 1140s. According to the author of the *Historia Selebiensis Monasterii*, in 1143 a kinsman of Henry of Lacy and former soldier, Elias Paynel, was elected abbot of Selby and went on to distinguish himself by defending the estates of his abbey during a disastrous war which overran the region.[115] The fighting began when Henry of Lacy, who held an extensive lordship centred on Pontefract immediately to the north and west of the abbey, 'after taking counsel from [Elias], began to build a castle at Selby. A week had not passed before Count William of Aumale, who was in contention with Henry, learnt of this and hurried to lay siege to the castle which was in the course of construction.'[116] After a siege of several days William's forces captured the castle and proceeded to plunder the surrounding countryside.[117] The war is most likely to have taken place shortly after Henry of Lacy's succession to the honour of Pontefract in *c.* 1142, and the earl of York's involvement is probably to be explained by his territorial ambitions.[118] Situated as it was on the Ouse, Selby castle threatened not only the trading ships on their way to York, but also the earl's hundredal manor of Howden and the archiepiscopal wapentake manor of Sherburn in Elmet which he aimed to control. Several estates belonging to Sherburn, including land in Selby itself, were already held of the archbishop by the abbot of Selby, and were under the *de facto* control of Henry of Lacy.[119] Although the abbey was directly subject to the arch-

---

[115] *Selby Coucher*, I, [33]. For the connections between the Lacys and the Paynels, see *EYC*, VI, 4–5, 38, 59.

[116] *Selby Coucher*, I, [33]. The text of the *Historia Selebiensis Monasterii* published in the *Selby Coucher* is based upon a mid-seventeenth-century transcript of an imperfect copy of the original manuscript, and has a lacuna where the toponymic surname of 'Count William' should be. However, a different copy of the original manuscript, made only a few years later in or about 1180, gives the toponymic surname as 'Albe Marie' which is evidently a distortion of 'Albe Marle', the Latin for Aumale: P. Janin, 'Note sur le manuscrit Latin 10940 de la Bibliothèque Nationale de Paris, contenant l'*Historia Selebiensis Monasterii* et les *Gesta Abbatum Sancti Germani Autissiodorensis*', *Bibliothèque de l'école des chartes*, 27 (1969), 214–24.   [117] *Selby Coucher*, I, [34]-[39].

[118] At this time the honour of Pontefract was probably under attack by Roger of Mowbray and Gilbert of Gant who, because of family connections with the Lacys, may have fostered rival claims to some of its estates. See Wightman, *Lacy Family*, 78–80, 87–8; *The Chartulary of St. John of Pontefract*, ed. R. Holmes, 2 vols. (Yorks. Arch. Soc. rec. ser., 1899–1902), II, no. 400; *Mowbray Charters*, xxvii–xxviii and notes, nos. 229, 255; *EYC*, III, nos. 1499, 1504; *Complete Peerage*, VII, 672–3; English, 'Counts of Aumale', 381, no. 126.

[119] *DB*, I, 302b; *VCH, Yorkshire*, II, 210 note 5; *Episcopal Acta*, nos. 4, 5, 21.

bishop, the election of Abbot Elias, who was deposed by Archbishop Henry Murdac in 1152, had been conducted without reference to archiepiscopal authority, and probably at the direction of Henry of Lacy.[120] Here again Earl William had a convenient excuse with which to cloak his private ambitions.

A further example of Earl William's readiness to exploit the York archiepiscopal election dispute for private advantage, against the wishes of the king, is provided by his relationship with St Peter's Hospital, York, whose master, Robert, was one of the group of heads of religious houses in Yorkshire opposed to the election of William Fitz Herbert. In 1140, as we have seen, Stephen commanded Earl William that Robert and his men should have the king's peace and not be impleaded concerning their lands until the consecration of a new archbishop.[121] The order implies that William was manipulating his judicial position at York in order to deprive St Peter's of its property, and it appears that it went unheeded. A letter of Alberic, cardinal bishop of Ostia, dated 1142 and addressed to the reforming party opposing Fitz Herbert, reveals that their houses and property were about to be confiscated, their orders were under threat of expulsion and their lives were in danger. The following year St Bernard himself wrote to the pope warning him that the destruction of the monasteries was imminent, and that the abbots and monks were prepared to go into exile rather than submit to a simoniacal archbishop.[122] Bernard's warnings are given substance by a series of papal, royal and archiepiscopal charters granting protection to the houses opposing the election of Fitz Herbert.[123] In one document Archbishop Theobald of Canterbury offered a release of twenty days penance to all who, for the provision of lodgings and repair of buildings, would make grants to St Peter's Hospital which was unable to house and support the sick because of the destruction of its buildings, plunder of its animals, depopulation of its towns and devastation of its lands.[124]

By 1149 there are indications that Earl William had withdrawn

---

[120] For the subjection of Selby Abbey to the archbishops of York, see *Episcopal Acta*, no. 20 and note; Hugh the Chantor, 8–9; Henry of Huntingdon, 216; *Selby Coucher*, I, [31]–[32], [44]–[45]; *EYC*, I, nos. 43, 126; *Historians of York*, III, 66; Dobson, 'Origins of Selby', 174; Burton, 'Religious orders', 10–17.   [121] *Regesta*, III, no. 991.
[122] C. H. Talbot, 'New documents in the case of Saint William of York', *CHJ*, 10 (1950–2), 4–5.
[123] *Regesta*, III, nos. 983, 991; *EYC*, I, nos. 173–4, 179–81, 184–8.
[124] *EYC*, I, no. 183.

his allegiance from the ecclesiastical party supporting William Fitz Herbert at York, and he is known to have engaged in open military conflict against the king at this time. In 1148, superficially at least, he was still toeing the royal line. He was implicated with the treasurer of York, Hugh du Puiset a nephew of the king, in organising opposition to the new archbishop, Henry Murdac, who had been consecrated at Trèves in 1147 by Pope Eugenius III after the deposition of Archbishop William Fitz Herbert. When Archbishop Henry arrived in Yorkshire in 1148 to take up his appointment the city of York refused to acknowledge him, and he was forced to retire to Ripon from where he excommunicated the citizens of York, Hugh du Puiset and the earl of York. In defiance of the anathema, Hugh maintained the performance of ecclesiastical services in York and pronounced his own excommunication of the archbishop. Before the end of the year, however, the situation was already changing. Hugh du Puiset left York to look after the bishopric of Winchester during the absence of the bishop in Rome, and 'on his removal to this distance, his associates became more moderate in their opposition to Archbishop Henry'.[125] There are indications that the drift of support away from the king continued in the following year. In 1149 Stephen came to York to oppose the allied forces of King David of Scotland, Henry of Anjou and Ranulf earl of Chester who, probably at the instigation of Archbishop Henry, planned to capture the city. At some point the allies abandoned the campaign and Stephen stayed on for a time in Yorkshire to suppress 'the hostilities that were on the increase round York', a programme involving the destruction of hostile castles and construction of others in more suitable places, before going on to Lincolnshire in order to campaign against Ranulf earl of Chester.[126] After his departure his son Eustace came to York to find 'the sacred offices discontinued', implying that the supporters of Archbishop Henry, who had placed the city under an interdict, were gaining the upper hand there.[127] It may have been at this time, and in response to the archiepiscopal excommunication, that coins of Stephen Type I minted at York were defaced.[128] If Earl William was still

---

[125] Symeon, *Opera*, II, 322. [126] *Gesta Stephani*, 216–22 (quotation from p. 218).
[127] Symeon, *Opera*, II, 324.
[128] P. J. Seaby, 'King Stephen and the interdict of 1148', *BNJ*, 50 (1980), 50–60; *idem*, 'The defaced pennies of Stephen from Sussex mints', *BNJ*, 56 (1986), 102–7. For an alternative interpretation, see Archibald, 'Stephen's first type', 19–20.

supporting William Fitz Herbert all this is difficult to explain. His switch of allegiance to Archbishop Henry is also suggested by his establishment at Meaux of a Cistercian daughter house of Fountains Abbey where Henry had been abbot. The foundation arrangements were almost certainly underway before the archbishop's reconciliation with the king in 1151.[129]

It is possible that the earl had become involved in the 1149 alliance. His family connections with the Scottish royal house and aristocracy may have encouraged him to transfer his allegiance to King David.[130] At some point in the 1140s he had also married his sister, Agnes, to the eldest son of William I of Roumare, earl of Lincoln, half-brother of Ranulf earl of Chester, and had endowed the young couple with the royal hundredal manor of Warter.[131] It was doubtless this close family relationship that motivated the earl of York to support his relatives in a war fought in the period *c.* 1149 × *c.* 1151 against King Stephen and his new earl of Lincoln, Gilbert of Gant, who had been set up in opposition to Roumare. In response to Gilbert's capture of his Lincolnshire *caput* and castle of Bytham the earl of York, assisted by Eustace Fitz John constable of Chester, destroyed the Gant castle of Hunmanby, the administrative centre of *Turbar* hundred in the East Riding and may have confiscated the Gant estates within the vicinity (Map 24).[132] Whether William was fighting simply out of family loyalty or because he had become involved in the great alliance of 1149 is unclear. What is certain is his pursuit of territorial and jurisdictional ambitions in opposition to the king, and the detrimental impact of this opposition on royal authority. Even before the outbreak of open war against the king, Stephen's presence in Yorkshire in 1149, his attempt to tax the citizens of York and

---

[129] See *Chronica de Melsa*, I, 76–83. Friendly relations between Archbishop Henry and Earl William are indicated by the former's grant of land and ferry rights to Meaux Abbey: *ibid.*, 93. See also the archbishop's confirmation (1147 × *c.* 1151) of the gifts made by William II of Roumare and his wife, Agnes of Aumale, to the canons of Warter Priory: *EYC*, x, no. 67; *Episcopal Acta*, no. 128.

[130] William's grandmother, Adelaide, married (as her second husband) Lambert, count of Lens, and by him was the mother of Judith, who was the mother of King David's wife Matilda. William's niece, Eufemia, married Robert II of Brus, lord of Annandale. See English, *Holderness*, 10; White, 'Stephen's earldoms', 52; *EYC*, III, no. 1352.

[131] King has tentatively dated the marriage to *c.* 1145: King, 'Parish of Warter', 51.

[132] *Chronicle of Langtoft*, I, 485; *Gesta Stephani*, 220–2; Dalton, 'Ranulf of Chester', 124–6. Gilbert of Gant was made earl of Lincoln in or shortly after 1149: Abbot, 'Gant family', 45, 312 (no. 59). Hunmanby was by far the most valuable manor in *Turbar* hundred in 1066, and had berewicks or sokelands in at least five neighbouring vills: *DB*, I, 326a. For the possible confiscation of Gant estates, see *EYC*, I, no. 362 and note.

Beverley, the disturbed state of the countryside, the proximity of adulterine castles to York and the royal castle construction programme reflect a king struggling to maintain control.[133]

The evidence suggests that Stephen came close to losing control of Yorkshire in the period 1149–51, and that his reconciliation with Archbishop Henry Murdac early in 1151 was forced upon him by a growing crisis. Although he retained control of York, the city was almost certainly a tiny royal island amidst a hostile sea, and the extent of the emergency is demonstrated by Stephen's decision to leave his son in charge there.[134] Even in better days the territorial extent of royal influence in Yorkshire was limited. For all his power the earl of York had been unable to prevent the election of Archbishop Henry at Richmond in 1147, even though Earl Alan had died the previous year, and the new incumbent was able to secure shelter within the ecclesiastical jurisdictional liberties of Beverley and Ripon. It was at Beverley that the king himself tried and failed to build a castle in 1149.[135] Thereafter it appears that, with the exception of the royal chancellor, Robert of Gant, and the king's nephew and canon of York, Hugh du Puiset, who remained in control of York, Stephen could count on little aristocratic support in Yorkshire.[136] The chroniclers are silent, but the royal charters indicate that the northern magnates, like the majority of their counterparts in the south, stayed away from Stephen's court. Gilbert of Gant and his brother Robert, who obtained a grant of the Paynel heiress and honour from Stephen, appear to have been the only magnates in Yorkshire openly loyal to Stephen at this time.[137] His opponents were probably many. Roger of Mowbray supported the great alliance of 1149, while William II of Percy and Henry of Lacy may have been at least sympathetic towards it.[138] The nadir came in 1151 when King

---

[133] The castle of Wheldrake was situated only ten miles to the south-east of York, and had been harassing the city: Symeon, *Opera*, II, 323.   [134] *Ibid.*, 324–5.
[135] *Ibid.*, 323–4.   [136] *Ibid.*, 320–2.   [137] *EYC*, VI, 33.
[138] For Mowbray, see *Mowbray Charters*, xxvi–xxvii. William II of Percy was lord of Wheldrake, the site of the castle which had been harassing York and which was seized by Stephen in 1149: Symeon, *Opera*, II, 323; *DB*, I, 322b. For the close links of the Percy family with the Scots and the earl of Chester, see *EYC*, XI, 2–3; VI, 33; VII, 4–8; *Chester Charters*, nos. 35, 73. Henry of Lacy had close links with the allies of 1149. His estates centred on Clitheroe to the west of the Pennines were at the mercy of the Scots, who had beaten his forces there in 1138 and controlled Cumberland and northern Lancashire: *VCH, Lancashire*, I, 286, 313–14; G. W. S. Barrow, 'King David I and the honour of Lancaster', *EHR*, 70 (1955), 85–9. See also *Chester Charters*, no. 69. Henry's brother, Jordan, witnessed a charter of William Fitz Duncan issued at Skipton 1146 × 1153: *EYC*, VII, no. 14.

David of Scotland confirmed his nephew William Fitz Duncan in the lordship of Skipton in Craven.[139] The wolves were closing in, and there was no choice but to turn to Archbishop Henry and the church for help.

Although the reconciliation with Archbishop Henry appears to have eased the tension in the north, and Stephen was able to recover the loyalty of Mowbray and Lacy, his problems were far from over.[140] The chapter of St Peter's remained divided, as it had been for most of the reign, between those supporting and those opposing the election of royal candidates to episcopal offices in the north. In 1153 the election of Hugh du Puiset as bishop of Durham provoked a fresh crisis. It was opposed by Archbishop Henry, who was expelled from York by the citizens on the grounds of contempt of the royal prerogative. Despite the efforts of Stephen's son Eustace, who came to Henry at Beverley to persuade him to return, the archbishop remained in exile until his death later in the year. Moreover, Stephen's rift with the earl of York may well have been permanent. With the exception of the treaty of Westminster in 1153 it is impossible to date any royal charter addressed to the earl or witnessed by him with certainty to the period 1149–54. William is conspicuously absent from the records of 1153, and it is significant that Henry of Anjou did not campaign against him. The earl appears to have balanced his willingness to sanction the resurgence of monarchical authority with a determination to preserve the local power he had built up in Yorkshire. In 1155 this determination brought Henry II on the first of very few excursions to the north.[141] Although securing William's submission the new king was forced to compromise. William was allowed to retain the royal hundredal manor of Driffield and the Brus estate of Danby for the rest of his life, secured control of the custody of the Fossard heir and lordship of the important barony of Copeland in Cumberland and received

---

[139] Symeon, *Opera*, II, 326.

[140] Mowbray recognised Stephen's title in a charter issued on 17 April 1153: *EYC*, III, no. 1823. His support for Stephen is also suggested by Henry II's elevation, at Roger's expense, of the Stutevilles, and by the fact that the Norman estates Roger held of the count of Eu, who had submitted to the Angevins in Normandy by 1149, were not confirmed to him until August 1154: *Mowbray Charters*, xxix–xxxi, no. 19. Henry of Lacy's support for Stephen is indicated by the fact that Henry felt it necessary to obtain two separate pardons from Henry II: *EYC*, III, nos. 1449–50.

[141] Henry appears to have visited York only six times in his long reign – 1155, 1158, 1163, 1175, 1180, 1181: R. W. Eyton, *Court, Household, and Itinerary of King Henry II* (London, 1878), 5, 33, 62, 230, 242.

many other privileges from Henry II throughout his long reign.[142]
The new king's concern for Yorkshire in 1155, and his concessions
there, provide an additional measure of both the power of Earl
William and the relative vulnerability of royal authority in the
county during the reign of Stephen.

The disintegration of royal authority in Yorkshire began in
1138 when Stephen was forced to place the royal administration,
castles, rights and demesne in the hands of William count of
Aumale. In the decade that followed royal authority took second
place to William's private ambitions. The institutions of government were either allowed to decay, as in the case of exchequer
practice, or were exploited for the earl's own purposes, as with the
coinage. A close analysis of William's involvement in the internal
politics of the county betrays the same priority of self-interest.
That so many royal wapentake, hundredal and soke manors, with
their associated castles and forests, fell into his hands in a county
where the king was a distant, almost anonymous, figure and
everything depended upon a personal relationship was a recipe for
disaster (Map 24). When the relationship was amicable, as it was
for part of Stephen's reign, the king could afford to leave
Yorkshire to itself, but when the relationship disintegrated, as it
did in 1142 and 1149, Stephen was forced to campaign in the north
in order to reassert his authority. His presence, however, could
never be more than short-lived, and consequently his success was
limited. Exercised at second hand through the agency of William
earl of York, royal authority could not compete with the plethora
of territorial and family rivalries stimulating war and disorder in
Yorkshire. All this does not square easily with Warren's thesis that
Stephen aimed to introduce a new decentralised style of government based upon the upgraded authority of earls. If Stephen
alienated governmental authority to the powerful men of the

---

[142] For Driffield and Danby, see *PR 25 Henry II*, 16, 23; *PR 26 Henry II*, 74; *EYC*,
II, 12. For the Fossard custody, see *Chronica de Melsa*, I, 104; *EYC*, II, 12–13, 328–9. It
is possible that Henry II also allowed William to retain custodianship of the manor and
castle of Scarborough. The farm of the manor was not accounted for by the sheriff until
1163–4; and Robert of Ros, William's steward, accounted for works on the castle of
Scarborough in 1157–8 and 1160–1: *PR 10 Henry II*, 12; *PR 2–4 Henry II*, 146; *PR 7
Henry II*, 36. Henry II also pardoned a large debt of 100 marks owed by William in
1157–8, and may subsequently have cancelled another debt of 400 marks: *PR 2–4
Henry II*, 146; *PR 6 Henry II*, 15; *PR 7 Henry II*, 36; *PR 8 Henry II*, 51; *PR 9 Henry
II*, 57–61. Henry II also appears to have allowed William to mint coins of Stephen Type
VII at his trading borough of Hedon in Holderness: Mack, 'Anarchy', 55–8. The
borough was granted privileges equal to those of York: *Recueil des Actes*, I, no. 334.

localities he did so out of necessity rather than choice. In Yorkshire the policy created more problems than it solved. The most critical assessment of the extent of the failure is that of William of Newburgh. For him William earl of York was 'more truly the king beyond the Humber than King Stephen'.[143]

THE DOMINATION OF THE ARISTOCRACY

William earl of York took charge of the royal government of Yorkshire during the reign of Stephen, and secured control of a large number of the county's wapentake and hundredal seats. It was one thing, however, to possess administrative and judicial authority, and quite another to make this authority effective. In order to achieve this William required the support of his fellow nobles, especially the lesser aristocracy who held land in Yorkshire as subtenants, and who were probably resident within the county for a good proportion of their time. In contrast to the tenants-in-chief, whose honours often encompassed lands in several counties, these lesser nobles tended to hold lands in only one or two shires and were able to administer them more directly. It was often they rather than their lords who were the force to be reckoned with in the localities, and by the mid-twelfth century many of the more influential of them were in the process of becoming independent from seignorial control. They were building their own castles and monasteries, establishing their own courts, households and patronage networks, commanding the allegiance of many lesser families and forging social, familial and tenurial relationships with their neighbours which cut across the ties of seignorial allegiance.[144] If the earl of York was going to transform his control of royal government, wapentakes, hundreds and soke centres into effective authority over the countryside and its occupants, it was essential for him to dominate his fellow magnates and the most powerful of the local knights. It remains to consider his degree of success in doing so.

---

[143] *Chronicles of the Reigns*, I, 103.
[144] See below, Chapter 7; C. J. Wales, 'The knight in twelfth-century Lincolnshire' (Univ. of Cambridge, PhD thesis, 1983); J. C. Holt, 'Feudal society and the family in early medieval England: I. The revolution of 1066', *TRHS*, 5th ser., 32 (1982), 209; E. Miller, 'The background of Magna Carta', *Past & Present*, 23 (1962), 79–80; Cheney, *Hubert Walter*, 28; Colvin, *White Canons*, Chapter 2.

One method of domination was the use of military power, which William appears to have possessed in abundance. Describing his participation in the battle of the Standard in 1138, which earned William his comital title, Ailred of Rievaulx refers to him as 'juvenis tunc strenuissimus et in armis multum exercitatus, habens secum, tam de Morinis quam de Ponciis, milites plurimos non minus astutia militari quam animi virtute praestantes'.[145] This statement was echoed by the monks of Whitby, who were sufficiently impressed by William's destruction of a number of their villages near Scarborough for the purpose of making a hunting chase to refer to him as 'vir strenuissimus et magnae militiae et potestatis'.[146] It was a power Earl William used to deal with a number of his more important Yorkshire neighbours. In 1143 he captured the Gant foundation of Bridlington and converted it into a castle, and in 1149 he battered the Gant castle of Hunmanby to the ground. Although Gant appears to have remained strong in neighbouring Lincolnshire, where both he and the earl held other important estates, his authority in Yorkshire must have been seriously undermined by these losses. Further west, the earl was successful in at least checking the military power of Henry of Lacy when he destroyed the castle of Selby in the early 1140s. There is also some evidence to suggest that it was by military action that William forced Eustace Fitz John to come to heel. Immediately after the battle of the Standard, 'some of the barons, with a portion of the army, marched to Eustace's town, called Malton ... and having destroyed the suburb, they laid siege to it, because, during the fight, the soldiers had sallied forth from it by orders of their lord and set fire to many villages'.[147] If, as seems likely, William was present among the siege army, and the siege was successful, it might explain how the earl apparently managed to secure control of the wapentake/soke manors of Knaresborough and Aldborough, which in 1130 had been in Eustace's charge. William's attachment to the lord of Malton is also suggested by the assistance Eustace provided in the destruction of the Gant castle of Hunmanby in 1149, by his attestation of two charters of William issued in the periods 1150 × 1153 and 1130 × 1157, and by the coins issued in his name at York.[148]

---

[145] *Chronicles of the Reigns*, III, 182. [146] *Cartularium de Whiteby*, II, 517.

[147] *Chronicles of the Reigns*, III, 165.

[148] *EYC*, III, no. 1381; Bodleian Library Dodsworth MS 100, fol. 84d. Eustace may have been acting for Ranulf earl of Chester at Hunmanby. Ranulf had made Eustace his

The earl of York's relations with Eustace Fitz John suggest the formation of one of those non-tenurial forms of association based upon pacts, fealty and recognitions of superiority which appear to have flourished during the reign of Stephen, and which in some ways appear to foreshadow thirteenth-century affinities.[149] Another magnate attached to Earl William's affinity was Adam II of Brus, who succeeded as a minor to fifteen knights' fees in the county after the death of his father, Adam I, in 1143.[150] By means unknown the earl of York appears to have acquired custody of the young heir, which belonged by right to Adam's mother, Juetta of Arches, married him to his sister, Agnes, and deprived him of a number of his most important Yorkshire estates.[151] The manipulation of Adam and his lands is also reflected in William's acceptance between 1150 and c. 1160 of a life grant from Agnes of her *maritagium*, 'for my assistance and my support'.[152] Dr Hyams suggests that William may have been selling his protection to Adam and his wife for profit.[153] What he had done, in effect, was to marry his sister without losing control of the lands alienated to provide for her. The language William used to describe this transaction is the language of domination. It raises questions about the circumstances in which the marriage between another of his female relatives, Eufemia, and Robert II of Brus, Adam II's uncle, took place.[154]

The earl of York's political satellites in Yorkshire may also have included Robert III of Stuteville, who held approximately eight knights' fees in the county in 1166, and William I Fossard, who held twenty-eight fees and an additional five and a half 'on the demesne'.[155] The Stuteville *caput* and castle of Cottingham was situated in the hundred of Welton, only four miles outside the wapentake of Holderness. The Fossard castle of Mountferrant was in the hundred of *Scard*, about twenty-five miles west-north-west of the earl of York's castle of Skipsea. And both Stuteville and

constable and principal counsellor between 1144 and 1145: Dalton, 'Ranulf of Chester', 122–6.

[149] D. Crouch, 'Comment' on P. R. Coss, 'Bastard feudalism revised', *Past & Present*, 131 (1991), 175; *idem*, 'A Norman *conventio* and the bonds of lordship in the reign of Stephen', in *Studies Presented to Sir James Holt*, ed. J. Hudson and G. Garnett (forthcoming); E. King, 'Dispute settlement in Anglo-Norman England', *ANS*, 14 (1992), 115–30.   [150] *Red Book*, I, 434.   [151] See above, p. 166.

[152] *EYC*, III, no. 1352.

[153] P. R. Hyams, 'Warranty and good lordship in twelfth century England', *LHR*, 5 (1987), 449 note 40.   [154] *EYC*, II, 15.   [155] *Red Book*, I, 407–8, 429.

Fossard held many other estates within the East Riding.[156] Stuteville attested a charter issued by Earl William in favour of Meaux Abbey between 1150 and 1153, and with Fossard and Fossard's tenant, Ralph Fitz Wimund, was among the earliest benefactors of that foundation.[157] It is more than likely to have been at the earl of York's direction that coins bearing Stuteville's name were issued at York. It was possibly due to him also that one of Stuteville's nephews, Roger, obtained tenancies in the Brus manor of Burton Agnes and the royal demesne manor of Warter.[158] Close relations between Earl William and the Stutevilles continued into the reign of Henry II. When William received a royal licence to destroy the Fossard castle of Mountferrant in revenge for the seduction of his daughter by William II Fossard, he gave the fortress timbers to Robert of Stuteville, who gave them in turn to the Aumale foundation of Meaux Abbey.[159] It may also have been during this reign that Robert of Stuteville's grandniece, Agnes, was married to Herbert II of St Quintin, one of the count of Aumale's most important tenants.[160]

Two more Yorkshire tenants-in-chief who came into contact with the earl of York during Stephen's reign deserve a brief mention. The first is Richard of Curcy who married Alice Paynel, daughter of William I Paynel lord of Drax, in or before 1147, and who may have been one of the king's leading agents in Yorkshire and Lincolnshire.[161] Richard probably fought with the earl of York at the battles of the Standard and Lincoln, attested two of the earl's charters issued between 1138 and 1142, and, together with the earl, witnessed three more charters of the king granted at York.[162] The second tenant-in-chief is William 'de Clerfai', who appears as the first witness to a charter of the earl issued in favour of the canons of Bytham in c. 1150, and is possibly the same man

---

[156] *EYC*, IX, 5, 74–5; II, 325–426; *Chronica de Melsa*, I, 104–5.

[157] *EYC*, III, nos. 1381, 1383, 1388; *Regesta*, III, nos. 583–4; *Chronica de Melsa*, I, 99.

[158] Along with William II of Roumare and Roumare's wife, Agnes of Aumale (Earl William's sister), Roger of Stuteville is said to have confirmed the grant of Blanchemarle grange in Warter, which appears to have been named after the earl of York's continental county: *Chronica de Melsa*, I, 172. See also *EYC*, IX, 28–34.

[159] *Chronica de Melsa*, I, 104–5.   [160] *EYF*, 79–80.

[161] *EYC*, VI, 31–2 and notes. Richard attested a number of charters issued by Stephen at York and Lincoln: *Regesta*, III, nos. 114, 442, 624, 803, 981, 985. For notes on his family, the genealogy of which is very complex, see Green, *Government*, 242–3; *EYC*, III, 468–71.

[162] *EYC*, III, nos. 1313–14. These charters were probably issued on the same occasion. See also *Regesta*, III, nos. 100 (dated 1138 × 1154), 803 (dated 1138 × 1143), 981 (dated August 1138 × 1143).

as the William de Clerfeith who fought for the king at the battle of Lincoln in 1141, escaped from the field to his castle of Tickhill and from there harassed the earl of Chester and his company.[163]

In addition to maintaining links with these tenants-in-chief Earl William was able to exercise some form of influence over a large number of lesser nobles, many of whom held lands of him in Yorkshire and Lincolnshire and attested his charters during the reign of Stephen. Dr Farrer tentatively listed over thirty families as tenants of the ten knights' fees which were stated to have been held by William of Aumale in Yorkshire in 1166.[164] Of these, members of at least sixteen families attested charters issued by the earl during Stephen's reign.[165] Moreover, the marital and tenurial connections of these families with other lords and honours served as channels through which the earl of York could extend his influence over the aristocracy outside Holderness.

A good example is provided by the family of Ros, who were among William's principal tenants in Holderness. Everard I of Ros attested one of William's charters issued in *c.* 1150, and his younger brother and heir, Robert I of Ros, who succeeded him in or before 1153, witnessed another charter in favour of Meaux Abbey at about the same time.[166] Everard and Robert were nephews of Walter Espec, lord of Helmsley, their father Peter having married one of Walter's three sisters and co-heiresses. It is significant that Earl William may well have been on good terms with Walter in Stephen's reign, and that Robert of Ros secured the lion's share of the Espec inheritance, which passed to the eldest surviving sons of Walter's sisters, including the Yorkshire and Northumberland *capita* of Helmsley and Wark, after Walter's death in 1154 or 1155.[167] Robert may even have been in control of this inheritance while Walter was still alive.[168] Whether this was due to the power of the earl of York must remain open to question, but there can be no doubt that it increased the earl's influence within an important Yorkshire lordship.

At least five more important Holderness families were well

---

[163] *Registrum Antiquissimum*, III, no. 1018; Symeon, *Opera*, II, 308.

[164] *EYC*, III, 34.

[165] *Ibid.*, nos. 1306, 1313–14, 1379–81; Clay, 'A Holderness charter', 340–2; *Registrum Antiquissimum*, III, no. 1018.

[166] Clay, 'A Holderness charter', 342; *EYC*, III, no. 1380 (dated by Farrer *c.* 1150); *EYF*, 78. [167] *EYC*, X, 143–6; *Complete Peerage*, IX, 90; English, *Holderness*, 151.

[168] Between 1147 and 1153 Robert issued a charter confirming Walter's gifts to Rievaulx Abbey: *Cartularium de Rievalle*, 21–2.

connected with other honours. The St Quintins, who probably held a knight's fee of the earl of York, were tenants of the Scrutevilles and Brus, and were related by marriage to the Arches family. The Fauconbergs, who held a knight's fee in Holderness, had also married into the Arches family who were important tenants of the honours of Mowbray, Lacy, Percy and Skipton, and related to the families of Brus, Foliot and the stewards of the honour of Percy.[169] The Meaux family, who held approximately a twelfth of a knight's fee of the earl of York, were tenants of the archbishop of York in an eighth of a knight's fee, and of William II of Percy in three-quarters of a knight's fee of the new enfeoffment.[170] The Scures family, who held a half knight's fee in Holderness, were East Riding tenants of Stephen Fitz Herbert the Chamberlain, great-grandson of Osbert the sheriff.[171] And finally, the Foliots, whose holdings outside Holderness included one of the largest tenancies on the honour of Lacy, and additional estates held of the Percys.[172]

As well as making use of the familial and tenurial connections of his own tenants to extend his influence over the aristocracy outside his honour, Earl William sought to achieve this by a more direct method: the exercise of patronage. As we have seen, two of the most prominent 'knightly' recipients of his favour were Thomas Fitz Ulvieth, an important citizen of York and a joint tenant of a knight's fee held of the lordship of Chauncy in Swaythorpe in the hundred of Burton Agnes, and Robert of Octon, sometime sheriff of Yorkshire and an East Riding subtenant in the Fossard vill of Octon.[173]

The lesser nobles attached to the earl of York's influence also included John Arundel, who attested the important charter issued by the earl recording the exchange of Bewick for Meaux in *c.* 1150.[174] John was almost certainly one of the principal tenants of the honour of Percy. He was among the most prominent witnesses to charters of Alan I of Percy issued towards the end of Henry I's reign, and to a charter of William II of Percy granted between *c.*

---

[169] *EYF*, 1–2, 26–7, 33–5, 79–80 and notes; *EYC*, XI, 153–4; VII, 183–5; English, *Holderness*, 147–50.   [170] *EYF*, 59–60; *Red Book*, I, 425.   [171] *EYF*, 82–3.
[172] *Ibid.*, 33–4. Jordan Foliot the head, or son of the head, of the family attested a charter of Earl William issued around 1150: *Registrum Antiquissimum*, III, no. 1018. For the Foliot family, see *EYF*, 33–4.
[173] Clay, 'A Holderness charter', 340–2; *EYC*, II, 374.
[174] *EYC*, III, no. 1379. John also attested a charter issued by William in the period *c.* 1150 × 1160: *ibid.*, no. 1352.

1147 and 1154. In 1166 William Arundel, who was probably his son, held a knight's fee of the old enfeoffment and a share in a third of a knight's fee of the new enfeoffment of William II of Percy, consisting of lands in Foston on the Wolds, Nafferton, Auburn and Scorborough just outside the boundaries of Holderness, and in Sneaton which formed part of the liberty of Whitby Strand.[175]

Although the network of wapentake/hundredal centres and aristocratic support constructed by the earl of York in Stephen's reign is impressive, it fell a long way short of encompassing the whole county. William's effective authority was largely confined to the East Riding and the eastern part of the North Riding. In the West Riding the only soke or wapentake centres under his control may have been Knaresborough and Aldborough, and his influence among the aristocracy appears to have been minimal. With the one exception of his success at Selby in *c.* 1143, the earl appears to have failed to make much of an impression on the powerful lordship of Henry of Lacy, which dominated a compact group of six wapentakes extending from Skyrack in the north to Osgoldcross and Staincross in the south (Map 24). There is no evidence that he ever managed (or wanted) to secure control of William III of Warenne's important estate of Conisbrough, which dominated Strafforth wapentake, or of the lordships of Skipton and Percy, which incorporated most of Cravenshire. In the North Riding the lords of Richmond and Mowbray were probably primarily responsible for keeping him out of Richmondshire and the wapentakes of Allerton, *Maneshou*, Birdforth, Halikeld and *Bolesford*. They had every reason to cooperate in doing so. While Alan was competing with William for control of important wapentakes and the custody of wealthy heirs, Roger was William's rival for control of the castle of York and (probably) the honour of Brus.[176] In addition, Alan and Roger were bound to each other by strong tenurial and familial ties, and appear to have been on good terms in Stephen's reign.[177] It may have been in order to stem the earl of York's advance into the North Riding that Roger built a castle at Myton some ten miles north-west of York, and destroyed the bridge over the River Swale there.[178]

---

[175] *EYC*, XI, 196–202.

[176] *Mowbray Charters*, xxiv–xxv, xxvii, xxx, and nos. 255, 263. Mowbray granted the tenancies and services of Peter and William Mauleverer, which belonged by right to the Brus fee, to Eustace Fitz John: see below, pp. 242–3.

[177] See above, p. 168 note 102.   [178] *Mowbray Charters*, no. 318.

ANARCHY BELOW: THE LIMITATIONS OF ARISTOCRATIC DOMINATION

The picture which has been portrayed of Yorkshire in Stephen's reign is that of a county where royal authority devolved into the hands of a powerful earl, who often acted in his own interests rather than those of the king, and who competed with other powerful magnates for the domination of large regions by securing control of wapentake and hundredal centres, and by commanding the allegiance of the local nobility. In determining the success of these magnates in building up aristocratic support we are forced to rely on the witness clauses of charters, evidence for marriages and religious benefactions and chance references in the chronicles. It would be dangerous to make too much of this. We do not know whether the men who attested the charters, married the daughters or sisters and granted lands to the religious houses of magnates like William of Aumale, Henry of Lacy and Roger of Mowbray did so as their subordinates or as their equals. The lesser nobles could be dominated by the magnates, but they were also capable of going their own way.

Here it is useful to draw comparisons between mid-twelfth-century Yorkshire and the eleventh- and twelfth-century Mâconnais region of France, which has been studied in detail by Professor Duby. In the Mâconnais, Duby illustrated that aristocratic relationships could be transformed by the breakdown of central authority, and, in turn, could influence the way in which that authority was exercised. In the late tenth century the counts of Mâcon began to lose control over their *pagus*. The institutions of central government began to disintegrate as the counts lost both their control over the powerful men who held their castles and demesne estates, and their rights over the immunist churches. In order to retain a vestige of control and to secure service the counts were forced to alienate their demesne estates, forests and seignorial rights. As the castellans competed for the spoils, rival claims were often abandoned in return for fealty, and lesser men sought the protection and support of the great: resulting in the formation of chains of vassalage. In the absence of central control society came to be regulated by homage and the fee, and looser forms of affinity based upon oaths and non-tenurial alliances. The regulation only worked, however, where a powerful man enfeoffed or took the homage of a weak one. Between men of more equal rank it was less effective. The relationships that did work ensured the organisation of the lower nobility, who attached themselves to the lord of the local castle, became his *milites castri*, provided him with castle-guard and suit of court, and so brought about the emergence of territorial lordships. The knights, however, were rarely the tenants of a single lord, and along the frontiers of the military districts neighbouring lords had to compete for service through the offer of protection and easier terms of tenure. The frontiers, therefore, became blurred and by the end of the eleventh century the general situation was that

The enfeoffed knight, belonging to several bands of vassals, protected by each of his patrons against all the others, was virtually free of the strictest of military and judicial obligations. He was, in fact, not subject to distraint. Feudal duties without question weighed more heavily on the petty aristocracy than on the great. They did not succeed in genuinely subjecting the vassal to his lord ... In spite of their power and their ability to confiscate the fief of a faithless vassal, the lords had little grip on their men ... The most powerful enjoyed total independence. The lesser nobles, more restricted by the service owed for their fiefs, still had an air of great freedom; for if they committed a crime, there was no definite court to judge them nor power to punish them. For the upper class feudalism was a step toward anarchy.[179]

In terms of the failure of central control, the concomitant growing power of a competitive higher nobility and the formation of looser non-tenurial forms of affinity, there are clear comparisons to be drawn between Duby's picture of the Mâconnais, and Yorkshire in Stephen's reign. And this is also true of the behaviour of the lesser nobility. In both regions some of them sought to exploit their ties with several lords to secure freedom from the regulative constraints of lordship. In Yorkshire this is illustrated by the careers of two magnates from the second rank of noble society, Peter of Goxhill and Adam Fitz Swain.

Peter of Goxhill held important estates of three tenants-in-chief in both Yorkshire and Lincolnshire. His Yorkshire holdings were incorporated within the earl of York's lordship of Holderness, and it is clear that Peter was among his most important tenants. In Farrer's conjectural list of knights' fees held of the honour of

---

[179] G. Duby, 'The nobility in eleventh- and twelfth-century Mâconnais', in *Lordship and Community in Medieval Europe*, ed. F. L. Cheyette (New York, 1975), 137–55, quotation from pp. 144–5.

Holderness, Peter of Goxhill is ranked as the holder of the fifth largest tenancy, with a fee of half a knight.[180] Each of the four men with larger estates held no more than one knight's fee.[181] It is possible that Peter also held land of Earl William in the vill of Goxhill in Lincolnshire, a portion of which was sokeland of the earl's neighbouring manor of Barrow.[182] It was also in Lincolnshire that Peter's lands held of other lords were situated. In addition to an estate of five knights' fees of the old enfeoffment held of Ralph of Bayeux in Goxhill, Newhouse, Brocklesby, Habrough and elsewhere, Peter also held a half knight's fee of the old enfeoffment of William I of Roumare, earl of Lincoln, situated partly in Killingholme.[183]

In the reign of Stephen, Peter may have been able to take advantage of the problems and mutual rivalries of his lords in order to advance his position at their expense.[184] Ralph of Bayeux's estates were a matter of dispute. They had been held at the Domesday survey by Alan of Lincoln and had passed to Ralph in marriage to Alan's daughter and heiress, Margaret. In Stephen's reign, however, a rival claim to Alan of Lincoln's honour was advanced by Ranulf II earl of Chester, the half-brother and ally of William I of Roumare, on the basis that Alan was his mother's uncle; and the honour was bestowed upon the earl by Duke Henry of Normandy in the early months of 1153.

Very much in the thick of things Peter of Goxhill was not a man to miss his opportunities. His aspirations are reflected by the castle and abbey he built at Newhouse. The charter recording the original endowment to Newhouse Abbey indicates that Peter had granted land in Killingholme, belonging to the tenancy-in-chief of William I of Roumare, as if it belonged to the lordship of Ralph of Bayeux. The irregularity is reflected in the confirmation charter issued by the bishop of Lincoln, which lists Peter's gifts with no attempt to distinguish between those held of Roumare and those held of Bayeux. The charter simply records that both magnates had given their concession, and may well reflect an attempt to keep the church's options open in a bid to guarantee the gift

---

[180] *EYC*, III, 34. For notes on the Goxhill family, see *Ibid.*, 61.

[181] By the end of the twelfth century, knight's fees on the lordship of Holderness were unusually large, consisting of forty-eight carucates: English, *Holderness*, 142–3.

[182] See *EYC*, III, nos. 1339, 1341.

[183] *Red Book*, I, 376, 387; *Monasticon*, VI, 865–6.

[184] For the discussion of Peter's career which follows, see Dalton, 'Ranulf of Chester', 116–17 and notes.

against future disputes. Roumare himself may have laid claim to the Bayeux portion of Newhouse.

There is at least a suggestion here that Peter of Goxhill was exploiting, perhaps even provoking, the rivalry of his overlords. William of Roumare may well have been competing for his service. In or about 1145 he granted Peter ten librates of land, including five within the soke of his Lincolnshire *caput* of Bolingbroke, for the service of one knight, and added another knight's fee situated in several other Lincolnshire vills. He also confirmed Peter's gifts to Newhouse Abbey, and those of Geoffrey of Turs who held land in Newhouse of his fee; and appears to have promoted an alliance between Peter and one of his leading tenants, Roger of Benniworth, by which Peter secured an additional interest in the Roumare honour. The terms of this alliance were agreed in the later years of Stephen's reign in the presence of William of Roumare at his *caput* of Bolingbroke. There Roger and Peter made mutual promises to share the expense of recovering the estate of Odo of Benniworth, after which Peter was to hold half of Roger, Roger was to hold half in demesne and Gervase of Halton was to hold the whole estate of them both for the rest of his life. Roger was put in seisin of Gervase's service by William of Roumare's marshal, took the homage of Peter and put him in possession of his half of the estate. The terms of this agreement were used by Professor Stenton to illustrate the supremacy of lordship, but it was a supremacy which was more apparent than real. Although William of Roumare may have been able to exercise some form of influence over Peter, the latter had no justifiable claim to the estates of Odo of Benniworth. Peter's encroachment on Roumare estates, his interference in the descent of the Benniworth fee and the grants made by Roumare to secure his service reflect his local power. With his castle, monastery and abundant supply of money it is likely that he, rather than his distant seignorial overlord, was the force to be reckoned with in the region of Newhouse in Stephen's reign.[185]

The career of Adam Fitz Swain closely resembles that of Peter of Goxhill. At the outset of Stephen's reign Adam was one of the most important tenants of Henry of Lacy's lordship of Pontefract. In 1086 his grandfather, Ailric, held twelve manors of Ilbert I of

---

[185] It has recently been suggested that Peter of Goxhill may have abandoned his castle at Newhouse in favour of a more comfortable and commodious residence nearby: Pounds, *Medieval Castle*, 9–10.

Lacy in at least ten vills in the West Riding, and his father, Swain, held an additional five manors.[186] In 1166 William of Neville held almost eight knights' fees of Henry of Lacy in right of his wife Amabel, Adam's eldest daughter and co-heiress.[187]

Like Peter of Goxhill, Adam Fitz Swain appears to have exploited the political weakness of his lord for his own advantage. The estates of Henry of Lacy were under threat from Scottish attack in Stephen's reign. In 1138 a Scottish force commanded by William Fitz Duncan, nephew of King David, attacked and defeated an English force at Clitheroe in Lancashire and laid waste to the surrounding area.[188] Clitheroe was the site of the *caput* and castle of an extensive conglomeration of Lacy estates in Blackburnshire and Bowland.[189] Together with Cumberland and Cravenshire it may well have been subject to Scottish control for the remainder of Stephen's reign.[190] If so, the Lacy estates in the West Riding of Yorkshire were also vulnerable to attack.

For Adam Fitz Swain the hostility of the Scots and Lacys confronted him with a dilemma. Together with his brother, Henry, he had been enfeoffed by Henry I in a number of important estates in the Vale of Eden in Cumbria, which was dominated by the Scots after 1136.[191] Continued possession of these estates depended on loyalty to King David, something which could only threaten the security of Adam's Lacy estates. In spite of this dilemma, however, Adam not only maintained control of all his lands, but was able considerably to augment his possessions and authority within both the Scottish and Lacy spheres of lordship.

Adam's success in maintaining friendly relations with the Scots is clear from King David's confirmation (*c.* 1141) of his grant of land in Wetheral to St Mary's Abbey, York, and by Adam's attestation of a charter issued by David in or around 1147.[192] Adam's brother, Henry, attested two more charters of David and a charter of David's son, Henry, in the period 1141 × 1152.[193] It may have been Adam's close relationship with David which accounts for his acquisition (by 1158) of the custodianship of Doncaster, an extensive and valuable settlement which had been granted to David's son by King Stephen in the first treaty of

[186] *DB*, I, 316a–17b.   [187] *Red Book*, I, 423; *EYC*, III, 317–19; VII, 177–8.
[188] Symeon, *Opera*, II, 291; *Chronicles of the Reigns*, III, 156.
[189] *VCH, Lancashire*, I, 312–14.   [190] See below, pp. 203–19.
[191] Wightman, *Lacy Family*, 317–18; *EYC*, VII, 177–8.   [192] *ESC*, nos. 140, 187.
[193] *Ibid.*, nos. 138, 141, 244.

Durham in 1136.[194] The same relationship probably also explains Adam's acquisition of one of the largest tenancies to be created after 1135 in the lordship of Skipton in Craven, over which King David's nephew, William Fitz Duncan, appears to have exercised some form of influence or control in Stephen's reign.[195] In addition to a direct tenancy of a knight's fee of the new enfeoffment of the honour of Skipton, Adam secured an important subtenancy in another military fee held by the Fleming family in an outlying portion of the honour close to the estates he held of the Lacys in south Yorkshire.[196] Adam's enfeoffment here may reflect an attempt by William Fitz Duncan to guarantee the security of isolated portions of his honour vulnerable to seizure by the Lacys, by placing them in the hands of Lacy tenants who had power within the area. Within a few miles of this outlying part of the honour of Skipton, Adam Fitz Swain held a castle at Mirfield and constructed a monastery at Monk Bretton (c. 1153 × 1154).[197]

The careers of Peter of Goxhill and Adam Fitz Swain suggest that some of the men of second rank were able to exploit or profit from the disturbances of Stephen's reign to advance their power within the localities; that competition for the service of these men was intense; and that the lordship of the magnates from whom they held their lands was weakening. It will be argued in a later chapter that the anarchy was not solely responsible for these developments, that other factors promoting them were already at work before 1135. But the particular contribution of the disturbances of Stephen's reign in accelerating these developments cannot be doubted. This can be seen most clearly perhaps in the foundation of monasteries. In other areas of the country it has been shown that one of the methods used by some of the magnates of Stephen's reign to strengthen their control of lands and to acquire possession of the lands of their rivals was the advancement of claims to advowsons over monasteries; and that these claims reflect a proprietary pattern of thought, represent 'siege warfare of a subtle and insidious kind' and resulted in destabilisation and the breakdown of lordship.[198] In Yorkshire both the greater and the

---

[194] *PR 2–4 Henry II*, 179.
[195] The estates forming this tenancy were all situated in Cravenshire: *EYC*, VII, 177–8.
[196] *Ibid.*, 178–9, 189, 193–7.
[197] Michelmore, 'Township gazetteer', 455–6; *West Yorkshire*, III, 736, 740–1; King, *Castellarium Anglicanum*, II, 522; *Chartularies of Monkbretton*, v; *EYC*, III, no. 1475.
[198] E. King, 'The foundation of Pipewell Abbey, Northamptonshire', *Haskins Society Journal*, 2 (1990), 167–77, quotation from p. 176.

lesser magnates appear to have been advancing similar claims. This was true of William II of Roumare at Warter, Roger of Mowbray at Byland and Newburgh, Henry of Lacy at Nostell and possibly Gilbert of Gant at Bridlington and Eustace Fitz John at Malton; and it was probably true of Adam Fitz Swain at Monk Bretton.[199]

This might explain the confusion surrounding the constitutional status of Monk Bretton in relation to its mother house, Pontefract Priory. Although a charter issued between 1153 and 1159 by Adam Fitz Swain, and a confirmation charter of Roger archbishop of York, suggest that (in accordance with normal Cluniac practices) the head of the priory of Monk Bretton was to be appointed by the head of its mother house (albeit with Adam's advice), a letter of 'G' the prior of La Charité, the French mother house of Pontefract, written between 1154 and 1159 indicates that a rather different and irregular procedure may have been in operation at some time between these dates. The letter is addressed to 'my special friend ... Adam Fitz Swain', and reveals not only that Adam (the 'advocate') was expected to choose a suitable prior and convent, but also that the prior of Pontefract was only to be involved in the process of election when he was 'requisitus'.[200] One possible explanation for this contradiction is that the letter of Prior 'G' was written shortly after Adam's foundation of Monk Bretton and reflects the disturbed conditions of the anarchy, when churchmen were sometimes forced to submit to the proprietary pretensions of secular lords, whereas the charters of Adam and Archbishop Roger were written after the accession of Henry II and the return of normal circumstances.[201] Whatever the case, there is more than a suggestion in Prior 'G''s letter that at some time between the foundation of Monk Bretton *c.* 1153 × 1154 and Adam Fitz Swain's death in 1159, Adam sought to exercise the same kind of proprietary power over monastic foundations that some of his more powerful neighbours were seeking to exercise during the troubles of Stephen's reign.

It would appear, therefore, that Duby's study of the Mâconnais has some relevance to an understanding of aristocratic politics in

---

[199] For Roumare, see King, 'Parish of Warter', 49–54; Denholm-Young, 'Warter Priory', 212–13; *EYC*, x, nos. 66–7. For Mowbray, see *Monasticon*, v, 350, 353; *Mowbray Charters*, xlii. For Lacy, see *EYC*, III, no. 1497. For Gant's reference to 'my canons' of Bridlington, see *EYC*, II, nos. 1156–7. For Eustace Fitz John's use of similar terms to describe the canons of Malton, see BL Cotton Claudius D xi, fol. 34.

[200] *EYC*, III, nos. 1669–71.

[201] The letter is discussed in Burton, 'Religious orders', 70–4.

Yorkshire in Stephen's reign. In both societies central authority disintegrated, and the limitations of the seignorial authority which replaced it encouraged the emergence of independent or semi-independent lesser nobles, whose activities appear to have been at least partly unrestrained; a situation which might be described as anarchic. But the image of anarchy must be qualified in three important respects. First, the evidence illustrating anarchic conditions is drawn from a limited number of lordships and from the activities of a small group of magnates and 'knights', and it is possible that many lords and their retainers were not prepared to engage in activities which created instability. Secondly, although the civil war of Stephen's reign may have accelerated the process by which the lesser nobles were establishing their independence from their lords, it did not create it; seignorial lordship was limited before Stephen became king.[202] Thirdly, despite the disintegration of central and seignorial control other forces came into play to limit the level of aristocratic conflict. Davis has traced a network of baronial treaties made in the later years of Stephen's reign designed to promote peace and limit destruction, and King has illustrated that the leading ecclesiastical figures were having some success in bringing spiritual pressures to bear to achieve the same goals.[203] The same territorial, tenurial, familial and ecclesiastical influences that produced division and conflict within society could also serve to unify and pacify. So it was in Yorkshire.

THE LIMITATIONS OF ANARCHY AND THE ESTABLISHMENT
OF PEACE

A charter of Roger of Mowbray issued between 1142 and *c.* 1154 reveals that although he had seized property and extracted castle works and illegal taxes from the abbey of St Mary's, York, he was prepared to admit and make reparation for his wrongs.[204] In addition, the charter confirms a tenurial settlement made between the abbey and one of Roger's principal tenants, William of Arches, by 'the oath of twelve lawful men ... in the presence of Augustine prior of Newburgh and the men of William of Arches, to whose fee the [disputed land] pertains ... who at my command were present on the appointed day'. William of Arches and his tenants

---

[202] See below, pp. 259–81.
[203] Davis, *King Stephen*, 108–11; King, 'Anarchy', 133–54.
[204] *Mowbray Charters*, no. 318; *English Lawsuits*, I, no. 345.

had made a settlement through legal procedure rather than force of arms, and they had done so in a court which had been convened by the authority of their lord. The settlement had then been confirmed by the lord in a document described as an 'agreement and pact', to which the lord bound himself in the hands of his retainers. It is a document which reveals that, at least in this area of Yorkshire, lordship was far from entirely defunct, and that it could be strengthened by other forces, such as those of religion and neighbourhood, promoting regulation and order within society.

Just as he had made his peace with St Mary's, Roger of Mowbray provided similar recompense to several other religious houses he had offended. At some time between *c.* 1143 and 1153 Selby Abbey obtained a grant of Middlethorpe near York, because of the damage Roger had done to the house; and on 17 April 1153 Roger offered compensation for the harm he had done to St Peter's, York.[205] The church was to have similar successes with many of Roger's neighbours, among them the earl of York, who came in turn to repent their sins and to accept the settlement of the succession crisis.[206]

If the churchmen were responsible in part for bringing the secular magnates to terms, they also appear to have been intent on healing the divisions within their own ranks. When William Fitz Herbert returned to Yorkshire as archbishop in 1154 he did so after calling at the abbey of Meaux and its mother house, Fountains, which had opposed his election in 1141. That the purpose of the visit was reconciliation is clear from his promise of compensation to Fountains for the damage done when his supporters burnt the abbey during the election dispute, and from the charter he issued for Meaux confirming land in Wawne which belonged to the archbishop's fee.[207] At about the same time he issued confirmation charters in favour of Nostell Priory and the priory of Kirkham, which had also firmly rejected his authority.[208] It is significant that the Kirkham charter was attested by Cuthbert prior of Guisborough, another of the archbishop's former opponents.[209] Churchmen as well as laymen were prepared in the long run to lay aside their differences in the interests of peace.

[205] *English Lawsuits*, I, nos. 255, 322; *EYC*, III, no. 1823.

[206] Those issuing similar charters include Gilbert of Gant: Abbot, 'Gant family', 377 (no. 123), 381 (no. 126).

[207] D. Knowles, 'The case of Saint William of York', *CHJ*, 5 (1936), 174; *Chronica de Melsa*, I, 94, 116–17. For the burning of Fountains, see *Memorials of Fountains*, I, 101.

[208] *Episcopal Acta*, nos. 91, 97.   [209] *Ibid.*, no. 91.

CONCLUSION

Viewed from one perspective the history of Yorkshire between 1135 and 1154 embodies all the elements in the traditional interpretation of Stephen's reign as a period of anarchy. It was home to a body of aggressive and expansionist magnates who competed for wealth and power at the expense of the church and king. The result was the limitation, and almost the failure, of central control. And yet if we attempt to penetrate behind the actions of the barons, and to explore the motives that gave rise to them, we obtain a rather different impression of aristocratic society and politics in Yorkshire at this time. In one sense Earl William and his neighbours were typical of the nobility of their era, responding to pressures and pursuing ambitions common to their class. These, above all, were tenurial and familial, and they were not confined to the reign of Stephen. It was natural for magnates under constant pressure to alienate their resources and provide for their families, to try and replenish these resources through the acquisition of lands and rights. And it was natural that their attempts to do so should result in competition and conflict between them.[210] This was just as true of the period before 1135 as it was to be during the anarchy. What was different about Stephen's reign, at least so far as Yorkshire is concerned, was that the restraints imposed by the operation of royal administration and justice on this conflict were disintegrating, leading to the development of widespread disorder. In large part this disintegration resulted from the breakdown of the central administrative system of Henry I, and the replacement of this system with the local authority of William earl of York, who appears to have been more intent on serving his own interests rather than those of the king, and whose private ambitions were sometimes pursued at the expense of royal authority and public order. But the deterioration of this authority and order was never complete. King Stephen managed to retain control of York until 1154, and outside the city baronial aggression was occasionally tempered by respect for religion, ties of neighbourhood and the force of lordship. This is reflected most clearly perhaps in the career of the earl of York himself. Although prepared to undermine royal authority and public order, in the later years of Stephen's reign

[210] See below Chapter 7.

194

William either sanctioned or instituted a series of measures which promoted their restoration, including the treaty of Westminster, the provision of recompense for the priory of Bridlington (which he had converted into a castle) and the foundation of a Cistercian monastery at Meaux with monks drawn from the abbey of Fountains (which had opposed his attempt to secure the election of William Fitz Herbert to the archbishopric of York).[211] It was not that the earl had changed, that an anarchist had suddenly seen the error of his ways, become a monarchist and discovered religion, but rather that the political environment had changed and that William, along with many of his fellow magnates, had altered his policy accordingly. There was to be no place under Henry II for the type of independent and aggressive local potentate who had dominated large areas of England under Stephen.

---

[211] *Regesta*, III, no. 272; *EYC*, III, no. 1306; I, no. 362; *Chronica de Melsa*, I, 76–83.

Chapter 5

THE SCOTS IN THE NORTH

In the reign of Stephen Yorkshire resumed its early eleventh-century position as a frontier county. The king was unable to prevent Scottish incursions into Cumbria, Northumberland and Durham in January 1136 and January 1138; and his retaliatory campaign of February 1138 did nothing to provide security against further attacks. The Scots were ceded the lordship of Carlisle in the first treaty of Durham in 1136, and the earldom of Northumbria in the second treaty of Durham in 1139. In Yorkshire Stephen placed royal administrative and military power in the hands of a single magnate, William earl of York; a policy which resembles the frontier strategy of previous English kings in the marcher counties on the border with Wales. It was a policy which failed to safeguard Yorkshire from a further extension of Scottish authority and influence.

This chapter will elucidate and explain the growth of Scottish power in the far north of England and Yorkshire in Stephen's reign, and King David's ultimate aims within the region. It will reveal that the scope of Scottish ambitions in England during the anarchy may have been much broader than has hitherto been realised. Its premise is that by 1135 there was a tradition of close political, tenurial and religious ties between northern England and Scotland, and that although these ties were redefined after the Norman conquest and colonisation of the north, the tradition was maintained into the twelfth century and exploited by the Scots in Stephen's reign to increase their authority within Cumbria and Northumberland. Having achieved this, the Scots were then able to use similar ties which existed between the 'border' counties and the shires immediately to the south of them, to expand their influence further into England. They were able to strengthen relationships with the magnates and monastic houses of Yorkshire which they had already begun to construct in the reign of Henry I, and to exploit these relationships to build up their territorial and political influence within the county. And they went further. In 1138 and again in 1149 King David of Scotland launched armed invasions of Yorkshire. If these invasions had been successful, and if David had been able to come to terms with the powerful earl of York, they might have resulted in the incorporation of Yorkshire, and possibly the archbishopric of York, within the kingdom of Scotland.

THE ANGLO-SCOTTISH 'BORDER' BEFORE 1135

Before the arrival of the Normans, and for many years after 1066, the boundaries of Scottish influence and authority in northern England were situated considerably further south than the much later border, which followed the lines of the Tweed in the east and the Solway and Sark in the west. In the seventh and eighth centuries the region between the Rivers Tyne and Forth formed a cultural and, frequently, political unity, and it was only after the decline of Northumbria in the ninth century that the Scots of the Scoto-Pictish kingdom north of the Forth began to move south, and that the line of the Tweed became important.[1] It was not, however, in any sense a fixed border. Before the arrival of the Normans in England successive Scottish kings attempted to secure control of Northumbria below the Tweed by military force, and although ultimately unsuccessful were able to forge and maintain links with the Anglo-Scandinavian nobility of the region, some of whom were employed in the administration of the Scottish lowlands.[2] In the period after 1066 King Malcolm III of Scotland launched four separate invasions of northern England, in one of which he penetrated as far south as Cleveland, and hoped to strengthen his influence in the region further by attempting (unsuccessfully) to arrange a marriage between his daughter, Edith, and the powerful Breton lord of Richmond, Count Alan I.[3]

Scottish influence in what was to become English Cumbria was even stronger than in Northumbria. Its origins lay in the eighth and ninth centuries when the British kingdom of Cumbria began to expand southwards from the Clyde valley, stretching eventually from Glen Falloch to the Rere Cross on Stainmore. In 945 King Edmund of Wessex overran Strathclyde and committed the

---

[1] Barrow, 'Anglo-Scottish border', 21–42.   [2] Barrow, 'Cumbria', 132.
[3] Kapelle, *Norman Conquest*, 93, 122–4, 139, 147–54, 174; Searle, *Women*, 30–6.

Conquest, anarchy and lordship

Cumbrian kingdom to the charge of Malcolm I king of Scots. Although the Britons threw off Malcolm's overlordship, Scottish rule was restored on the death of the last Briton king in 1018 and, with the possible exception of a few years before 1055, was to remain in force for the next three-quarters of a century.[4]

The coming of the Normans eventually resulted in the termination of Scottish control over Cumberland and Westmorland, and the extension of the direct authority of the English kings to the lines of the Solway, Sark and Tweed.[5] Although the Conqueror made some progress towards integrating Northumbria beyond the Tees into his kingdom by launching a brutal campaign against the nobility of the region, by appointing his men to the bishopric of Durham and earldom of Northumbria and by constructing castles at Durham and Newcastle, the major task of conquest and colonisation was left to his sons.[6] In the east, Rufus endowed Guy of Balliol with baronies in upper Teesdale and Bywell in the Tyne valley, and may have been the king responsible for granting the Northumberland lordships of Prudhoe/ Redesdale, Mitford and Callerton to the Umfravilles, Bertrams and la Vals respectively.[7] In the west, he invested his steward, Ivo Taillebois, with a lordship stretching from Ribblesdale to Kendale and with lands in the upper Eden, established castles and towns at Carlisle and (probably) Church Brough, brought in knights and peasants from the south to colonise them and placed the region under the ecclesiastical jurisdiction of the bishop of Durham.[8] His efforts were consolidated by Henry I who established Eustace Fitz John, Walter Espec, Ranulf of Merlay and several other continental magnates in important Northumberland lordships; gave extensive baronies in Cumbria to Robert of Trivers, Forne Fitz Sigulf, Richer of Boivill and the Meschin brothers, Ranulf and William; fortified the walls of Carlisle; directed the foundation of a new priory and bishopric centred

---

[4] Barrow, 'Anglo-Scottish border', 24–30.   [5] Ibid., 26–8, 37–9.
[6] Symeon, Opera, II, 211; Kapelle, Norman Conquest, 120–42.
[7] Austin, 'Barnard castle', 50–6; Hedley, Northumberland Families, I, 26–8, 145–7, 203–5, 208–11; Kapelle, Norman Conquest, 147–54; L. Keen, 'The Umfravilles, the castle and the barony of Prudhoe, Northumberland', ANS, 5 (1983), 171; Sanders, Baronies, 25–6, 109, 131.
[8] Farrer, Kendale, I, viii–x, 1; M. W. Beresford, 'Medieval town plantation in the Carlisle area', Archaeological Journal, 115 (1958), 216; ASC, s.a. 1092; Barrow, 'Cumbria', 121; H. H. E. Craster, 'A contemporary record of the pontificate of Ranulf Flambard', Archaeologia Aeliana, 4th ser., 7 (1930), 37–9, nos. iii, v; Regesta, I, nos. 463, 478; Episcopal Acta, no. 2 and note.

198

upon the city; and through his sheriffs and itinerant justices brought the region within the royal financial and judicial system.[9]

Although the Normans had made great strides towards the integration of Northumberland and Cumbria with the English kingdom by 1135, the process was far from complete.[10] The settlement of Northumberland was still in progress in the reign of Henry II when the barony of Langley in south Tynedale, west of Corbridge, was first organised.[11] Moreover, the region retained strong ties with Scotland. Although the northern boundaries of the new Norman baronies extended as far as the Solway, Sark and Tweed, they never constituted a sharp barrier between Scottish and English political, territorial and familial influence. This is clear from the composition of King David's court which was something of a magnet for the sons of important Northumbrian nobles, who were sent there to acquire an upbringing, education and career. Among the more famous young men who served their apprenticeships there were Ailred, son of Eilaf II the last hereditary priest of Hexham, and King David's stepson, Waldef, grandson of Waltheof earl of Northumbria.[12] In Cumbria the ties were even stronger. The kings of Scotland retained control of the Cumbrian barony of Gilsland, and at least the northern part of Tynedale.[13] They also maintained close links with the Anglo-Scandinavian families of the area, who witnessed their charters, served in their administrations and married the sons and daughters of their

[9] The date at which most of the continental lords of Northumberland and Cumbria were established in their lordships cannot be established with absolute precision. It is possible that some of them were granted their lands by Rufus rather than Henry I. What is certain is that they were in possession by 1135. See, Sanders, *Baronies*, 65, 103, 115, 149; Symeon, *Opera*, II, 291; *PR 31 Henry I*, 35; *VCH, Cumberland*, I, 303–6; Barrow, 'Cumbria', 121. For the establishment of continental lords in the far north generally, see J. A. Green, 'Anglo-Scottish relations, 1066–1174', in *England and Her Neighbours, 1066–1453. Essays in Honour of Pierre Chaplais*, ed. M. Jones and M. Vale (London, 1989), 57, 60, 63–4. For the fortification of Carlisle and establishment of a priory and bishopric there, see Symeon, *Opera*, II, 267; *PR 31 Henry I*, 140–1; *Regesta*, II, nos. 572, 1431, 1491; J. C. Dickinson, 'The origins of the cathedral of Carlisle', *TCWAAS*, 45 (1945), 134–43; *idem, Austin Canons*, 246–50; H. S. Offler, 'A note on the early history of the priory of Carlisle', *TCWAAS*, 65 (1965), 176–81; Nicholl, *Thurstan*, 146–50. For the extension of English royal justice, see *PR 31 Henry I*, 24, 27, 31, 33, 35–6, 131–2, 142–3.

[10] J. A. Green, 'Aristocratic loyalties on the northern frontier of England, *c.* 1100–1174', in *England in the Twelfth Century*, ed. D. Williams (Woodbridge, 1990), 84–94.

[11] Kapelle, *Norman Conquest*, 130.

[12] *Vita Ailredi*, xiii, xxxii, xxxiv–xxxv, xl–xli, lxxi; F. M. Powicke, 'The dispensator of King David I', *SHR*, 23 (1926), 34–41.

[13] Kapelle, *Norman Conquest*, 130–1 and notes.

magnates. According to Professor Barrow, the invasion of
northern England by King David of Scotland in 1136 'merely
brought back under Scottish rule many landowners and peasants
who can hardly have had time to accept the Solway as the fixed
and immemorial border between the northern and southern
kingdoms'.[14]

THE REINFORCEMENT OF SCOTTISH INFLUENCE IN THE
NORTH 1100–35

The first three decades of the twelfth century witnessed a
substantial reinforcement of Scottish influence in northern England. By far the most important element in this reinforcement was
the marriage in 1113 or 1114 of David of Scotland to Matilda, the
daughter and heiress of Waltheof earl of Northumbria and
Countess Judith, the Conqueror's niece. This marriage brought
David control of the earldom of Huntingdon (and possibly
Northampton), and lordship of the important 'shire' of Hallam in
Yorkshire.[15] It was arranged by King Henry I, at whose court
David had been brought up, educated and knighted.[16] Henry I
cultivated further tenurial and family ties between the northern
shires of England and the Scottish lowlands, through his generosity
to the magnates of the region. He gave the granddaughter and
heiress of Osbert the sheriff (of Yorkshire and Lincolnshire),
Milisent, together with her lands in Yorkshire and Lincolnshire, in
marriage to Herbert, lord of Kinneil, who in *c.* 1136 became King
David's chamberlain.[17] He also granted the extensive Northumberland lordship of Beanley to Gospatric, earl of Dunbar, who was
the son of Gospatric earl of Northumbria (d. 1074–5), the probable
half-brother of Waldeve, lord of Papcastle (Cumb.), and a close
relative of several women who married important nobles from
either Cumbria or Scotland.[18]

[14] Barrow, 'Anglo-Scottish border', 29.
[15] *ASC, s.a.* 1114; Barrow, 'Scottish rulers and religious orders', 85; *Complete Peerage*, VI,
641; IX, 662–3; Freeman, *Norman Conquest*, IV, 301, 524, 601.
[16] Orderic, IV, 274–6; Barrow, *David I*, 17–18.
[17] For Osbert's terms of office, see Green, *Sheriffs*, 54, 89. For his lands in Yorkshire and
Lincolnshire, see W. Farrer, 'The sheriffs of Lincolnshire and Yorkshire, 1066–1130',
EHR, 30 (1915), 277–85; Green, *Government*, 171, 189, 195–6, 199–200; *EYC*, XI,
213–17.
[18] For notes on the descendants of Earl Gospatric, see Hedley, *Northumberland Families*, I,
238–41; Hodgson, *Northumberland*, 24–31 and pedigree facing p. 104; Sanders, *Baronies*,
106, 134. The sisters or half-sisters of Gospatric included Gunnilda, who married the
powerful Copeland tenant, Orm Fitz Ketel; and Etheldreda, who married King

The traffic in patronage was far from all one way. From 1107, when he first assumed control of Scotland south of the Forth and Clyde as 'sub-king', David began to import Anglo-Norman magnates to colonise and administer the area.[19] The majority of these immigrants, many of whom attested David's charters and those of his son Henry with some regularity, were drawn mainly from the honour of Huntingdon, West Wessex, Normandy, Yorkshire and other parts of northern England.[20] The 'northerners' included Robert I of Brus, lord of extensive estates in north-east Yorkshire and in the region immediately to the north of the River Tees, who appears to have become associated with the future King David in the second (possibly the first) decade of the twelfth century, and who in *c.* 1124 was granted the Scottish barony of Annandale.[21] Other Anglo-Norman beneficiaries of David's patronage included men from more old-established families, like Alan of Percy, an illegitimate son of Alan I of Percy lord of Topcliffe (Yorks.), who received lands in Roxburghshire; Hugh of Morville (a relative of the Morvilles who held considerable estates in Huntingdon, Yorkshire, Cumberland, Westmorland and elsewhere), who obtained the lordships of Cunningham and Lauderdale; and William of Somerville, a tenant of the Lacy family in the West Riding of Yorkshire, who secured the baronies of Linton in Roxburghshire and Carnwath in Lanarkshire.[22] And in addition to granting them lands, King David attracted these magnates to his court, and employed them in his service.[23] Several more important Northumbrian barons are to be found among the witnesses to charters issued by David in *c.* 1113, *c.* 1124 and *c.* 1131 × 1136, including Eustace Fitz John, lord of

Duncan II of Scotland and by him was the mother of William Fitz Duncan. Waldeve's daughters, Gunnilda and Octreda, married Uhctred Fitz Fergus, lord of Galloway, and Ranulf of Lindsey, one of King David's closest companions, respectively. See *ESC*, 406; *Register of St. Bees*, nos. 3, 4, 32, 52, 223, 232 and notes, pp. ix, 339, 384, 465; *Register of Holm Cultram*, 34, nos. 49, 49d, 210; G. Washington, 'The parentage of William de Lancaster, lord of Kendal', *TCWAAS*, 62 (1962), 95–100.

[19] Barrow, *Anglo-Norman Era*, Chapters 2–4.

[20] G. W. S. Barrow, 'Scotland's "Norman" families', in Barrow, *Kingdom of the Scots*, 315–36; idem, *Anglo-Norman Era*, 97–117.

[21] For the Brus estates in Yorkshire, see *EYC*, II, 16–19; *Red Book*, I, 434–5. For Robert's early connections with David, see Green, 'Aristocratic loyalties', 95. For the grant of Annandale, see *ESC*, no. 54.

[22] *EYC*, XI, 3; Barrow, *Anglo-Norman Era*, 97 note 23, 70–84, 107–9, 177, 193–4; Young, *William Cumin*, 12.

[23] *ESC*, nos. 50, 54, 87, 121–3, 131, 137, 141, 145, 163, 172, 177, 179, 182, 187, 195, 236, 244; *Regesta Scottorum*, I, nos. 11–12, 17, 24–5, 28–9, 31, 34–6, 41–2, 44.

Alnwick and Malton, and Walter Espec, lord of Wark and Helmsley.[24] The close ties between David and the baronage of Northumbria and Cumbria are reflected again in the military assistance given to David by Walter Espec and several other northern lords, in defeating a Scottish rebellion led by the earl of Moray in 1134; assistance which helped David to expand his authority in Scotland beyond that of any of his predecessors.[25]

The last fifteen years of Henry I's reign also witnessed the beginnings of important new religious links between northern England, especially Yorkshire, and Scotland. King Alexander and King David were intent on importing Norman monasticism as well as Norman magnates. The first moves were made in 1120 when Alexander invited the Yorkshire Augustinian priory of Nostell to provide canons for the establishment of a priory at Scone. Four years later the prior of Nostell, Robert, was elected bishop of St Andrew's in succession to Turgot (1109–15), who had been prior of the Benedictine house of Durham.[26] Robert's successor at Nostell, Adelulf, became the first bishop of the new diocese established at Carlisle in 1133, and brought in Augustinian canons to serve the priory there.[27] Scottish links with Nostell were further reinforced when Waldef, stepson and courtier of King David, entered the house as a novice, possibly around 1130.[28] By the end of 1139 at the latest Waldef had become prior of the Augustinian house of Kirkham in the East Riding of Yorkshire, and possibly owed his election to the founder, Walter Espec, who exercised important influence within the house, and who, as we have seen, had assisted King David to establish his authority in Scotland in the early 1130s.[29] David's decision to send one of his household officials, Ailred, on a diplomatic mission to Yorkshire at about this time, and Ailred's decision during the mission to visit Walter Espec at his castle of Helmsley and to join Walter's new Cistercian abbey of Rievaulx, smacks of something more than coincidence.[30] To what extent Walter was acting under the

[24] *ESC*, nos. 35, 54, 98; *Regesta Scottorum*, I, no. 9.
[25] Ritchie, *Normans in Scotland*, 230–3. [26] Nicholl, *Thurstan*, 136.
[27] *VCH, Yorkshire*, III, 234; *VCH, Cumberland*, II, 150.
[28] *Vita Ailredi*, lxxi and note 2.
[29] D. Baker, 'Legend and reality: the case of Waldef of Melrose', in *Church, Society and Politics*, ed. D. Baker (Oxford, 1975), 59–82, esp. 75, 79. See Dickinson, *Austin Canons*, 123 note 3; *EYC*, x, no. 105.
[30] *Vita Ailredi*, xliii, 10–17; M. L. Dutton, 'The conversion and vocation of Aelred of Rievaulx: a historical hypothesis', in *England in the Twelfth Century*, ed. D. Williams (Woodbridge, 1990), 31–49.

influence of the Scottish king is difficult to say, but what is certain is David's determination to employ his secular contacts in Yorkshire to promote monastic ties between Scotland and northern England. In the years that followed, this determination grew in strength, and the ties that were formed assumed a new and important political significance.

Although the establishment of a French aristocracy north of the Tweed in the 150 years after 1102 was described by Ritchie as a 'Norman conquest' of Scotland, it also increased the pre-existing influence of the Scots kings in the north of England and elsewhere, and strengthened the foundations upon which they might have established their direct control of these areas had the political opportunity to do so arisen.[31] One opportunity came with the death of Henry I and the accession of Stephen in 1135, and King David wasted little time in seizing it. The seeds of Scottish influence that had been sown throughout northern England were to grow and develop rapidly during the next fifteen years, and come to a dangerous fruition which threatened radically to change the course of the history of the entire region.

NORTHUMBRIA AND CUMBRIA IN KING STEPHEN'S REIGN: THE RISE OF SCOTTISH DOMINATION

In the words of Professor Davis, 'Waiting for the death of Henry I must have been like waiting for the Bomb.'[32] When the bomb exploded the shock-waves were probably felt as strongly at the Scottish court as anywhere. As Barrow has stated, 'There can be no question that David and the Scots had a vested interest in the Angevin succession.'[33] David had been a friend of Henry I, had benefited greatly from his patronage and had been the first of his magnates to swear an oath to accept the succession of Empress Matilda in 1126.[34] Although he had been forced to accept the consolidation of Norman territorial and military control in Northumberland and Cumbria, he was compensated with the grant of English estates and judicial powers, the formation of even closer ties with the northern English magnates and English assistance in strengthening and expanding his own authority within Scotland. In King Stephen he faced a potentially dangerous prospect, who threatened to exclude him from the prosperous

[31] Ritchie, *Normans in Scotland*, xi–xv. [32] Davis, *King Stephen*, 12.
[33] Barrow, *David I*, 17. [34] *Historia Novella*, 4.

community of Norman England and English Normandy. And yet, if Stephen's accession created new problems, it also offered new opportunities. Here at last was a chance for David to throw off the Anglo-Norman overlordship of Scotland first established at Abernethy in 1072, and to recover Cumbria and secure control of Northumbria, which he almost certainly regarded as rightly belonging to his dominions. David pursued both these ambitions during the next two decades, and Barrow has argued that his ultimate goal was the creation of a new political entity, 'a Scoto-Northumbrian kingdom whose southern boundary was to run, however indeterminately, along the Tees, across Stainmore, and either through the Howgill and Shap Fells to reach the western sea by the River Duddon, or else, more ambitiously, to take in the whole of Westmorland and Lancashire as far as the Ribble'.[35] The following paragraphs will elucidate David's attempt to extend his control over the far northern shires of England after 1135, the nature of the authority he sought to exercise and his degree of success. They will reveal that his ambitions extended beyond the Tees and Ribble to include Yorkshire, and that his ultimate goal may have been the domination of the whole of England north of the southern boundary of Yorkshire; in other words, the old earldom of Northumbria.

David responded quickly to the death of Henry I. As soon as he heard of Stephen's accession he invaded England, seized the fortresses of Carlisle, Wark, Alnwick, Norham and Newcastle, and received allegiance and security from the northern magnates that they would maintain their fealty to the empress. However, in a peace conference with Stephen, held at Durham in February, David restored nearly all the castles he had seized, and allowed his son, Henry, to perform homage to Stephen at York in return for a grant of Carlisle and Doncaster, a confirmation of the earldom of Huntingdon and a promise that if Stephen decided to create an earl of Northumbria he would first consider Henry's claim.[36]

It is clear that David did not consider the treaty of Durham as a bar to the pursuit of his ambitions in northern England. In 1137, taking advantage of Stephen's visit to Normandy, he set out to lay waste to Northumbria, and was only prevented from doing so by the assembly of an English force at Newcastle and the diplomacy of Archbishop Thurstan, who managed to negotiate a suspension

---

[35] Barrow, *David I*, 18.
[36] Symeon, *Opera*, II, 287; *Chronicles of the Reigns*, III, 145–6.

of arms.[37] In 1138, after Stephen's return to England, the fragile peace was quickly broken. Stephen's refusal, early in January, to grant the earldom of Northumbria to Henry of Scotland provoked a Scottish invasion of the region. David's forces poured south across the Tweed, besieged Wark and ravaged the countryside as far south as Durham. Although a retaliatory English campaign forced the Scots temporarily back across the Tweed, Stephen was unable to consolidate his success, and David launched another invasion of Northumberland after Easter. It was during this second attack that a detachment of Scottish troops under the command of David's nephew, William Fitz Duncan, reached Clitheroe in Lancashire, defeated an English force under the command of Ilbert II of Lacy and went on to devastate Cravenshire. Although the Scots themselves were subsequently defeated at the battle of the Standard in August 1138, they were only brought to terms eight months later through the agency of Stephen's queen at Durham in April 1139.[38] In the treaty agreed there King Stephen granted Henry of Scotland the earldom of Northumbria (with the exception of Newcastle, Bamburgh, Hexhamshire and the territory of St Cuthbert's, Durham), the possession of two settlements in southern England which were of equal value to Newcastle and Bamburgh and the hand in marriage of Ada the sister of William III of Warenne. In return Henry attended Stephen's court throughout the summer, surrendered hostages and probably renewed his homage.

The second treaty of Durham provoked antagonism among elements of the English baronage, and has been seen by some historians as one of Stephen's failures.[39] But what did it mean for Scottish authority in the north? Were the Scots able to transform their nominal control of the 'border' counties into a practical reality? It is certainly true that the extension of Norman rule in northern England made David's task of ruling easier. The arrival of new lay and ecclesiastical personnel, together with new castles and church buildings, betokened the emergence of a 'feudal' society with the organisation and stability to be taken over. And in taking them over David appears to have interpreted the grants made to Henry of Scotland in the two treaties of Durham as having included the authority to exercise regalian rights throughout the 'border' counties.

[37] Symeon, *Opera*, II, 288; *Chronicles of the Reigns*, III, 150–1.
[38] Symeon, *Opera*, II, 300.   [39] Davis, *King Stephen*, 46.

In Northumberland Henry of Scotland appears to have established control of the royal boroughs and castles of Newcastle and Bamburgh, despite their apparent exclusion from the 1139 treaty. He granted demesne land and other possessions in Newcastle, together with the property of Aslach (described as 'burgensem meum de Novo Castello'), to St Bartholomew's Priory, Newcastle; and he issued charters in the borough in favour of the monasteries of Durham and Tynemouth.[40] It was to Newcastle that King David had the future William I conducted in 1152 after the death of Henry of Scotland, in order to take the pledges of the magnates of Northumberland and 'subject them to the young man's government'.[41] Scottish control of Bamburgh is indicated by the issue of charters, and possibly coins, there by Henry of Scotland.[42] These charters and coins suggest that Henry and his father were seeking not only to control the centres of English royal authority in Northumberland, but also to exercise regalian rights throughout the region. The charters were addressed by Henry in royal style to his justice, constable, sheriff and barons of Northumbria, and sometimes refer to this region as a *comitatus*, or as the area *inter Tinam et Twedam*. In one charter, issued in favour of Tynemouth Priory, Henry confirmed King Henry I's grant of the right to hold a court, released the priory from the obligation of maintaining the castle of Newcastle and all other castles in Northumberland, and excused its demesne peasants from army and escort service within the county for the defence of the earl's land.[43] Behind Henry there was the shadow of King David. As if to underline the fact, Henry was styled 'son of the king of Scotland' in nearly all of his comital charters, and David himself, despite receiving no direct authority over Northumbria in the 1139 treaty, issued his own charters from Newcastle confirming Henry I's gifts to Tynemouth Priory and granting it his peace.[44]

There is evidence that the Scots were also seeking to exercise regalian rights in Cumbria. King David made the royal borough and castle of Carlisle the principal seat of his court and administration, minted coins there and issued charters from the city addressed in royal style to his ministers, sheriffs and justices of Cumberland, Cumbria, Westmorland and Copeland; charters in

---

[40] *Regesta Scottorum*, I, nos. 32, 23, 27, 43.   [41] Symeon, *Opera*, II, 327.
[42] *Regesta Scottorum*, I, no. 28; Mack, 'Anarchy', 99–101.
[43] *Regesta Scottorum*, I, nos. 11, 22, 24–8, 32, 43; *ESC*, nos. 129, 137.
[44] *Regesta Scottorum*, I, nos. 30–1.

which he exercised rights which the English kings would have claimed as their preserve.[45] In addition, David encouraged the establishment of his Scottish nobles in Cumbrian baronies. His nephew and ally, William Fitz Duncan, secured control of the lordship of Copeland after the death of Ranulf Meschin in the period 1135 x 1140, and issued charters addressed to the men of the honour disposing of lands belonging to it, and confirming the gifts of the Meschin lords and their tenants to the abbeys of St Bees and Furness.[46] Fitz Duncan was also to succeed his cousin, Alan Fitz Waldeve (who probably died *c.* 1150), in the lordship of Papcastle, despite the fact that Alan had two married sisters who survived him.[47] Further east, David's constable, Hugh of Morville, received the lordship of Westmorland, which he was still holding when Henry II resumed the 'border' counties from the Scots in 1157.[48]

It was one thing to claim royal and baronial authority in the 'border' counties, and quite another to make this authority effective; and it remains to consider how far King David and his son were able to transform their nominal control of the region into practical reality. William of Newburgh, writing in the late twelfth century, stated that David of Scotland kept the region as far south as the Tees in peace in Stephen's reign; and there is evidence that David was able to do so because he was successful in securing the support of some of the local aristocrats, on whom real authority depended.[49] In Northumberland Robert Bertram, lord of Mitford, served for a time as Earl Henry's sheriff, and Gilbert of Umfraville, lord of Prudhoe/Redesdale, appears to have acted as Henry's constable.[50] Gilbert's nephew, Odinel, is known to have been dear to Henry and was brought up at his court.[51] There he would have witnessed visits by several other powerful Northumberland magnates who are known to have attested Scottish royal *acta*. In addition to his father and the lords of Bertram they included Eustace Fitz John, lord of Alnwick, Walter of Bolbec, lord of Styford, Ralph and Roger Merlay, successive lords of Morpeth,

[45] B. H. I. H. Stewart, 'An uncertain mint of David I', *BNJ*, 29 (1958–9), 293–6; Mack, 'Anarchy', 97–8; *ESC, passim*; *Regesta Scottorum*, I, *passim*; *Chronicles of the Reigns*, III, 170; Symeon, *Opera*, II, 322–3, 326, 328. For the charters addressed to the officials of Cumberland, Cumbria and Copeland, see *ESC*, nos. 123, 126, 140, 187.
[46] *Register of St. Bees*, nos. 16, 40; *EYC*, VII, 11.
[47] Hedley, *Northumberland Families*, I, 238–41; Sanders, *Baronies*, 134.
[48] Barrow, *Anglo-Norman Era*, 71–3.   [49] *Chronicles of the Reigns*, I, 70.
[50] *Regesta Scottorum*, I, no. 27; *ESC*, no. 257; Hedley, *Northumberland Families*, I, 191–2.
[51] *Jordan Fantosme's Chronicle*, ed. R. C. Johnston (Oxford, 1981), 44–6.

Odard, sheriff of Bamburgh, and Reginald de Muschamp, lord of Wooler.[52] These men were sometimes joined by the magnates of Cumbria. The most prominent among them were King David's nephew, William Fitz Duncan, who acquired the lordships of Copeland and Papcastle, and Adelulf, bishop of Carlisle, with whom David was reconciled in 1138.[53] Thereafter the bishop is to be found among other Cumbrian witnesses to the charters of David and his son Henry, who included Walter, prior of Carlisle, Alan Fitz Waldeve, lord of Papcastle, Gospatric Fitz Orm, lord of Workington, Adam and Henry Fitz Swain who between them held most of the Eden valley, and members of the Engaine family who may have been related to Ranulf Engaine, the husband of the heiress to the lordship of Burgh by Sands.[54]

Too much, however, should not of be made of these charter attestations. In some cases they were very infrequent, and even when regular are hardly sufficient to prove that King David and his son 'controlled' these magnates. They have to be balanced against other evidence which indicates that the Scots were having to compete for the allegiance of the northern magnates, and that some of these magnates were going their own way. This can be seen in the case of Bernard of Balliol, lord of Bywell (Northumb.) and Barnard (Yorks.), and Robert I of Brus, lord of Annandale in Scotland and Skelton (Yorks.), who came to David immediately before the battle of the Standard to plead with him not to engage the English army, and withdrew their homage and fealty to him when he refused.[55] Although both lords appear to have restored their relations with the Scots before 1142, Bernard is known to have attended the Scottish court only once after 1138, and Robert's decision to grant Annandale to the younger of his two

---

[52] *ESC*, nos. 35, 104, 123, 129, 131–3, 137, 172, 177, 184, 199, 247, 271; *Regesta Scottorum*, I, nos. 11–13, 21, 23, 30, 32–3, 41, 52. For notes on these families and their estates, see Keen, 'The Umfravilles', 166–82; *Red Book*, I, 427; Sanders, *Baronies*, 65, 84–5, 131, 184; *ESC*, no. 247; Hedley, *Northumberland Families*, I, 15, 24–6, 37–9, 142–3, 191, 196–8, 198–200.

[53] For Fitz Duncan's Cumbrian estates and relations, see Sanders, *Baronies*, 115; Hedley, *Northumberland Families*, I, 241. For David's reconciliation with Adelulf, see Symeon, *Opera*, II, 298; *Chronicles of the Reigns*, III, 170.

[54] *ESC*, nos. 138, 141, 146–7, 182, 187, 244–5, 257; *Regesta Scottorum*, I, nos. 28, 39; Sanders, *Baronies*, 23; Barrow, *Anglo-Norman Era*, 98 and note 34. For notes on the secular Cumbrian lords and their lands, see *Register of Holm Cultram*, 34; *Register of St. Bees*, 60 note 1, 317 and notes to nos. 22, 52, 223, 232; Hedley, *Northumberland Families*, I, 236–41; Hodgson, *Northumberland*, 26–31; *Register of Wetherhal*, nos. 196, 198; *EYC*, III, 317–18; Washington, 'William de Lancaster', 95–100.

[55] *Chronicles of the Reigns*, III, 161–2, 192–5.

sons, Robert II (who fought on the Scottish side at the Standard), while reserving the bulk of his estates in Yorkshire and the region of Hartlepool for his eldest son, Adam, may have been made partly in order to overcome the difficulty of serving two hostile lords.[56]

Another 'border' magnate with interests in Yorkshire whose support David had to compete for was Eustace Fitz John, lord of Alnwick (Northumb.) and Malton (Yorks.), who had served as one of Henry I's principal administrative officials in the northern shires.[57] Although Eustace fought for King David at the battle of the Standard in 1138, is described as having 'long secretly favoured the king of Scotland' and appears to have been rewarded for his loyalty with the grant of extensive estates belonging to the honour of Huntingdon to hold on very favourable terms, he is not known to have offered the Scottish king any further military service, or to have attended David's court more than once after 1141.[58] The apparent withdrawal of Eustace from the circle of Scottish influence was almost certainly due partly to a need to protect his estates in Yorkshire, which had been attacked after the battle of the Standard, and partly to a desire to acquire and retain the valuable and extensive honour of the constableship of Chester, the overlordship of which was held by King David's bitter rival for control of the lordships of Carlisle and Lancaster, Ranulf II earl of Chester.[59] The constableship fell vacant in 1143 or 1144, and

---

[56] *Regesta Scottorum*, I, no. 21. In 1153 Bernard issued a charter in favour of the abbey of Kelso referring to David as his lord, which David confirmed: *ESC*, nos. 258–9. For Brus, see *EYC*, II, 11–13, 15. Between 1139 and 1142 Robert I and his son attested a charter of Earl Henry of Northumberland in favour of Eustace Fitz John, issued at Selkirk: *Regesta Scottorum*, I, no. 11. It is uncertain whether the 'Robert of Brus' who witnessed many other charters issued by Henry and David of Scotland is Robert I or Robert II. See *ESC*, nos. 35, 46, 57, 59, 65, 71, 84, 86, 89, 90, 98, 104, 112, 115; *Regesta Scottorum*, I, nos. 3, 6, 7, 9–12, 22, 30–5.

[57] *PR 31 Henry I*, 24, 27, 31, 33, 35, 131–2, 142–3; Green, *Government*, 182, 251–2.

[58] The quotation is from *Chronicles of the Reigns*, III, 158. Eustace witnessed a charter of Henry of Scotland which has been dated to *c.* 1136. He may already have been an adherent of the Scots when King Stephen terminated his custody of Bamburgh castle during the northern campaign in February 1138: *ESC*, no. 115; Symeon, *Opera*, II, 291–2. For the grant of the demesne manors belonging to the honour of Huntingdon, which occurred between 1139 and 1142, see *Regesta Scottorum*, I, nos. 11–12, 14, and p. 103. The only charter definitely issued by the king of Scotland or Earl Henry and attested by Eustace after 1141 was a confirmation charter of Henry to Brinkburn Priory, granted at Corbridge between 1150 and 1152: *ESC*, no. 247; but see also no. 177, and p. 399.

[59] *The Chronicle of John of Worcester 1118–40*, ed. J. R. H. Weaver (Oxford, 1908), 52; *Chronicles of the Reigns*, III, 165.

Eustace had a claim to it through his wife, a sister and co-heiress of the last constable. His claim was eventually realised when Earl Ranulf granted him the office and honour of the constableship and made him his principal counsellor, at some point between 1144 and 1145.[60] Thereafter Eustace went on to witness six of the earl's surviving charters, some of them issued by Ranulf on his death-bed at or near Castle Gresley in Derbyshire in December 1153.[61]

Even more aloof from the Scottish court was Eustace Fitz John's former partner in the northern administration of Henry I, Walter Espec. Like Eustace, Walter's principal tenurial interests were divided between Northumberland, where he was lord of the lordship of Wark, and Yorkshire, where he held the lordship of Helmsley. Until 1138 Walter remained loyal to King Stephen. His garrison of Wark resisted a series of Scottish attacks, and Walter himself fought with the English at the battle of the Standard. Towards the end of 1138, however, when a truce between the kings of England and Scotland was about to expire, Walter despatched William, abbot of his Cistercian foundation of Rievaulx, to negotiate with King David the terms of a surrender for his town of Wark, which was dismantled after an agreement was reached.[62] Thereafter, in the remaining fifteen years or so of his life, Walter appears to have remained aloof from the courts of both the kings of England and Scotland, and to have taken no further active part in northern politics. If King David ever hoped to employ Walter to help him control and govern Northumberland, it is probable that he hoped in vain.

When we cut through the rhetoric of the charters issued by King David and Earl Henry, and examine the relationship of these rulers with the northern magnates on whose support real authority depended, it emerges that their power in the English 'border' counties may not have been as great as it appears at first sight. It would be wrong, however, to dismiss Scottish royal authority altogether, and to regard it as being confined to Northumberland and Cumbria. The disparate tenurial, familial and religious interests of the magnates which worked against the establishment of Scottish control in these counties served at the same time to promote the extension of Scottish influence beyond them. This was true in the region between Tyne and Tees where David was able to use some of his English baronial contacts to

---

[60] *Chester Charters*, no. 73 and note.   [61] *Ibid.*, nos. 34, 81, 90, 103, 115, 118.
[62] *Chronicles of the Reigns*, III, 170–2; Symeon, *Opera*, II, 292.

influence the course of the episcopal election dispute, which began after the death of Bishop Geoffrey in 1141. In the early stages of the dispute David's candidate, his chancellor William Cumin, received the support of Eustace Fitz John, Robert of Brus, Herbert of Morville and Bernard of Balliol who, in addition to being tenants of the bishopric, held extensive baronies either in Scotland or in Northumberland and Cumbria. And when David withdrew his support from Cumin, after it became clear that the clergy of Durham would never elect him, it is significant that some of these same magnates were instrumental in negotiating the truces which paved the way towards the settlement of 1144 and the installation of the new bishop, William of Ste Barbe.[63] And just as David was able to exploit the connections of the far northern magnates to extend his influence in the region between Tyne and Tees, he was also able to do so in Yorkshire where these connections were at least as strong.

THE SCOTS IN YORKSHIRE 1138–51

The list of magnates who held important estates in the 'border' counties and Yorkshire simultaneously is an impressive one. In addition to Eustace Fitz John and Walter Espec it includes Cecily of Rumilly, lady of Skipton, Roger of Mowbray, lord of Kendal and Thirsk, and Bernard of Balliol, lord of Bywell and Barnard. Of these magnates King David probably came to exercise the greatest influence over Cecily of Rumilly, and through the agency of his nephew and ally, William Fitz Duncan, appears to have secured control of her estates in Yorkshire and those of her husband in Cumbria.

Cecily of Rumilly married William Meschin, lord of the Cumbrian barony of Copeland, in the reign of Henry I. William died in or shortly before 1135, and his son and heir, Ranulf, was dead by the end of 1140. This left the Meschin estates to be divided amongst Ranulf's three sisters (Avice, Maud and Alice); while the honour of Skipton was in the charge of Cecily of Rumilly.[64] The Meschin and Skipton lands were a natural target for Scottish ambitions, and King David attempted to secure control of those of them which were situated in Yorkshire and Cumbria. This was

---

[63] Young, *William Cumin*, 8–29, esp. 12–14, 24, 27. Only one charter issued by David and Henry dealing with the region between Tyne and Tees resembles those illustrating their administration of Northumberland and Cumbria: *Regesta Scottorum*, I, no. 23.

[64] *EYC*, VII, 4–8.

almost certainly the purpose behind the marriage of his nephew, William Fitz Duncan, to Alice of Rumilly, which brought Fitz Duncan the lordship of Copeland, and which probably occurred either during or shortly after a military campaign conducted by Fitz Duncan in northern Lancashire and Cravenshire in 1138.

According to John of Hexham, while King David of Scotland was occupied with the siege of the castle of Norham in Northumberland in 1138:

William Fitz Duncan, as he was slaying and ravaging about Clitheroe, encountered an array of English soldiers, which met him in four bands. Putting them to flight by the energy of his first attack, he put them to the sword, and bore off much booty and a number of prisoners. This fight between the English, the Picts, and the Scots, took place at Clitheroe, on Friday, the fifteenth day before the Nativity of St John the Baptist [10 June].[65]

Richard of Hexham supplies a few more details.

[King David] despatched his nephew, William Fitz Duncan, on an expedition into Yorkshire, with the Picts and a portion of his army. When they had arrived there and had gained the victory... they destroyed by fire and sword the main part of the possessions of a splendid monastery situated in Southerness, and in the district called Craven. Then ... they first massacred ... children and kindred in the sight of their relatives, masters in the sight of their servants, and servants in the sight of their masters, and husbands before the sight of their wives; and then ... they carried off, like so much booty, the noble matrons and chaste virgins, together with other women.[66]

Although Sir Charles Clay suggested that the marriage of William Fitz Duncan and Alice of Rumilly had probably already taken place before the Scottish attack on Cravenshire, there is no evidence for this. It is more likely that the marriage was a consequence of the attack; and that it formed part of Fitz Duncan's campaign objectives.[67] The situation is complicated by the fact that the date of the death of Alice's longest surviving brother, Ranulf, cannot be established with certainty, and could have occurred at any point in the period 1135–40.[68] As long as Ranulf Meschin was alive, Alice had no claims to the Meschin fee, and it is unlikely that a magnate of the status of William Fitz Duncan would have married her. Although Alice's sisters had

[65] Symeon, *Opera*, II, 291.   [66] *Chronicles of the Reigns*, III, 156–7.
[67] *EYC*, VII, 11. Whether William Fitz Duncan entered the region of Skipton is not absolutely certain. See the comments on Cravenshire in Thorn, 'Hundreds and wapentakes', 57.   [68] *EYC*, VII, 7.

married powerful English lords before 1135, the betrothal of Alice to a man who was the son of one Scottish king and the nephew of another must still be regarded as extraordinary.[69] It is a reasonable assumption, therefore, that when William Fitz Duncan married Alice, Ranulf Meschin was dead, and that through this marriage William was aiming to secure title to the lordship of Copeland, to which his wife was a co-heiress, and of which he had probably already established *de facto* control. If the marriage had already taken place when William campaigned in 1138, it is difficult to explain his decision to devastate the Cravenshire estates of his mother-in-law; and the difficulty increases when it emerges that securing control over these estates formed another part of his ambitions.

An important fact to bear in mind when investigating the circumstances in which Alice of Rumilly was married is her acquisition of the lion's share of the inheritance of her parents, despite the seniority of her two sisters, Avice and Maud.[70] After the death of her brother, Ranulf Meschin, Alice acquired the honour of Copeland, held for one knight's service, together with a further one and a half or two knights' fees in Lincolnshire, and a half knight's fee in Northamptonshire. Her two sisters were already married, and whatever they received would have been added to their *maritagia*. Avice is subsequently known to have held seventeen knights' fees formerly belonging to the Meschin fee, situated mainly in Lincolnshire and Northamptonshire; while Maud's share of the possessions of her parents amounted to one knight's fee in Northamptonshire, seven carucates in Cheshire, and a small interest in Huntingdonshire.[71] In terms of the number of knights' fees it appears that Avice inherited far more lands than her sisters; but this may be an illusion. There are indications that the greatest share of the inheritance went to Alice. Although held for the service of only one knight, and situated in a poor upland region, Alice's honour of Copeland was a geographically extensive

---

[69] Avice married William II of Curcy, who held the lordship of Stogursey in Somerset which appears to have incorporated almost thirty knights' fees in 1166, and who may have been a steward of Henry I. After Curcy's death (*c.* 1125 × 1130), Avice went on to marry William I Paynel, lord of Drax (Yorks.). Maud's first husband was Philip de Belmeis of Tong (Salop.), the founder of Lilleshall Abbey; and her second was the powerful Hugh de Mortimer of Wigmore. See *EYC*, VII, 7–8; Sanders, *Baronies*, 143, 98–9; *Red Book*, I, 225.

[70] The seniority of Avice and Maud is suggested by the fact that Avice was married *c.* 1125 × 1130, and Maud by 1135 at the latest.

[71] *EYC*, VII, 7–12, 38–42; III, 468–9; *Red Book*, I, 225.

lordship. Its importance is reflected by William Meschin's construction of a castle at Egremont and a monastery at St Bees, which suggests that William may have regarded it as his chief seat.[72] The bias in favour of Alice is more apparent when we consider the descent of the Rumilly estates of her mother Cecily, centred on the lordship of Skipton, after Cecily's death in the early 1150s. Whereas Alice inherited the Yorkshire estates, constituting over 200 carucates and including the *caput honoris* and castle at Skipton, and an additional ten and a half (or more) fees strewn across six other counties, Avice secured only small interests in Devon, and Maud inherited only two knights' fees in Devon and Dorset.[73]

How is this disparity to be explained? Why did the youngest of the three daughters of William Meschin and Cecily of Rumilly succeed to the majority of the lands of her parents? Given the fact that Alice was married to William Fitz Duncan, and that he had ravaged Cravenshire in 1138, it is more than possible that the Scots were in some way responsible.[74] William Fitz Duncan must have been in Cravenshire in 1138 for a reason. And what better reason than to try and secure the hand of a woman who had recently become a co-heiress to the Meschin fee, which included the lordship of Copeland, and who might one day become a co-heiress to the honour of Skipton? His army is described as carrying off the noble matrons and chaste virgins of Cravenshire, descriptions applicable to the widowed Cecily of Rumilly and her unmarried daughter Alice. It is not inconceivable that the descent of the Meschin fee could have been the result of Scottish coercion. The case, of course, is circumstantial. But it is strengthened by other evidence which illustrates that William Fitz Duncan already had designs on the honour of Skipton during Cecily of Rumilly's lifetime, and which suggests that Cecily may have been subject to his authority.

William's designs on Skipton are reflected in charters issued in the reign of Stephen in which, either in conjunction with his wife or mother-in-law, or by himself, he disposed of property

---

[72] *EYC*, VII, 5; *Register of St. Bees*, nos. 1–3, 5, 6.

[73] *EYC*, VII, 7–12, 42–8; III, 468–9. Clay pointed out that the lands outside Yorkshire may have belonged either to Alice's mother or father, and that they were probably attached to the honour of Skipton when Alice succeeded her mother, and certainly before 1166.

[74] It should be noted that we know little about the usual arrangements concerning partibility of estates among daughters in the early Norman period. The subject is currently being investigated by Dr Judith Green.

belonging to the lordship.[75] As Clay suggested, these charters indicate that Alice of Rumilly had been designated as heir to the honour of Skipton during her mother's lifetime. They suggest also that William Fitz Duncan was actually present within the honour at some point between 1138 and 1154, and that he was involved in its administration. A charter issued by Cecily of Rumilly, granting the vill of Kildwick and land in Stirton to Embsay Priory, states that Cecily and her *gener*, William Fitz Duncan, had offered the gifts on the altar of the priory.[76] Clay thought it unlikely that William 'was in a position to take part in the present transaction between the battle of the Standard in 1138 and his probable return to Craven in 1151', and tentatively suggested that the charter was issued after 1151 and before the latest probable date of Cecily of Rumilly's death in 1153.[77] On the same grounds he was inclined to place other charters issued by William Fitz Duncan and his wife, illustrating their administration of the honour of Skipton, within the same limits of date.[78] There is evidence, however, that although William was in Cravenshire only briefly in 1138, he may have exercised some form of control within the honour of Skipton thereafter, and that each of the charters printed by Clay could have been issued at any point in the period 1138–53.

The next reference made by the chroniclers to William Fitz Duncan's presence in Cravenshire after 1138 relates to the year 1151 when, according to John of Hexham, King David 'with his army confirmed his nephew, William Fitz Duncan, in the lordship of Skipton in Craven, and stormed a fortress which had been constructed by the enemy, and having expelled the garrison he overthrew it'.[79] The use of the term 'confirmed', rather than 'restored', suggests that Fitz Duncan had enjoyed some form of authority within the honour of Skipton since 1138. The suggestion is strengthened by the fact that neighbouring north Lancashire was almost certainly still subject to Scottish authority in 1149, and by the nature of the plan hatched at that time by King David, Ranulf II earl of Chester and Henry of Anjou to capture York.[80] It was a plan which would have taken David's army through Lonsdale and the valley of the Ribble into Cravenshire, and from there probably

---

[75] *EYC*, VII, nos. 9, 12–15.   [76] *Ibid.*, no. 9 and note.   [77] *Ibid.*, 59.
[78] *Ibid.*, nos. 14–15.   [79] Symeon, *Opera*, II, 326.
[80] *Ibid.*, 323; Barrow, 'Honour of Lancaster', 85–9; J. A. Green, 'Earl Ranulf II and Lancashire', in *The Earldom of Chester and its Charters: A Tribute to Geoffrey Barraclough*, ed. A. T. Thacker (Journal of the Chester Arch. Soc., 1991), 97–108.

along Wharfedale to York. Lonsdale was under Scottish control in 1149, and Roger of Mowbray, lord of the castle of Burton in Lonsdale and several estates within Cravenshire, appears to have supported the invasion.[81] The Scots were probably also able to count on the assistance of another important Cravenshire tenant-in-chief, William II of Percy, who had close links with both Scotland and the earl of Chester, and who during the course of 1149 may have been attacking York from the nearby castle of Wheldrake.[82] King David had probably chosen the easiest line of march into Yorkshire, along which he could expect to receive help and reinforcements from the nobility of the local lordships; and it is possible that one of these lordships was Skipton.

Although the campaign was eventually abandoned, there is evidence that the allies assembled at Lancaster and came close enough to York to force Stephen, who had arrived at the request of the citizens to defend the city, to take action against them.[83] When Stephen came upon the Scots they withdrew 'to safer positions', and eventually dispersed and returned to their homes.[84] Stephen stayed on for a time in Yorkshire 'suppressing the hostilities that were on the increase round York', a programme involving the destruction of the castles of his enemies, and the construction of others in more suitable places.[85] The enemies described by the *Gesta Stephani* are anonymous, but it is not inconceivable that some of them were occupying the castle of Skipton.

It should not be assumed from the silence of the chroniclers that William Fitz Duncan never visited Skipton, and held no power there in the period 1139–50. Scottish authority in Cumbria, where William's wife was lady of Copeland, and where many of her mother's Cravenshire tenants held interests, must have enabled William to exercise influence in Skipton from a distance. And there is evidence that he attempted to strengthen this influence by granting estates in Cravenshire to magnates already subject to his authority in the honour of Copeland and elsewhere in Cumbria. One of the most powerful of these magnates was Adam Fitz

---

[81] *Mowbray Charters*, xxvi–xxvii.
[82] For the Percy holdings in Cravenshire and in Wheldrake, see *EYC*, XI, 11–16, 186–96; *DB*, I, 322b. It is significant that Wheldrake was held from the Percys in 1086 by the Colville family who came to be associated with King Malcolm IV and Scotland in the 1150s: *EYC*, XI, 303, 305; VI, 168–70; Barrow, *Anglo-Norman Era*, 177.
[83] Symeon, *Opera*, II, 323; *Chester Charters*, no. 88 and note.
[84] *Gesta Stephani*, 216.　　　　　　　　[85] *Ibid.*, 218.

Swain, lord of Kirkland, Melmorby and Ainsleth in Cumbria, Hornby and Croxton in Lancashire, and a large estate held of the Lacy family centred on the castle of Mirfield in the West Riding of Yorkshire.[86] In view of the proximity to Carlisle of the estates belonging to Adam and his brother Henry in the Eden valley, it is hardly surprising that the two men came to be associated with the Scots in Stephen's reign. Adam witnessed a charter issued by King David in or around 1147, and between 1141 and 1152 his brother Henry attested two more, as well as a charter of Earl Henry.[87] Neither Adam nor Henry are known to have been connected with the honours of Skipton and Copeland before 1138, and it was probably at the direction of William Fitz Duncan that Adam received land in Copeland, a new enfeoffment tenancy held of the honour of Skipton in several Cravenshire vills and a prominent position at the Rumilly honorial court.[88] William's influence may also explain Adam's grant of a subtenancy in his Skipton estates to Godard of Boivill, another tenant of the honour of Copeland.[89]

The establishment of Adam Fitz Swain in the honour of Skipton becomes even more understandable when his close connections with the honour of Lacy are considered. In 1166 Adam's descendants held nearly eight knights' fees of the honour of Lacy in the West Riding of Yorkshire.[90] A large number of the estates constituting the tenancy surrounded an outlying section of the honour of Skipton in the parish of Wath upon Dearne. The parish was situated to the south-west of the castle of Pontefract, deep inside territory dominated by the Lacy family.[91] Ilbert II of Lacy and his son Henry had good cause to hate the Scots, who had attacked their forces at Clitheroe in 1138, and probably annexed their estates in Blackburnshire shortly afterwards.[92] When examined in this context, there are grounds for believing that William Fitz Duncan's enfeoffment of Adam Fitz Swain in Cravenshire and Copeland may have been an attempt to compete for Adam's service, for his assistance in protecting the outlying

---

[86] *EYC*, VII, 177–8; *West Yorkshire*, III, 736.   [87] *ESC*, nos. 138, 141, 187, 244.
[88] *Register of St. Bees*, nos. 39–41; *EYC*, VII, 177–9, and nos. 9, 12–14, 17–18.
[89] *EYC*, VII, 182, 187–8.   [90] The Neville fee: *Red Book*, I, 423.
[91] For the estates held of Lacy by Adam's father in 1086, see *DB*, I, 316b–17b.
[92] It is difficult to determine the policy adopted by the Lacys in Stephen's reign. Although it is possible that they may have supported the Scottish invasion of Yorkshire in 1149, and that the enfeoffment of their tenants in the honour of Skipton is another reflection of an alliance with David, it appears that at the close of Stephen's reign they were supporting the English king and hostile to the Scots. See above, pp. 175–6.

Skipton estates in south Yorkshire from the Lacy threat.[93] The same objective may also explain the establishment of the Fleming family, tenants of the honour of Copeland, in the largest new enfeoffment Skipton tenancy, which was composed almost exclusively of estates within the same outlier. It is certainly interesting that the Flemings established Adam Fitz Swain as one of their subtenants, and that he, rather than they, exercised effective lordship within the region.[94]

The policy of providing for the security of another outlying portion of the honour of Skipton, near Barwick in Elmet in the West Riding, may also explain the new enfeoffment tenancies granted by the lord of Skipton to Hervey of Reineville, Helto Fitz William of Arches, Osbert the archdeacon, Peter of Marton and Simon of Mohaut. Like Adam Fitz Swain, the first three men were important tenants of the Lacys, holding estates not only in the region of Wath upon Dearne, but also in that of Barwick.[95] Marton and Mohaut, on the other hand, were tenants of Alice of Rumilly's sister, Avice, in lands immediately to the north-west of Barwick.[96] Avice herself cultivated ties with retainers of the Lacys, and was well placed to protect her sister's estates near Barwick; and it is possible that she may have been supported in this by Walter of Somerville, who held estates of Lacy close to and within Barwick, and whose younger brother, William, held land in Scotland, and witnessed charters of King David and Henry of Scotland in Stephen's reign.[97] Growing Scottish influence in the

---

[93] *EYC*, VII, 178, 189.

[94] The tenancy incorporated one and a half knights' fees: *Red Book*, I, 431; *EYC*, VII, 193–7, nos. 126, 131–2. A Reiner the Fleming witnessed charters issued by William Meschin before 1130, and by Cecily of Rumilly in the period 1131 × 1140. In some of these he is styled *dapifer*. His son witnessed charters of William Fitz Duncan and Alice of Rumilly. See *EYC*, VII, 195–7, 199–200, nos. 9, 13, 15, 17–18. For the lands held by Adam of the Flemings, and the lands they held of him, see *EYC*, VII, 180–1, 193–4, 207–8.

[95] The half knight's fee held by Reineville was one of the largest new enfeoffment tenancies on the honour of Skipton. Hervey's elder brother, William, held four knights' fees of Henry of Lacy in 1166. The several branches of the Arches family were closely connected with the honours of Copeland, Skipton, Percy and Lacy. Osbert the archdeacon held military tenancies of both the honours of Skipton and Lacy in 1166. He appears for the first time in the records of the honour of Skipton in charters of William Fitz Duncan and Alice of Rumilly. See *Red Book*, I, 422, 424, 431; *EYC*, VII, 212–13, nos. 13–14, 17–18; III, 248–53, nos. 1503–4, 1527, 1529, 1582, 1667.

[96] *Red Book*, I, 224–5; *EYC*, III, 474; VII, nos. 16–17.

[97] A charter issued by Avice between 1147 and *c.* 1152 was witnessed by Adam Fitz Peter of Birkin who, as well as holding lands of her in Horsforth, was a Lacy tenant in the region of Wath upon Dearne. The charter was also attested by Adam of Montbegon

region may provide at least part of the explanation for Henry of Lacy's fortification, with royal approval, of a castle at Barwick.[98]

Scottish power in north-west Yorkshire and the region to the north of it is not only reflected in the new enfeoffments made on the honour of Skipton, but in those made on other neighbouring lordships. Roger of Mowbray, who held Kendale, Lonsdale and most of Ribblesdale, granted his entire interest there to William Fitz Gilbert of Lancaster for the service of four knights. Dr Greenway suggests that the charter of enfeoffment seems to illustrate Roger's recovery of his lands in these areas from the Scots, as a result of his participation in the alliance of King David, Ranulf II earl of Chester and Henry of Anjou in 1149, and dated it *c.* 1149 accordingly.[99] Another possibility is that when Roger issued the charter the estates which it conveyed were still under Scottish control, that he was forced by King David to alienate them as the only way of retaining a vestige of his interest and that he never recovered direct control over the lands until the reign of Henry II. William Fitz Gilbert was a tenant of the honour of Copeland, a distant relative of William Fitz Duncan and (if anybody's man) David's man not Roger's.[100]

The Scots may also have been able to use their connections with magnates holding lands in the 'border' counties to extend their influence within the more central regions of Yorkshire. In the late twelfth century Duncan, earl of Fife, an important Scottish noble, held two carucates in the vill of Plumpton in the West Riding from the Vescy descendants of Eustace Fitz John.[101] The land had been held in 1086 by Gilbert Tison, and it is unclear how the Vescys and Duncan acquired their interests. Plumpton, however, was close to Knaresborough castle which was in the custody of Eustace in 1129–30 and probably later, and it is possible that

who was the first husband of Maud, a co-heiress of Adam Fitz Swain: *EYC*, III, nos. 1864, 1871 and notes. For the Somervilles, see *EYC*, III, 307; Barrow, *Anglo-Norman Era*, 107–8, 194.

[98] Public Record Office, Duchy of Lancaster 41/1/36; Wightman, *Lacy Family*, 10, 78–80, 244–5. But see also the comments in *West Yorkshire*, II, 257, 315; III, 735.

[99] *Mowbray Charters*, no. 370, p. xxvi and note 8.

[100] For William's lands and family connections, see Washington, 'William de Lancaster', 95–100; Green, 'Earl Ranulf II', 101–2 notes 26 and 27; *ESC*, 406; *Register of St. Bees*, nos. 3, 11, 223, 232–3, note to no. 32, and pp. 339, 465. William's cousin, Orm Fitz Ketel, married Gunnilda, half-sister of Etheldreda, the mother of William Fitz Duncan: Hedley, *Northumberland Families*, I, 239, 241. His uncle, Ketel, witnessed charters of William Meschin, lord of Copeland, and granted land in Workington and Preston to St Bees: *Register of St. Bees*, nos. 1–4, 7, 9.

[101] For Duncan's importance, see Barrow, *David I*, 16.

Eustace may have secured control of his part of the vill at this time, and that he granted the estate to Duncan at the behest of King David.[102]

The tentacles of Scottish influence also extended into south Yorkshire. In 1136 King Stephen granted Henry of Scotland the strategically important fortified town and port of Doncaster, situated at the point where the Great North Road crossed the River Don; and there is evidence that the Scots were able to exercise some control over the settlement.[103] Between 1136 and 1152 Henry of Scotland issued a charter addressed to his burgesses and ministers of Doncaster, notifying them of his gift to St Peter's Hospital, York, of a toft by the river in Doncaster.[104] The charter was probably issued at nearby Wadworth.[105] Although Barrow suggests that Henry lost Doncaster after 1141, the Scots may have been able to retain some form of control through the agency of Adam Fitz Swain, who rendered account for the farm of the town in 1158.[106]

King David's desire to control Doncaster may have been part of a plan to establish Scottish influence in a solid block of territory in south Yorkshire. Situated only a day's ride to the south-west of the town was the great manor of Hallam, to which were attached berewicks in sixteen neighbouring vills, which may have incorporated a castle, and which belonged to King David in right of his wife.[107] Whether the manor was under Scottish control in Stephen's reign cannot be ascertained, but it is significant that after the conclusion of the Durham election dispute, when David and William Cumin were probably not on the best of terms, the former Scottish chancellor was taken prisoner and tortured by Richard of Lovetot, who was David's tenant in the soke of Hallam.[108] Nearby also was the castle and soke of Conisbrough, held by William III of Warenne. Although Warenne was a loyal adherent of King Stephen, and his estates passed to his son-in-law, William, Stephen's youngest son, after his death in 1148, it is not

---

[102] *EYC*, XII, 19–20, no. 53.

[103] *Chronicles of the Reigns*, III, 146; Symeon, *Opera*, II, 287; King, *Castellarium Anglicanum*, II, 530, 534.   [104] *Regesta Scottorum*, I, no. 17, also printed as *EYC*, II, no. 1004.

[105] *Regesta Scottorum*, I, 142 note 6.   [106] *Ibid.*, 142 note 4; *PR 2–4 Henry II*, 179.

[107] *DB*, I, 320a. The vills probably belonging to Hallam are identified in *VCH, Yorkshire*, II, 256. The castle may have been at Sheffield which was one of the outliers of Hallam: King, *Castellarium Anglicanum*, II, 530. In 1086 the manor and soke of Hallam had belonged to Countess Judith, the mother of David's wife. See Freeman, *Norman Conquest*, IV, 301, 524, 601.

[108] Symeon, *Opera*, II, 317; *VCH, Yorkshire*, II, 166; *EYC*, III, 4–5.

impossible that the Scots harboured designs towards Conisbrough. In the second treaty of Durham, Henry of Scotland had secured the hand in marriage of Warenne's sister, Ada, and it may have been Henry's father David who enfeoffed a number of tenants attached to the lordship of Conisbrough in Scottish estates.[109]

Another Yorkshire tenant to secure lands in Scotland in the reign of Stephen was Walter of Ryedale, who was granted estates in Roxburghshire by King David between 1139 and 1153, and who witnessed several of David's charters and those of his son Henry.[110] Walter was a tenant of the former sheriff of Yorkshire, Bertram of Bulmer, who may have had good reason to resent the decline of royal authority in Yorkshire after 1135, and to support the Angevin party and their Scottish associates. It is possible that Bulmer was one of the magnates holding lands of the bishopric of Durham who supported the policy of King David in the episcopal election dispute during the early 1140s; and it is interesting to note that he was employed by Henry II as sheriff of Yorkshire during the early years of his reign.[111]

King David's attempt to build up his influence within Yorkshire was not confined to secular lordships. He was also intent after 1138 on reinforcing the close ties he had formed in the reign of Henry I with the church, especially with the reformed monasteries. His motives were political as well as religious, and his ultimate aim was almost certainly to establish control of the archbishopric of York. In order to understand the policy it is necessary to place it within the context of the history of Anglo-Scottish ecclesiastical relations.

King David's ecclesiastical policy was essentially the same as that of his predecessor, Alexander: the establishment of the independence of the Scottish bishoprics from the metropolitan authority of the archbishops of York.[112] Everything depended upon the decision of the papacy. In 1119 and 1121 Pope Celestine

---

[109] Symeon, *Opera*, II, 300; *EYC*, VIII, 11; Barrow, 'Cumbria', 132; *Regesta Scottorum*, I, 226, 265; II, 125, 314, 363; Barrow, 'Scotland's families', 328.

[110] *Regesta Scottorum*, I, no. 42; *ESC*, nos. 179, 186, 195, 222, 234, 244, 248, 250. For Walter's lands and family, see *Red Book*, I, 428; *EYC*, II, 111–20; VI, 119–21, 143–4, nos. 13, 21, 38–9, 44–5.

[111] Young, *William Cumin*, 24. In 1166 Bertram's son, William, held five knights' fees of the bishopric of Durham: *Red Book*, I, 417. Bertram was sheriff of Yorkshire from January 1155 until 1163: J. H. Round, 'Neville and Bulmer', in *Family Origins and Other Studies*, ed. W. Page (London, 1930), 54–9. Bulmer had been sheriff of Yorkshire in the later years of Henry I's reign, but it is not clear if he retained his office under Stephen: Green, *Sheriffs*, 90.

[112] For the following details, see Nicholl, *Thurstan*, 79–107.

II issued declarations stating that the Scottish bishops were to be suffragans of York; but these were resisted in Scotland. The case was heard again in Rome in 1126, and postponed. During the postponement Henry I and David persuaded Archbishop Thurstan to accept a compromise. In 1127 Robert bishop of St Andrew's was consecrated by Thurstan at York, but withheld the usual oath of obedience sworn to the metropolitan. The issue was then left to rest until 1130 when a schism occurred in the papacy between Innocent II, who had the support of St Bernard and the reformers within the church, and Anacletus II. David's decision to support Anacletus isolated the Scottish church and invited the hostility of Innocent, who was on good terms with King Stephen. In 1131 Innocent issued letters commanding Bishop John of Glasgow and the other Scottish bishops to perform due obedience to Archbishop Thurstan of York. Five years later Innocent sent further letters to Thurstan and King Stephen encouraging them to bring the bishop of Glasgow to acknowledge his subjection to York. The letter to Stephen urged the king to develop the see of Carlisle, which incorporated territory formerly belonging to the bishopric of Glasgow, and the organisation of which was opposed by David, who may have expelled its bishop, Adelulf.[113] However, when the schism ended with the death of Anacletus in 1138, David took the opportunity to make his reconciliation with Innocent during a visit of the papal legate, Alberic bishop of Ostia, to Carlisle. David restored Bishop Adelulf to his see, and in return the legate recalled John bishop of Glasgow from the monastery of Tiron, where he was sheltering after resigning his bishopric in the face of Innocent's threats of excommunication.[114]

The year 1138 marks an important turning point in the ecclesiastical policy of King David. After opposing the reforming elements within the church, he now became their ally and sought to use them to further his ecclesiastical interests. An opportunity came in the early 1140s when Stephen attempted to secure the archbishopric of York for his nephew, William Fitz Herbert. William's election in 1141 appeared to be uncanonical and incited the hostility of the heads of the reformed Augustinian and Cistercian houses in Yorkshire who, with the backing of St Bernard, appealed to Rome against the election, and eventually secured William's deposition by the Cistercian pope, Eugenius III,

[113] For the question of Adelulf's expulsion, see Green, 'Anglo-Scottish relations', 63 and note 64. [114] Symeon, *Opera*, II, 298; *Chronicles of the Reigns*, III, 170–1.

in 1147.[115] There is evidence that King David, who had already established ties with several of these houses, became involved in their programme of opposition and sought to use it to establish either his own candidate at York, or at least a reformer sympathetic to his ecclesiastical policy.

King David may have been behind the candidature of Waldef, prior of the Augustinian house of Kirkham, who stood against William Fitz Herbert in 1141 and became one of his principal opponents. Waldef was David's stepson, and it was because of his Scottish connections that Stephen vetoed his election.[116] It is significant that Waldef's candidacy, and his subsequent decision (made at the instigation of David's former courtier, Ailred of Rievaulx) to leave Kirkham and join the Cistercians, occurred only shortly after a visit to Yorkshire in 1139 by the archbishop of Armagh, Malachy, who was on his way from Ireland to Clairvaux and Rome. Before reaching Yorkshire Malachy almost certainly paid a visit to King David, and on arriving at York received assistance from Waldef.[117] In the light of these events it is more than possible that Waldef's Cistercian conversion was made under the influence of King David, and deliberately calculated to win the support of St Bernard (and his connections at Rome) for his candidacy in the York election. Such a policy would certainly explain the hostility of Waldef's brother, Simon II of Senlis, earl of Northampton, a magnate loyal to King Stephen and a rival of Henry of Scotland for control of the earldom of Northumbria, to the conversion. Simon forced Waldef to leave the Bedfordshire monastery of Wardon, in which he had begun his Cistercian novitiate.[118] But he failed to suppress Waldef's determination to become a white monk. In 1148 the former Augustinian prior became a Cistercian abbot; and it is another reflection of his connections that he did so at Melrose in Scotland.[119]

It is possible that Malachy provided a vital communications link between St Bernard (who took a great interest in the York election

---

[115] The houses involved were Rievaulx, Fountains, Kirkham and Guisborough: Symeon, *Opera*, II, 311, 313; Knowles, 'Saint William of York', 162–77, 212–14; Talbot, 'Saint William of York', 1–15; A. Morey, 'Canonist evidence in the case of St William of York', *CHJ*, 10 (1950–2), 352–3.

[116] *Acta Sanctorum*, I, August 3rd, 256–7; *Vita Ailredi*, xliv, xiii, xxxii; Nicholl, *Thurstan*, 240.

[117] *Vita Ailredi*, lxxi–lxxv; J. Wilson, 'The passages of St. Malachy through Scotland', *SHR*, 18 (1921), 72–3; Nicholl, *Thurstan*, 235.

[118] *Vita Ailredi*, lxxii–lxxiii. Waldef took refuge at Rievaulx.   [119] *Ibid.*, lxxv.

dispute, and was vehemently opposed to William Fitz Herbert), the party of reformed houses in Yorkshire and the Scottish court. Malachy probably already had close ties with the Scottish court before his first journey to Rome, and these ties would certainly have been greatly strengthened on his return from that journey, when he is said to have healed David's son Henry from a potentially fatal illness. It is significant that Malachy's second journey to Clairvaux by the same route was made in 1148, in the year after the election to the archbishopric of the reformers' candidate, Henry Murdac, and in the year before King David's second invasion of Yorkshire; an invasion which was probably undertaken partly with the intention of establishing the new archbishop in York.[120] During this journey Malachy stayed for a time at the Augustinian priory of Guisborough, which was one of the reformed houses leading the opposition to the election of William Fitz Herbert, and which had béen founded by the Brus family who were close adherents of King David. It is a stark reflection on the relative strength of David and Stephen in the north that, in his *Life* of Malachy, Bernard of Clairvaux describes the saint as coming to Guisborough after 'traversing Scotland [and turning aside] at the very gate-way of England'.[121]

King David's connections with Rievaulx Abbey, another member of the group of religious houses opposed to the election of William Fitz Herbert, were as close as those he had with Kirkham. After the arrival at Rievaulx in the early 1130s of David's household official, Ailred, the ties between the house and Scotland were strengthened. In 1136 King David himself founded a daughter house of Rievaulx at Melrose, and six years later in 1142 established another at Dundrennan.[122] In 1138 it was Abbot William of Rievaulx, a former secretary of St Bernard, who came north to negotiate peace with David and arrange the surrender of Walter Espec's castle of Wark.[123] Meanwhile at Rievaulx itself, Ailred was rising within the ranks, and in 1142 represented the house in complaining about the election of William Fitz Herbert before the pope in Rome.[124] That he maintained his ties with Scotland is clear from his visits to Rievaulx's daughter houses of

[120] Symeon, *Opera*, II, 321.
[121] Wilson, 'St. Malachy', 77–82. The quotation is from A. Brian Scott, *Malachy* (Dublin, 1976), 64.   [122] *Vita Ailredi*, lxx, 45 note 4.
[123] Symeon, *Opera*, II, 291–2; *Chronicles of the Reigns*, III, 171; Nicholl, *Thurstan*, 231.
[124] Knowles, 'Saint William of York', 167; Talbot, 'Saint William of York', 2.

Melrose and Dundrennan, and from his later writings which reveal both a powerful devotion to King David and his son Henry, and a political attitude reflecting ideas almost certainly prevalent at the Scottish court. Ailred believed that the kings of Scotland were the true successors of the English kings, and that King David was the chief representative of the West Saxon house. He saw the inhabitants of old Northumbria, incorporating both southern Scotland and northern England, as a single race with a common culture. Englishmen and Normans were united, whether they looked to King David or King Stephen for lordship.[125] With its close ties with Northumberland, Cumbria and Scotland, Yorkshire provided ideas of this kind with a fertile environment in which to grow.[126]

King David also appears to have been cultivating links with the Cistercian abbey of Fountains. In or about 1147 the Percy family founded a daughter house of the Northumberland priory of Newminster, itself a daughter of Fountains, at Sallay in Cravenshire.[127] When viewed in the light of the close connections of the Percys with the Scottish court, the location of the house and its dedication to St Andrew is significant.[128] At about the same time another daughter house of Fountains was founded by Henry of Lacy at nearby Barnoldswick, before being removed to Kirkstall; and it is interesting that the abbots of both Kirkstall and Sallay were among the witnesses to a charter issued by William Fitz Duncan before 1153, which notified Archbishop Henry Murdac of a gift to Embsay Priory.[129] Henry Murdac had been abbot of Fountains, and his relations with the Scots appear to have been particularly close. This is probably reflected in the support offered to Murdac by Adelulf bishop of Carlisle at the archiepiscopal election held at Richmond in 1147.[130] At some point within the next two years, and not long after Malachy's second visit to Yorkshire and the election of David's stepson, Waldef, as abbot of

---

[125] *Vita Ailredi*, lxxv, xcii, xlii, xlvi–xlvii, 45–6, 74.

[126] Ailred's ideas were echoed by other northern chroniclers, such as Jocelin of Furness and William of Newburgh: *Acta Sanctorum*, August 1st, 248, d, c; *Chronicles of the Reigns*, I, 105–6.

[127] *Sallay Chartulary*, I, no. 1, reprinted as *EYC*, XI, no. 12. But see also the comments in *EYC*, XI, no. 13 note; Burton, 'Religious orders', 222.

[128] The house probably took its name from the well of St Andrew to which it was closely situated. Cistercian houses were usually dedicated to St Mary.

[129] *Kirkstall Coucher*, ix–xii; *Foundation of Kirkstall*, 169–208; *EYC*, VII, no. 15.

[130] Symeon, *Opera*, II, 320–1.

the Cistercian house of Melrose, Murdac came north to meet David at Carlisle, where they may have negotiated the plans for the Scottish invasion of Yorkshire launched in 1149.[131] David's nephew, William Fitz Duncan, whose Cravenshire estates were to provide the point of entry into Yorkshire for the invading army, was also well disposed to Murdac. In addition to giving land to Fountains Abbey, he was probably responsible for granting one of the largest new enfeoffment tenancies on the honour of Skipton to Archdeacon Osbert, one of the leading opponents of William Fitz Herbert, Murdac's rival for the archbishopric of York.[132]

The strength of King David's influence in the ecclesiastical politics of Yorkshire almost certainly provides part of the explanation for Stephen's concern to construct his own party of religious support within the county. Stephen needed a counterbalance to the reformers. The party he organised to do this included the heads of two of the old Benedictine houses illdisposed towards the new reformed monasticism, Severinus of St Mary's Abbey, York, and Benedict of St Hilda's Abbey, Whitby, both of whom supported the candidature of William Fitz Herbert for the archbishopric of York when the case was tried at Winchester in 1143.[133] Fitz Herbert's supporters also included King Stephen's nephew, Hugh du Puiset, and his chancellor, Robert of Gant, who were promoted by Fitz Herbert to their respective offices of treasurer and dean within the chapter of York.[134] When Fitz Herbert was deposed in 1147, Puiset and Gant took the lead in opposing the election of the reforming candidate, Henry Murdac, and refused to admit him to York after his appointment, until his reconciliation with the king in 1151.[135]

We can only speculate about what might have happened had Henry Murdac gained entry to York with the help of King David in 1149. It is just possible that Murdac had agreed during the negotiations with David in 1148 or 1149 either to promote the independence of the Scottish church at Rome or, like the bishop of

---

[131] *Ibid.*, 322–3; Davis, *King Stephen*, 104.

[132] *EYC*, VII, no. 14, pp. 216–17; *Red Book*, I, 431. Osbert was accused of murdering Archbishop William in 1154: Nicholl, *Thurstan*, 244–5; C. T. Clay, 'Notes on the early archdeacons in the church of York', *YAJ*, 36 (1944–7), 277–9; Morey, 'St William of York', 352–3; *EYC*, VI, 158–9.

[133] Symeon, *Opera*, II, 315. The heads of certain Benedictine houses are also to be found among those who witnessed a charter issued by William as archbishop: *Episcopal Acta*, no. 100, dated *c.* 1143 × 1144.   [134] Symeon, *Opera*, II, 320.

[135] *Ibid.*, 320–2, 325.

Carlisle, to govern his see under the overlordship of the king of Scotland. If this was the case, David's ambitions received a set-back when Stephen and the archbishop were reconciled in January 1151. But David never abandoned his ambitions, and a few months later when the papal legate, John Paparo, arrived at Tynemouth, the Scottish king hurried north from Cravenshire to meet him at Carlisle, won his favour and persuaded him to request the pope to grant the *pallium* to St Andrew's.[136] In the following year David permitted Henry Murdac to conduct his archiepiscopal duties in the region to the north of Yorkshire, and heard his complaints at Carlisle.[137] The Scottish king and the archbishop of York were cooperating, and that they could do so after Murdac's reconciliation with King Stephen is a reflection not only of the close relationship David had established with the reformed papacy, but also of the influence he had built up within the reformed monastic houses of Yorkshire.

CONCLUSION

David of Scotland took advantage of the weakness of royal authority in northern England during Stephen's reign to expand the Scottish influence in the region which had its origins far back in the Anglo-Scandinavian past, and which, in a modified form, had survived the arrival of the Normans. Before 1135 David himself formed close links with the Norman secular and ecclesiastical aristocracy of the northern shires, by granting its members lordships and ecclesiastical offices in Scotland, and by establishing his own courtiers in the reformed religious houses of England. After Henry I's death he used these links, in conjunction with his military campaigns, to increase his authority within Northumbria and Cumbria. Although it would be unsafe to say that David controlled the nobility of the 'border' counties, it is almost certain that he was able to strengthen their attachments to him, and to use their disparate tenurial, familial and religious interests to extend or consolidate his influence in the shires that lay further south.

Perhaps the greatest step in this direction was taken in 1138, when David's nephew, William Fitz Duncan, invaded Lancashire and Cravenshire. The influence William appears to have been able to exercise within the honour of Skipton thereafter suggests that

---

[136] Symeon, *Opera*, II, 326–7; *The Historia Pontificalis of John of Salisbury*, ed. M. Chibnall (London, 1956), 70–2.   [137] Symeon, *Opera*, II, 328.

the Scottish annexation of northern Lancashire and Lonsdale should be dated to 1138, rather than 1141.[138] William's victory at the battle of Clitheroe in 1138, ignored by most historians, must now assume a new and crucial significance. It paved the way towards Scottish domination of Lancashire and Cravenshire, where William consolidated his military success by enfeoffing Cumbrian magnates already subject to his authority.

Scottish power was not confined to Cravenshire. By a variety of methods the tentacles of David's influence were extended to several other regions within Yorkshire, including Wath upon Dearne and Doncaster, and possibly even Hallam and parts of the honour of Conisbrough. Nor was the influence confined to the secular world. It can also be traced within the reformed religious houses which were firmly opposed to Stephen's attempts to manipulate the York archiepiscopal election, and which eventually brought about the promotion of Archbishop Henry Murdac, with whom David was on good terms.

Viewed against this background, King David's invasion of Yorkshire in 1149 begins to look like a manifestation of a preconceived programme, intended to reinforce Scottish power within the county. It was launched soon after negotiations with Henry Murdac, channelled through Cravenshire, supported by Yorkshire magnates with Scottish ties and directed towards the acquisition of York.[139] What King David's plans for Yorkshire were had the invasion been successful is open to question, but it is not inconceivable that he would have demanded permission from Henry of Anjou, who may already have sworn in 1149 to allow him to control Newcastle and Northumberland, to add the county to his kingdom.[140] Ailred's writings suggest that Northumbria was perceived as incorporating the whole of the region to the north of the Humber, and was as much Scottish as English. It is a perception reflected in the Northumbrian campaigns of David's father, one of which had extended into Yorkshire and was probably aimed at far more than the collection of booty; and it should be remembered that in terms of political objectives David

---

[138] Dr Green has been working independently towards the same conclusion: 'Earl Ranulf II', 101.

[139] Those almost certainly supporting the invasion were Alice of Rumilly and William Fitz Duncan, Roger of Mowbray and William II of Percy.

[140] *Regesta Scottorum*, I, 5; *Chronica Rogeri de Houedene*, ed. W. Stubbs, 4 vols. (RS, 1868–71), I, 70; *Chronicles of the Reigns*, I, 70, 105. And see the comments in Warren, *Henry II*, 181–2 and notes.

was in every respect his father's son.[141] Even for those who may have regarded Yorkshire as more properly part of England, David had no shortage of family connections with which to manufacture a claim to govern the county. He was a descendant of the House of Wessex, a husband of a grandniece of the Conqueror, a brother of one English queen and an uncle of another.[142] Only an attempt to make his various claims a reality can explain David's two military invasions of Yorkshire in 1138 and 1149, and his willingness during one of these invasions to fight a pitched battle at Northallerton on one of the major roads south to York. Battles of this sort were rarely fought and usually avoided in the Anglo-Norman period.[143] King David's determination to fight one on Yorkshire soil leaves little doubt that he had no intention of confining his authority to the region north of the Ribble and Tees.

The extent of King David's success in building up his power within the northern shires is reflected most clearly in the urgency and thoroughness of Henry II's policy to reestablish English authority there. Only three years after his succession, Henry forced King Malcolm IV to surrender Northumberland and Cumbria into his hands, and took the abbey of Holm Cultram, which Henry of Scotland had founded c. 1150 as a daughter house of Melrose Abbey, with all its belongings into his custody.[144] He then proceeded to consolidate his authority in the 'border' counties by strengthening the castles there, establishing new men in the key lordships and reinforcing the loyalty of established families.[145] His determination to cut out the cancer of Scottish influence in the north is clear from his policy towards the honours of Skipton and Copeland. After the death of William Fitz Duncan, between 1153 and 1154, Henry was particularly careful to prevent the formation of any further family links between the Rumillys and the Scots, and to ensure that the lordships of Copeland and Skipton descended to trusted administrators.[146] In 1156 he married Alice of Rumilly to Alexander Fitz Gerold, one of his relatives and a tenant of one of the chamberlains of the exchequer. He took charge also of the custody of Alice's four children by William Fitz

---

[141] For King Malcolm III's invasion of the southern part of Teesdale and Cleveland in 1070 and its objectives, see Symeon, *Opera*, II, 190, and the commentary in Kapelle, *Norman Conquest*, 123.   [142] Barrow, *David I*, 17.

[143] J. Bradbury, 'Battles in England and Normandy, 1066–1154', *ANS*, 6 (1984), 1–3.

[144] Warren, *Henry II*, 178, 182–3; *Chronicles of the Reigns*, I, 105–6; *VCH, Cumberland*, II, 162–3.   [145] Green, 'Anglo-Scottish relations', 70–1.

[146] For what follows, see *EYC*, VII, 12–20.

Duncan, despite the fact that (according to the terms of Henry I's coronation charter) this privilege belonged by right to Alice or one of her relations.[147] The only male amongst the four, William, died sometime after 1163 while still in the wardship of the king. His three sisters were all betrothed at Henry's direction. Amabel married Reginald of Lucy, who was probably a close relative of the justiciar, Richard of Lucy, and succeeded to interests in Copeland and Allerdale. Alice married Gilbert Pipard, a sheriff and justice in several counties and a baron of the exchequer in Normandy, and succeeded to most of Allerdale, a portion of Copeland, Radston in Northamptonshire and a small interest in Skipton. And Cecily married William, count of Aumale, the former earl of York and a man well favoured by Henry II, and with her husband administered the honour of Copeland during her mother's lifetime. Nothing more clearly than these marriages highlights the contrast between the weakness of King Stephen and the power of King Henry II in Yorkshire. The year 1154 saw the succession of a new English king, and the return of the old English domination of the north. Had King David secured control of York in 1149, come to terms with the earl of York and lived a little longer, things might have been very different. As it was his dreams were left for his grandson, William the Lion, to pursue.

[147] *Select Charters*, 118. Alice lived until 1187.

Chapter 6

CARTAE BARONUM, NEW ENFEOFFMENTS AND THE NATURE OF THE HONOUR

In 1166 Henry II conducted a great inquest into military enfeoffment on the honours of his magnates, both laymen and clerics. He asked his tenants-in-chief to provide answers to three questions. First, how many knights were enfeoffed on their honours at the death of Henry I (the old enfeoffment). Secondly, how many knights had been enfeoffed since the death of Henry I (the new enfeoffment). And thirdly, how many knights would have to be armed and equipped from their private resources in order to fulfil the service quota or *servitium debitum* owed to the king, if they had enfeoffed fewer knights than were required. As Professor Holt has stated, the answers they provided, known as the *cartae baronum* because they were sent to the king in sealed letters, 'are a curiously neglected source in English history'.[1] What is particularly interesting about these letters is not so much the lists of military tenants and fees they contain, but the details which were either additional to or omitted from the information sought by the king. These additions and omissions reveal that some magnates were anxious about providing the information required of them, particularly the number of knights' fees of the new enfeoffment.

This chapter will first illustrate the anxiety displayed by the magnates in their *cartae*, and will then attempt to explain what the magnates were anxious about. It will argue that the magnates suspected the king of intending to use the 1166 inquest as the basis for moving away from artificial quotas, toward a more realistic and burdensome assessment based upon the actual number of knights enfeoffed. Although prepared to accept quotas of the old enfeoffment, some magnates refused to countenance the incorporation of those of the new enfeoffment. They saw the recording and taxation of many of these enfeoffments as financially

---

[1] J. C. Holt, 'The introduction of knight service in England', *ANS*, 6 (1984), 89.

oppressive, politically dangerous and legally disadvantageous. Their attitude helps to explain the questions asked by Henry II in the 1166 inquest, and throws light on the impact of the politics of Stephen's reign upon the honorial community. A study of the *cartae baronum* suggests that any coherence this community possessed was weakened by the anarchy. Viewed in conjunction with other evidence, it also indicates that this coherence was already weakening before 1135 as the Norman magnates and their tenants settled into the localities and established strong tenurial, religious and familial ties with their neighbours.

THE BARONIAL RESPONSE TO THE 1166 INQUEST

In a recent and important work, Professor Keefe offered a convincing challenge to the traditional interpretation of Henry II's scutage policy as a failure. He did so by undermining the significance of the primary piece of evidence upon which this interpretation is based: Henry II's relaxation in 1187 of the assessment of both ecclesiastical knights' fees in excess of the old service quotas, and lay fees of the new enfeoffment. Keefe revealed that the losses incurred by the 1187 settlement did nothing materially to alter the crown's potential yield through assessments from what was actually achieved by the aid and scutage levies of 1168 and 1172; and that these losses were greatly outweighed by the increased service Henry demanded from the lay knights' fees of the old enfeoffment surplus to the old quotas. The result was that Henry II increased the military service due from the tenants-in-chief by some 1,211 knights.[2]

One aspect of Keefe's thesis which may be questioned is his assessment of the baronial response to the increased burden of service. Despite acknowledging that the ecclesiastical tenants-in-chief refused to make payments on knights' fees in excess of their traditional service quotas, both of the old and the new enfeoffment, Keefe states that, 'a similar resistance attributed by many scholars to the lay baronage cannot be documented', and does not explain why Henry II abandoned the attempt to assess lay fees of the new enfeoffment in 1187.[3] It will be argued in this chapter that Henry II faced resistance in and after 1166 not only from the ecclesiastical

---

[2] Keefe, *Feudal Assessments*, 41–89, esp. 41–52, 59, 87–9.   [3] *Ibid.*, 41.

magnates, but also from the lay magnates of Yorkshire who were opposed to the assessment of fees of the new enfeoffment.

Although it is true that the lay magnates paid scutage on a far greater number of knights' fees after 1166 than before, that arrears were deleted from the rolls only after the sums had been paid or pardoned and that only a small percentage of the 1168 aid and the 1172 scutage remained unaccounted for by 1189, payment need not necessarily be equated with baronial acceptance.[4] In Yorkshire although the magnates eventually paid their new enfeoffment assessments for aid and scutage, payment coincided with Henry II's appointment to the county of his great justice Glanvill as sheriff and itinerant justice in 1175.[5] Glanvill had made his reputation as sheriff of Yorkshire in the previous decade, and it was doubtless a combination of this reputation, his familial connections with some of the most important Yorkshire magnates and his close ties with the king which brought about a rapid settlement of most of the long outstanding debts in the county.[6] This, at least, is the implication of an entry in the 1175–6 pipe roll, which states that Henry of Lacy rendered account before the pleas of Hugh of Cressy and Ranulf Glanvill.[7] It would appear that, having avoided payment for nearly ten years, many of the barons of Yorkshire were only brought to heel in 1175–6 by a special royal administrative and judicial effort.

Baronial knowledge of, and opposition to, some of Henry II's intentions in 1166 is also clear from the remarks included by some of the barons in their *cartae*. The archbishop of York, for example, appears to have been particularly anxious about the fact that the number of knights' fees on his estates was far in excess of his *servitium debitum*: 'We have indeed more knights enfeoffed than are necessary for [the royal] service as you may learn from what follows. For our predecessors enfeoffed more knights than they owed to the king, and they did this, not for the necessities of the royal service, but because they wished to provide for their relatives and servants.'[8] For good measure the archbishop attempted to minimise the significance of the excess knights' fees by declaring that he was claiming more service from some of his military tenants than they were currently performing, and that others were 'keeping back services which are said to be due, not to themselves,

---

[4] *Ibid.*, 41–2.   [5] *PR 22 Henry II*, 99, 101–3; *PR 23 Henry II*, 71.
[6] F. J. West, *The Justiciarship in England, 1066–1232* (Cambridge, 1966), 54–5.
[7] *PR 22 Henry II*, 103.   [8] *Red Book*, I, 413.

but to the table and demesne of the archbishop '.[9] Finally, he asked the king that his *carta* 'may not be allowed to do harm to me or to my successors by preventing the church from recovering or preserving its legal rights'.[10] The archbishop was clearly suspicious that his *carta* might be used to increase the level of his assessment, and to undermine his position in legal disputes.

As for the lay magnates, although most of them cooperated in the 1166 inquest, some of those who did so may have acted under duress. Others may have been more obstructive, including a number of lords from Yorkshire who appear to have returned no *cartae* (Table 10).[11] At the end of the Yorkshire section of the *cartae baronum* appear brief entries for seven lords which record only the total number of knights fees on their lordships in Yorkshire in 1166. The possibility that these entries were the result either of the loss of the original *cartae* by the time the Red Book of the exchequer was compiled in the early thirteenth century, or of abbreviations made by the scribe or scribes who copied the *cartae* into the Red Book and another manuscript which served as its exemplar, is ruled out by evidence from the pipe rolls of Henry II's reign.[12] An entry at the end of the Yorkshire section of the pipe roll account for the aid levied for the marriage of the king's daughter in 1167–8 lists the same seven lords under the statement that, 'The same sheriff renders account of the fees of the barons and knights who hold of the king in chief in his bailliage who have not sent charters to the king concerning their tenements.'[13] It is possible that these barons had not returned *cartae* because they enjoyed a special relationship with the king, or considered themselves to be exempt, or had been unable to provide the information required of them because of administrative confusion: a confusion resulting either from a lack of knowledge about the number of military tenancies on their lands, or from uncertainty about the meaning of the king's questions.[14] It is equally possible,

---

[9] *Ibid.*, 415.   [10] *Ibid.*   [11] *Ibid.*, 434–5.

[12] Hall argued that the *cartae* were copied into the Black Book of the exchequer *c.* 1206 by the exchequer official Alexander de Swereford, that in or about 1212 Swereford began a new and more extensive compilation (no longer extant) based upon the Black Book which became the exemplar of the Red Book, and that various elements which compose the Red Book were bound together *c.* 1230: *Red Book*, I, liii–lxiii.

[13] *PR 14 Henry II*, 90. In the scutage account in the pipe roll for 1171–2 six of the seven were listed under a heading 'De His Qui Cartas ne Miserunt': *PR 18 Henry II*, 62. The one absent name was that of Conan, lord of Richmond, who died in February 1171.

[14] Keefe notes that some of those who failed to return *cartae* were *curiales* or royal relatives: *Feudal Assessments*, 47–8. Several tenants-in-chief had to resort to asking old

however, that at least some of them did not return *cartae* because they were suspicious of the king's inquisition and opposed to it.

Even when magnates were prepared to submit *cartae* there are indications that the information they provided may often have been incomplete, imprecise or inaccurate, and that in some cases this was probably deliberate. Of the 189 or so lay tenants-in-chief who returned *cartae* in 1166, no less than eighty either failed to record new enfeoffments or denied that any had been made.[15] Although many of these denials may have been genuine, it is difficult to believe that this was so in the case of those made by magnates of the status of the bishop of Winchester and the abbot of Abingdon, who possessed large estates hardly likely to have been fully encumbered with sitting tenants in 1135.[16] Although the level of enfeoffment probably declined markedly on most honours after 1135, the relatively underdeveloped state of military settlement in Yorkshire before that date makes it difficult to believe the accuracy of the large number of Yorkshire *cartae* which record only small numbers or fractions of knights' fees of the new enfeoffment (Table 10), in spite of the possibility that some of these fees were geographically larger than those created before 1135. Suspicion is also aroused by the *cartae* of Henry of Lacy and William of Vescy, both of which avoided reference to fees of the new enfeoffment. The former stated that sixty knights' fees of the old enfeoffment were owed to the king, and then listed the other fees on the lordship under the heading 'ipse et antecessores sui feodaverunt, et cum dominio suo serviunt'.[17] The Vescy *carta* began by referring to twenty knights' fees held by Vescy's father on the day Henry I was alive and dead, and then listed additional fees established by Vescy's grandfather and father, and by Vescy himself.[18] Although it may be that both these lords returned their *cartae* in this form because they either did not fully understand the king's instructions, or found it difficult to determine whether fees were created before or after 1135, another possible way of reading their returns is that they were anxious to avoid any increase in

---

men to discover the number of military tenancies on their lordships in 1166. The task of answering the king's questions must have been all the more difficult on those lordships which had been broken up and recast in the century following 1066.

[15] This figure is my own, and was arrived at by using the tabulated 1166 returns in Keefe, *Feudal Assessments*, 154–88.

[16] The bishop's *carta* simply records the names of the tenants in Henry I's day, and the names of the tenants in 1166: *Red Book*, I, 204–7, 305–6. [17] *Ibid.*, 421–4.

[18] *Ibid.*, 427–8.

what they saw as their *servitia* by the assessment of fees of the new enfeoffment. Several more magnates returned *cartae* similar in form to those of Lacy and Vescy, in which they were careful to state the quotas they thought they owed before listing the knights' fees on their honours.[19]

The lists themselves sometimes fail to record all the fees on the honour, and occasionally place fees in the wrong category of enfeoffment. The *carta* of Roger of Mowbray provides an example. It listed Robert III of Stuteville as holding eight knights' fees of the old enfeoffment and one knight's fee of the new enfeoffment, despite the fact that Mowbray had enfeoffed him with ten knights' fees in the period 1154–66.[20] Although it is possible that the grant of one fee had not been effective for some reason, it is difficult to explain with any degree of certainty why Roger designated the bulk of the Stuteville tenancy as being of the old enfeoffment, when it was clearly of the new enfeoffment.[21] Roger also appears to have been guilty of inaccuracy when it came to the tenancy of William Fitz Gilbert of Lancaster who was credited with two fees of the new enfeoffment, even though Roger had bestowed four upon him.[22] Another magnate who may also have been in error was the bishop of Durham who, in addition to avoiding specific references to old enfeoffment and new enfeoffment fees, appears to have omitted a knight's fee held by William of Vescy in Yorkshire. Although the bishop's *carta* records William holding fees only in the region between Tyne and Tees, a confirmation charter of Henry II, probably granted to William shortly after 1157, reveals that William held land of the bishop in Landmoth and High Worsall in Yorkshire.[23] The possibility that the absence of this land from the bishop's *carta* is to be explained by a recovery effected by the bishop before 1166 is weakened by a

---

[19] From outside Yorkshire they include the bishop of Lincoln and the abbot of Bury St Edmunds: *Red Book*, I, 376, 394.

[20] *Ibid.*, 419–20; *EYC*, IX, no. 42, calendared in *Mowbray Charters*, no. 386.

[21] One possibility is that it was an attempt to legitimise an enfeoffment which the king is known to have vetoed: *EYC*, IX, no. 42. Another is that the land alienated to Stuteville had already been granted out for military service before 1135.

[22] *Red Book*, I, 420; *Mowbray Charters*, no. 370. Roger appears to have left the Westmorland portion of the estate out of the reckoning. Given the political circumstances in which the enfeoffment was made (for which, see above, p. 219), it is difficult to believe that this was because Roger had forgotten the precise terms of his grant.

[23] *Red Book*, I, 417; Public Record Office, Chancery Miscellanea C 47/9/5, printed as an appendix to Hartshorne, *History of Northumberland*, cx.

tenurial survey of the early thirteenth century which records that a half knight's fee in Landmoth and High Worsall was held by Eustace of Vescy, the son and heir of William of Vescy.[24]

More evidence of the inaccuracy and incompleteness of some of the 1166 *cartae* can be derived from a comparison of the Percy *carta* with a tenurial record drawn up at the king's court at the Easter exchequer only eleven years later, in April 1175. The later document describes the partition of the lordship of William II of Percy between the husbands of his two daughters and co-heiresses, and shows that it was possible to collect far more detailed information than that required in the 1166 inquest.[25] What is most significant about this document is that it records a minimum of approximately fifty-three and a half knights' fees on the Percy honour in 1175, some nine and a half fees in excess of the total recorded in the 1166 *carta*.[26] Although it is possible that a proportion of the difference was due to new enfeoffments made in the intervening period, this proportion is unlikely to have been great because of the relative shortage of alienable resources on this honour in the second half of the twelfth century.[27] It is far more probable that the difference was mainly due to the omission of fees in the 1166 return.

Although in some cases the omissions and errors in the *cartae* may have been due to administrative confusion, or an honest

---

[24] *Book of Fees*, I, 24.

[25] *EYC*, XI, no. 89 and note. Although the 1175 survey does not attempt to distinguish between knight's fees of the new and old enfeoffments, it does appear to distinguish between tenancies assessed in knight's fees, those assessed in carucates and a variety of other estates.

[26] The total for 1175 is my own, and it may be too low. In addition to the fees explicitly described as held for the service of a certain number of knights, the partition document records a large number of tenancies where the service is not specified or which were described in terms of carucates and bovates, some of which may have been military. The unspecified service of Thomas de Arcy, for example, was assigned to the earl of Warwick's share of the Percy honour. Although Thomas is not listed in the 1166 *carta*, a document of 1184–5 records that his son held five knights' fees of William II of Percy in Lincolnshire: *EYC*, XI, 86; *Regesta*, III, no. 427. Clay's approximate total for the number of knights' fees on the Percy honour in 1175 was forty-three: *EYC*, XI, 81, 89. The 1166 total includes the thirty-six and a third or so knights' fees recorded in the actual *carta*, and an additional seven and a half knights' fees which the Percys held as subtenancies of the bishop of Durham, the earl of Richmond, Hugh of Port and Simon III of Senlis: *ibid.*, 335, 338–9, 353–6. By 1166 the Percys appear to have acquired the tenancy-in-chief of at least part of the lands held of the earl of Chester at the time of Domesday Book.

[27] By 1135 the Percy lords had already alienated over 60 per cent of the carucates on their Yorkshire estates: Dalton, 'Feudal politics', Appendix 2.

mistake on the part of a magnate whose knowledge of enfeoffment on his lordship was imprecise or incomplete, this is unlikely to have been so in every case. There is more than a suggestion in the evidence that the omissions and errors in some of the *cartae* were the result of a deliberate attempt to deceive the king into thinking that fewer fees (and especially fewer fees of the new enfeoffment) had been created than was actually the case; and that this deception was a manifestation of baronial opposition to the king.

MOTIVES FOR BARONIAL OPPOSITION

If, as has been argued, not only the ecclesiastical magnates, but also some of their lay counterparts were opposed to Henry II's demand for information in 1166, the grounds for their opposition need to be explained. Here the *carta* submitted by the archbishop of York is invaluable. It suggests that the archbishop regarded the 1166 inquest as financially, politically and legally dangerous. Each of these dangers will now be considered in turn.

Although scutage was only an occasional tax from which many of the greater magnates were often exempted by offering personal or alternative service, or subsequently pardoned, and some magnates had no excess fees for Henry II to assess, it is possible that actual increases in assessment, however small, might be bitterly opposed in a society which put great store by customary practice. In and after 1166 the magnates had no way of knowing how often Henry II would levy scutage on the basis of his new assessments, or if they would be exempted or pardoned when the levies were made. The experience of the 1150s and early 1160s could hardly have filled them with confidence. During the first eleven years of his reign Henry II took five scutages, sometimes in years when no military campaign was undertaken.[28] The military and political situation could change from year to year, and the king's mind and relationship with individual magnates along with it. Henry II's potential for using the greatly increased level of assessment to exploit his magnates, as much as the realisation of that potential, is likely to have provoked opposition to his policy in certain quarters.

It was a potential, moreover, which was not confined to scutage. The barons had also to face the prospect that the new

---

[28] C. W. Hollister, 'The significance of scutage rates in eleventh- and twelfth-century England', *EHR*, 75 (1960), 580 and note 1; Painter, *English Feudal Barony*, 34.

quotas would be employed as the basis of other forms of tax assessment. The 1166 inquest itself had been initiated with the purpose of levying an aid for the marriage of the king's daughter in 1168.[29] In addition, as Professor Warren has pointed out, the information provided in the *cartae baronum* gave the crown a

fair indication of the feudal resources of an honor, so enabling a realistic price to be put upon it when charging *relief* to an heir, putting it out to wardship, or marketing an heiress. Moreover, if by reason of escheat, or forfeiture or wardship an honor came into the hands of the crown, all the fief-holders on it became liable to the exchequer for the feudal dues which they would previously have rendered to their lord.[30]

Since many tenants-in-chief were also subtenants they, as much as their retainers, were set to lose out because of this liability.

There were other reasons why the increased level of assessment was potentially more burdensome to the magnates than might appear at first sight. It was an assessment which threatened to deprive those of them whose honours were heavily overenfeoffed of the important profits they could expect to make when the king levied scutage.[31] As the archbishop of York's *carta* implies, the increased level of assessment also made no allowance for the possibility that some tenants-in-chief were not obtaining the full service attached to their military fees. The complaints recorded in the *cartae* of many magnates suggest that there might be several possible reasons for this. One was that some of their tenants were not rendering the military service due from their tenements.[32] Another was that some tenants had alienated their lands to religious houses quit of secular services, sometimes without the consent or even the knowledge of their lords.[33] A third reason was that the operation of politics and patronage often required or encouraged lords to alienate land on favourable terms. On most honours it is likely that some tenancies had been granted out in return for only token military service, in order either to secure the favour of influential men, or to provide maintenance and rewards for family and loyal retainers. The king's failure to make allowance for these factors almost certainly explains why at least one magnate

---

[29] Keefe, *Feudal Assessments*, 13–14.
[30] Warren, *Governance*, 100–1; and see his *Henry II*, 280–1.
[31] Warren, *Henry II*, 278–9. See also Hollister, *Military Organization*, 202–3.
[32] See in addition to the return made by the archbishop of York, that of the bishop of Exeter: *Red Book*, I, 248–50.   [33] See below, pp. 266–72.

was careful to list certain knights' fees in his *carta* return under a separate heading of 'Relaxatio militum in eodem feodo'.[34] Any attempt to assess the magnates on fees either returning no service, alienated to religion or granted out on favourable terms was bound to be regarded as especially burdensome, and very likely to be opposed.

The financial dangers inherent within the 1166 inquest were accompanied by others of a political nature. These are evident in the archbishop of York's *carta*. He wrote to the king that 'there is also to be included in the return the names of all those, both of the old and new enfeoffments, because you wish to know if there are any who have not yet done you allegiance and whose names are not written in your roll, so that they may do you allegiance before the first Sunday in Lent'.[35] The king was asking his magnates to make public the names of those tenants who had not yet offered him their loyalty, and who probably included men who had opposed him during the reign of Stephen. If a royal charter issued between 1155 and 1162 concerning Robert Botevilein, dean of York, is any reflection of Henry II's general attitude towards those whose names were not on his rolls of allegiance, it is easy to understand why his barons were reluctant to provide him with the information he required in 1166. The charter implies that those who had never made an oath of fealty to the king's mother, or to the king himself, were normally outside his affections and liable to have their property confiscated.[36]

The archbishop of York's *carta* suggests another possible motive for opposition to Henry II's inquest: the fear that the information requested might be used against the magnates in legal disputes. In effect, by recording their military fees in sealed letters addressed to the king the magnates were committing themselves to what was potentially a legal record, and providing their tenants with a confirmation 'charter' which could be used against them in court.

From this analysis we can see that the 1166 inquest, and the revised tax assessment based upon it, posed a series of threats or potential threats to the magnate community. Although these threats probably provide a general explanation for the opposition which the inquest appears to have faced from some barons, they do not elucidate why many lay barons appear to have been particularly reluctant to record and pay scutage on knights' fees of

---

[34] *Red Book*, I, 378. [35] *Ibid.*, 412. [36] *EYC*, I, no. 140.

the new enfeoffment, and why the king was eventually willing to abandon the assessment of fees of this sort, despite continuing to assess the lay barons on the much more numerous excess fees of the old enfeoffment.[37] Professor Painter considered that the barons were opposed to the assessment of fees of the new enfeoffment because many of these fees may have been made under duress in the reign of Stephen, and that although refusing to accept their opposition Henry II recognised it by making the distinction between the old and new fees in the questions he asked in the 1166 inquest.[38] Against this, Keefe argues that

A protest from those barons who had new fees yet were not overenfeoffed is hard to imagine because they were unaffected by Henry II's policy. If the overenfeoffed barons entered a protest, it probably would have been connected with some increase in their obligation, and would not have pertained to whether the surplus fees had been created in a time of war versus a time of peace. One might also question whether the number of fees forcibly created in Stephen's reign was much higher than the number voluntarily granted out for the provision of friends, relatives, and retainers. William 'de Arches' does not seem to have acted under duress when he granted eight carucates of land to his kinsman Elias 'de Hou' (1140 × 1147). On the other hand, the "de novo fefamento" category covered all enfeoffments made from December 1135 through February 1166 and thus included twelve years of Henry II's reign in addition to Stephen's reign.[39]

Although Keefe's observation concerning the equation of fees of the new enfeoffment with surplus fees is unobjectionable, the same cannot be said of his assumption that a protest from the magnates who had fees of the new enfeoffment but who were not overenfeoffed is hard to imagine because they were unaffected by Henry II's policy. It was common in this period for magnates to regard antique and customary practice as one of the foundations of legitimacy in matters of law, and it can hardly be doubted that this was also true in matters of finance.[40] A magnate in 1166 whose father and grandfather had provided a certain amount of scutage to the crown is unlikely to have acquiesced readily to an attempt by the king to raise the level of this scutage, whether he was underenfeoffed or not. And this must have been especially true of

---

[37] Keefe illustrates that the new fees accounted for only 7.5 per cent of the entire enfeoffment: *Feudal Assessments*, 43.   [38] Painter, *English Feudal Barony*, 35.

[39] Keefe, *Feudal Assessments*, 16–17.

[40] For matters of law, see below, pp. 289–93.

the magnates who did not know their quotas, and who were unaware that they were underenfeoffed.

Another difficulty arises with the assumption that any opposition of overenfeoffed barons to Henry II's scutage policy was probably connected with the increased level of obligation, and did not pertain to whether the surplus fees had been created in a time of war versus a time of peace. If it were merely a question of increased levels of obligation, it is difficult to explain why the magnates appear to have succumbed to the assessment of large numbers of excess fees of the old enfeoffment, while remaining almost uniformly recalcitrant regarding payment on fees of the new enfeoffment, which accounted for only a small proportion of the total enfeoffment and added very little to their overall tax burden.[41]

There can be little doubt that many enfeoffments made after 1135 which appear at first sight to have been regular were actually made under duress. A case in point may be Keefe's own example of a 'voluntary' grant. William of Arches gave his eight carucates in Kirk Hammerton, Kirkby Ouseburn, Hebden and Appletreewick to his kinsman, Elias de Hou, to hold by the same acquittance as Robert Fitz Fulk held until the return of peace, when he was to perform the service of the fourth part of one knight ('Quando vero pax erit terramque suam plenarie possidebit, servitium de quarta parte militis faciet').[42] The terms of William's charter suggest that the acquittance of service was directly related to the warfare of Stephen's reign, that far from being 'voluntary' the enfeoffment was made in exceptional circumstances, and that it may have been intended to encourage a kinsman to protect land which was disputed and/or under threat of seizure.

An examination of some of the new enfeoffments made in Yorkshire in Stephen's reign by magnates who were unwilling to admit them in their *cartae* reveals that these enfeoffments were made for political reasons and were either illegal or unfavourable to the grantors. These grantors would have had good reason to avoid recognising such enfeoffments in the reign of Henry II, and to oppose being taxed upon them.

An example of one such new enfeoffment is the grant made in Stephen's reign by Roger of Mowbray to Eustace Fitz John,

---

[41] Keefe, *Feudal Assessments*, 43–4, 56–7, 87–8.   [42] *EYC*, I, no. 534.

constable of Chester, of fourteen knights' fees for the service of eleven knights.[43] In his 1166 *carta*, Roger lists Eustace's son and heir, William of Vescy, as the tenant in only two knights' fees of the new enfeoffment.[44] This was probably due to the fact that Roger's grant to Eustace appears to have been forced upon him by Ranulf II, earl of Chester (who captured him at the battle of Lincoln in 1141), and 'represented a serious loss of status'.[45] In effect, Eustace had been granted superiority over a number of existing Mowbray military tenancies, including one knight's fee held by Rolland Hachet, six knights' fees held by William Tison, and two knights' fees in the Lincolnshire vill of Gainsborough and elsewhere almost certainly held by a different branch of the Tison family.[46] Roger had probably already lost control of Gainsborough to the earl of Chester's half-brother, William I of Roumare, by 1141.[47] With the earl of Chester's death in 1153, and the accession of Henry II a year later, Roger had good reason to renege on the enfeoffment to Eustace. Not only did it pose a threat to his control of his own estates, it prevented him from obtaining the full service attached to the grant, and jeopardised his relationship with his old-established tenants, who would probably not have relished their demotion in the tenurial order. Moreover, because the enfeoffment included three knights' fees held by William and Peter Mauleverer, which belonged by right to the Brus tenancy-in-chief, it was likely to bring Roger into conflict with the Brus family and trouble with the king.[48] Indeed, this may actually have happened. This is certainly the implication of a charter in which Henry II commanded Roger to reseise William of Vescy of the tenancies and service of William and Peter Mauleverer if Vescy had been unjustly disseised.[49] When placed within this context it is easy to understand why Roger of Mowbray was willing to admit to William of Vescy's tenure of only two of the fourteen knights' fees granted to Eustace Fitz John, despite the fact that Vescy probably held, and certainly had a claim to, far more than two fees.[50]

---

[43] *Calendar of the Close Rolls, 1313–1318*, 286, calendared in *Mowbray Charters*, no. 397.
[44] *Red Book*, I, 420.   [45] *Mowbray Charters*, xxvii.   [46] *EYC*, XII, 11–13.
[47] Dalton, 'Ranulf of Chester', 117–18.
[48] *Mowbray Charters*, no. 397 and note; *EYC*, II, 13.
[49] Public Record Office, Chancery Miscellanea Bundle 9, no. 5, m. 2d.
[50] The two fees probably represented those estates which Roger had bestowed out of his own demesne. The Vescys are known to have retained an interest in some of the Tison estates into the thirteenth century: *EYC*, II, 323; XII, 32, 35–6, 38; *Selby Coucher*, II, no.

There are other examples of new enfeoffments which turn out on closer analysis to have been motivated by political designs. This appears to have been true of some of the new enfeoffments made in the region of Cravenshire by the three major magnate families holding lands there: the Mowbrays, Percys and lords of Skipton. As we have seen, the region became the focus of Scottish ambitions in Stephen's reign, and King David's nephew, William Fitz Duncan, was successful in establishing himself as lord of Skipton for at least part of the period 1138–54. It was probably at William's direction that in *c.* 1149 Roger of Mowbray granted William Fitz Gilbert of Lancaster four knights' fees, composed of estates in Cumbria, Lonsdale and Cravenshire.[51] William Fitz Duncan enjoyed the predominant tenurial interest in Cravenshire, and it was on his estates that the new enfeoffments there were most numerous. It is significant that although ten and a half of the twelve or thirteen knights' fees of the old enfeoffment recorded on the honour of Skipton in 1166 lay outside Yorkshire, most if not all of the entire eight or so knights' fees of the new enfeoffment were situated within Cravenshire.[52] To some degree this was doubtless a reflection of the fact that the Norman settlement of the north lagged behind that in other areas of the country, but it was probably also due in part to the unusual political circumstances of Stephen's reign. Several of the new enfeoffments are likely to have resulted from an attempt by William Fitz Duncan to try and consolidate his control of the honour, and to prevent its outlying estates from falling into the hands of hostile magnates, by granting land to tenants who were already subject to him in Cumberland. The examples of Adam Fitz Swain and the Fleming family have already been examined in some detail in the previous chapter. Many more new enfeoffments could have been granted by William in order to win the support of the established Skipton tenantry, who had already forged a complex network of family and neighbourhood ties with other honours, including those of Lacy and Mowbray, whose lords were potentially hostile to Scottish ambitions in Yorkshire and Lancashire.

Two families attached to the Lacys and Mowbrays whose

---

754. The fees held by Hachet, Tison, Mauleverer and the Tisons of Gainsborough amounted to twelve of the total of fourteen. The Mowbray *carta* records the holdings of these tenants as immediate tenancies of the old enfeoffment: *Red Book*, I, 418–21. See also *EYC*, XII, 11–13. [51] *Mowbray Charters*, no. 370.
[52] *Red Book*, I, 430–2; *EYC*, VII, 42, 90.

support William Fitz Duncan and his allies may have been competing for were the Arches and the Reinevilles. William of Arches witnessed charters of William Fitz Duncan and his mother-in-law, Cecily of Rumilly, in Stephen's reign, and his son Helto held three carucates of the new enfeoffment of the honour of Skipton in 1166.[53] William of Arches may have been connected with the Arches family who were tenants of the honour of Copeland, an honour controlled by William Fitz Duncan in Stephen's reign, and he was almost certainly related to Gilbert of Arches, who held one knight's fee of the old enfeoffment and three-quarters of a knight's fee of the new enfeoffment in Cravenshire and elsewhere of William II of Percy, a magnate who had close connections with the Scots.[54] The antiquity and strength of the connections of Gilbert's family with the honour of Percy are indicated by his tenure of an additional knight's fee of the old enfeoffment, his father's appearance in the witness lists of several charters issued by Alan I of Percy before 1135 and his own attestation of William II of Percy's charters thereafter.[55] Through his family he probably also had close links with the lands belonging to the honour of Lacy in Lancashire, which may have fallen under Scottish control in Stephen's reign.[56] In the case of the Reineville family, a junior member of which (Hervey) held a half knight's fee of the new enfeoffment of the honour of Skipton in 1166, the links with the honour of Lacy were even stronger. The senior line of the family held four knights' fees of the old enfeoffment of Henry of Lacy, consisting partly of lands close to the outlying section of the honour of Skipton in the region of Wath upon Dearne in south Yorkshire.[57]

Given the fact that the Lacys and Mowbrays were probably in competition with the Scots for control of land in northern Lancashire and Lonsdale respectively, and given the vulnerability of the outlying portion of the honour of Skipton situated deep inside territory dominated by the Lacys in south Yorkshire, the grant of new enfeoffments by the lord of Skipton and William II of Percy to members of the Arches and Reineville families, who had close links with these three regions and with the Lacy and

---

[53] *EYC*, VII, 272, and nos. 9, 12; *Red Book*, I, 432.
[54] See *Register of St. Bees*, nos. 4, 8, 9, 10 and notes; *Red Book*, I, 424, 426; *EYC*, XI, 146.
[55] *EYC*, XI, 146, 150–1, nos. 5–7, 10, 12, 14, 16–17, 20.
[56] See *EYC*, XI, 152–4, nos. 128–9, 133, 136; III, 256–79; VII, 183, no. 161; *Red Book*, I, 422.
[57] *EYC*, III, 248–9; VII, 212.

Mowbray estates within them, may have had a political purpose. Although it cannot be proved, it is more than possible that Fitz Duncan and Percy were using, perhaps being forced to use, the grant of new enfeoffments to win or reinforce the loyalty of powerful local families who might have been inclined to support their political opponents, and who were well placed either to defend or threaten their more vulnerable estates.[58]

On a wider plain it is even possible that the Scots employed their newly acquired lands in Cravenshire to attach the highly influential archdeacon of York, Osbert, to their interests. In 1166 Osbert held one of the largest new enfeoffment tenancies of the honour of Skipton, consisting of eleven carucates in a place where fourteen carucates made a knight's fee.[59] In view of Osbert's staunch opposition to William Fitz Herbert, the royal candidate for the vacant archbishopric of York, and his support for Henry Murdac, who is known to have been in close contact with the Scottish court, his enfeoffment in the honour of Skipton may well have been motivated by political concerns.

Competition for service was an endemic feature of King Stephen's reign.[60] If this competition dictated some of the enfeoffments made by the lords of Yorkshire to influential knights from outside their honours, this was probably also true of some of the enfeoffments they made to influential knights from within them: especially those knights with familial and tenurial ties with other lordships, whose loyalties may have been divided. One example is Roger of Mowbray's grant of one knight's fee to Robert of Daiville, who was one of Roger's most important old enfeoffment tenants, served as Roger's constable from *c.* 1154 until *c.* 1186 and married a sister of Roger's rival, Robert III of Stuteville. Another example is William II of Percy's grant of a half a knight's fee to his steward, Robert, who had tenurial and marriage ties outside the Percy honour with the families of Arches (tenants of the Mowbrays) and St Quintin (tenants of the counts of Aumale). And a third example is provided by William II of

---

[58] It is interesting that two mid-twelfth-century charters issued by the Percy tenant Peter of Arches, and concerning land in Cravenshire, were attested by Gamello and Orm, sons of Gospatric, who had connections with the Scots. They were probably grandsons of Orm Fitz Ketel, the ancestor of the Curwens of Workington. Orm Fitz Ketel was the husband of Gunnilda, half-sister of Etheldreda the mother of William Fitz Duncan. Fitz Duncan was the nephew of King David of Scotland. See *EYC*, XI, nos. 133, 136; VII, 282; Washington, 'William de Lancaster', 95–100; Hedley, *Northumberland Families*, I, 239, 241.   [59] *Red Book*, I, 431.   [60] King, 'Anarchy', 138–41.

Percy's grant of three-quarters of a knight's fee to Gilbert of Arches who, as we have seen, had family connections with several other Yorkshire honours.[61]

It is possible, therefore, that many new enfeoffments were created by lords in adverse or unusual political circumstances, and as such became unacceptable when the conditions that gave rise to them had passed away. New enfeoffments of this sort may often have undermined the authority of lords, placed them in danger of legal repercussions under Henry II, jeopardised their relationship with existing tenants and deprived them of lands and services which could have been put to more profitable use elsewhere.

What this study suggests is that the unusual nature of fees of the new enfeoffment, possibly a good number of which were made in adverse political circumstances, may have been an important factor responsible for stimulating the baronial opposition to Henry II's attempt to record and tax these fees in 1166. But it was not the only factor. This is suggested by the fact that the lay magnates appear to have acquiesced in the payment of scutage on all fees of the old enfeoffment, despite the fact that some of these fees may have been granted for the same or similar political reasons as the fees of the new enfeoffment. It is also suggested by the strong likelihood that, as Keefe points out, not all of the post-1135 enfeoffments were made under duress, especially those made in the period 1154–66. How, then, are we to explain the general reluctance of the Yorkshire magnates to pay scutage and aid on all new enfeoffments?

The key to answering this question is probably to be found in the distinctions made in the pipe roll accounts for the assessment of scutage and aid, between fees of the new and old enfeoffment held by lay magnates, and between fees 'acknowledged' (*recognoscit*) and 'not acknowledged' (*non recognoscit*) as eligible for taxation held by ecclesiastical magnates. According to Professor Warren, these distinctions show that Henry II anticipated resistance to his increased assessment, and structured the 1166 questions and the ensuing levies to facilitate a compromise: he was prepared to allow the ecclesiastics to pay on their *servitia* (that is, the fees they

---

[61] For Daiville, see *Mowbray Charters*, xxxiv, lx; *EYF*, 23. For notes on Robert the Steward, see *EYC*, XI, 89–97. For the Arches and St Quintin families, who were important tenants in Yorkshire of the Mowbrays and the counts of Aumale respectively, see *EYF*, 79; *Mowbray Charters*, xxv, xxxv. For notes on Gilbert of Arches, see *EYC*, XI, 146–55.

'acknowledged' as eligible to pay) and to record the rest as an unrequited debt, but would require payment from lay magnates on at least the total number of fees in existence in 1135.[62] Although this argument cannot be corroborated with documentary evidence, and has been criticised, it appears logical.[63] It is likely that Henry II worked out the questions asked of the barons in 1166 with the intention of maximising the income to be derived from the taxation of military tenements; an intention which would itself explain why the new fee category was not confined to the period 1135–54. And it is equally likely that Henry anticipated some form of opposition from his magnates; especially to his enrolment and taxation of fees of the new enfeoffment, many (but not all) of which had been made during the troubles of Stephen's reign. The king could not count on being able to record and tax the total enfeoffment, and had to formulate his questions accordingly. In addition to the total enfeoffment in 1166, therefore, it was necessary that these questions should provide him with information about the total enfeoffment at some other date on which the magnates were likely to accept taxation. He required a 'point of legitimacy' in the period 1066–1166 at which he could argue that all fees in existence owed scutage to the king. It was common in the Anglo-Norman period for points of legitimacy to be taken as the day on which the previous king had been alive and dead. It is a principle discernible in Domesday Book and in Anglo-Norman charters. The question for Henry II was which Anglo-Norman king to choose. The nearer the king's death to 1166, the greater the number of fees in existence, the more benefit to be derived by the king from scutage and aids assessed on the basis of knight service. Since Henry could not choose Stephen without acknowledging him as king and legitimating the alienations he had made from the royal demesne, the obvious choice was Henry I and 1135. And since Henry II had already decided to employ the general principle of tenure in his grandfather's reign as the basis of title in settling legal disputes, he could be confident of obtaining relatively comprehensive records of the number of fees in existence at this date from magnates concerned not to be seen to be disowning their tenancies.[64] Moreover, since, as Warren points

---

[62] Warren, *Henry II*, 279–80.
[63] For criticism of Warren, see Keefe, *Feudal Assessments*, 18.
[64] For the principle, see *The Chronicle of Robert of Torigni*, ed. R. Howlett, in *Chronicles of the Reigns*, IV, 177.

out, there is evidence that Henry I had already demanded payment from his magnates on the actual number of knights enfeoffed on their honours, Henry II's proposal to tax the total enfeoffment in 1135 was supported by the force of precedent.[65]

The distinction drawn by Henry II between new and old fees was a distinction designed to give him the potential to record and tax the total military enfeoffment of England in 1166, and, if that failed due to baronial opposition, to record and tax it in 1135, for which a more legitimate case could be made. Even the adoption of this fall-back position would substantially raise the level of service due to the crown. In the event it was a fall-back position which the king was forced by his magnates to accept. The magnates were probably generally opposed to the assessment of the fees of the new enfeoffment because they, like their king, were aware that 1135 had been established as the date of legitimacy in matters of custom and law, and that it might also be regarded as such in matters of finance.

THE DISINTEGRATION OF THE HONOUR

Analysis of the 1166 *cartae baronum* and the circumstances in which some of the fees recorded there were created, suggests that the importance attached by Professor Stenton and others to the honour in the social and political organisation of Anglo-Norman England may have been overestimated. Although recognising that some Anglo-Norman tenants might hold land of several lords, Stenton was convinced that honours usually incorporated 'a self-contained feudal community' of 'honorial barons' who 'belonged' to the honour, served in the lord's household, sat in his court and (apparently) held land exclusively of him.[66] The *cartae baronum* of 1166, however, reveal that it was common for military tenants, from both within and outside the seignorial household, to have tenurial ties with more than one lord. The analysis of the new enfeoffments above reveals that many of these cross-honorial ties were formed in Stephen's reign as magnates were forced to make enfeoffments under duress, or as they competed with each other

---

[65] Warren, *Henry II*, 280, citing Hollister, *Military Organization*, 203.
[66] Stenton, *First Century*, Chapters 2 and 3, quotations from pp. 55, 95, 98. In examining the honour of William Peverel of Nottingham, Stenton states that it was the Peverel tenants who held land of Peverel alone 'whom we should bear in mind when we are trying to form an impression of the honorial baronage of the eleventh century': *ibid.*, 100.

for the service of influential knights. The formation of such ties, however, was probably in progress within a short time of the arrival of the Normans in England, and was certainly older than Stephen's reign.

The honour of Percy provides a number of examples. In 1086 Osbert the priest was the tenant of William I of Percy in several estates in Yorkshire and Lincolnshire. In 1166 these estates formed part of a tenancy of two knights' fees held of William II of Percy by Stephen the chamberlain, the son of Osbert's granddaughter, Milisent. By the later years of the reign of Henry I, Osbert had acquired tenancies held of at least another nine magnates; probably on account of his close connections with the royal administration, in which he served as sheriff of Lincolnshire in the period 1093–1116, and sheriff of Yorkshire from December 1100 to *c.* 1115.[67] This was certainly the opinion of the Meaux chronicler, who attributed Osbert's acquisition of many lands from the earls and barons of England to the fact that he was in the king's household.[68]

The establishment of tenurial and familial ties which cut across honorial boundaries was a two-way process. Just as the old-established and influential Percy tenant families, like that of Osbert the sheriff, acquired lands beyond the Percy dominions, so influential tenant families originally based in other lordships acquired lands within these dominions. An example is provided by the family of Walter of Amundeville. In 1166 Walter's younger brother, Ralph, held a knight's fee of the old enfeoffment of William II of Percy, at least part of which is known to have been held by Walter before 1135. But the most important, and almost certainly the original, attachments of Walter's family were with other lordships. Walter succeeded his father, Goslin, in the stewardship of the bishop of Lincoln, to which was attached a fee owing the service of five knights. There is evidence to suggest that Walter's mother, Beatrice, was a daughter of the Yorkshire Domesday tenant-in-chief, Ralph Paynel; and Goslin and Walter are known to have held estates of the Paynel honour in Lincolnshire. Other interests held by Walter in Lincolnshire included a half knight's fee of the old enfeoffment held of Richard de la Haye, and estates belonging to the bishopric of Durham. It was in Lincolnshire also that Walter's brother, William, held three

---

[67] *EYC*, XI, 213–17; Farrer, 'Sheriffs of Lincolnshire and Yorkshire', 277–85; Green, *Sheriffs*, 54–5, 89.   [68] *Chronica de Melsa*, I, 85.

knights' fees of the old enfeoffment of the honour of Gant, another half knight's fee of Maurice de Craon, and several more estates attached to the bishopric of Durham and the lordship of the counts of Aumale. The important influence of Walter and his family in Lincolnshire is also reflected in Walter's tenure of the shrievalty there between Michaelmas 1158 and Michaelmas 1163.[69] It was this influence which probably accounts for Walter's enfeoffment on the honour of Percy.

The creation of cross-honorial ties could result from other causes besides the cultivation of influential men. One of these causes has been described by Dr Mortimer as a process of 'settling into the locality'.[70] It is a process which can be seen on the honour of Percy in the acquisition of estates by the Vavasour family, who were among the most important Percy tenants. In 1166 William the Vavasour held two knights' fees of the old enfeoffment of William II of Percy, a third of a knight's fee of uncertain provenance of the honour of Lacy, and an additional half knight's fee of the old enfeoffment of the honour of Skipton. Domesday Book reveals that the lands held in 1086 of the Percys and Lacys by William's grandfather, Malger, were situated in neighbouring vills in the region of Tadcaster. It was in this region also that the family was subsequently to acquire more lands from the honours of Bulmer and Mowbray.[71] Further 'settling in' had possibly also taken place by 1135 in the region of Addingham in Cravenshire, where the Vavasours held land of both the lords of Skipton and Percy.[72]

Taking the Percy tenants as a whole, of the twenty-nine listed as holding tenancies of the old enfeoffment in 1166, the predecessors of at least five, and possibly many more, held lands of one or more lords in addition to the Percys by 1135. Together these five men held eight and a half of the twenty-eight knights' fees of the old enfeoffment on the honour at that date, amounting to some 30 per cent of the total. They included two men whom Stenton would have classed as 'honorial barons', Robert the Steward and William the Vavasour. Robert was the principal official in the Percy household; and both he and William attested

---

[69] C. T. Clay, 'The family of Amundeville', *Lincolnshire Architectural and Archaeological Reports and Papers*, n. s., 3 (1939–52), 109–36.

[70] Mortimer, 'Honour of Clare', 186–7, 194–6, quotation from p. 187.

[71] *DB*, I, 321b, 316a; *EYC*, XI, 118–22, esp. 119 and notes 1 and 8; VII, 166.

[72] *EYC*, VII, nos. 104–7 and notes.

the charters of the Percy lords, and held larger estates than most of their fellow Percy tenants.[73]

What is even more significant is that, with the exception of the greater Percy tenants, it is almost certain that the membership of the Percy tenantry was unstable. Of the twenty-nine military tenants holding fees of the old enfeoffment in 1166, the familial descendants of only five can be identified as holding of the Percy lord in 1086. These five were the most important tenants on the honour, and held between them eleven of its twenty-eight knights' fees of the old enfeoffment.[74] Of the remaining twenty-four Percy tenants in 1166, the tenure of the familial descendants of six, who held a total of between five and six knights' fees in 1166, can be traced back to the reign of Henry I; and the tenure of the familial descendants of another two, who held one and a half knights' fees in 1166, can be traced back to the reign of Stephen. This leaves sixteen 1166 tenants holding lands of the old enfeoffment, who held a total of nine and a half knights' fees.[75] Although it is possible that some of the ancestors of these sixteen had been enfeoffed by the Percys by 1086, this cannot be proven. It is more likely that the membership of the lesser tenantry changed rapidly over time as new tenants were periodically enfeoffed. The enfeoffment of twenty-one or so Percy military tenants is known to have taken place between 1135 and 1166; and Clay noted the instability in the personnel and estates of the smaller Percy tenantry in the period 1166–75.[76] Although some of this instability may have resulted from the enfeoffment of knights from the Percy household, some of it was almost certainly due to the granting of estates to men from outside the Percy honour, who were just as anxious as the old-established Percy tenants to secure good lordship.

The same process of 'settling into the locality' is reflected in the pattern of religious benefaction on the honour of Percy and several other Yorkshire lordships. Although it was common for tenants to assist their lords in founding monasteries, their religious patronage

---

[73] *EYC*, XI, 89–96, 118–20, nos. 1–3, 5, 7, 11–12, 14, 16–20. The other men included in the group of five were Ralph of Amundeville, whose predecessor and elder brother, Walter, held of several other lords; Stephen the chamberlain, whose ancestor, Osbert the sheriff, held land of at least nine other tenants-in-chief; and Henry Fitz Apolitus, whose father was also a tenant of the Trussebuts. See *EYC*, XI, 137–8, 146, 172–3, 180–1, 202–3, 207–8, 213–15, 222–6, 232–4, 243–4, 248–9, 252–3; *EYF*, 33–4.

[74] Robert the Steward, Robert of Percy, William the Vavasour, William Fitz Hugh and Stephen the Chamberlain: *EYC*, XI, 93–6, 105–7, 118–19, 137–9, 213–17.

[75] *Ibid.*, *passim.*　　　　　　　　　　[76] *Ibid.*, 88.

was by no means always confined within the honour.[77] On the lordship of Percy at some time in the reign of Henry I, Picot, an important old enfeoffment tenant and possible relative of Alan I of Percy, gave the church of Bolton Percy (which he held of Alan) to the nearby Lacy foundation of Nostell Priory.[78] Picot's son, Robert, was equally prepared to look beyond the Percy foundations of Sallay and Whitby in satisfying the demands of piety, and at some point before 1153 gave the church of Carnaby to the nearby Gant priory of Bridlington.[79] Between *c.* 1140 and 1150 another Percy tenant, Hugh Fitz Everard, whose sons held a knight's fee of the old enfeoffment of the honour in 1166, gave his Percy estates in Stainton in Cravenshire to the abbey of Selby in return for specified facilities for himself and his wife on the occasion of their visits there.[80] And just as the Percy tenants gave lands to the monasteries founded by other lords, so the monasteries founded by the Percys attracted the patronage of tenants from outside the Percy honour. The confirmation charter granted by King Stephen to Whitby Abbey in February 1136 included gifts from the fees of Brus, Fossard and Eustace Fitz John.[81] The Fossard and Fitz John estates are known to have been granted between *c.* 1120 and 1135 by a tenant of these lordships, Durand of Butterwick, who became a monk at Whitby by 1150, and whose descendant held two knights' fees of the Fossards in 1166.[82] By the reign of Henry II Whitby had also secured the church of Barmston in Holderness from Alan of Monceaux, whose son held approximately one knight's fee of the lords of Holderness in 1166, and who was a regular witness of the charters of William, count of Aumale. Alan's establishment of local roots can also be seen in his grant of land in Holderness to the Gant foundation of Bridlington Priory, and in the construction of his own religious house at Nun Coton in Lincolnshire by 1153.[83] These examples can easily be multiplied.[84]

If the pattern of tenure and religious benefaction often cut across honorial boundaries, so did the pattern of marriage. Marriages between families who held their principal tenements of different lords were common in the first half of the twelfth century, and

---

[77] See Burton, 'Religious orders', 126, 180, 182–4, 200–2, 223, 225, 254–78, 331.
[78] *EYC*, XI, 105, 107, no. 97.   [79] *Ibid.*, 107 and note to no. 101.
[80] *Ibid.*, no. 123; *EYF*, 52.   [81] *Regesta*, III, no. 942.   [82] *EYF*, 11–12.
[83] *Ibid.*, 61.
[84] See Burton, 'Religious orders', 29–30, 83, 90, 126, 184, 209–10, 331.

examples can be found on the honour of Percy. It was almost certainly at the command of Henry I that Milisent, the grand-daughter and eventual successor of the Percy Domesday tenant, Osbert the sheriff, married Herbert, lord of Kinneil, the chamberlain of the king of Scotland, who held office in the period *c.* 1136–*c.* 1160.[85] At some point before *c.* 1150, Robert Fitz Fulk, steward of the honour of Percy, married Alice of St Quintin whose father, Herbert of St Quintin, was one of the most important retainers of the lords of Holderness and earls of Gloucester, and whose mother, Agnes of Arches, was the sister of one of the principal tenants of the honour of Mowbray, William of Arches. Because of the other inter-honorial marriages of the Arches family, it was an association which attached Robert Fitz Fulk to a broad familial as well as tenurial network. After Herbert of St Quintin's death (not later than 1129), Agnes of Arches went on to marry in succession Robert de Fauconberg, another tenant of the counts of Aumale, and William Foliot, who held five knights' fees of the Lacys; and at some point before 1143 Agnes's niece, Juetta of Arches, married the tenant-in-chief Adam I of Brus.[86] Another Percy tenant to make an important marriage outside the honour was Geoffrey of Valognes who, at some point before 1163, married Emma the daughter and eventual heiress of Bertram of Bulmer, and probably acquired through her a tenancy of four knights' fees held of the honour of Fossard.[87] Inter-honorial marriages of this kind can be found on several other Yorkshire lordships throughout the first century of Norman rule.[88]

When viewed against the background of the political enfeoffment in progress in the reign of Stephen, and the cross-honorial tenurial, religious and familial ties which were developing throughout the Anglo-Norman period, some honours look more like artificial constructs than functioning self-contained communities around which society and government were principally organised. Although there is some evidence that magnates were able to surround themselves with a nucleus of more important tenants whose loyalties lay principally with them, who served in their households, attended their courts regularly, made benefactions to their religious houses, witnessed their charters and looked to them for assistance, outside this select group (and

---

[85] *EYC*, XI, 214.   [86] *Ibid.*, 94–5; *EYF*, 26, 33–4, 79.   [87] *EYC*, XI, 180.
[88] See *ibid.*, XII, 8–9, 145; X, 143–5; IX, 5, no. 17 and note; *Mowbray Charters*, lx; *EYF*, 21–2, 23, 78.

sometimes even within it) the coherence of the honour was undermined by multifarious political allegiances, complicated patterns of tenure and strong ties of neighbourhood and family.

CONCLUSION

This chapter has argued that the scutage policy of Henry II was opposed not only by ecclesiastical magnates, but also by at least some of their lay counterparts. There is evidence that several lay magnates who held lands in Yorkshire failed to return *cartae* to the king in 1166, that several of those who did return *cartae* made no reference to fees of the new enfeoffment and that others made errors or omissions in their returns. While some of these failures, errors and omissions may have been due to administrative confusion rather than deliberate opposition to the king, it is difficult to believe that this was true of them all. The *carta* submitted by the archbishop of York indicates that he was concerned that the information required from him would be used in a variety of ways to his disadvantage; and it is more than likely that some of the lay magnates of Yorkshire shared the archbishop's concerns. In the case of the recording of fees of the new enfeoffment there was all the more reason to be concerned, since many of these enfeoffments appear to have been made in unusual or adverse circumstances during the reign of Stephen, and were sometimes a source of regret or embarrassment after the return of peace in 1154. The magnates appear to have avoided the payment of aid and scutage on fees of the new enfeoffment for several years after 1166, and were only brought to account as the result of a special royal administrative and judicial effort, involving the appointment of the powerful Ranulf Glanvill as sheriff of Yorkshire. It was an effort, however, which was not maintained, and in 1187 the king abandoned his attempt to assess both ecclesiastical fees in excess of the *servitium debitum* and lay new fees. While it is certainly true that Henry II succeeded in substantially raising the level of assessment, his success need not necessarily be equated with an absence of baronial opposition. In formulating his questions to the magnates in 1166, Henry may well have anticipated resistance to the assessment of the total enfeoffment at that date, and allowed himself the alternative possibility of assessing the barons on the total enfeoffment in 1135, for which a more legitimate case could be made.

As well as illuminating the baronial response to, and logic behind, the questions asked by the king in 1166, a detailed study of the *cartae baronum* throws a good deal of light on the nature of the honour in the first century of Norman rule, and some of the factors which could serve to undermine its coherence. One of the most important of these factors was the development of diverse ties of tenure, family, religious benefaction and political allegiance, which pulled tenants in different ways and diluted the strength of their links with their original lords. It was a development which resulted from the ever present competition for good lordship and good service, and from the settlement of tenants into the localities in which they lived. It was a development which, as many of the new enfeoffments reveal, accelerated in the troubled reign of Stephen as magnates were either forced by more powerful men, or pressurised by the need to compete for the service of influential knightly families, into accepting tenants from outside their honours, and as their existing tenants became attached to other lords and went their own way.

This portrait of the Anglo-Norman honour suggests that the strength and autonomy of seignorial lordship in this period has been overestimated. It is a suggestion supported by the testimony of the barons themselves in the *cartae* they submitted to the king in 1166. Some of them claimed that they were having trouble securing the services due from their retainers, requested the intervention of the king's justice to obtain these services and declared their uncertainty as to what these services should be.[89] Some of them admitted, in other words, that their lordship was limited and that they needed help from outside the honour to enforce their authority. Although limited in number, the importance of these admissions should not be underestimated. They have very serious implications for the history of the 'first century of English feudalism' and the origins of the English Common Law.

[89] See *Red Book*, 1, 385–6 (Etocquigny), 412–13 (archbishop of York), 248 (bishop of Exeter), 370 (abbot of Ramsey).

Chapter 7

THE FIRST CENTURY OF ENGLISH
FEUDALISM

Over the past sixty years or so the nature of baronial lordship in Anglo-Norman England, and the impact upon that lordship of the Angevin legal reforms, have become the subject matter of an important and vigorous historical debate. The origins of the debate lie in Professor Stenton's classic Ford Lectures of 1929, published under the title *The First Century of English Feudalism*. The society portrayed by Stenton was a 'seignorial world', dominated by baronial lordship rather than royal control. Although careful to point out that the crown had an overriding supervision of law and aristocratic affairs, Stenton implied that this supervision was exercised intermittently and selectively, and that, generally speaking, the greater baronial lordships were autonomous jurisdictional entities free from the interference of the crown.[1] Referring to a document recording an agreement made in the 1140s between two Lincolnshire tenants in the presence of their lord, William I of Roumare, Stenton stated that the king,

[could not] intervene in the internal affairs of a great honour. The supreme authority here is not the king, but William de Roumara, earl of Lincoln. The present agreement was made at Bolingbroke, the head of his fief, and witnessed by a group of his leading tenants; the heir to the land at issue was put in seisin by his marshal. The feudal order illustrated here was independent of the king's direction or control. The honour of Bolingbroke was a feudal state in miniature. Within it the peers of the fee were tenants in chief, and any arrangement on which they were agreed needed no sanction except that which their lord could give. A few years later the process had begun which was to open all but the greatest honours to the king's justices.[2]

Stenton's portrait of the 'seignorial world' has been accepted and built upon by the legal historians Professor Thorne and Professor

---

[1] Stenton, *First Century*, 37–42.   [2] *Ibid.*, 51, and see 52, 54.

Milsom, who have attempted to explain how this world evolved into a thirteenth-century society in which royal justice had come to predominate, and a tenant property right closely linked to heritability had become a reality. In this evolution these historians have discovered the origins of the English Common Law. Although their views might differ in detail, the salient point is that they have both seen the legal reforms of Henry II as the fundamental dynamic of change.[3] Although Henry II intended only to correct abuses and 'make the seignorial structure work according to its own assumptions', the reforms undermined the legal sovereignty of the aristocracy and, as an accidental by-product, brought down the 'seignorial world'.[4]

Although the work of Thorne and Milsom has recently been supported and modified by Professor Palmer, other historians have either not accepted, or have taken issue with, a number of their arguments; particularly those concerning the development of heritability, and the role of the Angevin legal reforms in promoting the power of royal justice at the expense of the justice exercised by magnates in their seignorial courts.[5]

The first major problem with the approach of Thorne and Milsom is its acceptance of Stenton's portrait of the 'seignorial world', which is open to various objections. The second is its almost exclusive reliance on late twelfth-century legal records, which often bear little or no relation to the early twelfth-century

---

[3] S. E. Thorne, 'English feudalism and estates in land', *CLJ*, 6 (1959), 193–209; Milsom, *Legal Framework*, 8, 14, 26–39, 42, 63, 66, 105, 176–86; *idem, Historical Foundations*, 99–104, 107, 110–13, 120–2, 128–9, 133–4, 142–3, 151, 167.

[4] Milsom, *Legal Framework*, 34–7, quotation from p. 186.

[5] R. C. Palmer, 'Feudal framework of English law', *Michigan Law Review*, 79 (1981), 1130–64; *idem*, 'The origins of property in England', *LHR*, 3 (1985), 1–50, esp. 1–22. For works presenting very different arguments to those of Thorne, Milsom and Palmer, see Holt, 'Politics and property', 3–52; *idem*, 'Feudal society and the family in early medieval England: II. Notions of patrimony', *TRHS*, 5th ser., 33 (1983), 193–220; *idem, What's in a Name? Family Nomenclature and the Norman Conquest* (The Stenton Lecture 1980: Univ. of Reading, 1981); *idem*, 'Magna Carta 1215–1217: the legal and social context', in *Law in Medieval Life and Thought*, ed. E. B. King and S. J. Ridyard (Univ. of the South, 1990), 1–19; P. R. Hyams, review of Milsom, *Legal Framework*, in *EHR*, 93 (1978), 856–61; *idem*, 'Warranty', 437–503; M. T. Clanchy, 'A medieval realist: interpreting the rules at Barnwell Priory, Cambridge', in *Perspectives in Jurisprudence*, ed. E. Attwooll (Glasgow, 1977), 176–94; *idem, England and its Rulers*, 150; J. Biancalana, 'For want of justice: legal reforms of Henry II', *Columbia Law Review*, 88 (1988), 433–536; J. Hudson, 'Milsom's legal structure: interpreting twelfth-century law', *Tijdschrift Voor Rechtsgeschiedenis*, 59 (1991), 47–66; *idem*, 'Life-grants of land and the development of inheritance in Anglo-Norman England', *ANS*, 12 (1990), 67–80.

society they are sometimes employed to illuminate.[6] This lack of relationship is not simply a matter of time, it is also a matter of record. There could be a significant discordance in this period between what these legal records tell us *should* have happened, and what *actually* happened in practice.

This chapter seeks to make a contribution to the debate concerning the nature of Anglo-Norman baronial lordship, and the impact of the Angevin legal reforms upon that lordship, by examining what happened in practice. It will use charter and chronicle evidence drawn mainly from Yorkshire in the period 1066–1166. It will reassess Stenton's conception of the 'seignorial world', and the thesis on the origins of the Common Law which has been built upon this conception. It will begin by examining each of the three main props which have been identified as buttressing the legal sovereignty and power of the aristocracy before 1154: the disciplinary and proprietary jurisdiction of the seignorial courts; the power of lords to regulate the alienations made by their tenants; and seignorial control of succession to fiefs. It will illustrate that these props were not nearly as steady as has hitherto been supposed; that in the first half of the twelfth century there was already a fundamental discordance between the idealised society dominated by tenurial lordship and actual tenurial and social reality. The second part of the chapter will go on to explain this discordance against the background of certain dynamic tenurial and social processes in progress within society throughout the first century of Norman rule, which were tending to undermine tenurial lordship; in particular the pressure on lords to alienate their lands. It will be argued that, although dramatically quickening the pace of change, the legal reforms of Henry II were to some extent a reflection of these processes, of a society that was already changing.

EARLY TWELFTH-CENTURY SOCIETY: A 'SEIGNORIAL WORLD'?

There is no doubt that from time to time on some (and probably many) honours in the Anglo-Norman period, lordship functioned according to the expectations of Stenton and the legal historians who have accepted his ideas. The power of lords and their courts

---

[6] Milsom admits this: *Legal Framework*, 1, 8.

is attested by a number of sources. Consider, for example, the charters issued between 1109 and 1114 by Nigel d'Aubigny, lord of Thirsk, when he thought he was dying, which reveal that he had deprived several of his tenants of their estates.[7] Many more examples of the effectiveness of seignorial authority may have been lost to us because there was no need to record events which were regarded as normal; a fact which must be borne in mind when considering the sources which appear to illustrate the limitations of the power of lords and their courts. Although tenure was gradually superseded by other forms of retinue based upon money and office-holding, tenurial lordship remained important in the functioning of social, political and economic relationships throughout the twelfth century and beyond. Many honorial courts, the key to Stenton's 'seignorial world', continued to function and exercise strong control over tenurial affairs throughout the reigns of Henry II and his successors. In 1201, for example, a dispute between Hervey de Lofthus and the abbey of Kirkstall, concerning land held of the Lacy family, was settled by a duel and agreement before the honorial court at the Lacy *caput* of Pontefract.[8] The resilience of the tenurial element in the relationship between lord and man is illustrated by the importance attached to homage for land in the late twelfth and early thirteenth centuries.[9] It is also apparent from an examination of the entourages of some of the leading barons of the same period.[10] In John's reign we can find some of these magnates imposing their legal authority in even the outlying regions of their honours, albeit with the help of royal justice. In the pleas heard at York in 1204, for example, Adam of Staveley, a tenant of William of Mowbray, lord of Thirsk, remitted to his lord 'The gallows and ordeal pit which the aforesaid Adam claimed to have in Sedburgh',

---

[7] *Mowbray Charters*, nos. 2–7.

[8] *EYC*, III, no. 1526. For more evidence illustrating the functioning and importance of seignorial courts in the late twelfth and thirteenth centuries, see *ibid.*, II, no. 1226; V, nos. 245, 309; IX, no. 157; *Mowbray Charters*, lvii; Stenton, *First Century*, 45; Milsom, *Legal Framework*, 70–1; *idem*, *Historical Foundations*, 126; Clanchy, 'A medieval realist', 189, 191–2; N. Denholm-Young, *Seignorial Administration in England* (London, 1937), 97; M. Altschul, *A Baronial Family in Medieval England: The Clares, 1217–1314* (Baltimore, 1965), 219–22.

[9] For homage, see *Glanvill*, 103–11; T. F. Plucknett, *A Concise History of the Common Law* (5th edn, London, 1956), 546; *Rolls of the Justices*, 398–9; *EYC*, XI, 189–90; III, no. 1400; *Mowbray Charters*, no. 364; English, *Holderness*, 168.

[10] See, for example, K. J. Stringer, *Earl David of Huntingdon 1152–1219: A Study in Anglo-Scottish History* (Edinburgh, 1985), 132, 164–5, 172–6.

a vill some fifteen miles from the nearest Mowbray castle at Burton in Lonsdale, and over forty miles from Thirsk.[11] The importance of tenurial ties in determining the actions of the tenants of the greater magnates can also be seen in the rebellion of 1215, when many of these tenants sided with their lords against the king.[12]

Tenurial lordship could be strong, and it could be durable. But Stenton's assumption that this was generally true of all honours throughout his 'First Century' is open to serious objections. The charters and chronicles of early twelfth-century Yorkshire reveal that on some honours, at least, the concept of a 'seignorial world' dominated by tenurial lordship is in need of revision. The social conventions underlying lordship were frequently either ignored, exceeded or actively undermined. Many lords were struggling to maintain effective control of both their estates and tenants. The seignorial charters which appear at first sight to boast of the efficacy of tenurial lordship, on closer analysis often reveal that there was little substance behind the show. This lack of substance can be seen in each of the three major cornerstones considered by Thorne and Milsom to have been the foundations on which the 'seignorial world' rested; and it can be seen before the legal reforms of Henry II.

SEIGNORIAL JURISDICTION

Milsom divided seignorial jurisdiction into two categories: disciplinary and proprietary. The former concerned cases where an accepted tenant had defaulted in some way on the obligations he owed his lord in return for his tenure. The latter concerned tenurial disputes about rights to land; about who should be accepted as the lord's rightful tenant. Both forms of jurisdiction were exercised through the seignorial court, and for Milsom this court was at the very core of the 'seignorial world'. It was here that rights 'are created, exist, and can be ended; and a decision of that court, whether in admitting an heir or sanctioning a grant or settling a dispute, will be final'.[13] So far as disciplinary jurisdiction was concerned, in the 'seignorial world' honorial courts held the balance between the tenant's right to the tenement and the lord's

---

[11] *Pleas before the King or his Justices 1198–1212*, III, ed. D. M. Stenton (Selden Soc., 1967, for the year 1966), 136. I am grateful to Professor Holt for this reference.
[12] Holt, *Northerners*, 36.   [13] Milsom, *Legal Framework*, 183.

right to his dues, and these rights were interdependent. Only when the provision of the writ of right and other new legal remedies in the reign of Henry II accidentally deprived the seignorial courts of the power of final decision did these rights become independent and property emerge.[14] This deprivation was also responsible for undermining the proprietary jurisdiction of seignorial courts. It took away from lords 'the ultimate control over lands within their lordships, leaving them with the fixed economic rights of our picture. Tenants became owners, subject only to these fixed rights, because lords and their courts lost their power of final decision.'[15]

The first problem with this view of the disintegration of seignorial jurisdiction is the main premise upon which it based: 'Until a generation before 1200, [the lord's] own was indeed the only relevant legal system, and there was no outside authority to which the tenant could regularly look for help.'[16] It is clear, however, that long before the Angevin legal reforms, tenants and lords were looking beyond the honour for legal aid in both disciplinary and proprietary cases. As early as 1086 a dispute between William I of Percy and his lord, Hugh I earl of Chester, concerning the abbey of Whitby's right to hold land in Fyling had been brought to the attention of royal officials, and is recorded in Domesday Book.[17] County courts are known to have frequently heard arguments about warranty obligations during the course of the Domesday survey, and were probably quite familiar with them by 1135.[18] More evidence of the removal of cases from seignorial courts is provided by the writs of Henry I. In a writ issued between 1109 and 1111, for example, the king commanded that disputes between the vavasours of two lords concerning 'the boundaries of their land', were to be settled in the county courts.[19] Another clause in the same writ, directing that similar cases between vavasours of the same lord should be heard in the seignorial court, suggests that removals of this nature may have been common. It is a suggestion which receives some support from a charter of Henry I, which was either forged or interpolated by the monks of St Mary's, York, between 1112 and 1121. The charter prohibits the men of the abbey from going to the court of the shire, wapentake or hundred, and commands sheriffs and their officials in dispute with these men to obtain right in capital pleas

[14] *Ibid.*, 34–5, 183–4. [15] *Ibid.*, 66; and see Milsom, *Historical Foundations*, 142–3.
[16] Milsom, *Legal Framework*, 11. [17] *DB*, I, 373a.
[18] Hyams, 'Warranty', 466. [19] *Select Charters*, 122.

('ibi teneant rectum de capitali placito suo') in the abbey court.[20] Many more lords in other areas of the country were experiencing similar problems concerning the removal of cases from their courts, and were having to rely on royal writs and royal power to exercise their disciplinary and proprietary jurisdiction over their tenants.[21] Royal writs, and payments made to the exchequer for the king's support in warranty cases, reveal that many of these tenants were also seeking royal aid in securing tenure of tenements where their rights were challenged by their lords. One such writ was issued by Henry I between *c.* 1126 and 1129. It commands Robert Fossard to do right to the abbot of Ramsey, respecting the church of Bramham. It was almost certainly issued as a result of a complaint made in the royal court by the abbot of Ramsey, who must have been aggrieved at Robert Fossard's grant of Bramham church to Nostell Priory, without regard for his father's earlier grant of the same church to Ramsey Abbey.[22] What this charter and others like it suggest is that the removal of cases from the seignorial to the county court or *curia regis* was already a common phenomenon by 1135.[23] And not just to the royal courts: tenants occasionally took their cases to the courts of powerful neighbours.[24]

Baronial charters add further weight to this argument. In her study of the charters of the honour of Mowbray, Dr Greenway illustrated that although the seignorial court was dealing with all manner of tenurial business well into the second half of the twelfth century, after 1150 its jurisdiction was becoming increasingly subject to outside interference. As early as 1145, Roger of Mowbray appears to have been concerned that his tenants might take their suits out of his court. In his concession to Uctred Fitz Dolfin of the land of Uctred's grandfather, Roger seems to anticipate possible disputes, and commands that, 'predictus Ucthred hanc terram teneat in pace, quod pro nullo calumpniatore in placito ponatur nisi in presencia mea, quia inde homo meus est et ego ei presidium'.[25] By the 1160s royal officials were involving themselves in the proceedings of the Mowbray court,

---

[20] *Regesta*, II, no. 1276, and see nos. 529–30, 1516, 1630, 1662.
[21] For disciplinary cases, see Biancalana, 'Legal reforms of Henry II', 440, 448, 452; *English Lawsuits*, I, nos. 162, 164, 206. For what appear to be proprietary cases, see *English Lawsuits*, I, nos. 145, 165, 174, 182, 187, 220, 227, 272.
[22] *Regesta*, II, nos. 1627, 1630 and notes; *EYC*, II, no. 1002.
[23] Biancalana, 'Legal reforms of Henry II', 452–66.
[24] Hyams, 'Warranty', 466–7. [25] *Mowbray Charters*, no. 392.

and some Mowbray tenants were already pursuing their suits and making their affidavits in the courts of the sheriff or the chapter of St Peter's, York. From 1169 onwards 'the Pipe Rolls reveal an increasing number of land suits against Mowbray'.[26]

Just as tenants were prepared to look beyond the honorial structure for justice, so also they came increasingly to rely on their own resources to provide it. The charters of the late eleventh and early twelfth centuries reveal that tenants were seeking and obtaining not just land, but also jurisdictional rights over land. They were securing the right to have their own courts. The devolution of jurisdictional rights was encouraged by the practical problems confronting the organisation of seignorial courts. In theory these courts were to meet every three weeks, and were to be attended by all the honorial tenants, but difficulties of tenure, cost, time and space must often have made this impossible.[27] The result was that jurisdictional authority came to be exercised by tenants independently of the authority of their lords. This, at least, is the impression to be derived from a charter issued by Gilbert of Gant, lord of Hunmanby (Yorks.) and Folkingham (Lincs.), in the period 1146 × 1149. The charter prohibits the abbot of Rufford Abbey from dealing with, or answering to, a certain Ralph Fitz Wichard concerning lands given to the abbey by Gilbert (from his demesne) which Ralph was claiming. Gilbert declared that, 'if Ralph or somebody else claims anything from my demesne or my almoign, let him come before myself and I shall do him full right'.[28] He was determined, in other words, to protect the jurisdiction of his court against agreements made without reference to its authority by his tenants; and in doing so he was admitting that the power of the seignorial court was not only under pressure from above, but also from below.

The independent jurisdiction exercised by Norman tenants may have had its origins in the pre-conquest past. Lennard believed that when pre-conquest kings conferred jurisdictional privileges upon their thanes, they were 'not appointing an official, but conferring a piece of property'.[29] Although he found it 'hard to say whether before the Norman Conquest property in land was in itself considered to imply any jurisdictional power', Lennard considered that 'under the Normans it was clearly recognised that every

---

[26] *Ibid.*, lvii–lviii.
[27] Lennard, *Rural England*, 35; Milsom, *Legal Framework*, 14, 16.
[28] *English Lawsuits*, I, no. 324.   [29] Lennard, *Rural England*, 23.

landlord had the right to hold a court for his tenants'.[30] It is possible to stand his logic on its head, and to posit that jurisdictional rights implied property in land, and that they were not confined to tenants-in-chief (lords). With the devolution of land went the devolution of jurisdictional rights attached to the land; rights commonly articulated in the expressions *curia, placita, forisfacturae* and *soc, sac, tol, tem et infangenthef*.[31] Stenton believed that although the latter expression might be 'evidence of a man's standing in his lord's court rather than a delegation of a lord's rights of justice', it usually conveyed permission to hold a court and take its profits, to extract payment for the sale of livestock and goods and to do justice on thieves caught red-handed.[32] Dr Roffe believes it conveyed much more: not only jurisdiction, but full economic rights over land. He argues that land held in this way was akin to pre-conquest bookland, which was hereditary and freely disposable. By the early twelfth century (and perhaps on some lordships by 1086) the lords who held it included not only the tenants-in-chief, but their most powerful retainers, the 'honorial barons'.[33]

As well as undermining the argument that seignorial courts were universally autonomous before the legal reforms of Henry II, the evidence set out above also undermines the argument that they were universally strong. Even with the outside assistance of the crown, some lay magnates were clearly having difficulty exercising their proprietary jurisdiction over the tenantry in the late eleventh and early twelfth centuries. This was also true of some ecclesiastical lords. William of St Calais and Ranulf Flambard, successive bishops of Durham, were forced to appeal for royal assistance to secure the recovery of estates in Yorkshire, which had been encroached upon by royal agents and their own tenants after William's quarrel with William Rufus in 1088, and Ranulf's temporary exile from England in 1101.[34] These appeals were made after the bishops were restored to royal favour, and although successful appear to have had little practical effect. The number of royal directives commanding the restoration of episcopal property reflects the persistent ignorance of those directives and seignorial

---

[30] *Ibid.*, 24.
[31] On the alienation of justice, see Maitland, *Domesday Book*, 83 and notes.
[32] Stenton, *First Century*, 101–2, 106, quotation from p. 106. See also Maitland, *Domesday Book*, 79–152.   [33] Roffe, 'Thegnage to barony', 157–76, esp. 165–7.
[34] Symeon, *Opera*, I, 171–4, 179–80.

authority by the men occupying the estates.[35] It appears that in
some cases the best the bishops could hope for was a compromise
arrangement, in which these men were allowed to retain the lands
they occupied as tenancies held of the bishopric.[36] Compromises
of this and a variety of other forms, rather than strict decisions
emanating from courts of law, appear to have been a common,
and probably the preferred, method of settling disputes between
men in the Anglo-Norman period; an observation which serves to
strengthen the impression that the emphasis placed by some legal
historians on the power and 'final decision' of seignorial courts in
determining tenurial claims, and in providing the basis of title to
land, in this period is seriously misplaced.[37]

GRANTS

According to Thorne, before *c.* 1200 tenants required the consent
of their lords before they could alienate land to a third party, and
cannot, therefore, be seen as owners.[38] Although modifying this
logic to some extent, Milsom's interpretation of tenant alienations
is essentially very similar.[39] It is an interpretation closely bound up
with his view of inheritance, which is heavily influenced by what
is perhaps the central premise of his thesis: that in the 'seignorial
world', only the acceptance of a lord could make a tenant, and that
this acceptance was all the title there could be.[40] Milsom argues
that the lord in the 'seignorial world' could not have a tenant he
did not want forced upon him as the result of a grant.[41] The

---

[35] *Regesta*, II, nos. 540–1, 545–6, 560–1, 575, 589–90, 642–3, 660, 767, 1124, 1181;
Mowbray Charters, nos. 2–5.

[36] *EYC*, XI, 335. The Fossard family, who had been granted control of the sokelands of
the bishop's manor of Howden, were still in possession of a knight's fee held of the
bishop there in 1166: *Red Book*, I, 416.

[37] The author of the *Leges Henrici Primi* stated that 'Agreement triumphs over the law and
love over judgement', that litigants could choose between friendship and legal process,
and that if they chose friendship 'that shall be as firm as a judgement of a court': *LHP*,
p. 164 cl. 49, 5a, p. 172 cl. 54, 3. See also *Glanvill*, 129; M. T. Clanchy, 'Law and love
in the middle ages', in *Disputes and Settlements: Law and Human Relations in the West*,
ed. J. Bossy (Cambridge, 1983), 47–67; King, 'Dispute settlement', 115–30; Tabuteau,
Transfers of Property, 228–9; White, *Custom, Kinship and Gifts*, 71–2; P. R. Hyams, 'The
charter as a source for the early Common Law', *JLH*, 12 (1991), 174, 180, 182.

[38] Thorne, 'Estates in land', 194–5, 205, 208–9.

[39] Milsom, *Legal Framework*, 103–21; *idem*, *Historical Foundations*, 110–16, 143.

[40] Milsom, *Legal Framework*, 66, 103–10, 163–4, 170, 173, 176–7, 181, 183–4; *idem*,
Historical Foundations, 100–3, 127, 133–4, 167.

[41] Milsom, *Legal Framework*, 105.

consent of the lord was required before a tenant could make a grant by substitution, that is substitute another tenant in his place.[42] In the case of a grant by subinfeudation, although Milsom acknowledges that this could 'obviously be made without the participation of the grantor's lord', he considers that when it reserved less service than that owed to the lord for the land, 'it is likely that such a grant would not be made unless the immediate and all other lords up to the king were willing to confirm it'.[43] This confirmation, he argues, was a customary part of sub-infeudations before the thirteenth century. It 'would not just add some marginal advantage to a self-sufficient gift. The gift was unthinkable without it.'[44] As long as this was so, tenants cannot be seen as owners. What undermined this need for confirmation or consent, according to Milsom, was the assize of *novel disseisin*, which (he considers) deprived the lord's court of its means of removing unwanted tenants, and the assize of *mort d'ancestor*, which 'allowed an heir to feel that he entered in his own right rather than under a grant to himself from the lord'.[45] The result was that by the beginning of the thirteenth century tenants were no longer seeking the confirmation/consent of their lords for their gifts to religious houses; and Milsom suggests that this reflects an underlying change in which the tenant was 'beginning to think of himself as having a sort of ownership which he can transfer'.[46]

Milsom's interpretation of alienation corresponds closely in some respects to that advanced by Maitland eighty years earlier. Like Milsom, Maitland had been careful to distinguish between alienation by substitution and by subinfeudation, postulating that seignorial control may have been stronger in the former case, and that were it not for an assertion made by Bracton to the contrary, 'we should probably have come to the opinion that a new tenant ... could not be forced upon an unwilling lord'.[47] More specifi-cally, Maitland stated that 'the tenant may lawfully do anything that does not seriously damage the interests of his lord. He may make reasonable gifts, but not unreasonable. The reasonableness of the gift would be a matter for the lord's court'.[48] Maitland concluded that in the Anglo-Norman period there was

[42] *Ibid.*, 103–10; Milsom, *Historical Foundations*, 111.
[43] Milsom, *Historical Foundations*, 111, 113.   [44] Milsom, *Legal Framework*, 120–1.
[45] *Ibid.*, 115–21, quotation from p. 120; Milsom, *Historical Foundations*, 143.
[46] Milsom, *Legal Framework*, 120.
[47] Pollock and Maitland, *English Law*, I, 332 note 1, 345.   [48] *Ibid.*, 343.

an indeterminate right of the lord to prevent alienations which would seriously impair his interests, a right which might remain in abeyance so long as there was plenty of scope for subinfeudation and the liberty of endowing churches was not abused, a right on which the king's court was seldom if ever called upon to pronounce, since the lord could enforce it in his own court, a right which was at length defined, though in loose terms, by the charter of 1217.[49]

Many charters appear at first sight to provide evidence that certain lords in Anglo-Norman Yorkshire were able at certain times to exercise some form of control over alienations by substitution, and those alienations by subinfeudation which threatened to impair their services. One such charter records that when Rainald Puher sold his land in Middlethorpe to the monks of Whitby between *c.* 1147 and *c.* 1154, effectively substituting his tenancy, he resigned all his right to the land into the hand of his lord, Roger of Mowbray, to the use of the monks, to whom Roger then gave it, putting them in seisin by the same rod by which the resignation had been made.[50] Another charter, dealing with a subinfeudation, issued before 1130 by Herman and Brian the Breton (subtenants of the honour of Richmond), announces that their grant of land in Little Danby to the abbey of St Mary's, York, had been made with the counsel and assent of their lord 'Wigani'.[51] However, there is always the possibility that charters of this nature were drawn up by beneficiaries who were anxious to strengthen the security of their tenure, and who in doing so were either tampering with the terms of original charters or manufacturing forgeries.[52] It would be dangerous, therefore, to accept charters referring to, or actually conveying, seignorial confirmations/concessions of tenant alienations at their face value.[53]

Some of Maitland's comments on seignorial confirmation charters provide further reason to pause for thought. Maitland noted that many confirmations of gifts in frankalmoign 'will often appear to be confirmations and something more'. He pointed out that these confirmations frequently incorporate other clauses threatening penalties against those who might disturb the donees, or willing that the donees enjoy sake and soke and other liberties,

---

[49] *Ibid.*, 346.   [50] *Cartularium de Whiteby*, I, 203; *Mowbray Charters*, no. 290.
[51] *EYC*, v, no. 351. For more examples, see *EYC*, IV, nos. 94–6; v, no. 384.
[52] See J. C. Holt, 'More Battle forgeries', *Reading Medieval Studies*, 11 (1985), 75–86.
[53] Milsom appears to accept such charters as evidence of seignorial control: Milsom, *Legal Framework*, 120.

or granting acquittance from services.[54] In the case of royal confirmations he also observed that religious houses tended to wait until they had a number of gifts before securing a charter.[55] Maitland's observations suggest a number of possibilities: that many seignorial confirmations were only sought long after the original grant, and that in seeking them the primary concern of tenants was to secure protection and to offer the lord a mark of respect, rather than to obtain consent. Similar ideas have been expressed more forcefully in Professor Tabuteau's study of eleventh-century Norman land transfers. Noting that seignorial consent to alienation was often only granted after (sometimes long after) alienation had occurred, Tabuteau suggests that such consent was not legally necessary, that even in cases of substitution it was only sought in order to make arrangements about the service to be performed, or to secure the support of the lord in defeating rival claims, or to assure the security of the grant.[56]

The necessity of seignorial consent is also called into question by evidence drawn from Yorkshire. Here again we find examples of confirmations issued some time after the original alienation.[57] Here also we find tenants who in making land grants appear to have been prepared to act without the permission, or even the knowledge, of their lords. One such tenant was Agnes of Arches, who held land of William count of Aumale. In the reign of King Stephen, Archbishop William of York issued a charter which reveals that Agnes may have granted the nuns of Nunkeeling a half carucate in the vill there, without involving her lord directly in the transaction. Agnes had promised that she would pay the services due from the land until she could petition the count to acquit them; a promise which suggests that although Agnes had some respect for the services due to her lord, she was prepared to undertake the alienation of land held from him without his knowledge or consent.[58]

Even if lords had some form of abstract right to control tenant alienations, there is the question of whether they were able in practice to enforce it. This obviously depended upon a range of factors, including the relative power and influence of lord and tenant, the nature of the personal relationship between them and

---

[54] Pollock and Maitland, *English Law*, I, 341.   [55] *Ibid.*, 342.
[56] Tabuteau, *Transfers of Property*, 171–94, esp. 184.
[57] *EYC*, II, nos. 656, 1135 and notes; III, nos. 1340, 1502 and notes; IV, no. 8; VIII, no. 7.
[58] *EYC*, III, no. 1332, dated 1143 × 1154.

the geographical distance of the tenement from the centres of seignorial authority. One lord who was clearly having problems controlling the alienations made by a powerful Yorkshire tenant on the peripheries of his lordship was Hugh Bigod, earl of Norfolk. In the early years of the reign of Henry II, Hugh was forced to engage in a legal suit against Henry of Lacy, lord of Pontefract, for recovery of the West Riding vill of Barnoldswick, which Henry had alienated, without Hugh's knowledge or consent, to the abbey of Fountains for the purpose of founding a daughter house. Despite the fact that Hugh won his case, and issued his own charter granting Barnoldswick to Fountains, it is significant that the monks continued to regard the land as a Lacy benefaction in all subsequent confirmations.[59]

The limitations of seignorial control over alienation are also reflected by the common occurrence of what might be termed 'double grants', that is grants made either by a lord and his predecessor/wife/son/tenant(s), or by two or more tenants, of the same piece of property to two or more religious houses. The history of the churches of Hooton Pagnell (Yorks.) and Roxby and Irnham (Lincs.), which were bestowed by members of the Paynel family and their tenants on a number of religious houses, provides a striking example of this phenomenon. Between 1090 and 1100 the churches were granted by Ralph Paynel to Holy Trinity Priory, his new foundation at York.[60] At some point in the 1130s Ralph's son and heir, William I Paynel, gave them to his new Augustinian priory at Drax. Roxby church was also confirmed to Drax Priory by a Paynel tenant, Walter of Scoteny, who later gave it to Roche Abbey. Later still, Robert of Gant, who married the daughter and heiress of William I Paynel, Alice, was also to make a conflicting grant of Irnham church to Drax Priory and Bardney Abbey (Lincs.). He made a similar mistake with the church of Swinstead, granting it to a certain clerk named Guy, in ignorance of a previous grant by William I Paynel to Drax Priory. In a letter to the abbots of Vaudey and Fountains, Robert declared that he had been unaware of his predecessor's gift. Naturally these discordant grants were apt to result in conflicts between the rival grantees and their lords. In an assize of *darrein presentment* in 1201 conflicting claims to Roxby church were made

---

[59] *Foundation of Kirkstall*, 173–4; *Kirkstall Coucher*, ix–x, 188–9; Wightman, *Lacy Family*, 109–10.

[60] For this and what follows, see *EYC*, VI, 167 and nos. 1, 13, 74–5, 80.

by three religious houses. Many more examples of double grants made in the twelfth century could be cited.[61] They illustrate the practical problems of controlling the process of land grants. If lords like Robert of Gant were experiencing difficulties in keeping track of even the grants made from the seignorial demesne, their chances of successfully supervising all the grants made by their tenants and subtenants must have been remote, especially where the subtenants themselves had been installed without their knowledge or consent.

The same problems are reflected in the provisions that lords began to make within their charters, apparently from the time of the Conqueror, governing the alienation of land and rights by tenants.[62] In the case of ecclesiastical lords, although these provisions were dictated by the restrictions placed upon the alienation of church possessions by canon law, they would hardly have been necessary if unauthorised alienation had not been a reality. At some point between the late 1140s and 1166, Abbot Richard of Whitby threatened to excommunicate those who alienated the town of South Fyling from the abbey demesne without his permission.[63] Similar restrictions on alienation appear in lay charters, such as the one issued between 1142 and 1154 by Walter of Percy granting land in Wold Newton to Erneis Fitz Besing.[64] The licence issued by Earl Simon III of Senlis, allowing Rievaulx Abbey to acquire lands from his men, marks another attempt at secular regulation.[65] It may be that such regulations reflect the limitations rather than the strength of seignorial control in matters of alienation.

It may also be that these limitations are mirrored by the increasing use of seals by men below the rank of tenant-in-chief. This phenomenon, which first appears in the mid-twelfth century, was brought to the attention of the justiciar, Richard of Lucy, who

---

[61] See *EYC*, III, no. 1359 and note; VI, xii; I, no. 555; X, xvii–xviii; *Mowbray Charters*, nos. 325 and notes, 359, 377; Wardrop, *Fountains Abbey*, 57; *Chronica de Melsa*, I, 103–4; Notts. County Record Office, DDSR 102/35, printed in Abbot, 'Gant family', 352–3 (no. 100, and see no. 98); BL, Cotton Vespasian E xviii, fol. 99v; BL, Cotton Charter xvi. 37; Norwich Dean and Chapter, Scampton Charters, 1254–6, calendared in Abbot, 'Gant family', 367–9 (nos. 113–15), 377–9 (nos. 123–5).

[62] Holt, 'Notions of patrimony', 202–3; J. A. Robinson, *Gilbert Crispin Abbot of Westminster* (Cambridge, 1911), 38; *English Lawsuits*, I, no. 164.

[63] *EYC*, II, nos. 880, 887–8.   [64] *Ibid.*, no. 1201.

[65] *Ibid.*, no. 1232, dated by Farrer *c.* 1170 × 1184. See also a charter issued in favour of the daughter house of St Martin's, Sées, at Lancaster, in the period 1092 × 1094: Thompson, 'Norman Lancashire', 203, 209–11.

declared that, 'It was not the custom in the past for every petty knight (*militulum*) to have a seal. They are appropriate for kings and great men only.'[66] The more substantial honorial tenants often had their own seal before (or in) the reign of Henry II.[67] By the 1170s, and probably earlier, men of quite lowly status were borrowing the seals of ecclesiastical foundations to attach to their charters, rather than seeking the seals of their lords.[68] And by *c.* 1200, 'for almost anyone above the level of peasant', the owning of a seal matrix 'had become a necessity'.[69] Charters frequently refer to the affixing of seals in terms such as *confirmavi, corroboravi, testatur* and *securitatem*, and they were used to authenticate documents and guarantee their contents.[70] Sometimes reference to seals in charters is linked directly to the warranty or affidation clause. An agreement between two Percy tenants who lived in Yorkshire in the 1180s concluded: 'Hanc convencionem ad tenendam ego predictus Ricardus affidavi predicto Alano et heredibus suis et sigillo meo confirmavi'.[71] Seals were a symbol of lordship, and their proliferation in the mid- and late twelfth century may be an indication that many tenants viewed themselves as their own men, as lords in their own right, with independent authority to alienate lands.

Although the evidence illustrating the theoretical and practical limitations of seignorial control over alienation may to some extent reflect the exceptional rather than the normal (because charters tell us only about grants which were made, rather than the cases where lords were successful in preventing alienation), it is sufficient to suggest that it was possible, perhaps even common, for tenants to make grants without the consent or even the knowledge of their lords. Whatever the legal theory on the basis of tenant title might be, in practice lords were sometimes forced to accept, or at least to compromise with, tenants they did not want; and they were forced to do so before the inception of the Angevin legal reforms.

---

[66] *The Chronicle of Battle Abbey*, ed. and trans. E. Searle (Oxford, 1980), 214.
[67] *EYC*, I, nos. 534, 567; II, nos. 692, 814, 817, 1073; III, nos. 1302, 1339, 1354, 1529, 1663, 1771; V, nos. 174, 218, 367; VI, no. 151; VII, nos. 83–4, 176; VIII, nos. 111, 124, 126, 138; IX, no. 161; X, no. 52; XI, nos. 93, 96, 108–9, 181, 183; XII, no. 112; *Furness Coucher*, II, 522.   [68] *EYC*, VII, nos. 120–1. See also *ibid.*, II, no. 758.
[69] T. A. Heslop, 'Seals', in *English Romanesque Art*, ed. G. Zarnecki *et al.* (London, 1984), 299.   [70] *Ibid.*, 298.   [71] *EYC*, XI, no. 148.

INHERITANCE

The legal historians who have accepted Stenton's interpretation of the Anglo-Norman world believe that it was a world in which inheritance right had no place. Although acknowledging the strong regularity of tenant succession which is discernible before the Angevin legal reforms, they argue that the only absolute right a tenant had to a tenement for most, if not all, of the twelfth century was the acceptance of his lord, and that this did not amount to a property interest in the land:

As between the parties, proprietary language is out of place. There is a relationship of reciprocal obligations ... [the lord] buys services and pays directly in land. But of course the land is not transferred out-and-out: the basic purchase is of a life's service for a life tenure ... [the lord] owes the tenant enjoyment of his tenement as long as he lives; and when he dies the lord and his court will make a new arrangement with a new man.[72]

Because, for reasons of convenience, the new man tended to be the heir of the deceased tenant, and familial succession became regular, heirs came to be seen as having a right to the tenement; but this was only a customary right 'existing within the lord's court and availing against the lord, just a claim to be put in', rather than a 'direct property interest in the land, availing against the world'.[73] 'So long as there was only the lord's court, the canons of inheritance, however clearly settled and however consistently followed, were criteria for making a choice. They were not rules of law conferring an abstract right on the heir, but customs about whom the lord's court should choose; and it was their choice that mattered'.[74] It was only after the inception of the Angevin legal reforms that title ceased to be based upon the acceptance of the lord and became an abstract right 'existing in the sky'.[75]

As Dr Hudson has pointed out, the definition of heritability adopted by the legal historians who have put forward this thesis, 'implicitly distinguishes Common Law heritability from landholding in their postulated pre-inheritance world in three con-

---

[72] Milsom, *Legal Framework*, 39. Compare Thorne, 'Estates in land', 195–209, esp. 195–9. On the regularity of succession generally, see Holt, 'Politics and property', 30–7; R. DeAragon, 'The growth of secure inheritance in Anglo-Norman England', *JMH*, 8 (1982), 381–91. [73] Milsom, *Legal Framework*, 41.
[74] *Ibid.*, 180, and see 66, 109–10, 183; Milsom, *Historical Foundations*, 106–7, 120–1; and compare Thorne, 'Estates in land', 195–9, who gives a more precise chronology for the emergence of heritability. [75] Milsom, *Historical Foundations*, 129.

nected ways, relating to custom, thought, and seignorial authority'. First, 'customary succession must not be automatically
equated with heritability' because it was not dictated by the law,
and tenants had only a life interest in their tenements; secondly,
such succession 'need not have involved abstract rules'; and
thirdly, 'before the existence of the true Common Law inheritance
the heir only entered upon the tenement with the lord's
authority'.[76] While noting the possibility that there may have
been important differences between landholding on ecclesiastical
and lay honours, Hudson has illustrated that as far as the estates of
Ramsey Abbey are concerned these three assumptions about the
nature of the 'seignorial world' are all flawed, and that, at least on
ecclesiastical estates, the development towards inheritance had
progressed further by 1135 than some legal historians would
allow.[77]

As Professor Biancalana has argued, lords and tenants might
have rival perceptions concerning inheritance. This is clear from
the methods used to justify inheritance claims in legal suits
concerning ecclesiastical foundations. It was common in disputes
between monasteries and their tenants for the tenant to justify a
claim that a certain piece of land was his inheritance by the fact of
ancestral seisin, and for the monastery to resist on the grounds that
the tenant's ancestor had not received the lands heritably.[78]
Occasionally, when they found their own tenure threatened, the
monasteries themselves resorted to claims of long-term occupancy
in their defence. Claims of this nature undermine the assumption
of some legal historians that in the 'seignorial world' only the
acceptance of the lord's court could make a tenant, and that
inheritance was only a customary right availing against this court
which might be either accepted or rejected. These assumptions are
weakened further by the failure of lords to invoke any right to
choose a new tenant when defending or prosecuting their tenurial
cases, and by the frequency with which such cases ended in
compromise agreements. Some lords were even ready to accept
that gifts made in fee and inheritance to tenants entitled the heirs
of these tenants to succeed to the tenements. Their willingness to
do so reinforces an argument advanced by Holt, that inheritance in
the Anglo-Norman world was more of a primordial right than a
seignorial concession, and that (although varying in strength

---

[76] Hudson, 'Development of inheritance', 71.   [77] *Ibid.*, 67–80.
[78] Biancalana, 'Legal reforms of Henry II', 498–9, and the cases cited on pp. 500–1.

according to who was inheriting and what was being inherited) it was a right based upon abstract notions of heritability; notions which all historians seem to agree were crucial to the existence of abstract notions of property.[79]

Evidence from a number of Yorkshire lordships, both lay and ecclesiastical, serves to reinforce the arguments of Hudson, Biancalana and Holt, and suggests that the Angevin legal reforms, which are supposed to have created heritability, merely reflected a society in which heritability was already an abstract right. Consider, for example, the charters issued by Nigel d'Aubigny, lord of Thirsk, when he thought he was dying in the second decade of the twelfth century. These charters made recompense for Nigel's dispossession or tenurial demotion of several of his tenants, and reveal that he considered these actions to be offences.[80] As Holt has noted, Nigel used one word to describe what he had done. His tenants had been 'disinherited'.[81] Nigel's assessment of his own behaviour reflects what Biancalana has termed 'the strong secular presumption in favour of continuity of familial seisin'.[82] It is a presumption which is also mirrored in the provisions made by lords in their own lifetimes for their relatives to succeed them after their deaths. William I Paynel, lord of Drax, was engaging in a common practice before his death (*c.* 1145 × 1147) in planning to divide his cross-Channel honour between his two eldest sons.[83] Childless magnates less fortunate than William might even resort to the expedient of designating their brothers, or some other male relative, as their successor, in order to secure the descent of their estates within the family. This was the course adopted by Nigel d'Aubigny, who had no children at the time of his illness, and who designated his brother, William, as his heir ('honoris mei et rerum mearum constitui heredem') and asked him to supervise the restorations he had made to the church.[84] Even bishops could

---

[79] Holt, 'Notions of patrimony', 218, 207–8; *idem*, 'Politics and property', 20–5. For a debate concerning Holt's arguments, see S. D. White, 'Succession to fiefs in early medieval England', *Past & Present*, 65 (1974), 118–27; J. C. Holt, 'Politics and property in early medieval England: a rejoinder', *Past & Present*, 65 (1974), 127–35.

[80] *Mowbray Charters*, nos. 2–8.   [81] Holt, 'The revolution of 1066', 212.

[82] Biancalana, 'Legal reforms of Henry II', 498.

[83] *EYC*, VI, nos. 15 and note, 19. See also, J. S. Beckerman, 'Succession in Normandy, 1087, and in England, 1066: the role of testamentary custom', *Speculum*, 47 (1972), 258–60; J. Le Patourel, 'The Norman succession, 996–1135', *EHR*, 86 (1971), 225–50.

[84] *Mowbray Charters*, no. 3. Roger of Mowbray had probably not been born when Nigel made this provision. Glanvill later stated that men could not 'make' heirs other than sons or daughters of their own bodies: *Glanvill*, 70–1.

designate heirs. Between 1136 and 1145, Alan III, earl of Richmond, gave and conceded to Alexander bishop of Lincoln 'et heredibus suis' the vill of Kneeton (Notts.), 'in feudum et hereditatem scilicet tenendam de me et de heredibus meis per servicium unius militis, et nominatim Robertus de Aluers filius neptis ejusdem Alexandri episcopi sit heres ejus nisi ipse alicui alii heredum suorum eam in vita sua in hereditatem concesserit'.[85] The alienations made by some fathers with the consent of their children, and by some children either with their fathers or on their own initiative in their father's lifetime, probably reflect other examples of designation. Between *c.* 1121 and 1130, for example, Serlo of Burg restored land in Ellenthorpe to St Mary's Abbey, York, with the concession of his son, Osbert, and 'sine omni calumpnia heredum meorum'; and between 1127 and *c.* 1135 Alan of Monceaux, a tenant of the lordship of Holderness, gave two bovates and two acres in the vill of Winkton to the poor of the hospital of Bridlington Priory with the concession of Robert 'filius et heres meus'.[86] In Stephen's reign, both Alice of Rumilly and her husband, William Fitz Duncan, made grants and confirmations of land belonging to the honour of Skipton during the lifetime of Cecily of Rumilly, Alice's mother, to whom the lordship rightly belonged.[87] And towards the end of the reign, Robert I of Ros, the eldest son of one of the sisters (and co-heiresses) of Walter Espec, issued a charter confirming Walter's gifts to Rievaulx Abbey while his uncle was still alive.[88]

If the assumptions made by some legal historians about the rights of seignorial courts over succession are open to question, this is also true of their assumptions about the power of these courts to enforce these rights, and about the degree of seignorial autonomy. The argument that seignorial courts dominated succession, and provided the only superior jurisdiction to which tenants could regularly appeal for help, does not square easily with the evidence. Appeals were frequently made by even very powerful lords to higher lords, or to the crown, for support against men who were clearly attempting by a variety of means to weaken seignorial control. These means might include retaining tenements for

---

[85] *EYC*, IV, no. 15.

[86] *Ibid.*, V, no. 128; III, no. 1328 (the dating of the latter charter is Farrer's). For more examples, see *ibid.*, II, nos. 727, 970, 1209; III, nos. 1326, 1329, 1332; V, nos. 156–8, 231, 343, 358, 367, 384; X, no. 67; XI, nos. 5, 14.

[87] *Ibid.*, VII, 10–11, nos. 9, 12–16.

[88] *Cartularium de Rievalle*, 21–2 (dated 1147 × 1153).

longer than the agreed or justifiable period of tenancy, succeeding to life tenements held by their ancestors, passing tenements held on terms of life-grant to their heirs, and securing the succession of heirs who were not their natural children. In 1129–30 William, count of Aumale, paid Henry I 100 marks 'that he may not plead against his men about the land which his father had held in demesne'.[89] In the reign of Henry II the Lincolnshire tenant, Roger of Benniworth, lord of Benniworth (Lincs.) and Anlaby (Yorks.), felt it necessary to seek the assistance of his lord, William I of Roumare, to ensure that land he had granted to his brother, Matthew of Benniworth, should revert to his demesne if Matthew died without an heir by his wife.[90] In some cases, tenant succession appears to have been taking place without reference to the seignorial court. It may have been this which prompted William Fitz Nigel, constable of Chester and lord of Flamborough in Yorkshire, to go to the death-bed of his tenant, Hugh Fitz Odard, at Keckwick (Ches.) in or shortly before 1130 in order to enfeoff the stricken man's son with Hugh's lands.[91]

Even where private charters appear to illustrate seignorial control over succession, there may have been little substance behind the show. It should be remembered that, when issued by laymen other than the king before 1150, such charters are 'likely to exist because they treat the unusual case'.[92] Moreover, charters might be as much propaganda tools as land deeds, often intended for the consumption of a wide audience.[93] Lords had a natural interest in propagating the rights pertaining to their lordship, thereby helping to preserve and reinforce their authority. As such they may often have portrayed in their charters a very distorted or incomplete picture of the world, describing as a perquisite of lordship only what they wanted to see as a perquisite of lordship. A charter issued between 1138 and 1154 by Roger of Mowbray to one of his tenants, Ralph Fitz Aldelin, appears at first sight to illustrate the seignorial court controlling succession. Roger re-stores, gives and concedes to Ralph the land of his father, Aldelin, for the fourth part of the service of one knight.[94] It appears that

---

[89] *PR 31 Henry I*, 29.
[90] *Documents Illustrative of the Social and Economic History of the Danelaw*, ed. F. M. Stenton (British Academy, 1920), no. 504.
[91] G. Ormerod, *The History of the County Palatine and City of Chester*, 3 vols. (2nd edn, London, 1882), I, 690. It is possible that William was simply behaving as a good lord should.   [92] Hyams, 'The charter as a source', 176, and see 178.
[93] See, for example, *EYC*, II, no. 1105.   [94] *Mowbray Charters*, no. 383.

Roger may already have granted a portion of Aldelin's lands in Winterburn to a certain William Graindorge, and that this portion was not included in the restoration made to Ralph.[95] The language of Roger's charter, with its emphasis on restoration, the lord's power to give the tenement and the descent of Winterburn are features completely at odds with the existence of heritability. On closer analysis, however, all is not quite as it might at first appear. When viewed in the context of several other charters concerning the Fitz Aldelin fee, Roger of Mowbray's charter is open to more than one possible interpretation. Ralph may have challenged William Graindorge's tenure of Winterburn. Between c. 1149 and 1166 Roger of Mowbray gave Winterburn to Furness Abbey, declaring that the monks were to retain the vill in alms if William Graindorge forfeited anything.[96] William's own gift of Winterburn to the monks may have been an attempt to enlist their support to maintain his influence there, or at least to prevent Ralph Fitz Aldelin from realising his claim: the reality of which is clear from the quitclaim to Winterburn which Ralph issued in favour of the monks at some point after 1154.[97] There is more than a hint in all this that Roger of Mowbray was unable (or at least unwilling) to guarantee the tenure of Graindorge, and to control the actions of Fitz Aldelin; that the language of seignorial power expressed in Roger's restoration charter to Fitz Aldelin was empty rhetoric; and that the charter may have been a compromise measure fashioned in a bid to settle a dispute and promote peace and friendship. Ralph's lands are specifically stated to have been 'terram patris sui', and he was to hold them 'in feudo et in hereditate et heredibus suis'. Here again we come back to the mentality of tenants. Ralph Fitz Aldelin saw the tenure of all his father's lands as his hereditary right, no matter what his lord might think or do.

If the power of seignorial courts in matters of succession is open to doubt, so is their degree of autonomy. Just as lords were prepared to appeal to the crown and higher clergy for support in inheritance cases, so were the tenants or would-be tenants with whom they were in dispute. Anglo-Norman charters reveal that these tenants often succeeded in taking such cases out of the jurisdiction of their lords and into the courts of the king and

---

[95] Greenway believes that Winterburn probably passed to the Graindorge fee after c. 1149: *Mowbray Charters*, notes to nos. 150, 383. [96] *Furness Coucher*, II, 373.
[97] *Ibid.*, 372, 375; *Mowbray Charters*, nos. 152–3, 150.

bishops.[98] In the reign of Henry I, for example, after the death of their father the sons of Osbert the sheriff offered the king large sums of money to intervene on their behalf to prevent one of Osbert's lords, Stephen count of Aumale, from recovering Osbert's tenement into his demesne.[99] Similar appeals for royal aid by potential heirs or claimants to inheritances probably also lie behind the numerous fines recorded in the 1129–30 pipe roll paid to the king by tenants for the recovery of lands.[100] In the realm of inheritance, therefore, as in that of jurisdiction, seignorial justice was open to outside interference long before the Angevin legal reforms.

This view of inheritance is in accord with recent research on the related topic of the development of warranty. Professor Hyams has noted that warranty 'can presumably outlast the joint life of the original principals only when the tenurial and vassalic relationships are perceived to be long lasting or permanent, a point with obvious implications for the heritability of land tenure'; and that, 'in the developed common law, warranty was as fully transmissible as the property right it represented'.[101] He has challenged Thorne's contention that the extension of warranties to the heirs of the parties only occurred around 1175 when heirs began to enjoy royal assistance in their suits on a regular basis, and when the assize of *mort d'ancestor* began to enforce not only warranty but the recovery of seisin. And he has concluded that the emergence of Common Law warranty was 'a gradual affair, best understood in terms of the gradual hardening of tenurial customs into a set of legal rules about ownership and inheritance rights'; an affair less dependent upon royal intervention than Thorne implied.[102] As with heritability, so with warranty, the Angevin legal reforms transformed existing customary inheritance rights into something stronger and more formalised.[103]

In conclusion, it is clear that the concept of the 'seignorial world', and the thesis on the origins of the English Common Law

---

[98] Milsom acknowledges that kings had intervened in inheritance cases before the reforms, but appears to regard this as exceptional: Milsom, *Legal Framework*, 179–80. For the regularity of such intervention in practice, see Biancalana, 'Legal reforms of Henry II', 490–1, 495–7; Hudson, 'Development of inheritance', 77–80.

[99] *Chronica de Melsa*, I, 86. See also Green, *Government*, 189.

[100] *PR 31 Henry I*, 10, 11, 33, 38, 54; Barlow, *Rufus*, 250–1.

[101] Hyams, 'Warranty', 467.   [102] *Ibid.*, 467–74, quotation from p. 468.

[103] *Ibid.*, 473–4. For an alternative view of the origins of warranty, see D. Postles, 'Gifts in frankalmoign, warranty of land, and feudal society', *CLJ*, 50(2) (1991), 330–46.

which has been constructed upon it by some legal historians, must be heavily qualified. Although lordship undoubtedly dominated some Anglo-Norman estates, on others the power of seignorial courts over matters of jurisdiction, land grants and inheritance was limited. The importance attached by some historians to the Angevin legal reforms in undermining that power appears to have been overestimated. While it must be taken into account that the charters on which such conclusions are partly based may sometimes (perhaps often) record the exceptional rather than the ordinary, when viewed in conjunction with pipe roll and chronicle evidence these charters suggest that many of the developments attributed to Henry II's legal reforms were already underway before 1154. We can already discern that limitation of active tenurial lordship, that independence of service and tenure and that insulation of tenants from lords which some legal historians consider essential to property, but can only accept as the outcome of a late twelfth-century bureaucratic regulation of a supposedly pre-property 'seignorial world'.[104] We can also discern the existence of conflicting views about the related rights of lords and tenants in the realms of jurisdiction and inheritance which, although not set down in statute books and not part of an established legal code, were firmly inscribed in men's minds and continually reinforced by practice.[105] Although not legal rights in the modern lawyer's strict definition, although 'open to different [contemporary] interpretations, no one of which was distinctly privileged', and although perhaps 'strengthened, defined and formalized' by the Angevin legal reforms, for the men of the Anglo-Norman world these flexible and sometimes competing customary rights or social norms were far more important in governing their behaviour, and legitimating their actions, than the consistent application of formal and strictly defined legal rules.[106]

The importance of customary rights in regulating Anglo-Norman society is reflected above all perhaps in the frequency with which tenurial disputes were settled in this period by compromise agreements. These agreements, and the disputes between lord and tenant that often lay behind them, reflect in turn

[104] Milsom, *Legal Framework*, 33–9; *idem*, *Historical Foundations*, 99–100.
[105] For the existence of abstract ideas of landholding, see Hudson, 'Development of inheritance', 74–7.
[106] White, *Custom, Kinship and Gifts*, 69–76, 81, 84, 144–9, quotation from p. 73. The second quotation is from Hyams, 'Warranty', 474. On the existence of competing views of customary rights, see also Hudson, 'Milsom's legal structure', 61.

the existence of a concept of property which, although more flexible, was as real in its own day as our own. If, as Dr Reynolds suggests, 'The rights or claims of property ... are the rights to use and manage the thing concerned and to receive its produce or income; the right to pass it on to one's heirs and the right to dispose of it to others [and] ... to have one's title protected', then there can be no doubt that tenant property right existed in England in the century after 1066.[107] Not only is the external enforcement-based definition of property, put forward by some legal historians, open to a range of technical criticisms, its premise that before the introduction of the Angevin reforms the decision of the seignorial court was the only basis of tenurial title that there could be, does not square with the actions and attitudes of Anglo-Norman tenants.[108] The frequency with which they challenged that decision, the methods they employed to do so and the willingness of their lords to come to some form of compromise with them, reinforces the argument that property rights independent of lordship were already part of the natural order of things before the reign of Henry II. The problem now is to explain how this natural order came about: how tenurial lordship came to be limited and how property emerged.

THE LIMITATION OF TENURIAL LORDSHIP AND CONCEPT OF PROPERTY IN ANGLO-NORMAN YORKSHIRE: POLITICS, PERSONALITIES AND TENURIAL AND SOCIAL DYNAMICS

As Hyams has noted, 'The historian wishing to determine the location of "ownership" of land in anything resembling the modern lawyer's sense needs to assess [the] rough balance of power between lord and man with care. As this shifted according to political circumstance, so too in a sense did "ownership".'[109] It was a balance which depended also upon a range of economic,

---

[107] S. Reynolds, 'Bookland, folkland and fiefs', *ANS*, 14 (1992), 212–13, quotation from p. 213. Similar ideas were expressed by Lennard: *Rural England*, 23.

[108] Milsom does not consider seisin by a lord as a delivery of property because service had to be performed: Milsom, *Legal Framework*, 24. Although acknowledging that 'a single plot of land may have been in some sense the property of several different people: a peasant, the lord of his manor, the lord's lord, the king', Milsom does not regard this to be property in the full sense of the word. It appears that for him true property only came into being when 'General rules came to be enforced, and the rights of tenants other than those holding immediately of the king himself came to be protected by the king's courts': Milsom, *Historical Foundations*, 99–100.

[109] Hyams, 'Warranty', 440.

social, tenurial and even personal factors, which might vary widely within an individual honour from estate to estate and from time to time. A detailed analysis of all of these factors is beyond the scope of this survey, particularly the influence of general twelfth-century economic trends, which is not considered because it is the subject of a detailed debate.[110] What follows is an attempt to illustrate some particular examples of, and to make some tentative generalisations about, the ways in which politics, personal factors and tenurial and social dynamics might have brought about the limitation of tenurial lordship, and promoted the emergence of property right, on certain estates in Anglo-Norman Yorkshire.

Politics could have a powerful influence on the effectiveness of tenurial lordship. This effectiveness varied according to the relative status, patronage contacts and landed wealth of lord and tenant. In cases where the balance was clearly in favour of the lord, his authority over his tenants may have been similar to that assumed by Stenton to have been characteristic of all the greater magnates. This was probably true of Nigel d'Aubigny, lord of Thirsk, whose close and ruthless control of his tenants in Yorkshire, reflected in his effective disinheritance of a number of them, almost certainly reflects his position as the lord of an extensive barony composed of eighty-eight knights' fees extending across nearly ten counties, and his powerful links with the king's government, in which he served for a time as a northern justiciar.[111] The reality of seignorial power on some lordships is also illustrated by three charters issued in favour of Nostell Priory in the reign of King Stephen by the Yorkshire tenant Osbert Salvein, a former sheriff of Nottingham and Derby. The charters notify the three lords above Osbert in the tenurial chain (Adam Tison, Roger of Mowbray and King Stephen) and the dean and chapter of York of his gifts, and beg their aid to confirm and maintain the donation in the event of anyone molesting the canons. It is significant, as Hyams observes, that Osbert 'never mentioned legal action in his attempts to provide a comprehensive safeguard for his relatively minor gift ... [knowing] that in the event of future challenge, the maintenance of great men was all-important'.[112] Just how important is clearly

---

[110] For the debate, see P. D. A. Harvey, 'The English inflation of 1180–1220', *Past & Present*, 61 (1973), 3–30; R. C. Palmer, 'The economic and cultural impact of the origins of property: 1180–1220', *LHR*, 3 (1985), 375–96; Harvey, 'The knight and knight's fee', 31–43; Holt, 'Magna Carta 1215–1217', 17–18.

[111] *Mowbray Charters*, xvii–xxv, xxxiii, xxxvii, nos. 2–7.

[112] Hyams, 'Warranty', 450, and the sources cited there.

demonstrated by the fate of the canons of Warter Priory, who were evicted from their lands in 1175–6 after Henry II gave the manor of Warter to Geoffrey Trussebut.[113]

In other cases the scales of power were tilted in favour of the tenant, who might either be a greater landholder than his lord, have powerful backers or alternative lords, or hold an important office. In such cases the authority of the lord and effectiveness of his lordship diminished accordingly. From the very early days of the Norman settlement tenants could hold lands of several lords, and this undoubtedly served to dilute, and in some cases to undermine, seignorial authority. The growth of multiple tenancies was itself the product of aristocratic competition for good service, and the competition of their tenants for good lordship. The greater magnates had not only to compete for service with the king and each other, but also with the 'new men' who were rising through the ranks of the nobility via royal service, and establishing their own networks of tenants. The 'new men' themselves often rose to local prominence partly through the tenurial patronage of a county aristocracy anxious to win their support and influence.[114] This form of competition 'must have worked to break up the honour as a self-sufficient unit almost from its inception', especially as the land supply diminished during the course of the twelfth century and the crown became better (or even better) placed than the magnates to offer patronage to the county 'knights' in terms of offices, marriage and wardship.[115] The problems of dealing with a well-connected tenant are illustrated by the relationship between Roger of Mowbray and one of his men, Ralph Fitz Aldelin, in the very early years of the reign of Henry II. The ability of Ralph to preserve a claim to a portion of his father's estates which had been granted by Roger to a new tenant, and, apparently, to force Roger to admit the insecurity of the new tenant's tenure, may have been due to the fact that his brother, William, was a steward of Henry II.[116] Outside Yorkshire more

---

[113] King, 'Parish of Warter', 49–54. There were important differences between the lordship exercised by laymen over their lay and ecclesiastical tenants, and it would be unsafe, therefore, to make generalisations about relations between laymen and their lay tenants from this example.   [114] See above, Chapter 2.

[115] D. A. Carpenter, 'Comment' on P. R. Coss, 'Bastard feudalism revised', *Past & Present*, 131 (1991), 186–9, quotation from p. 189.

[116] *Mowbray Charters*, no. 383 and note. Henry II himself issued a confirmation of Roger of Mowbray's restoration charter to Ralph, probably in January 1156, which suggests that William may have brought the case to the king's attention. See *Chartulary of Fountains*, I, 23 (2); *EYC*, III, 299–300; *Recueil des Actes*, Introduction, 478.

tenants were exploiting similar advantages to force their lords to accept tenancies they did not want.[117]

A second major cause of the limitation of lordship was geography. In a land with only a rudimentary communications network, where forty miles was probably the best a man could hope to travel in a day, lords with many estates strewn across several counties had no hope of achieving the regular presence which undoubtedly helped them to maintain their authority.[118] Delegation was unavoidable, and it might only be a short step from there to independence. The difficulties which arose when tenants held land at some distance from the administrative centre of the honour were already apparent to the author of the *Leges Henrici Primi* in the second decade of the reign of Henry I.[119] They were difficulties which cost the earls of Norfolk and Chester effective control of at least some of the outlying estates of their great lordships situated in Yorkshire.[120]

The personal and administrative abilities or disadvantages of individual lords and their officials, was another important factor determining the strength or weakness of lordship. Although our sources rarely provide us with direct information on these subjects, an example of what could happen to lordship when placed in the wrong hands is illustrated in the account given in the *Historia Selebiensis Monasterii* of the chequered career of Abbot Herbert of Selby, in the third decade of the twelfth century. This overly pious man 'did nothing about, nor gave thought to, the property and wealth of the monastery', with the result that the abbey's fields, barns and messuages were ruined.[121] On the advice of the papal legate, John of Crema, who informed him that his personal qualities were incompatible with lordship, Herbert resigned. His successor, Durand, enjoyed a far more successful term of office, restoring the abbey's estates and wealth, and was suitably credited

---

[117] For some examples, see *English Lawsuits*, I, nos. 10, 220, 266.
[118] Stenton, 'Road system', 16–17.   [119] *LHP*, p. 172 cl. 55, 1a.
[120] For Bigod, see above, p. 270. In 1086 a major portion of the lands belonging to the earl of Chester in Yorkshire were held by William I of Percy. Although William and his son, Alan I, may have continued to recognise Chester overlordship until the early twelfth century (see *EYC*, II, nos. 855, 857), in 1166 William's grandson, William II, returned as tenant-in-chief details of knights' fees incorporating estates formerly held of the earls of Chester: *Red Book*, I, 424–5; *EYC*, XI, 223–5, 213–14. By this date it is also probable that the tenancy-in-chief of other Chester estates in Yorkshire had passed to the Brus family. In 1168 Adam II of Brus paid scutage directly for two knights' fees held of the earl of Chester: *PR 14 Henry II*, 90.
[121] *Selby Coucher*, I, [26]–[28], quotation from p. [26].

by the author of the history of the abbey with the qualities of jurisdictional skill, shrewdness, eloquence and nobility. Qualities of this nature, or the lack of them, undoubtedly had an important influence on the efficacy of lordship, something which must also have been true in the secular world. There lordship might also be weakened by the failure of the seignorial dynasty, and by the succession of new lords who lacked the benefit of old-established personal ties with their tenants.

The factors limiting tenurial lordship outlined above are concerned with the particular, with individual lords, tenants and estates at specific times. In addition, it may be possible to identify dynamics at work within society in the century after 1066 which were tending to promote a more general limitation of lordship, and a concomitant emergence of property. These dynamics were essentially tenurial and social, and they will now be examined in turn.

One factor tending towards the limitation of seignorial authority in the twelfth century was the constant pressure on men to alienate their lands. It derived from, among other things, the extension of Norman settlement and military control, the interference of the king and opportunism of his officials, the demands of family and good lordship, the obligations of piety, the need to secure service and political influence and the provision of security for debts. The severe drain upon tenurial resources resulting from the cumulative impact of all the forces compelling lords to alienate their lands is illustrated on the honour of Percy, the component estates of which were situated mainly in Yorkshire and Lincolnshire. By 1135 at least 60 per cent (and probably far more) of the demesne carucates had been granted by the lords to their relatives, tenants and religious houses.[122] A similar erosion of resources on many more lordships is suggested by the down-turn in the amount of land alienated by successive lords as the twelfth century progressed. One index of this is the ratio of fees of the old enfeoffment to fees of the new enfeoffment recorded in the *cartae baronum* of 1166.[123] Although assarting and other forms of land

---

[122] Dalton, 'Feudal politics', Appendix 2.

[123] Keefe, *Feudal Assessments*, 43. The amount of land alienated is not directly proportional to the number of knights' fees. Some of the knight's fees, or fractions of fees, created after 1135 may have been much larger than those created before that date. On this, see Mortimer, 'Honour of Clare', 190; Harvey, 'The knight and knight's fee', 31–43. Despite this, the disparity between the level of enfeoffment before and after 1135

reclamation certainly provided a degree of relief, it is unlikely to have been sufficient to stem the consistent overall drain upon resources.

The pressures influencing men to alienate lands help to explain the loss of seignorial control over alienations, and the emergence of tenant ownership. Even in those cases where the lord's consent was sought and given, the result was that the tenurial chain became one link longer, the occupant of the land one step removed from the lord. In this way land and lordship gradually separated. By the mid-twelfth century the formation of long tenurial chains was already well advanced on some Yorkshire estates, where anywhere between three and five men might have some form of interest in the same piece of land, and where the control of the man at the top was clearly in a state of decay.[124] The vill of Wentworth near Wath upon Dearne in the West Riding provides an example. Before 1159 a portion of the vill was held of the lord of Skipton by Reiner the Fleming, as part of one and a half knights' fees of the new enfeoffment.[125] Reiner's tenant in Wentworth, and several nearby vills, was Adam Fitz Swain, who enfeoffed in turn John Fitz Assolf. Between c. 1170 and 1200 Fitz Assolf made a gift to Monk Bretton Priory of land in Wentworth which Hugh Fitz Henry had held of him, together with the service of the land which Fitz Assolf had done to Adam Fitz Swain: that is, homage, suit of court every three weeks, a boon-plough in Lent and a boon-reaper in autumn.[126] Despite his position as the third tenant in the tenurial chain, Adam Fitz Swain clearly had the right to hold a court and to take the homage of John Fitz Assolf. The latter makes no mention of either Reiner the Fleming or the lord of Skipton in his charter. Fitz Assolf saw Adam Fitz Swain as the lord of the estate, and refers to Adam not as 'domini mei' but as 'domino de Newhalla', a nearby vill also forming part of the estate held by Adam of Reiner the Fleming, and probably the site of Adam's court. Here at Wentworth the attachment of tenant to tenement, at least in the eyes of one contemporary, had become more

---

remains striking. For the decline in tenurial resources generally, see Wightman, *Lacy Family*, 67, 70, 75, 109–12, 210–11; Wardrop, *Fountains Abbey*, 140–3, 146, 150–1, 166, 169, 183; Miller, *Ely*, 165, 174–5; S. Raban, *The Estates of Thorney and Crowland: A Study in Medieval Monastic Land Tenure* (Univ. of Cambridge Dept of Land Economy Occasional Paper, no. 7, 1977), 32–44.
[124] For multiple mesne tenancies, see *EYC*, I, no. 601 and note; II, no. 916 and note; *Mowbray Charters*, no. 392.   [125] *Red Book*, I, 431; *EYC*, VII, 193–6.
[126] *EYC*, VII, nos. 131–2 and notes, 126.

important than the attachment of tenant to lord. For men of the status of John Fitz Assolf and Hugh Fitz Henry, the lord of Skipton and Reiner the Fleming were distant, possibly anonymous figures, of only minor local significance, and Adam Fitz Swain was the owner of the estate. Who can doubt but that Adam himself shared their views?

Milsom noted another way in which progressive subinfeudation could lead to a breakdown of seignorial control: the introduction into the tenurial chain of tenants without courts, who had no means of distraining for lack of services or other obligations, and who would have to look to the royal officials to enforce their rights.[127] There is no need, however, to regard the intrusion of central justice into private tenurial relations as integral to this development: alienation, or, in the case of ecclesiastical tenancies, a combination of alienation and the ideological impact of church reform upon ecclesiastical landholding, provided the primary stimulus. As we have seen, progressive alienation could result in the increasing independence of occupancy and lordship before the legal reforms of Henry II had time to take effect; and there is evidence that it had the same impact on the relationship between tenement and dues.[128] In securing grants from lay landholders the church was anxious that the lands acquired should be free from secular services and exactions. Thus, when tenants made grants in alms to ecclesiastical foundations the actual occupant of the land would not be responsible for the payment of the dues for which the land had originally been alienated, and there was a danger that these dues might be completely lost to the lord. This separation of tenement and dues, and the threat to seignorial authority posed by it, is clear from a charter issued by Ranulf of Greystoke in the 1160s. It confirms a gift by his Yorkshire tenant, William Fitz Theobald, of land in Folkton to Rievaulx Abbey quit of all services except the provision of one pound of cumin each year.[129] It provides that should William omit these services Ranulf would claim them directly from him rather than troubling the monks. The potential threat to Ranulf's lordship posed by this alienation to Rievaulx is also evident from William's affidavit and offer of warranty in the hand of Alexander and in the presence of Simon

---

[127] Milsom, *Legal Framework*, 33–5.
[128] I am grateful to Dr Hudson for reminding me that the process of distraint by fee, and much of *Glanvill*, show that land and services were still regarded as interdependent in theory.　　　　[129] *EYC*, II, nos. 1250–1.

de Sigillo, two canons of St Peter's, York. At one end of the scale we have the lord, who feared the loss of his rights, and who had been unable to confine the business of alienation to his own court. At the other we have the monks of Rievaulx, securely entrenched at Folkton with their two charters, warranty promise, support of important churchmen and nominal service obligation. On many estates vertical alienation was more advanced than at Folkton. If the fundamental basis of lordship was a personal relationship, it is easy to understand the vulnerability of that relationship on estates of this kind.

The pressure on lords and tenants to alienate lands could also undermine lordship by stimulating conflict between tenants which led to disputes being removed from the seignorial courts. This was particularly true when lords and tenants attempted to accommodate new tenants within the existing body of alienated lands. The accommodation could take two forms, each of which is clearly discernible in the early twelfth century. First, the granting of the same estates to more than one beneficiary ('double grants'), and secondly the creation of mesne tenancies. We have already seen how the conflicting grants of the church of Roxby in Lincolnshire by the Paynel lords and their tenants in the early twelfth century led to legal disputes in the royal court between the various beneficiaries in the reign of John. 'Double grants' concerning property in the Yorkshire vill of Bramham show that such cases were already being taken outside the seignorial courts in the reign of Henry I. A grant by Robert Fossard to Nostell Priory of the church of Bramham, made without regard for his father's charter bestowing it upon Ramsey Abbey, resulted in direct royal intervention. Although the king confirmed the church to Nostell, he issued a writ commanding Robert to do right to the abbot of Ramsey.[130] In the case of the creation of mesne tenancies, relations between mesne and sitting tenants could be uneasy. The trouble might begin with an attempt by the mesne tenant to convert his rights to services into actual occupancy of the land. An example of what could happen is illustrated on the Mowbray estate of Acaster Selby in the reign of Stephen. It was then that Roger of Mowbray issued a charter which established the abbey of Selby in the tenurial chain of Acaster Selby, and notified Leising and Chetell and his men of Acaster that the land there had been given to the monks.

---

[130] *Ibid.*, no. 1002; *Regesta*, II, nos. 1627, 1630.

The possibility for conflict is implicit in the statement made in the charter that if the monks were disseised by anyone Roger would reseise them by his charters.[131] Although there is more than one possible interpretation of this charter, it may be evidence that the monks had been expelled by the resident Mowbray tenants, and it is significant that in a separate act Roger restored Acaster to them.[132]

In the twelfth century, therefore, the pressure on lords to alienate lands served to undermine lordship, not only by elongating tenurial chains, but also by complicating tenurial relationships. It has been said that 'To hold of many different lords was, in some ways, to hold of none and to enjoy a measure of political independence.'[133] Such a multiplication of tenurial relationships was common from the very earliest years of Norman rule. It might result not only in the dilution of lordship, but also in a shift in the balance of political power from lord to tenant. In the first century of Norman rule in Yorkshire 'knightly' families holding lands of several lords were forging social, familial and tenurial relationships with their neighbours which cut across the ties of seignorial allegiance.[134] The same process has been observed by Dr Wales throughout the estates of Lincolnshire, and by Dr Mortimer on the lordship of Clare.[135] By the mid-twelfth century in many parts of Yorkshire and elsewhere the honour had become little more than an artificial construct. The tenurial chain, like any other chain, was only as strong as its weakest link.

It has been argued above that property existed in the minds of men long before it came to be protected by the courts. Even in the thirteenth century there is evidence that men with a genuine claim to land looked to the courts not to provide title, but as one method of securing or preserving the rights attached to a title which (they considered) already existed. If the courts failed to do so their decisions were sometimes either ignored or contradicted, and the

---

[131] *Mowbray Charters*, no. 254.

[132] *Ibid.*, no. 256, dated September 1143 × 1147, or October 1153 × June 1154. For another possible interpretation of these charters, see above, pp. 168–9. For more examples which probably illustrate conflict between mesne and sitting tenants, see *Mowbray Charters*, no. 392 (dated 1138 × *c*. 1145); *EYC*, II, nos. 1036–8 (dated 1186 × 1187, *c.* 1148 × 1154, and *c.* 1150 × 1165 respectively). Before 1165 the monks of Rievaulx were clearly concerned about the creation of mesne fees in the vill of Stainton where the tenurial chain was already long: *ibid.*, III, nos. 1842–5. See also *ibid.*, XI, 186–90.

[133] Holt, *Northerners*, 36.   [134] See above, pp. 249–54.

[135] Wales, 'Twelfth-century Lincolnshire'; Mortimer, 'Honour of Clare', 177–97, esp. 178–90, 194–6.

claim continued.[136] What, then, was the basis of title? For Holt there is no doubt: title 'derived not from jurisdiction but from the social conventions within which the jurisdiction was set to work'.[137] Integral to these social conventions was the concept and practice of inheritance. For Holt inheritance was already well established in Normandy before 1066, and was more of a 'primordial right' than a seignorial concession.[138] When it reemerged in fully developed form in England in the early twelfth century, inheritance did not depend upon seignorial acceptance.[139] Inheritance was informed by 'notions of patrimony', the family attachment to its lands:

property law was family law ... the family retained an interest [in land] until the relationship between collateral branches became so tenuous that it ceased to have any relevance, and this only occurred after the lapse of several generations. The family always sought to ensure reversion. Possession always left a residual family claim, strong or weak, depending on the length and terms of tenure and the distance of the relationship.[140]

A lord might override it but the family claim was there nevertheless. Symptomatic of these proprietary notions is the toponymic family surname common in Normandy before 1066, and reemerging rapidly in England before the legal reforms of Henry II. This was 'not just name but title'.[141]

Holt's thesis receives support from the extant sources of eleventh- and early twelfth-century Yorkshire. That the Normans arrived in England with a well-developed conception of inheritance is implicit in some of the clauses of the Yorkshire Domesday, and explicit in the language of the early Yorkshire charters.[142] The same charters also illustrate the strong sense of family attachment to land. It was common in Yorkshire for men

---

[136] See, for examples, *EYC*, XI, 252–3 and no. 36; English, *Holderness*, 40–6.
[137] Holt, 'Notions of patrimony', 218. [138] *Ibid.*, 199.
[139] *Ibid.*, 207. See also Tabuteau, *Transfers of Property*, 63–4, 75–100.
[140] Holt, 'Politics and property', 20–1. See also *idem*, 'Notions of patrimony', 193–220, esp. 207–11.
[141] Holt, 'The revolution of 1066', 200; *idem, What's in a Name?*; *idem*, 'Magna Carta 1215–1217', 13–15.
[142] The six carucates in Elvington which William I of Percy was holding were testified to the use of Robert Malet 'because his father had them': *DB*, I, 373b. For antecessorial succession as a legitimate basis of title in Domesday Book, see P. R. Hyams, '"No register of title": the Domesday inquest and land adjudication', *ANS*, 9 (1987), 127–41; Fleming, *Kings and Lords*, Chapters 4–5; Roffe, 'Thegnage to barony', 167–8. For charters illustrating the early use of inheritance language before 1135, see *Mowbray Charters*, no. 3; *EYC*, II, nos. 883, 970, 1012, 1071; IV, no. 9.

to make hereditary claims to land which their ancestors had either seized or held only for life.[143] In the reign of John, William II de Forz, count of Aumale, claimed the royal demesne manor of Driffield, even though Henry II had granted his predecessor only a life tenure; and the Stutevilles continued to pursue tenurial claims against the Mowbrays first advanced in Stephen's reign, despite having been deprived of the disputed lands by Henry I.[144] Royal directives did not necessarily bar the preservation of a family claim, and this was also true of the exercise of seignorial jurisdiction and the interference of lords in the process of succession, even when there had been a failure of the direct family line.[145] We have seen how lords who died without issue were quite prepared on their own initiative to designate brothers or even sons-in-law as their heirs, in order to preserve the family attachment to its lands.[146] Even when the succession had been taken out of the hands of these lords, and the land had passed under the effective control of a new family, their close relatives were often still prepared to fight on after their deaths. This was true of Robert of Gant who, after the death in 1156 of his elder brother, Gilbert of Gant lord of Hunmanby, saw the Gant tenancy-in-chief and the hand of Gilbert's infant daughter and only child, Alice, pass by royal command to Simon III of Senlis, the former lord of Huntingdon. Despite securing the Gant honour and its heiress from the king, Simon was anxious to publicise a claim that his tenure was based on an agreement with Gilbert.[147] For his part, Robert of Gant proved to be no friend of Simon, and upon eventually succeeding to the honour himself in 1185 made strenuous and costly efforts to recover the estates Simon had alienated from the Gant patrimony.[148] The policy of both lords leaves little doubt that land and family were seen as inseparable.

This view of inseparability is also reflected in the determination of some married women to preserve their family name and its association with their inherited estates, in spite of their marriages. This was particularly true of Cecily of Rumilly, lady of Skipton, and her daughters and granddaughters, who continued to use the Rumilly name, and issued charters jointly with their husbands

---

[143] This had also been true in Normandy. See Tabuteau, *Transfers of Property*, 99–100.

[144] S. Painter, *The Reign of King John* (Baltimore, 1949), 330; *Monasticon*, v, 351–5; *Mowbray Charters*, xxviii–xxx; *EYC*, ix, nos. 41–4 and notes.

[145] See the case of Ralph Fitz Aldelin above, pp. 277–8.

[146] *Mowbray Charters*, no. 3.   [147] Abbot, 'Gant family', 53–8.

[148] *PR 32 Henry II*, 76; *PR 3 and 4 Richard I*, 4, cited by Abbot, 'Gant family', 107–8.

which reveal a concern to preserve their rights.[149] The same determination was displayed by the daughters and co-heiresses of William II of Percy, and by Hawisa, daughter and heiress of William count of Aumale.[150] In Hawisa's case it is particularly striking. She attempted to resist King Richard's desire to have her marry one of his military captains, William I de Forz, and after the death of her third husband, Baldwin de Béthune, in 1212 she offered King John the enormous sum of 5,000 marks in order to secure possession of her inheritance and her dowers, and to obtain a privilege allowing her not to be married again against her will.[151] Her desire to retain her own identity is also clear from the seal she used when married to her first husband, William de Mandeville, earl of Essex, which was inscribed with the legend HAWIS DE ALBEMARLA COMITISSE ESSEXE.[152] For Hawisa being an Aumale was just as important as being a countess.

The tenacity of family tenure is also illustrated in the attitude of men toward land sold or exchanged. Here again neither form of conveyance was necessarily regarded as a bar to the preservation of the family claim. In the period 1107–15, for example, Nigel d'Aubigny was still claiming land in Crowle (Lincs.) which had been sold to Selby Abbey by his 'quartus antecessor', Geoffrey de La Guerche.[153] A similar resolve was displayed by William Fitz Ucce, a tenant of Nigel d'Aubigny's son and successor, Roger of Mowbray, who appears to have maintained his claim to the vill of Bagby, despite the fact that Roger granted him an exchange for it in nearby Ampleforth.[154] The reluctance of other tenants to relinquish claims to exchanged lands is reflected in the carefully worded clauses woven by their lords into charters granting or confirming these exchanges, which were designed to prevent reversion of the lost estates by the tenants and their descendants. In his charter of *c.* 1150, granting John of Meaux the vill of Bewick in exchange for that of Meaux, William count of Aumale stipulated that John had surrendered Meaux with a knife, 'solutam et quietam de se et heredibus suis; et hanc redditionem juravit tenendam sic quod ecclesia fundata in Melsa sicut elemosina erit quieta et sine omni calumpnia tam de Johanne de Melsa quam de heredibus suis imperpetuum'.[155] The count's awareness of the

---

[149] *EYC*, VII, 3–20, nos. 2–3, 10–11, 13–16.   [150] *EYC*, XI, 5–7, 45 and note 2.
[151] English, *Holderness*, 30, 35.   [152] *Ibid.*, Plate 8.
[153] *Mowbray Charters*, no. 1.   [154] *Ibid.*, nos. 59, 73, 399 and notes.
[155] *EYC*, III, no. 1379. Farrer dated the charter 1149 × 1150.

strength of the family tenurial attachment is also clear from the
fact that the charter begins by applying the surname 'de Melsa'
to John, but concludes by referring to him as 'de Bewyc'.

The importance of family attachment to lands in providing
title, especially when it was of some antiquity, is further illustrated
by the fact that where no such attachment existed it might be
invented. In the 1140s, when William I of Roumare secured
control of the East Riding royal demesne manor of Warter,
probably as a result of a gift from William count of Aumale, he
appears to have manufactured a claim that his father had held the
manor in the late eleventh century.[156]

Closely related to notions of patrimony, and symptomatic of
the limitation of lordship they helped to promote, was a process of
aristocratic cultural popularisation, involving the gradual devolution through the social hierarchy of the cultural patterns of
those in the upper ranks. At the core of this culture, and basic to the
concept of *nobilitas*, was family dynastic feeling, the veneration of
ancestors, a sense of lineage. The process has been said to be
discernible on the continent in the tenth and eleventh centuries.[157]
In England, it was probably one of the most important of a
complex series of influences responsible for the widespread
adoption of the notions and attributes of *nobilitas* by men below
the rank of tenant-in-chief. Although one of these attributes, the
castle, had already been adopted by 1086, this probably owed
more to the military exigencies of the conquest period than to a
desire to imitate the greater magnates.[158] It was only gradually
over the next two generations that other attributes, such as family
toponymic surnames, notions of heritability, independent jurisdiction, seals and monasteries, appear to have been adopted.[159]

[156] King, 'Parish of Warter', 49–54. For more examples of the tenacity of family tenure,
see *EYC*, VII, 14–27; IX, 65–7; X, 12–19; XI, no. 36 and note, and 253–4; Wightman,
Lacy Family, 66–70, 88–93.

[157] G. Duby, 'The diffusion of cultural patterns in feudal society', *Past & Present*, 39 (1968),
3–10.

[158] It has been suggested that the 500 or so castles in the hands of lesser nobles in the early
Anglo-Norman period were in the hands of men, 'who could hardly sustain seigneurial
pretensions from their own landed resources without direct aid and patronage from
their lords', and that, 'such assistance ... was unlikely to be forthcoming after the initial
phase of Norman settlement': Eales, 'Royal power and castles', 62.

[159] Holt, 'The revolution of 1066', 209. A very large majority of the religious foundations
made by men of second rank in Yorkshire occurred in the period 1140–65.
They include the Benedictine houses of Nunkeeling (1143 × 1154), Nun Monkton
(c. 1147 × 1153), Marrick (1154 × 1158) and Yedingham (*ante* 1158); the Cistercian
houses of Jervaulx (1145), Roche (1147), Nun Appleton (c. 1148 × 1154), Swine

As the twelfth century wore on, such attributes came to be acquired by 'knights' of a progressively lower social status.[160] Although this process of aristocratic cultural popularisation was by no means the only factor responsible for the occurrence and timing of these developments, there can be little doubt that the 'knights' of the twelfth century viewed themselves principally as lords in their own right, rather than as tenants; and that they did so before the Angevin legal reforms.[161] This much, at least, is suggested by the tradition preserved by the monks of Jervaulx Abbey (established 1145) about their founder, Acaris Fitz Bardolph, a tenant of the lords of Richmond. Towards the end of the twelfth century they remembered him as 'a knight of generous stock ... a great lord of land and possessions in the county of York'.[162] Although probably coloured to some degree by the monks' concern for the reputation of their own house, there can be little doubt that this memory also reflects the aspirations of their founder. Acaris Fitz Bardolph liked to see himself not just as a knight, but also as a lord; and a lord of lands and possessions. He liked to see himself, in our words, as an owner.

The way in which the monks of Jervaulx perceived their founder suggests that the dynamics promoting the emergence of property were not confined to the secular world. The church may also have had a significant influence. Its buildings included the mausoleums and libraries that gave tangible substance to the concepts of lineage and family title.[163] The church encouraged the donation of land by tenants, often without the knowledge or consent of their lords, on terms specifically designed to limit

(*c.* 1143 × 1153), Wykeham (*ante* 1153) and Basedale (*c.* 1162); the Premonstratensian house of Easby (1151 × 1152); the Cluniac house of Monk Bretton (1153 × 1154); and the Templars' preceptory of Temple Hirst (1152). Many of these houses were poor, indicating that the aspirations of their founders may have outstripped their resources. See *EYC*, I, nos. 480–1, 546, 612, 614; II, 125 and nos. 784, 787 and note, 1133; IV, no. 23 and note; V, no. 372; XI, 7–8; *Cal. Chart. Rolls*, IV, 291; *Monasticon*, V, 568–74; Wardrop, *Fountains Abbey*, 20 and note 68; *VCH, Yorkshire*, III, 248–9, 251; Burton, 'Religious orders', 199, 256–69, 276–7.

160 For an example, see the case of the Lenhams: *VCH, Yorkshire*, III, 249–50. For the same trend in a wider context, see Cheney, *Hubert Walter*, 28.

161 There was far more to this process than the percolation down the social scale of ideas of nobility and lordship. This can be seen in the case of monastic endowment, which occurred in order to satisfy a variety of social and religious needs: Burton, 'Religious orders', 254–78.   162 *Monasticon*, V, 568.

163 The surviving thirteenth-century gate-house of Kirkham Priory in the East Riding still bears the coats of arms of several of the families who made grants to it, including the Ros family, who were the successors of the founder, Walter Espec.

secular control and guarantee tenure.[164] It has been suggested that
the percolation of these and other ecclesiastical ideas into the
secular world may have contributed to the development of
abstract ideas about landholding, and the evolution of the standard
charter language important in the emergence of Common Law
warranty.[165] The monks of Byland were well aware of the benefits
that could accrue from implanting the idea of *nobilitas* into the
minds of the local tenantry. We are told that when certain veteran
knights of Roger of Mowbray retired to their house and brought
them lands: 'straightaway after their entry they spread abroad
throughout the province that the new habitation was wonderfully
supported by noble men and generous people, whereby the
devotion of those who heard this was inclined towards the
place'.[166] When combined with abstract ecclesiastical ideas about
landholding, these notions of nobility posed an even greater threat
to seignorial authority. It has even been suggested that such a
combination lay behind and shaped a constitutional principle
which existed in England long before 1154, encouraged tenants to
take their legal cases out of the courts of their lords and into those
of the church and king and guided Henry II and his officials in
developing their legal reforms.[167] Once again, the Angevin
reforms which are supposed to have initiated social change appear
on close analysis to reflect a society that was already changing.

CONCLUSION

This study of seignorial jurisdiction, alienation and inheritance
suggests that the interpretation of the 'seignorial world' dominated by tenurial lordship, and of its transformation into the
Common Law society of property rights, which has been
advanced by some legal historians, is in need of substantial
revision. Although on some honours, and parts of honours,
tenurial lordship could be strong and durable, on others it could be
weak and transient. The efficacy of the relationship between lord
and tenant could vary over distance and time, depending upon a
complex interaction of mutable factors. When viewed against this
background the attribution of the bringing down of the 'seignorial

[164] For examples, see *EYC*, II, nos. 739, 762. See also the discussion in Hyams, 'Warranty',
472, 474–5.
[165] Hudson, 'Development of inheritance', 75–6; *idem*, 'Milsom's legal structure', 63, 65;
Hyams, 'Warranty', 474–6.   [166] *Monasticon*, V, 350.
[167] Biancalana, 'Legal reforms of Henry II', 433–56 (esp. 436–7), 485–6, 501–4, 506–7.

world' to the legal reforms of Henry II appears too simplistic. Although contributing towards the limitation of tenurial lordship, the reforms, specifically designed as they were to protect the tenure of the weak, were to some extent merely the reflection of a lordship which on many honours was already crucially limited. Henry I had already made some progress towards the provision of the legal remedies of his grandson, and his court was already interfering in the private jurisdiction of his magnates on a far more regular basis than some historians have assumed.[168]

This is not to deny that the Angevin reforms introduced new and revolutionary advances in jurisdictional procedure, greatly increased the volume of judicial business coming into the royal courts and had important effects on society which substantially quickened the pace of change.[169] However, the argument that the reforms brought down the 'seignorial world' and promoted the emergence of the Common Law society not only ignores the importance of the fundamental tenurial and social dynamics already changing society before 1154, which actually helped shape the reforms, but also presupposes a level of availability and effectiveness for the twelfth-century Angevin royal courts which is open to question. The pipe rolls illustrate that litigation could be an expensive game, and raise questions about the number of tenants able to afford the new remedies. And the records of legal disputes reveal that in some cases fair treatment may have proved elusive. Well into the thirteenth century many (perhaps most) cases continued to be settled by out-of-court compromises, and even when this was not the case the decisions of some courts could have more to do with political manipulation than legal rules.[170] These facts highlight the dangers of making historical assumptions

[168] Henry I developed an *ad hoc* writ resembling the later writ of right to deal with rival claims to tenure: see for examples, *Regesta*, II, nos. 1630, 1672; *English Lawsuits*, I, nos. 165, 188, 227. One royal charter issued between 1131 and 1133 appears to foreshadow the rule that no man need answer without a royal writ: *Regesta*, II, no. 1819. Other early royal writs reflect at least the procedural points of what later became the writ of *novel disseisin*: Glanvill, 167–8; *Regesta*, II, nos. 611a, 1080, 1825; III, nos. 228, 286, 354, 525, 534, 545–9, 620, 766, 866; *English Lawsuits*, I, nos. 212 (B), 282. See also R. C. Van Caenegem, *Royal Writs in England from the Conquest to Glanvill* (Selden Soc., 1959), 84, 271–7.

[169] For the impact of the reforms, see Brand, 'Henry II and the Common Law', 197–222; Biancalana, 'Legal reforms of Henry II', 441–2, 449–50, 461–6, 467, 482, 484, 508–12, 534; Clanchy, *England and its Rulers*, 150; Hyams, 'The charter as a source', 179; Holt, *Magna Carta*, 124–5.

[170] Hyams, review of Milsom, *Legal Framework*, 861; Holt, *Magna Carta*, 153–4; Clanchy, 'A medieval realist'. See also Clanchy, *England and its Rulers*, 150–2.

about the social impact of legal change purely on the basis of legal records. If the history of tenurial lordship in Anglo-Norman Yorkshire is reconstructed from contemporary or near contemporary chronicles, charters and pipe rolls, rather than from late twelfth-century legal records, the 'Angevin leap forward' begins to look more like a logical next step.[171]

Although inspired partly no doubt by the need for the restoration of order after the anarchy of King Stephen's reign, the legal reforms of Henry II were to some extent the natural progression of a royal policy initiated before the anarchy and designed to deal with the problems associated with far more fundamental changes within society.[172] These changes were already undermining tenurial lordship, promoting ownership and stimulating the need for royal judicial guarantees long before the Angevin legal statutes. The 'seignorial world' was already giving way to the Common Law world before the accession of Henry II; and while 'there is no means of weighing the respective influence, at the same time or at different points of time, of economic and constitutional changes, of the growth of legal doctrine or the advance of what we might call technical education' on the transformation of lordship, one thing does seem clear.[173] Although, as Milsom states, 'The law does not passively follow social change any more than it can actively cause it', and the interaction between the two is extremely complicated, legal change could reflect as well as influence social change, and it is primarily within social change rather than legal regulation that we should seek the origins of property in the 'first century of English feudalism'.[174]

[171] The quotation is from D. M. Stenton, *English Justice between the Norman Conquest and the Great Charter 1066–1215* (London, 1965), 22–53.

[172] For a discussion of the results of the anarchy in influencing Henry II's reforms, see Milsom, *Legal Framework*, 178–9; Biancalana, 'Legal reforms of Henry II', 439, 450–1, 466–74, 478–9, 500–4; Palmer, 'Origins of property', 18–24.

[173] The quotation is from Miller, *Ely*, 278.

[174] Milsom, *Historical Foundations*, 151.

TABLES

Table 1 *The value of the estates of the Yorkshire lay tenants-in-chief in Domesday Book*

Name of tenant-in-chief	Value of Yorkshire estates in 1066 (£)	Value of Yorkshire estates in 1086 (£)
Hugh earl of Chester	260.0	10.5
Robert count of Mortain	239.3	83.4
Count Alan of Brittany	211.7	80.2
Robert and Berengar of Tosny	21.3	21.0
Ilbert of Lacy	313.3	159.9
Roger of Bully	134.1	76.5
Robert Malet	29.6	9.3
William of Warenne	18.0	40.0
William of Percy	91.9	54.8
Drogo de la Beuvrière	553.8	93.3
Ralph of Mortemer	22.5	10.0
Ralph Paynel	22.0	5.1
Geoffrey de la Guerche	4.0	1.5
Geoffrey Alselin	16.0	4.5
Walter of Aincourt	6.0	2.0
Gilbert of Gant	12.0	3.0
Gilbert Tison	47.4	26.6
Richard Fitz Arnfastr	5.5	3.2
Hugh Fitz Baldric	96.5	70.4
Erneis of Burun	23.7	10.8
Osbern of Arches	53.5	23.2
Odo the Crossbowman	4.5	4.8
Aubrey of Coucy	5.5	3.0
Gospatric	19.6	9.7
Roger the Poitevin	?	?

Table 2 *The resources of the lordship of Conisbrough in Domesday Book*

Resources	Demesne	Tenanted
Carucates	90.9	0
Ploughlands	59.0	0
Seignorial plough-teams	16.0	0
Peasant plough-teams	92.0	0
Villeins	95.0	0
Bordars	82.0	0
Sokemen	120.0	0
Other population	4.0	0
Total population	301.0	0
1066 value (£)	18.0	0
1086 value (£)	40.0	0
1086 value as a percentage of 1066 value	222.2	0

Table 3 *The resources of the lordships of William of Percy and Hugh Fitz Baldric in Domesday Book*

Resources	Demesne		Tenanted		Tenant resources as a percentage of total resources	
	Percy	Fitz Baldric	Percy	Fitz Baldric	Percy	Fitz Baldric
Carucates	161.6	286.8	141.6	91.3	46.7	24.1
Ploughlands	91.5	136.0	83.5	42.5	47.7	23.8
Seignorial plough-teams	26.0	34.0	26.0	15.5	50.0	31.3
Peasant plough-teams	44.5	121.8	52.5	51.5	54.1	29.7
Villeins	173.0	314.0	100.0	131.0	36.6	29.4
Bordars	50.0	13.0	38.0	2.0	43.2	13.3
Sokemen	1.0	1.0	0	0	0	0
Other population	6.0	0	2.0	0	25.0	—
Total population	230.0	328.0	140.0	133.0	37.8	28.9
1066 value (£)	41.3	83.3	50.6	13.2	55.0	13.7
1086 value (£)	28.6	59.2	26.1	11.2	47.7	15.9
1086 value as a percentage of 1066 value	69.2	71.1	51.6	84.9		

Table 4 *The number of tenants enfeoffed by Yorkshire lay tenants-in-chief by 1086*

Name of tenant-in-chief	Number of tenants enfeoffed
Hugh earl of Chester	2
Robert count of Mortain	4
Count Alan of Brittany	28 approx.
Robert and Berengar of Tosny	1
Ilbert of Lacy	38 approx.
Roger of Bully	4 approx.
Robert Malet	0
William of Warenne	0
William of Percy	17
Drogo de la Beuvrière	33 approx.
Ralph of Mortemer	0
Ralph Paynel	1
Geoffrey de la Guerche	0
Geoffrey Alselin	0
Walter of Aincourt	0
Gilbert of Gant	0
Gilbert Tison	9
Richard Fitz Arnfastr	0
Hugh Fitz Baldric	8
Erneis of Burun	7
Osbern of Arches	15 approx.
Odo the Crossbowman	0
Aubrey of Coucy	0
Gospatric	0
Roger the Poitevin	0

Table 5 Bossall and its neighbouring estates in 1086

Resources	Manor of Scrayingham and berewicks	Manor of Buttercrambe and berewicks	Two manors of Heslington and berewicks	Manor of Sand Hutton	Manor of Langton and berewicks	Manor of Norton and berewick	Manor of Buckton Holms	Two manors of Scrayingham	Manor of North Grimston
Carucates	15.0	6.3	5.0	7.0	39.0	4.4	3.0	12.0	2.3
Ploughlands	7.5	3.0	2.0	3.5	20.0	2.0	1.5	6.0	1.0
Demesne seignorial plough-teams	0	2.0	0	0	3.0	2.0	0	5.0	2.0
Tenanted seignorial plough-teams	3.0	0	0	1.0	3.0	0	0	0	0
Peasant plough-teams	15.5	0	2.0	2.0	15.0	4.0	0	6.5	1.0
Villeins	29.0	2.0	3.0	11.0	43.0	12.0	0	15.0	6.0
Bordars	0	0	0	0	4.0	0	0	0	0
Sokemen	0	0	0	0	1.0	0	0	0	0
Other population	0	0	0	0	0	0	0	0	0
1066 value	50s	21s	42s	32s	£12	60s	?	60s	20s
1086 value	60s	60s	20s	30s	£6	60s	Waste	100s	30s
Mill value	—	20s	—	—	5s	10s	—	20s	—
Church	1.0	0	0	0	2.0	1.0	0	0	0
Priest	1.0	0	0	0	2.0	1.0	0	0	0

Table 6 *The resources of the lordships of Richmond, Pontefract, Holderness and Tickhill in Domesday Book*

Resources	Demesne				Tenanted				Tenant resources as a percentage of total resources			
	R	P	H	T	R	P	H	T	R	P	H	T
Carucates	391.0	433.8	375.5	234.5	768.8	301.0	146.0	7.4	66.3	41.0	28.0	3.1
Ploughlands	334.6	275.0	365.5	149.0	525.9	209.5	137.0	4.0	61.1	43.2	27.3	2.6
Seignorial plough-teams	28.0	41.5	23.5	55.0	72.5	77.5	37.0	6.5	72.1	65.1	61.2	10.6
Peasant plough-teams	77.4	135.0	61.8	163.3	184.4	123.5	32.5	5.0	70.4	47.8	34.5	3.0
Villeins	150.0	260.0	224.0	362.0	441.0	276.0	164.0	12.0	74.6	51.5	42.3	3.2
Bordars	38.0	90.0	42.0	158.0	126.0	190.0	72.0	11.0	76.8	67.9	63.2	6.5
Sokemen	7.0	5.0	33.0	36.0	0	9.0	9.0	—	0	64.3	21.4	—
Other population	2.0	76.0	0	31.0	6.0	6.0	0	—	75.0	7.3	—	—
Total population	197.0	431.0	299.0	587.0	573.0	481.0	245.0	23.0	74.4	52.7	45.0	3.8
1066 value (£)	103.3	164.0	481.8	132.1	108.4	149.3	72.0	2.0	51.2	47.7	13.0	1.5
1086 value (£)	28.4	90.3	64.1	74.5	51.8	69.6	29.2	2.0	64.6	43.5	31.3	2.6
1086 value as a percentage of 1066 value	27.5	55.1	13.3	56.4	47.8	46.6	40.6	100.0				

R = lordship of Richmond; P = lordship of Pontefract; H = lordship of Holderness; T = lordship of Tickhill.

Tables

Table 7 The resources of the lordship of Robert of Mortain in Domesday Book

Resources	Demesne	Tenanted	Tenant resources as a percentage of total resources
Carucates	187.0	618.9	76.8
Ploughlands	80.5	348.5	81.2
Seignorial plough-teams	9.0	48.0	84.2
Peasant plough-teams	43.1	163.8	79.2
Villeins	100.0	351.0	77.8
Bordars	4.0	90.0	95.7
Sokemen	1.0	86.0	98.9
Other population	8.0	18.0	69.2
Total population	113.0	545.0	82.8
1066 value (£)	49.9	188.9	79.1
1086 value (£)	14.6	68.9	82.5
1086 value as a percentage of 1066 value	29.3	36.5	

Table 8 *The resources of the embryonic lordships in Domesday Book*

Resources	Demesne			Tenanted			Tenant resources as a percentage of total resources		
	T	To	P	T	To	P	T	To	P
Carucates	77.1	130.2	85.4	46.5	17.5	8.0	37.6	11.8	8.6
Ploughlands	42.0	89.6	45.5	31.0	13.0	4.0	42.5	12.7	8.1
Seignorial plough-teams	11.5	15.4	3.0	4.5	6.0	1.0	28.1	28.0	25.0
Peasant plough-teams	22.0	41.5	7.0	8.0	4.0	2.0	26.7	8.8	22.2
Villeins	79.0	111.0	26.0	33.0	28.0	7.0	29.5	20.1	21.2
Bordars	25.0	47.0	0	15.0	0	0	37.5	0	—
Sokemen	4.0	8.0	2.0	0	0	0	0	0	0
Other population	3.0	17.0	2.0	2.0	1.0	0	40.0	5.6	0
Total population	111.0	183.0	30.0	50.0	29.0	7.0	31.1	13.7	18.9
1066 value (£)	22.4	19.2	18.0	25.0	1.6	4.0	52.7	7.7	18.2
1086 value (£)	16.6	18.8	3.1	10.0	2.0	2.0	37.6	7.7	39.2
1086 value as a percentage of 1066 value	74.1	97.9	17.2	40.0	125.0	50.0	37.6	9.6	

	Demesne		Tenanted		Tenant resources	
	M	C	M	C	M	C
Carucates	102.0	42.3	0	135.3	0	76.2
Ploughlands	55.0	34.0	0	93.0	0	73.2
Seignorial plough-teams	5.5	0	0	9.0	0	100.0
Peasant plough-teams	13.3	1.0	0	28.0	0	96.6

	B	A	B	A	B	A
Villeins	57.0	1.0	0	84.0	0	98.8
Bordars	0	0	0	4.0	0	100.0
Sokemen	0	0	0	17.0	0	100.0
Other population	2.0	0	0	1.0	0	100.0
Total population	59.0	1.0	0	106.0	0	99.1
1066 value (£)	22.5	48.0	0	212.0	0	81.5
1086 value (£)	10.0	0	0	10.5	0	100.0
1086 value as a percentage of 1066 value	44.4	0	—	4.9		

	B	A	B	A	B	A
Carucates	57.1	54.7	20.9	89.1	26.8	62.0
Ploughlands	30.5	52.5	11.5	81.3	27.4	60.8
Seignorial plough-teams	6.0	7.0	3.0	7.5	33.3	51.7
Peasant plough-teams	11.0	12.0	2.0	26.0	15.4	68.4
Villeins	30.0	29.0	12.0	61.0	28.6	67.8
Bordars	12.0	13.0	1.0	22.0	7.7	62.9
Sokemen	2.0	0	0	1.0	0	100.0
Other population	0	1.0	0	1.0	—	50.0
Total population	44.0	43.0	13.0	85.0	22.8	66.4
1066 value (£)	18.1	22.0	5.7	31.5	23.9	58.9
1086 value (£)	7.8	7.7	2.8	15.5	26.4	66.8
1086 value as a percentage of 1066 value	43.1	35.0	49.1	49.2	66.4	

T = lordship of Gilbert Tison; To = lordship of Robert and Berengar of Tosny; P = lordship of Ralph Paynel; M = lordship of Ralph Mortemer; C = lordship of Hugh earl of Chester; B = lordship of Erneis of Burun; A = lordship of Osbern of Arches.

Table 9 *The charters of Henry I addressed to, witnessed by or concerning Walter Espec*

Number of charter in Regesta, II	Place of issue	Addressed [a]	Other addressees [b]	Judicially active [c]	Judicially active with [d]	Witnessed [e]	Other witnesses [f]	Affairs of which county [g]	Notif. gift conf. [h]	Specific instruction [i]	Non-Yorks. witnesses [j]
1264	Woodstock	+	F, O					co. Dur. Northumb.		+	
1279	Winchester	+	D, F, O			+	A, RB, F	Northumb.	+		+
1312	?					+	T, EFJ	Yorks.	+		+
1326	Nottingham		T			+	F	Yorks.	+		+
1332	York		T			+	GM, NF, P, EFJ	Yorks.	+		+
1333	York		T			+		Yorks.	+		+
1335	York					+	D, W, A, RB	Yorks.	+		
1336	York		B			+		Yorks.		+	
1357	Windsor		T, A, B	+				Yorks.	+		+
1451	Brampton					+	RB	Beds.	+		+
1459	Rockingham					+	T, EFJ, P, B	Yorks.	+		+
1463	Rockingham					+	T, D, P	Yorks.	+		+
1464	Woodstock		T			+	EFJ, RB	Yorks.	+		+
1491	Worcester		T			+	A	Cumb. Westmld.	+		+
1494	Portsmouth		T			+	A, F	Yorks. Northumb.	+		
1532	Woodstock	+	B					Yorks.		+	+
1541	Winchester			+	B, F			Yorks.		+	
1557	Argentan	+	EFJ, F, BB				A	Yorks.	+		
1560	?	+	EFJ, O				T	Cumb.	+		
1561	?	+		+	EFJ			Northumb. co. Dur.	+		
1603	Portsmouth	+	T			+	A, GFP	co. Dur.	+		+
1604	Windsor	+	EFJ, GE					co. Dur.		+	+
1662	Trentham	+	EFJ					Yorks.		+	+

		a	b	c	d	e	f	g	h	i	j
1679	Westminster	+	EFJ, BB			+		Yorks.		+	+
1685	Rouen	+	EFJ		EFJ, W, GFP	+	+	Northumb.	+	+	+
1740	Windsor					+	+	Yorks.		+	+
1741	Windsor							Yorks.			+
1756	Oxford	+	EFJ							+	+
1759	Westminster		T		T, EFJ, GFP	+	+	Yorks. Hants.	+		
1760	Westminster		T, D		EFJ	+	+	Northumb.	+		
1825	?	+						co. Dur.	+	+	
1891	Oxford	+	EFJ					Yorks.	+	+	+

a Denoting whether or not Walter Espec was addressed in the charter.

b The names of other Yorkshire tenants-in-chief addressed in the charter.

c Denoting whether or not the charter commands Walter Espec to perform judicial duties.

d The names of other Yorkshire tenants-in-chief commanded in the charter to carry out the same judicial duty as Walter Espec.

e Denoting whether or not Walter Espec witnessed the charter.

f The names of other Yorkshire tenants-in-chief witnessing the charter.

g The county with which the charter deals.

h Denoting whether or not the charter is a simple notification, gift or confirmation.

i Denoting whether or not the charter conveys specific judicial instructions to the addressees.

j Denoting whether or not the witnesses of the charter include tenants-in-chief who held all their lands outside Yorkshire.

+ = affirmative

A = Nigel d'Aubigny	GFP = Geoffrey Fitz Pain
B = Anschetill of Bulmer	GM = Geoffrey Murdac
BB = Bertram of Bulmer	NF = Nigel Fossard
D = Ranulf Flambard, bishop of Durham	O = Odard sheriff of Northumberland
EFJ = Eustace Fitz John	P = Alan I of Percy
F = Forne Fitz Sigulf	RB = Robert of Brus
GE = Geoffrey Escolland	T = Thurstan archbishop of York
	W = William II of Warenne

Tables

Table 10 *The* cartae baronum *for Yorkshire: 1166*

Name of tenant–in–chief	Number of knights' fees of the old enfeoffment	Number of knights' fees of the new enfeoffment	Number of knights to be enfeoffed on the demesne
Archbishop of York	43.5	3.9	0
Bishop of Durham	64.7	5.1	0
Roger of Mowbray	88.3	11.7	0
Stephen Fitz Herbert	1.2	0.8	0
Henry of Lacy	66.5	18.1	0
William II of Percy	28.0	8.4	0
Amphrey II of Chauncy	4.0	0	1.0
William of Vescy	24.3	2.1	0
William of Bulmer	3.1	0.2	0
Robert III of Stuteville	8.0	0.1	0
William Paynel of Hooton	14.0	1.0	1.0
Alexander Fitz Gerold	12.0	8.0	0
Everard of Ros	6.1	2.3	0
Robert of Gant	10.5	3.5	2.5
Ranulf Fitz Walter	1.0	0	2.3
William count of Aumale	Said to have ten knights in Yorkshire		
Adam II of Brus	Said to have fifteen knights in Yorkshire		
William Trussebut	Said to have ten knights in Yorkshire		
Count Conan of Brittany	Said to have fifty knights in Yorkshire		
Robert II of Brus	Said to have five knights in Yorkshire		
Jocelin of Louvain	Said to have five and a half knights in Yorkshire		
'Honour of Tickhill'	Said to have sixty knights in Yorkshire		
William of Fougeres	Said to have one knight in Yorkshire		
Honour of Warter	Said to have 4.4 knights in Yorkshire		
R. constable of Chester	holds *Snehe* by one knight's fee		
Richard of Sproxton	holds Sproxton by four knights		

Source: **Red Book.**

SELECT BIBLIOGRAPHY

MANUSCRIPT SOURCES

Bodleian Library, Oxford

Dodsworth MS 20
Dodsworth MS 100

British Library

Add. MS 38816 (A collection of miscellaneous twelfth-century quires containing
information relating to St Mary's Abbey, York)
Add. MS 40008 (Cartulary of Bridlington Priory)
Cotton Charter xvi. 37
Cotton Claudius D xi (Cartulary of Malton Priory)
Cotton Vespasian E xviii (Cartulary of Kirkstead Priory)

Public Record Office, London

Chancery Miscellanea C 47/9/5
Duchy of Lancaster 41/1/36 (Catalogue of charters preserved at Pontefract in
1322)

PRINTED SOURCES

*Abstracts of the Charters and Other Documents Contained in the Chartulary of the
Cistercian Abbey of Fountains*, ed. W. T. Lancaster, 2 vols. (Leeds, 1915)
*Abstracts of the Charters and Other Documents Contained in the Chartulary of the
Priory of Bridlington in the East Riding of the County of York*, ed. W. T.
Lancaster (Leeds, 1912)
Abstracts of the Chartularies of the Priory of Monkbretton, ed. J. W. Walker (Yorks.
Arch. Soc. rec. ser., 1924)
Acta Sanctorum, ed. J. Bollandus *et al.* (Antwerp, 1643–1867)
Ailred of Rievaulx, *Relatio de Standardo*, in *Chronicles of the Reigns*, III, 181–99
The Anglo-Saxon Chronicle, ed. and trans. D. Whitelock *et al.* (London, 1961)
Calendar of the Charter Rolls, 6 vols. (London, 1903–27)
Calendar of Inquisitions Post Mortem ..., 16 vols. (London, 1904–74)
Cartularium Abbathiae de Rievalle, ed. J. C. Atkinson (Surtees Soc., 1889)
Cartularium Abbathiae de Whiteby, ed. J. C. Atkinson, 2 vols. (Surtees Soc.,
1879–81)

Select bibliography

Cartularium Prioratus de Gyseburne, ed. W. Brown, 2 vols. (Surtees Soc., 1889–94)

The Charters of the Anglo-Norman Earls of Chester, c. 1071–1237, ed. G. Barraclough (Rec. Soc. of Lancs. and Cheshire, 1988)

Charters of the Honour of Mowbray 1107–1191, ed. D. E. Greenway (British Academy, 1972)

The Chartulary of the Cistercian Abbey of St. Mary of Sallay in Craven, ed. J. McNulty, 2 vols. (Yorks. Arch. Soc. rec. ser., 1933–4)

The Chartulary of St. John of Pontefract, ed. R. Holmes, 2 vols. (Yorks. Arch. Soc., rec. ser., 1899–1902)

Chronica Monasterii de Melsa, ed. E. A. Bond, 3 vols. (RS, 1866–8)

The Chronicle of Pierre de Langtoft, ed. T. Wright, 2 vols. (RS, 1866–8)

Chronicles of the Reigns of Stephen, Henry II, and Richard I, ed. R. Howlett, 4 vols. (RS, 1884–9)

The Coucher Book of the Cistercian Abbey of Kirkstall, ed. W. T. Lancaster and W. Paley Baildon (Thoresby Soc., 1904)

The Coucher Book of Furness Abbey, vol. I (in three parts), ed. J. C. Atkinson (Chetham Soc., n.s., 1886–7); vol. II (in three parts), ed. J. Brownbill (Chetham Soc., n.s., 1915–19)

The Coucher Book of Selby, ed. J. T. Fowler, 2 vols. (Yorks. Arch. and Top. Ass. rec. ser., 1891–3)

Domesday Book seu liber censualis..., ed. A. Farley et al., 4 vols. (London, 1783–1816)

Dugdale, W. *Monasticon Anglicanum*, ed. J. Caley et al., 6 vols. in 8 (London, 1817–30)

Early Scottish Charters Prior to A.D. 1153, ed. A. C. Lawrie (Glasgow, 1905)

Early Yorkshire Charters, vols. I–III, ed. W. Farrer (Edinburgh, 1914–16); vols. IV–XII, ed. C. T. Clay (Yorks. Arch. Soc. rec. ser. extra ser., 1935–65)

The Ecclesiastical History of Orderic Vitalis, ed. M. Chibnall, 6 vols. (Oxford, 1969–80)

English Episcopal Acta, V: York 1070–1154, ed. J. E. Burton (Oxford, 1988)

English Lawsuits from William I to Richard I, ed. R. C. Van Caenegem, 2 vols. (Selden Soc., 1990–1)

Florence of Worcester, *Chronicon ex Chronicis*, ed. B. Thorpe, 2 vols. (Eng. Hist. Soc., 1848–9)

The Foundation of Kirkstall Abbey, ed. and trans. E. K. Clark, in *Miscellanea* (Thoresby Soc., 1895), 169–208

Gesta Stephani, ed. K. R. Potter and R. H. C. Davis (Oxford, 1976)

The Great Rolls of the Pipe for the Second, Third, and Fourth Years of the Reign of King Henry II, ed. J. Hunter (London, 1844)

Henry of Huntingdon, *Historia Anglorum*, ed. T. Arnold (RS, 1879)

The Historians of the Church of York and its Archbishops, ed. J. Raine, 3 vols. (RS, 1879–94)

Hugh the Chantor, *The History of the Church of York 1066–1127*, ed. and trans. C. Johnson (London, 1961)

Kirkby's Inquest, ed. R. H. Skaife (Surtees Soc., 1867)

Leges Henrici Primi, ed. L. J. Downer (Oxford, 1972)

Select bibliography

Liber Feodorum: The Book of Fees Commonly Called Testa de Nevill, 3 vols. (London, 1920–31)

The Life of Ailred of Rievaulx by Walter Daniel, ed. F.M. Powicke (Oxford, 1978)

Magnum Rotulum Scaccarii vel Magnum Rotulum Pipae de anno tricesimo-primo regni Henrici Primi, ed. J. Hunter (London, 1833)

Memorials of the Abbey of St. Mary of Fountains, ed. J. R. Walbran and J. T. Fowler, 3 vols. (Surtees Soc., 1863–1918)

Pipe Rolls 5 Henry II to 4 Henry III (Pipe Roll Soc., 1884–1987)

The Priory of Hexham, ed. J. Raine, 2 vols. (Surtees Soc., 1864–5)

Recueil des Actes de Henri II, Roi d'Angleterre et Duc de Normandie, concernant les Provinces françaises et les Affaires de France, ed. L. V. Delisle and E. Berger, 4 vols. (Paris, 1906–27)

Red Book of the Exchequer, ed. H. Hall, 3 vols. (RS, 1896)

Regesta Regum Anglo-Normannorum 1066–1154, ed. H. W. C. Davis, C. Johnson, H. A. Cronne and R. H. C. Davis, 4 vols. (Oxford, 1913–69)

Regesta Regum Scottorum 1153–1371, ed. G. W. S. Barrow *et al.*, 6 vols. (Edinburgh, 1960–87)

The Register and Records of Holm Cultram, ed. F. Grainger and W. G. Collingwood (Cumb. and Westmld. Ant. and Arch. Soc. rec. ser., 1929)

The Register of the Priory of St. Bees, ed. J. Wilson (Surtees Soc., 1915)

The Register of the Priory of Wetherhal, ed. J. E. Prescott (Cumb. and Westmld. Ant. and Arch. Soc. rec. ser., 1897)

The Registrum Antiquissimum of the Cathedral Church of Lincoln, ed. C. W. Foster and K. Major, 10 vols. (Linc. Rec. Soc., 1931–73)

Rolls of the Justices in Eyre for Yorkshire 1218–19, ed. D. M. Stenton (Selden Soc., 1937)

Select Charters and Other Illustrations of English Constitutional History from the Earliest Times to the Reign of Edward the First, ed. W. Stubbs (9th edn, Oxford, 1913)

Symeonis Monachi Opera Omnia, ed. T. Arnold, 2 vols. (RS, 1882–5)

Tractatus de Legibus et Consuetudinibus Regni Anglie qui Glanvilla vocatur, ed. G. D. G. Hall (London, 1965)

Visitations and Memorials of Southwell Minster, ed. A. F. Leach (Camden Soc., n.s., 1891)

Willelmi Malmesbiriensis Monachi De Gestis Regum Anglorum, ed. W. Stubbs, 2 vols. (RS, 1887–9)

William of Malmesbury, *Historia Novella*, ed. K. R. Potter (London, 1955)

William of Newburgh, *Historia Rerum Anglicarum*, in *Chronicles of the Reigns*, I *The History of English Affairs Book I*, ed. P. G. Walsh and M. J. Kennedy (Warminster, 1988)

The Yorkshire Domesday, ed. G. H. Martin and A. Williams (London, 1992)

Yorkshire Inquisitions of the Reigns of Henry III and Edward I, ed. W. Brown, 3 vols. (Yorks. Arch. Soc. rec. ser., 1892–1902)

Select bibliography

SECONDARY WORKS

Books

Anderson, O. S. *The English Hundred-Names* (Lund, 1934)

Barlow, F. *Durham Jurisdictional Peculiars* (London, 1950)
William Rufus (London, 1983)

Barrow, G. W. S. *The Kingdom of the Scots* (London, 1973)
The Anglo-Norman Era in Scottish History (Oxford, 1980)

Brooke, G. C. *A Catalogue of English Coins in the British Museum: The Norman Kings*, 2 vols. (London, 1916)

Cheney, C. R. *Hubert Walter* (London, 1967)

Chibnall, M. *Anglo-Norman England 1066–1166* (Oxford, 1986)

Clanchy, M. T. *England and its Rulers 1066–1272* (London, 1983)

Clay, C. T., and Greenway, D. E. *Early Yorkshire Families* (Yorks. Arch. Soc. rec. ser., 1973)

Colvin, H. M. *The White Canons in England* (Oxford, 1951)

Complete Peerage, by G.E.C., revised edn, V. Gibbs *et al.*, 13 vols. (London, 1910–59)

David, C. W. *Robert Curthose, Duke of Normandy* (Cambridge, Mass., 1920)

Davies, R. R. *Domination and Conquest* (Cambridge, 1990)

Davis, R. H. C. *King Stephen 1135–1154* (3rd edn, London, 1990)

Dickinson, J. C. *The Origins of the Austin Canons and their Introduction into England* (London, 1950)

The Domesday Geography of Northern England, ed. H. C. Darby and I. S. Maxwell (Cambridge, 1962)

Domesday Studies. Papers Read at the Novocentenary Conference of the Royal Historical Society and the Institute of British Geographers Winchester, 1986, ed. J. C. Holt (Woodbridge, 1987)

English, B. *The Lords of Holderness 1086–1260* (Oxford, 1979)

Farrer, W. *Records Relating to the Barony of Kendale*, ed. J. F. Curwen, 2 vols. (Cumb. and Westmld. Ant. and Arch. Soc. rec. ser., 1923–4)
Honors and Knights' Fees, 3 vols. (London and Manchester, 1923–5)

Fleming, R. *Kings and Lords in Conquest England* (Cambridge, 1991)

Freeman, E. A. *The History of the Norman Conquest*, 5 vols. and index (London, 1867–79)

Gransden, A. *Historical Writing in England c. 550 to c. 1307* (London, 1974)

Green, J. A. *The Government of England under Henry I* (Cambridge, 1986)
English Sheriffs to 1154 (London, 1990)

Hartshorne, C. H. *Memoirs Illustrative of the History and Antiquities of Northumberland*, Proceedings of the Archaeological Institute, Newcastle on Tyne, 1852 (London, 1858)

Hedley, W. Percy *Northumberland Families*, 2 vols. (Newcastle upon Tyne, 1968–70)

Hey, D. *The Making of South Yorkshire* (Ashbourne, 1979)
Yorkshire from AD 1000 (London, 1986)

Hodgson, J. C. *A History of Northumberland*, vol. VII: *The Parish of Edlingham. The*

Parish of Felton. The Chapelry or Parish of Brinkburn (Newcastle upon Tyne, 1904)

Hollister, C. W. *The Military Organization of Norman England* (Oxford, 1965)
 Monarchy, Magnates and Institutions in the Anglo-Norman World (London, 1986)

Holt, J. C. *The Northerners. A Study in the Reign of King John* (Oxford, 1961)
 Magna Carta (2nd edn, Cambridge, 1992)

Kapelle, W. E. *The Norman Conquest of the North: The Region and its Transformation, 1000–1135* (London, 1979)

Keefe, T. K. *Feudal Assessments and the Political Community under Henry II and his Sons* (Berkeley, 1983)

King, D. J. C. *Castellarium Anglicanum. An Index and Bibliography of the Castles in England, Wales and the Islands*, 2 vols. (Millwood, 1983)

Knowles, D. *The Monastic Order in England* (2nd edn, Cambridge, 1963)

Knowles, D. *et al. The Heads of Religious Houses: England and Wales 940–1216* (Cambridge, 1972)

Lennard, R. *Rural England 1086–1135* (Oxford, 1959)

Loyd, L. C. *The Origins of Some Anglo-Norman Families*, ed. C. T. Clay and D. C. Douglas (Harleian Soc., 1951)

Maitland, F. W. *Domesday Book and Beyond* (Cambridge, 1897)

McDonald, J., and Snooks, G. D. *Domesday Economy* (Oxford, 1986)

Miller, E. *The Abbey and Bishopric of Ely* (2nd edn, Cambridge, 1969)

Milsom, S. F. C. *The Legal Framework of English Feudalism* (Cambridge, 1976)
 Historical Foundations of the Common Law (2nd edn, London, 1981)

Nicholl, D. *Thurstan Archbishop of York (1114–1140)* (York, 1964)

North, J. J. *English Hammered Coinage*, 2 vols. (2nd edn, London, 1980)

Painter, S. *Studies in the History of the English Feudal Barony* (Baltimore, 1943)

Pollock, Sir F. and Maitland, F. W. *The History of English Law before the Time of Edward I*, 2 vols. (2nd edn, Cambridge, 1968)

Pounds, N. J. G. *The Medieval Castle in England and Wales: A Social and Political History* (Cambridge, 1990)

Preparatory to Anglo-Saxon England, ed. D. M. Stenton (Oxford, 1970)

Raine, J. *The History and Antiquities of North Durham* (London, 1852)

Raistrick, A. *West Riding of Yorkshire* (London, 1970)

Ritchie, R. L. G. *The Normans in Scotland* (Edinburgh, 1954)

Round, J. H. *Geoffrey de Mandeville* (London, 1892)

Sanders, I. J. *English Baronies: A Study of their Origin and Descent 1086–1327* (Oxford, 1960)

Stenton, D. M. *English Justice between the Norman Conquest and the Great Charter 1066–1215* (London, 1965)

Stenton, F. M. *The First Century of English Feudalism 1066–1166* (2nd edn, Oxford, 1961)

Tabuteau, E. Zack. *Transfers of Property in Eleventh-Century Norman Law* (Chapel Hill, 1988)

Van Caenegem, R. C. *Royal Writs in England from the Conquest to Glanvill* (Selden Soc., 1959)

Select bibliography

The Victoria History of the Counties of England (London, 1900– , in progress)
Wardrop, J. Fountains Abbey and its Benefactors 1132–1300 (Kalamazoo, 1987)
Warren, W. L. Henry II (London, 1973)
   The Governance of Norman and Angevin England 1086–1272 (London, 1987)
West Yorkshire: An Archaeological Survey to A.D. 1500, ed. M. L. Faull and S. A.
   Moorhouse, 3 vols. (Wakefield, 1981)
Whitaker, T. D. The History and Antiquities of the Deanery of Craven in the County
   of York, ed. A. W. Morant (3rd edn, Leeds, 1878)
White, S. D. Custom, Kinship and Gifts to Saints (Univ. of North Carolina, 1988)
Wightman, W. E. The Lacy Family in England and Normandy 1066–1194 (Oxford,
   1966)
Williams, A. The Fate of the Anglo-Saxons: The English and the Norman Conquest
   (forthcoming)
York Minster Fasti, ed. C. T. Clay, 2 vols. (Yorks. Arch. Soc. rec. ser., 1957–8)

Articles and Papers

Amt, E. 'The meaning of waste in the early pipe rolls of Henry II', EcHR, 44
   (1991), 240–8
Austin, D. 'Barnard castle, co. Durham. First interim report: excavations in the
   town ward, 1974–6', JBAA, 132 (1979), 50–73
Baker, L. G. D. 'The foundation of Fountains Abbey', Northern History, 4
   (1969), 29–43
Baring, F. 'The Conqueror's footprints in Domesday', EHR, 13 (1898), 17–25
Barrow, G. W. S. 'Scottish rulers and the religious orders, 1070–1153', TRHS,
   5th ser., 3 (1953), 77–100, reprinted as 'The royal house and the religious
   orders', in Barrow, Kingdom of the Scots, 165–87
   'King David I and the honour of Lancaster', EHR, 70 (1955), 85–9
   'The Anglo-Scottish border', Northern History, 1 (1966), 21–42, reprinted in
   Barrow, Kingdom of the Scots, 139–61
   'Scotland's "Norman" families', in Barrow, Kingdom of the Scots, 315–36
   'The pattern of lordship and feudal settlement in Cumbria', JMH, 1 (1975),
   117–38
   David I of Scotland (1124–1153): The Balance of New and Old (The Stenton
   Lecture 1984: Univ. of Reading, 1985)
Beddoe, J., and Rowe, J. H. 'The ethnology of West Yorkshire', YAJ, 19 (1907),
   31–60
Bethell, D. 'The foundation of Fountains Abbey and the state of St. Mary's York
   in 1132', JEH, 17 (1966), 11–27
Biancalana, J. 'For want of justice: legal reforms of Henry II', Columbia Law
   Review, 88 (1988), 433–536
Bishop, T. A. M. 'The Norman settlement of Yorkshire', in Studies in Medieval
   History Presented to Frederick Maurice Powicke, ed. R. W. Hunt et al. (Oxford,
   1948), 1–14
Blackburn, M. 'Coinage and currency under Stephen', in The Anarchy of King
   Stephen's Reign, ed. E. King (Oxford, forthcoming)

314

Select bibliography

Brand, P. '"Multis vigiliis excogitatam et inventam": Henry II and the creation of the English Common Law', *Haskins Society Journal*, 2 (1990), 197–222

Bridbury, A. R. 'Domesday Book: a re-interpretation', *EHR*, 105 (1990), 284–309

Chibnall, M. 'Robert of Bellême and the castle of Tickhill', in *Droit privé et institutions régionales: études historiques offertes à Jean Yver* (Paris, 1976), 151–6

'The Empress Matilda and church reform', *TRHS*, 5th ser., 38 (1988), 107–30

Clanchy, M. T. 'A medieval realist: interpreting the rules at Barnwell Priory, Cambridge', in *Perspectives in Jurisprudence*, ed. E. Attwooll (Glasgow, 1977), 176–94

'Law and love in the middle ages', in *Disputes and Settlements: Law and Human Relations in the West*, ed. J. Bossy (Cambridge, 1983), 47–67

Clay, C. T. 'The early treasurers of York', *YAJ*, 35 (1940–3), 7–34

'Notes on the early archdeacons in the church of York', *YAJ*, 36 (1944–7), 269–87, 409–34

'A Holderness charter of William count of Aumale', *YAJ*, 39 (1956–8), 339–42

Dalton, P. 'William earl of York and royal authority in Yorkshire in the reign of Stephen', *Haskins Society Journal*, 2 (1990), 155–65

'Aiming at the impossible: Ranulf II earl of Chester and Lincolnshire in the reign of King Stephen', in *The Earldom of Chester and its Charters: A Tribute to Geoffrey Barraclough*, ed. A. T. Thacker (Journal of the Chester Arch. Soc., 1991), 109–34

'*In neutro latere*: the armed neutrality of Ranulf II earl of Chester in King Stephen's reign', *ANS*, 14 (1992), 39–59

Denholm-Young, N. 'The foundation of Warter Priory', *YAJ*, 31 (1934) 208–13

Dickens, A. G. 'The "shire" and privileges of the archbishop in eleventh century York', *YAJ*, 38 (1952–5), 131–47

Dobson, R. B. 'The first Norman abbey in northern England. The origins of Selby: a ninth centenary article', *Ampleforth Journal*, 74 (1969), 161–76

Duby, G. 'The diffusion of cultural patterns in feudal society', *Past & Present*, 39 (1968), 3–10

'The nobility in eleventh- and twelfth-century Mâconnais', in *Lordship and Community in Medieval Europe*, ed. F. L. Cheyette (New York, 1975), 137–55

Eales, R. 'Royal power and castles in Norman England', in *The Ideals and Practice of Medieval Knighthood III*, ed. C. Harper-Bill and R. Harvey (London, 1990), 49–78

Ellis, A. S. 'Biographical notes on the Yorkshire tenants named in Domesday Book', *YAJ*, 4 (1877), 114–57, 215–48, 384–415

Farrer, W. 'The sheriffs of Lincolnshire and Yorkshire, 1066–1130', *EHR*, 30 (1915), 277–85

Finn, R. W. *The Making and Limitations of the Yorkshire Domesday* (Univ. of York, Borthwick Paper, no. 41, 1972)

Golding, B. 'Robert of Mortain', *ANS*, 13 (1991), 119–44

Graham, T. H. B. 'Turgis Brundos', *TCWAAS*, 29 (1929), 49–56

Select bibliography

Green, J. A. 'William Rufus, Henry I and the royal demesne', *History*, 64 (1979), 337–52

'The sheriffs of William the Conqueror', *ANS*, 5 (1983), 129–45

'Anglo-Scottish relations, 1066–1174', in *England and Her Neighbours, 1066–1453. Essays in Honour of Pierre Chaplais*, ed. M. Jones and M. Vale (London, 1989), 53–72

'Aristocratic loyalties on the northern frontier of England, *c.* 1100–1174', in *England in the Twelfth Century*, ed. D. Williams (Woodbridge, 1990), 83–100

'Earl Ranulf II and Lancashire', in *The Earldom of Chester and its Charters: A Tribute to Geoffrey Barraclough*, ed. A. T. Thacker (Journal of the Chester Arch. Soc., 1991), 97–108

'Financing Stephen's war', *ANS*, 14 (1992), 91–114

Harvey, S. P. J. 'The knight and the knight's fee in England', *Past & Present*, 49 (1970), 3–43

'The extent and profitability of demesne agriculture in England in the later eleventh century', in *Social Relations and Ideas. Essays in Honour of R. H. Hilton*, ed. T. H. Aston *et al.* (Cambridge, 1983), 45–72

Heslop, T. A. 'Seals', in *English Romanesque Art*, ed. G. Zarnecki *et al.* (London, 1984), 298–319

Holt, J. C. 'Politics and property in early medieval England', *Past & Present*, 57 (1972), 3–52, reprinted in *Landlords, Peasants and Politics in Medieval England*, ed. T. H. Aston (Cambridge, 1987), 65–114

What's in a Name? Family Nomenclature and the Norman Conquest (The Stenton Lecture 1980: Univ. of Reading, 1981)

'Feudal society and the family in early medieval England: I. The revolution of 1066', *TRHS*, 5th ser., 32 (1982), 193–212

'Feudal society and the family in early medieval England: II. Notions of patrimony', *TRHS*, 5th ser., 33 (1983), 193–220

'Feudal society and the family in early medieval England: III. Patronage and politics', *TRHS*, 5th ser., 34 (1984), 1–25

'Feudal society and the family in early medieval England: IV. The heiress and the alien', *TRHS*, 5th ser., 35 (1985), 1–28

'The introduction of knight service in England', *ANS*, 6 (1984), 89–106

'Magna Carta 1215–1217: the legal and social context', in *Law in Medieval Life and Thought*, ed. E. B. King and S. J. Ridyard (Univ. of the South, 1990), 1–19

Hudson, J. 'Life-grants of land and the development of inheritance in Anglo-Norman England', *ANS*, 12 (1990), 67–80

'Milsom's legal structure: interpreting twelfth-century law', *Tijdschrift Voor Rechtsgeschiedenis*, 59 (1991), 47–66

Hyams, P. R. review of Milsom, *Legal Framework*, in *EHR*, 93 (1978), 856–61

'"No register of title": the Domesday inquest and land adjudication', *ANS*, 9 (1987), 127–41

'Warranty and good lordship in twelfth century England', *LHR*, 5 (1987), 437–503

Select bibliography

'The charter as a source for the early Common Law', *JLH*, 12 (1991), 173–89

Keen, L. 'The Umfravilles, the castle and the barony of Prudhoe, Northumberland', *ANS*, 5 (1983), 165–84

King, E. 'The parish of Warter and the castle of Galchlin', *YAJ*, 52 (1980), 49–58

'The anarchy of King Stephen's reign', *TRHS*, 5th ser., 34 (1984), 133–53

'Waleran, count of Meulan, earl of Worcester (1104–1166)', in *Tradition and Change. Essays in Honour of Marjorie Chibnall*, ed. D. Greenway *et al.* (Cambridge, 1985), 165–81

'The foundation of Pipewell Abbey, Northamptonshire', *Haskins Society Journal*, 2 (1990), 167–77

'Dispute settlement in Anglo-Norman England', *ANS*, 14 (1992), 115–30

King, P. 'The return of the fee of Robert de Brus in Domesday', *YAJ*, 60 (1988), 25–9

Knowles, D. 'The case of Saint William of York', *CHJ*, 5 (1936), 162–77, 212–14, reprinted in *The Historian and Character* (Cambridge, 1963), Chapter 5

Latimer, P. 'Grants of "totus comitatus" in twelfth-century England: their origins and meaning', *BIHR*, 59 (1986), 137–45

Le Patourel, J. 'The Norman colonization of Britain', *I Normanni e la loro espansione in Europa nell'alto medioevo* (Centro Italiano di Studi sull'Alto Medioevo, Settimana xvi, 1968, Spoleto, 1969), 409–38

'The Norman conquest of Yorkshire', *Northern History*, 6 (1971), 1–21

Lewis, C. P. 'The king and Eye: a study in Anglo-Norman politics', *EHR*, 104 (1989), 569–87

'The formation of the honor of Chester, 1066–1100', in *The Earldom of Chester and its Charters: A Tribute to Geoffrey Barraclough*, ed. A. T. Thacker (Journal of the Chester Arch. Soc., 1991), 37–68

Liebermann, F. 'An English document of about 1080', *YAJ*, 18 (1904–5), 412–16

Mack, R. P. 'Stephen and the anarchy 1135–1154', *BNJ*, 35 (1966), 38–112

Michelmore, D. J. H. 'Township and tenure', in *West Yorkshire*, II, 231–64

'Township gazetteer', in *West Yorkshire*, II, 294–579

Morey, A. 'Canonist evidence in the case of St William of York', *CHJ*, 10 (1950–2), 352–3

Mortimer, R. 'Land and service: the tenants of the honour of Clare', *ANS*, 8 (1986), 177–97

Palliser, D. M. *Domesday York* (Univ. of York, Borthwick Paper, no. 78, 1990)

'An introduction to the Yorkshire Domesday', in *The Yorkshire Domesday*, ed. G. H. Martin and A. Williams (London, 1992), 1–38

'Domesday Book and the "harrying of the north"', *Northern History*, 29 (1993), 1–23

Palmer, R. C. 'The origins of property in England', *LHR*, 3 (1985), 1–50

Purvis, J. S. 'A foundation charter of Bridlington priory', *YAJ*, 29 (1927–9), 395

'The foundation of Bridlington Priory', *YAJ*, 29 (1927–9), 241–2

Reynolds, S. 'Bookland, folkland and fiefs', *ANS*, 14 (1992), 211–27

Roffe, D. R. 'Domesday Book and northern society: a reassessment', *EHR*, 105 (1990), 310–36

'From thegnage to barony: sake and soke, title, and tenants-in-chief', *ANS*, 12 (1990), 157–76

'The Yorkshire Summary: a Domesday satellite', *Northern History*, 27 (1991), 242–60

Round, J. H. 'The death of William Malet', *The Academy* (26 April 1884)

Sawyer, P. H. 'The royal *Tun* in pre-conquest England', in *Ideal and Reality in Frankish and Anglo-Saxon Society*, ed. P. Wormald *et al.* (Oxford, 1983), 273–99

Searle, E. *Women and the Legitimisation of Succession at the Norman Conquest* (California Institute of Technology Social Science Working Paper 328, July 1980)

Sheppard, J. A. 'Pre-conquest Yorkshire: fiscal carucates as an index of land exploitation', *Inst. of Brit. Geographers Trans.*, 65 (1975), 67–78

Stenton, F. M. 'The road system of medieval England', *EcHR*, 7 (1936), 1–21, reprinted in *Preparatory to Anglo-Saxon England*, ed. D. M. Stenton (Oxford, 1970), 234–52

Talbot, C. H. 'New documents in the case of Saint William of York', *CHJ*, 10 (1950–2), 1–15

Thompson, A. Hamilton 'The monastic settlement at Hackness', *YAJ*, 27 (1924), 388–405

Thompson, K. 'Monasteries and settlement in Norman Lancashire: unpublished charters of Roger the Poitevin', *Trans. Hist. Soc. of Lancs. and Cheshire*, 140 (1990), 201–25

Thorn, F. R. 'Hundreds and wapentakes', in *The Yorkshire Domesday*, ed. G. H. Martin and A. Williams (London, 1992), 39–70

Thorne, S. E. 'English feudalism and estates in land', *CLJ*, 6 (1959), 193–209

Washington, G. 'The parentage of William de Lancaster, lord of Kendal', *TCWAAS*, 62 (1962), 95–100

White, G. H. 'King Stephen's earldoms', *TRHS*, 4th ser., 13 (1930), 51–82

Wightman, W. E. 'Henry I and the foundation of Nostell priory', *YAJ*, 41 (1963–6), 57–60

'The significance of "waste" in the Yorkshire Domesday', *Northern History*, 10 (1975), 55–71

Wilson, J. 'The passages of St Malachy through Scotland', *SHR*, 18 (1921), 69–82

Yoshitake, K. 'The exchequer in the reign of Stephen', *EHR*, 103 (1988), 950–9

Young, A. *William Cumin: Border Politics and the Bishopric of Durham 1141–1144* (Univ. of York, Borthwick Paper, no. 54, 1979)

Theses

Abbot, M. R. 'The Gant family in England, 1066–1191' (Univ. of Cambridge, PhD thesis, 1973)

Burton, J. E. 'The origins and development of the religious orders in Yorkshire *c.* 1069 to *c.* 1200' (Univ. of York, DPhil. thesis, 1977)

Dalton, P. 'Feudal politics in Yorkshire 1066–1154' (Univ. of Sheffield, PhD thesis, 1990)

Select bibliography

English, B. A. 'The counts of Aumale and Holderness 1086–1260' (Univ. of St Andrews, PhD thesis, 1977)

Soulsby, I. N. 'The fiefs in England of the counts of Mortain, 1066–1166' (Univ. of Wales, Cardiff, MA thesis, 1974)

Wales, C. J. 'The knight in twelfth-century Lincolnshire' (Univ. of Cambridge, PhD thesis, 1983)

Cambridge Studies in Medieval Life and Thought
Fourth series

* Also published as a paperback

321

INDEX

Index

Index

Benedict of Stapleton, 133

Benniworth, 277

Berengar of Tosny, 54–5, 69, 75n, 298, 300, 305
  lordship of, *see* Robert of Tosny

Bernard of Balliol, 208, 209n, 211
  lordship of, *see* Balliol family

Bertram of Bulmer, sheriff of Yorks., 104, 106–7, 108n, 110, 153n, 221, 254, 306–7
  lordship of, *see* Bulmer family

Bertram family, 198, 207

Bertram of Verdon, sheriff of Yorks., 103

Béthune, 154

Beverley, 5, 6, 108, 139, 159n, 161, 175–6

Bewick, 183, 292

Biancalana, J., 274–5

Bigod fee, 166n

Birdforth wapentake, 75, 82, 184

Bjornulfr, 128n

Black Book of the exchequer, 234n

Blackburnshire, 189, 217

Blanchemarle grange, 181n

Blois, House of, 160, 170n; *see also* Adela, Emma, Henry (bishop of Winchester), Stephen (count), Stephen (king), William, count of Aumale

Bodin, 47n

Bolesford wapentake, 38, 91, 100, 108n, 121, 184

Bolingbroke, 188, 257

Bolton in Craven, 83–4, 129–30

Bolton upon Dearne, 123, 126

Bolton Percy, 65, 127, 253

Bonwick, 154

bookland, 265

Boroughbridge, 6

Bossall, 38, 301
  castle of, 38

Bowes, 6

Bowland, 189

Bracton, 267

Bradford, 6

Braithwell, 123

Bramham, 106, 263, 288

Brampton, 306

Brian the Breton, 268

Bridbury, A. R., 27

Bridlington, 6, 85–6, 99, 126, 139, 164–5, 179
  castle of, 164–6, 179, 195
  priory of, 13, 138n, 139–40, 164–5, 168, 191, 195, 253, 276

Brinkburn Priory, 209n

Brinsworth, 121, 123

Brocklesby, 187

Brompton, 57, 61, 99
  castle of, 61

Brough, 6

Brus family, 183, 224, 243, 284n; *see also* Adam I, Adam II, Agatha, Peter, Robert I, Robert II
  castlery of, 93–4
  lordship of, 70, 92–4, 108n, 166, 176, 180–1, 184, 201, 201n, 208–9, 243, 253, 284n, 308

Buckton Holms, 38, 301

Bulmer family, 129–30; *see also* Anschetill, Bertram, Emma, William
  lordship of, 100, 104, 106, 108n, 129–30, 221, 251, 254, 308

Burgh by Sands, lordship of, 208

Burghshire wapentake, 108n, 121, 157

Burniston, 136

Burnsall, 130

Burstwick, 48n

Burton, J., 16

Burton, J. E., 14, 137

Burton Agnes, manor of, 93–4, 103, 166, 181

Burton Agnes hundred, 86, 166, 183

Burton in Lonsdale, 83, 118–19, 125, 133, 144, 168, 216, 261
  castle of, 83, 133, 216, 260
  castlery of, 118, 125

Bury St Edmunds, 236

Buttercrambe, 301

Byland Abbey, 15, 138n, 191, 295

Bytham, 174
  abbey of, 181
  castle of, 174

Bywell, barony of, 198, 208, 211

Calderdale, 96

Calixtus II, pope, 141

Callerton, lordship of, 198

Cambridge, 10
  castle of, 10

Canterbury, cathedral of, 15

Carleton, 125

Carlisle, 6, 82, 148–9, 196, 198, 204, 209, 217, 222, 226–7
  bishopric of, 198, 202, 222
  castle of, 198–9, 204, 206
  priory of, 198–9, 202; priors of, *see* Walter

Carnaby, 121, 126, 253

Carnwath, barony of, 201

Index

Hornby, 217
Hornsea, 48, 48n
  castle of, 48
Horsforth, 218n
Houses on Toft Green, 154n
Howden, manor of, 4, 6, 171, 266n
Howden hundred, 167
Hudson, J., 273–5, 287n
Hugh I, earl of Chester, 54, 57, 69, 86,
  115, 115n, 120, 124, 237n, 262, 284n,
  298, 300, 305
  lordship of, *see* Chester
Hugh Bigod, earl of Norfolk, 270, 284,
  284n
Hugh the Chantor, 15
Hugh of Cressy, 233
Hugh Fitz Baldric, sheriff of Yorks., 9,
  34–8, 60n, 65–6, 71, 72n, 75, 75n,
  81–3, 93, 102, 117n, 135–6, 298–300
  castleries of, 82
  lordship of, 9, 34–8, 41n, 60n, 66, 71,
  72n, 75, 81–3, 93, 117n; date of
  formation of, 37–8, 65–6, 71;
  Domesday resources of, 35, 35n,
  36–8, 299; Domesday value of, 36–8,
  64, 298–9; enfeoffment on, 37–8,
  117n, 299–300; level of Norman
  authority on in 1086, 35–8, 71
Hugh Fitz Everard, 253
Hugh Fitz Henry, 286–7
Hugh Fitz Odard, 277
Hugh of la Val, 95, 110
  lordships of, *see* Clitheroe, Pontefract
Hugh of Lacy, 151
Hugh de Mortimer, 213n
Hugh of Morville, 201, 207
Hugh of Port, 237n
Hugh du Puiset, treasurer of York, bishop
  of Durham, 161, 161n, 173, 175–6, 226,
  308
hundreds, 80, 107, 168, 170
  administrative centres of, 8, 84, 84n, 85,
  91, 107–8, 112, 116, 156, 156n,
  164–5, 167, 170–1, 174, 178, 184–5
  control of by 'new men', 80, 86, 93–4,
  100, 103, 107–8, 108n, 112
  courts of, 262
  lands granted out by hundred, 71–2,
  72n, 73, 73n, 74–6, 78, 169
  relationship of to castleries, 76, 84, 91,
  93
  significance of in local authority, 2, 78,
  84, 87, 107, 156, 158
  see also Acklam, Burton Agnes,
  Howden, Hunthow, *Scard*,

Sneculfcros, Toreshou, Turbar, Warter,
  Weighton, Welton, William, count
  of Aumale
Hunmanby, 65, 84, 164–5, 174, 174n, 179,
  179n, 264, 291
  castle of, 84, 164, 174, 179
Hunter, J., 16
Hunthow hundred, 85–6, 91, 92n, 93n,
  162, 164, 166
Huntingdon, 10, 96, 201, 291
  castle of, 10
  earl of, *see* Waltheof
  earldom of, 200, 204
  honour of, 148, 201, 209, 209n
  see also Henry, Judith
Huntingdonshire, 213
Hutton Conyers, 168
  castle of, 168, 168n
Hutton Rudby, 53n, 91, 92n, 93
  castlery of, 91, 93
Hyams, P. R., 180, 279, 281–2

Ilbert I of Lacy, 21, 39, 41, 43–4, 47,
  66–7, 71, 75n, 76, 102n, 188–9, 298,
  300
  lordships of, *see* Clitheroe, Pontefract
Ilbert II of Lacy, 153n, 205, 217
  lordships of, *see* Clitheroe, Pontefract
Ilger Fitz *Roeri*, 124
infangenetheof, 135, 265
Ingelbert de Mainers, 133
inheritance/heritability, 29n, 144, 151,
  182, 213, 258
  control of lords over, 259, 266, 273–81,
  291
  debate concerning nature of, 266,
  273–81, 290–1, 295
  designation of heirs, 275–6, 291
  emergence of, 3, 258, 273–4, 290
  justifications for claiming, 274
  language of, 290, 290n
  notions of adopted by lesser aristocracy,
  293
  regularity of tenant succession, 273,
  273n
  rival perceptions/views concerning,
  274, 280
  see also Common Law, courts
  (seignorial), Domesday Book, Henry
  II (legal reforms), hereditary tenure,
  property right
Innocent II, pope, 222
Inquisitions Post Mortem, as a source, 13
Irnham, 270
Ivo Taillebois, 83, 102, 198

Index

Ivo of Vescy, 97

Jervaulx Abbey, 15, 293n, 294
Jocelin of Furness, 225n
Jocelin of Louvain, 308
John, bishop of Glasgow, 222
John, count of Eu, 176n
  lordship of, see Tickhill
John, king of England, 260–1, 288, 291–2
John, prior of Hexham, 14, 152, 162,
  164–5, 167, 212, 215
John Arundel, 183, 183n
John of Crema, 284
John Fitz Assolf, 286–7
John of Meaux, 292–3
John Paparo, 227
Jordan of Bussey, 151
Jordan Foliot, 183n
Jordan of Lacy, 175n
Jordan Paynel, 91
Judith, countess of Huntingdon, 96, 102n,
  174n, 200, 220
Juetta of Arches, 180, 254
justice, royal, 101, 103, 105–9, 111, 142,
  162, 194, 199n, 256, 258, 260, 287,
  306–7; see also court, king's, and
  courts (county, hundredal,
  wapentake), darrein presentment, mort
  d'ancestor, novel disseisin
justice, seignorial, 122, 258, 265, 279, 291,
  293, 295; see also courts (seignorial)
justices, royal, 230, 257, 271
  itinerant, 106, 108, 112, 149n, 199, 233
  local, 103, 105, 112, 138, 153, 206,
  230, 282

Kapelle, W. E., 17, 21
Karle, 9–10, 65, 69n, 130
Keckwick, 277
Keefe, T. K., 232, 234n, 241–2, 247
Kelso Abbey, 209
Kendal, 211
Kendale, 3, 83, 89, 102, 198, 219
Ketel, 219n
Ketill, 130
Kildwick, 215
Kilham, 157–8
Killerby, 47, 47n, 116, 124
  castle of, 47, 116
Killinghall, 157n
Killingholme, 187
King, E., 157, 174n, 192
King's Tofts, 154n
Kippax, 48, 48n, 67, 116
  castle of, 48, 67

Kirby Misperton, 58
Kirby Moorside, 38, 82, 100, 118
  castle of, 38
  castlery of, 82, 100, 118
Kirk Hammerton, 242
Kirkby Fleetham, 47, 47n, 116
  castle of, 47, 116
Kirkby Lonsdale, 6
Kirkby Malzeard, 83, 89, 118–19, 125
  castle of, 83
  castlery of, 89–90, 118, 125
Kirkby Ouseburn, 242
Kirkham, 100
  priory of, 100, 138n, 141, 193, 202, 223,
  223n, 224, 294n; priors of, see
  Waldef, William
Kirkland, 217
Kirkleatham, 124
Kirklevington, 166
Kirkstall, 7n
  abbey of, 15, 225, 260; abbots of, 225
Knaresborough, 90n, 99, 107, 109, 111,
  157, 158n, 179, 184, 219
  castle of, 99, 157, 219
Kneeton, 276
Knowles, D., 18

La Charité sur Loire Priory, 137
  priors of, see 'G'
la Val family, 198
Lacy family, 17, 76, 171n, 190, 201, 217,
  217n, 218, 244, 251, 253–4, 260; see
  also Henry, Hugh, Ilbert I, Ilbert II,
  Jordan, Robert I, Sibyl
  lordships of, 151; see also Clitheroe,
  Pontefract
Lagr, 8
Lambert, count of Lens, 174n
Lancaster, lordship of, 209
Lancaster, town, 216, 219, 271n
Lancaster, W. T., 13
Landmoth, 236–7
Langbargh wapentake, 75, 91–3, 108n,
  166
Langley, barony of, 199
Langton, 301
Lastingham, 136–7
Latimer, P., 146
Lauderdale, lordship of, 201
Laughton en le Morthen, 49, 67, 77
  castle of, 49, 67, 77
  castlery of, 77
Lazenby, 124
Le Patourel, J., 21
Lealholm, 93n

Index

Index

knights of, 308
priory of, 138n, 141, 174n, 283
Warter hundred, 57, 100, 108n, 128n
Warwick, 10
    castle of, 10
    earl of, 237n
waste, 19, 23–5, 33, 37, 40, 42, 42n, 43,
    45–7, 47n, 49, 51–2, 57, 60, 61, 61n,
    62, 77, 91, 95, 116–17, 145, 160, 160n
Wath upon Dearne, 88, 129, 217–18,
    218n, 228, 286
Wawne, 193
Wearmouth, 11, 69
Weaverthorpe, 170
Weighton hundred, 108n
Welton hundred, 167, 180
Wentworth, 286
Weobley, 151
West Coatham, 124
Westminster, 107, 148, 307
    treaty of, 156n, 176, 195
Westmorland, lordship of, 207, 236n
Westwick, 157n
Wetheral, 189
Wetherby, 6, 125
Wharfedale, 216
Wheldrake, 39, 39n, 128n, 175n, 216
    castle of, 39, 175n, 216
Whitaker, T. D., 16
Whitby, 4, 6, 69, 86, 120, 124, 134, 136,
    138
    abbey of, 69, 126, 136, 139, 179, 226,
    253, 262, 268, 271; abbots of, *see*
    Benedict, Richard; priors of, *see*
    Reinfrid
Whitby Strand, 184
White, G. J., 146, 158
Whitwood, 48, 48n
    castle of, 48
Whorlton, 53, 53n, 92n
    castle of, 53, 92n
Widdrington, T., 16
'Wigani', 268
Wiggington, 25
Wigglesworth, 121, 124
Wightman, W. E., 17, 20–1, 25, 44, 67,
    117
Wigmore, 213n
Willerby, 164–5
William, abbot of Rievaulx, 210, 224
William, count of Aumale, earl of York,
    133, 157, 177n, 186–7, 197, 230, 253,
    269, 277, 292–3, 308
    appointed earl of York, 2, 146, 152,
    179

attempts to influence York election,
    147, 154, 169–70, 172–4, 195
builds Scarborough castle, 156
in charge of administration of Yorks.,
    153–61, 177–8, 185, 194
in charge of castle and city of York,
    147, 153–4
charters of, 156n, 160, 166n, 179,
    181–3, 183n
domination of lesser aristocracy, 2, 147,
    178–85
excommunication of, 173
exploits custody of Brus heir, 166, 180
fortifies Bridlington, 164–6, 179, 195
founds Meaux Abbey, 174
geographical extent of power of, 184
hostility of to Henry of Lacy, 171, 179,
    184
hostility of to King Stephen and
    Gilbert of Gant, 174, 176, 179
lordships of, 164, 165n, 174, *see also*
    Aumale, Copeland, Holderness
military power of, 179
mints coins, 155, 161–2, 179, 181
promotes restoration of order, 195
provides recompense to church, 193,
    195
related to King Stephen, 160
rivalry with Alan of Richmond, 162–4,
    166–9, 184
rivalry with earl of Chester and Gilbert
    of Gant, 162–6
rivalry with Roger of Mowbray, 168,
    184
secures control of Yorks. hundreds and
    wapentakes, 2, 147, 156–9, 162–72,
    178–9, 184–5
self-interest of, 2, 147, 161–2, 165–74,
    176–7, 179, 185, 194
submits to Henry II, 156, 176
titles of, 155–6
William, count of Eu, 11, 82
William, count of Mortain, 80–1, 87, 91,
    93, 100
    lordship of, *see* Mortain
William I, king of England, 1, 9, 11, 19,
    21, 23–4, 33, 34, 39, 46, 48, 62, 64–8,
    71, 78–81, 86–7, 93, 102n, 103n, 112,
    130–1, 169, 200, 229, 271
chooses earls of Northumbria, 9–10
control of over conquest, 78
establishes overlordship over Scotland,
    12
imposes his authority on Northumbria,
    198

YALE COLLEGE
LEARNING RESOURCE CENTRE

Printed in the United Kingdom
by Lightning Source UK Ltd.
132473UK00001B/434/A

9 780521 524643